New Leadership *for* Today's Health Care Professionals

CONCEPTS AND CASES

Edited by

Louis G. Rubino, PhD, FACHE
Professor and Director of Health Administration Program
California State University, Northridge

Salvador J. Esparza, DHA, RN, FACHE
Assistant Professor
California State University, Northridge

Yolanda S. Reid Chassiakos, MD, FAAP, FACP
Clinical Assistant Professor
Pediatric David Geffen School of Medicine, UCLA
Director, Klotz Student Health Center
California State University, Northridge

D0109869

JONES & BARTLETT
LEARNING

World Headquarters
Jones & Bartlett Learning
5 Wall Street
Burlington, MA 01803
978-443-5000
info@jblearning.com
www.jblearning.com

Jones & Bartlett Learning books and products are available through most bookstores and online booksellers. To contact Jones & Bartlett Learning directly, call 800-832-0034, fax 978-443-8000, or visit our website, www.jblearning.com.

Substantial discounts on bulk quantities of Jones & Bartlett Learning publications are available to corporations, professional associations, and other qualified organizations. For details and specific discount information, contact the special sales department at Jones & Bartlett Learning via the above contact information or send an email to specialsales@jblearning.com.

Production Credits

Publisher: Michael Brown
Editorial Assistant: Chloe Falivene
Production Assistant: Leia Poritz
Production Assistant: Alyssa Lawrence
Senior Marketing Manager: Sophie Fleck Teague
Manufacturing and Inventory Control Supervisor: Amy Bacus
Composition: Laserwords Private Limited, Chennai, India
Cover Design: Scott Moden
Cover Image: © maxim ibragimov/ ShutterStock, Inc.
Printing and Binding: Edwards Brothers Malloy
Cover Printing: Edwards Brothers Malloy

To order this product, use ISBN: 978-1-284-02357-2

Library of Congress Cataloging-in-Publication Data
Rubino, Louis.
 New leadership for today's health care professionals : concepts and cases / Louis Rubino, Salvador Esparza, Yolanda Reid Chassiakos.
   p. ; cm.
 Includes bibliographical references and index.
 ISBN 978-1-4496-3431-5 (pbk.) — ISBN 1-4496-3431-1 (pbk.)
 I. Esparza, Salvador. II. Chassiakos, Yolanda Reid. III. Title.
 [DNLM: 1. Health Personnel—organization & administration—United States. 2. Leadership—United States. 3. Health Care Reform—trends—United States. 4. Professional Competence—United States. W 21]

 610.73068—dc23

2012041427

6048

Printed in the United States of America
17 16   10 9 8 7 6 5

Dedication

Louis Rubino: I dedicate this book to my wife of 27 years, Judy, who attempts to keep me balanced, and my Academic Assistant, Joo Kim, who keeps me organized.

Salvador Esparza: I dedicate this book to my wife, Caroline, for her constant love and support throughout my career.

Yolanda S. Reid Chassiakos: I dedicate this book to EG and Effie Stassinopoulos for their inspiration and motivation, and to my husband, Anastasios Chassiakos, for his patience and support.

Table of Contents

Foreword

Most observers of healthcare management have recognized that the complexity of managing healthcare organizations calls for new leadership skills. External forces, such as intensified competition, greater regulation, and tighter reimbursement, as well as internal challenges, such as improving clinical quality, promoting patient satisfaction, and fostering employee engagement continue to be vexing issues for healthcare leaders. Programs in healthcare management at the undergraduate and graduate levels are increasing their enrollments and expanding their curricula in response to the continuing demand for healthcare managers. Specifically, healthcare management programs are charged with ensuring that students possess the knowledge and skills to effectively lead their future organizations. Resources to address healthcare leadership at the undergraduate level, in particular, are few in number, so this book is a timely resource for faculty and students.

While the importance of healthcare leadership is widely acknowledged, the practice of healthcare leadership is in a state of flux. Organizational leaders are faced with a tough balancing act: meeting the needs of their communities and patients while achieving desired organizational metrics. These challenges are shaping new thinking about healthcare leadership, and, as a result, best practices in healthcare leadership are evolving. To fully understand today's best practices, students need to gain the perspective of the practitioner, and providing that perspective is a unique and key contribution of this book. The book's chapters on leadership concepts and practices are written by co-authors representing both academia and management practice; this novel approach provides a rich and balanced assessment of the current state of healthcare leadership.

This text fills an important gap in the healthcare management literature. Being an effective leader in health care requires exhibiting the knowledge, behaviors, and practices to lead staff to the desired level of performance.

As this book insightfully describes, leading others begins with leading oneself, which includes assessing and developing one's own knowledge and skills, and building on personal strengths. Much has been written recently about the importance of leadership and the desired competencies of effective leaders in healthcare management. That knowledge is expanding with new research that identifies and analyzes the success healthcare leaders have had in transforming individual services and organizations into high performers, and the strategies and tactics used to achieve those successful results. The chapter authors of this book highlight important current healthcare leadership concepts and practices. For example:

- *Cultural Competency.* Organizations are becoming more diverse in terms of professional and support staff, and the populations they serve. Leaders must fully recognize this trend and practice effective relationship management with key internal and external stakeholders.
- *Teamwork.* Effective delivery of care requires staff to work closely and interdependently. This process begins with the leadership team that shapes an organizational culture of teamwork, collaboration, and engagement.
- *Patient- and Family-Centered Leadership.* Patient- and family-centered care has been shown to impact patient satisfaction as well as quality and outcomes, and is now a key factor influencing reimbursement. Leadership in healthcare organizations is instrumental in achieving patient- and family-centered care.
- *Community Outreach.* Healthcare organizations fundamentally serve the community. Leaders must conceptualize and act on strategies and approaches to effectively engage in community outreach and development.
- *Leadership Under Healthcare Reform.* Health reform legislation at the state and federal levels brings about new demands and account-abilities for leading healthcare organizations. Leaders must embrace new knowledge and skills to effectively adapt their organizations to healthcare reform.

One major point that the academic and practice communities understand about healthcare leadership is that leadership must constantly change as the internal and external environments of healthcare organizations change. The call for new leadership by today's healthcare professionals is a needed and welcomed call; this book will challenge those of us who teach in healthcare management programs as well as our students to reconsider the practice of healthcare leadership and our expectations for healthcare leaders of the future.

Jon M. Thompson, PhD
Professor and Director
Health Services Administration Program
James Madison University
Harrisonburg, Virginia

Preface

There have been a number of books on leadership in a variety of fields, including health care. Some of these texts have been penned by researchers presenting rigorous empirical analyses; others are produced by industry practitioners who bring an experiential perspective to the material. Some books have been written with senior leadership in mind, and others target newly minted managers. Academic tomes tend to include complex theories and models, whereas workbooks may present simpler algorithms or formulas to demonstrate management approaches. All of these texts strive to capture the general nature of excellent leadership, its significance, and its contribution to organizational effectiveness—with variable success.

As professors of health administration and health services management, we have often struggled to find texts that are well suited to undergraduate students. Many textbooks are written at a level of content best suited for masters' students or readers with experience as practitioners in the field. For undergraduate students in health administration, we have had to create a patchwork quilt of readings and references so that we can provide meaningful and understandable information.

In our experience, the majority of undergraduate students we encounter have similar interests, needs, and profiles. These enthusiastic students are typically only 2 to 3 years beyond high school, have little work experience, and have no frame of reference as we dive into the complex and dynamic structure and function of health administration. A smaller number of our students are healthcare professionals with an Associate degree, license, or certification in a field such as nursing, radiologic technology, or respiratory therapy. These students are on the road to management positions in the healthcare workforce, and are seeking the necessary leadership training and degrees to promote their ambitions. Finally, a few of our students are aiming for professional schools such as medicine or pharmacy, and are pursuing an undergraduate degree in a healthcare field as a first step in the pipeline. Finding a health administration text that can effectively address the educational needs of these diverse populations can be challenging.

To tackle that challenge, the editors set out to merge the academic and the practitioner perspectives, and to develop a textbook that would combine the highlights and best practices from both critical worlds, creating a synergistic collaboration. They invited renowned professionals in academia and industry to partner in producing each content area, so that information, theories, and models provided are both academically rigorous and practically applicable. Textbook content, which addresses administration and leadership throughout the full breadth of healthcare disciplines, is presented in language and formats easily understandable by and relevant to these diverse groups of health administration undergraduates. We believe that leadership knowledge and skills must be developed in a sequential fashion, beginning with the foundation of "leading oneself," and then moving step-by-step to the higher echelons of leading other leaders. Our model of leadership development is shown in **Figure P.1**.

Using this model as a basis for promoting leadership development in our text, we begin Chapter 1 with a call for modern leadership, and provide the foundation and skills (such as self-assessment) required for entry into the world of management. Chapter 2 relays information on how healthcare leaders are developed today, and explores the characteristics of leadership excellence. Chapter 3 completes the basic instruction by introducing the culturally competent leader, and the strategies used to promote cultural competency.

The next level up in the model promotes skill building for future leaders. Chapter 4 establishes the importance of creating a culture of professionalism, which transcends from an individual responsibility to an organizational responsibility. Chapter 5 examines the strategies associated with effective personnel management, and the human resource implications of their implementation. Chapter 6 discusses the value of strategic

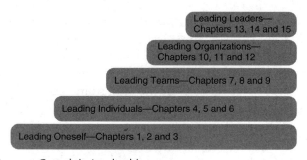

Figure P.1 Steps to Growth in Leadership

leadership in promoting an organization's success in the modern healthcare environment.

How to build and lead outstanding teams becomes the focus of Chapter 7, and Chapter 8 addresses the need for effective teamwork to successfully implement quality initiatives and continuous performance improvement. The skills and attributes of collaborative leadership, essential in the healthcare field, are highlighted in Chapter 9.

Chapter 10 offers a review of how leading organizations utilize transformational leadership via leaders who are change agents. Chapter 11 explores the new concept of patient- and family-centered care and the social and financial benefits for an organization that adopts this model. A detailed discussion of organizational financial management in Chapter 12 outlines the basics of this critical leadership function.

To be able to approach and understand the highest levels of leadership, students must learn how leaders can train and lead other leaders both within and outside of their organizations. Physician leaders are an important and unique constituency in healthcare organizations that are introduced in Chapter 13. High-level health administrators must also successfully interact with and answer to a governing body, such as board of directors or trustees, reviewed in Chapter 14. And, the critical role of external relationships and community outreach for organizational success is explored in Chapter 15.

Given the current era of groundbreaking healthcare reform, we have written the final chapter with the understanding that our students will be entering the healthcare industry in a time of historic change. Chapter 16 presents the newest models of healthcare delivery, and their impact on and implications for leadership. Additionally, to promote interactive student learning and to demonstrate the practical applications of the leadership principles presented in each chapter, the authors provide case studies based on their industry experiences that give students a glimpse of the current working environment as well as instructors' resources to help teach the concepts presented.

As the editors of this book, we have researched and reviewed the requirements for quality leadership in a variety of modern healthcare settings. We have ourselves served both as experienced administrators and academics as well as currently practicing healthcare leaders, and we have assembled a group of renowned contributors who have the academic understanding and the practice 'know-how' necessary for excellent leadership in today's healthcare industry.

Our students will take on the mantle of healthcare leadership in the coming decades and will have the opportunity to enhance our healthcare system for the benefit of our country and our population. We hope the strong foundation we provide in this book will help our students to develop into the outstanding healthcare leaders our country seeks and needs.

Louis Rubino
Salvador Esparza
Yolanda S. Reid Chassiakos

Acknowledgments

Our thanks go to our esteemed colleagues who contributed their time, talent, knowledge, and experiences to this work. It has been a privilege and an honor to work with each and every contributor. This project would not have been possible without their dedication to the field of health administration education.

Louis Rubino
Salvador Esparza
Yolanda S. Reid Chassiakos

About the Editors

Dr. Louis G. Rubino is Professor and Director of the Health Administration program at California State University, Northridge (CSUN). In the community, he serves as a governing board member at St. Francis Medical Center and is Chair of their Quality and Patient Safety Subcommittee. Prior to academia, Dr. Rubino served for 20 years as a hospital administrator and health system executive. Dr. Rubino holds a master's degree and PhD in Public Administration from the University of Southern California. His expertise is the study of integrated systems with special emphasis on the operation of acute hospitals, international comparative studies in hospital administration, and leadership. He is a recertified Fellow in the American College of Healthcare Executives. He is the co-editor of "Collaboration Across the Disciplines in Health Care."

Dr. Salvador J. Esparza has been teaching full-time in the Health Administration Program at California State University, Northridge since 2006. Prior to this time, Dr. Esparza was a practicing healthcare executive with extensive experience in hospital and ambulatory operations for a variety of healthcare organizations within and outside of California. He is a board-certified executive and Fellow of the American College of Healthcare Executives. Dr. Esparza started his career as a Registered Nurse and as a result has a great appreciation for the role and contribution of clinicians in healthcare organizations, and the strategic value they provide for the effective delivery of healthcare services. He serves as chairman of the board of a local, not-for-profit medical center and has contributed his governance expertise to other organizations in his community.

Dr. Yolanda S. Reid Chassiakos is the Director of the Klotz Student Health Center at California State University, Northridge, and a Clinical Assistant Professor of Pediatrics at the David Geffen School of Medicine, UCLA.

Dr. Chassiakos has also served as the Assistant Head of the Ambulatory Branch of the Department of Pediatrics at the Naval Hospital Bethesda; as the Project Director of the Preventive Services Initiative at the Office of Disease Prevention and Health Promotion in the U.S. Department of Health and Human Services; as the Chair of the Medical Staff at Ashe Health and Wellness Center, UCLA; and as Medical Editor for Lifetime Medical Television and Hospital Satellite Network. She is the co-editor of "Collaboration Across the Disciplines in Health Care."

Contributors

Hildegarde B. Aguinaldo, JD, MPH
Attorney
Lewis Brisbois Bisgaard & Smith LLP
Los Angeles, CA

Keith Benson, PhD
Associate Professor
Winthrop University
Rock Hill, SC

Nancy Borkowski, DBA, CPA, FACHE, FHFMA
Clinical Associate Professor and Executive Director
Health Management Programs
Chapman Graduate School of Business
Florida International University
Miami, FL

Dale Buchbinder, MD, FACS
Chairman Department of Surgery and Clinical Professor of Surgery
University of Maryland Medical School
Good Samaritan Hospital
Baltimore, MD

Sharon B. Buchbinder, PhD, RN
Professor and MS in Healthcare Management Program Coordinator
Graduate and Professional Studies
Stevenson University
Owings Mills, MD

Marsha Chan, PharmD, MBA, FACHE
Chief Administrative Officer
Cynosure Health
La Canada, CA

David E. Cockley, DrPH
Associate Professor of Health Administration
James Madison University
Harrisonburg, VA

Barbara Perez Deppman, FACHE
President itMD
Miami, FL

Ethel Elkins, DHSc
Assistant Professor
Health Services Administration
University of Southern Indiana
Evansville, IN

Brenda Freshman, PhD
Assistant Professor
Health Care Administration Department
California State University, Long Beach
Long Beach, CA

Andrew N. Garman, PsyD
Chief Executive Officer
National Center for Healthcare Leadership
Professor and Associate Chair, External Relations and Business Development
Rush University
Chicago, IL

Linda Joyce Gunn, PhD, CPHRM, ACC
Course Mentor
MBA Healthcare Management Programs
Western Governors University
Salt Lake City, UT

Mellisa Hall, DNP, ANP-BC, FNP-BC, GNP-BC
Family Nurse Practitioner
Tulip Tree Family Health and C.A. Goodman, LLC
Fort Branch, IN

Christopher R. Hummer, MHA
President
Carolinas Medical Center–Pineville
Charlotte, NC

Mary Lynne Knighten, DPN, RN, PN, NEA-BC
Senior Director
Patient Experience and Care Delivery
St. Francis Medical Center
Lynwood, CA

Christy Harris Lemak, PhD, FACHE
Chief Academic Officer
National Center for Healthcare Leadership
Associate Professor, Health Management and Policy
Director, Griffith Leadership Center
University of Michigan
Ann Arbor, MI

Thomas F. McIlwain, PhD, MPH
Professor and Director
MHA Program
Clayton State University
Morrow, GA

Mary Helen McSweeney-Feld, PhD
Associate Professor
Office of Collaborative Programs
Research Associate, Center for Productive Aging
Towson University
Towson, MD

Jeanne M. Melton, DHA
Director
Pre-Professional Health Studies
St. Louis University
St. Louis, MO

Carol Molinari, PhD, MBA, MPH
Associate Professor
University of Baltimore
Baltimore, MD

Craig Nesta, JD, MBA, MS, FACHE, FHFMA
Consultant
Performance Improvement and Healthcare Practice Management
Boston, MA

John A. Orsini, CPA
Chief Financial Officer
Presence Health
Des Plaines, IL

Victoria A. Parker, DBA, EdM
Associate Professor
School of Public Health
Boston University
Boston, MA

Timothy Putnam, DHA, MBA, FACHE
President/CEO
Margaret Mary Community Hospital
Batesville, IN

Beverly Quaye, EdD, RN, NEA-BC, FACHE
Vice President and Chief Nursing Officer
St. Francis Medical Center
Lynwood, CA

Nancy Rubin, MS
Vice President Human Resources
Motion Picture and Television Fund
Woodland Hills, CA

Laurie Shanderson, PhD, MPA
Assistant Dean
School of Health Sciences
Richard Stockton College
Galloway, NJ

John M. Shiver, MHA, FACHE, FAAMA
Assistant Professor
Department of Health Administration and Policy
George Mason University
Fairfax, VA

Michael O. Ugwueke, DHA, FACHE
Chief Executive Officer
Methodist North and South Hospitals
Memphis, TN

Brian O. Underhill, PhD
Founder and CEO
CoachSource LLC
San Jose, CA

Michael L. Wall, MHA, FACHE
Acting Chief Executive Office
St. John Hospital and Health Center
Santa Monica, CA

Chapter 1

A Call for New Leadership in Health Care

Salvador Esparza and Louis Rubino

LEARNING OBJECTIVES

By the end of this chapter, the student will be able to:

· Understand how healthcare reform in the United States is changing leadership.
· Describe the difference between leadership and management.
· Know the shared models of leadership in an environment of reform.
· Explain the importance of understanding yourself and others for effective leadership.

KEY TERMS

C-suite

Ethics

Healthcare value

Leadership competencies

Leadership models

Learning organization

Mental models

Patient Protection and Affordable Care Act (ACA)

Psychological contract

Will-Ideas-Execution

INTRODUCTION

We are living in historic times. Reform of the healthcare delivery system in the United States is actively underway. The **Patient Protection and Affordable Care Act (ACA)**, enacted in 2010, was upheld in June 2012 as constitutional by the U.S. Supreme Court and is now being implemented. Even though court challenges may continue for some of the ACA's provisions, most of the ACA's components are already becoming a reality in the U.S. healthcare industry. These vast changes to the healthcare industry will continue, motivated not only by legislative and legal processes, but also by market forces.

The ACA's scope extends beyond simple health insurance reform; it is the catalyst for additional reforms of our healthcare delivery system. For example, the ACA addresses quality and cost-effectiveness of care; public health, including disease prevention and wellness; the healthcare workforce; fraud and abuse; long-term care; biopharmaceuticals; elder abuse; and Indian Health Services (McDonough, 2012). New frameworks and structures, such as accountable care organizations, patient-centered medical homes, foundations, and health insurance exchanges, are being developed and implemented to enhance healthcare services and quality (McLaughlin, 2011).

The objective of these changes is to improve American **healthcare value** and accessibility. Even though the ACA does not provide for universal healthcare coverage, it does increase the availability of health insurance for most Americans, allowing more people to seek out and obtain medical care. "Value of services provided" is a more elusive goal. Cost-effective services,— that is, the provision of high-quality care at lower cost—will be critical to successful healthcare reform (Wachter, 2012).

Outstanding leadership is necessary to guide us well in this period of dynamic change. Strategies must be developed to achieve the performance benchmarks needed to survive in this new healthcare environment. Potential barriers to successful adaptation for healthcare organizations and their leaders include limited economic resources and increased government regulation. The healthcare workforce will be looking to their leaders and managers to steer them safely through these churning waters. Stakeholders from within and from outside healthcare entities will demand leadership that can appropriately address interests and concerns such as fiscal stability and sustainability. Healthcare reform will provide new opportunities for graduates entering the healthcare workforce who have the confidence, abilities, and skills to effectively lead under these challenging conditions.

LEADERSHIP AS A COURSE OF STUDY

Today's healthcare leaders must transform the way their organizations operate (Gabow, Halvorson, & Kaplan, 2012). A recent symposium, sponsored by the Robert Wood Johnson Foundation, invited more than 50 healthcare leaders from across the United States to meet and develop recommendations for pursuing opportunities to improve the health of the nation and create workable health solutions for the upcoming 2 decades (Japsen, 2012). Of the four key areas of focus that were identified, one was the cultivation of new leadership to promote a healthy society. In its discussion paper, *A CEO Checklist for High-Value Health Care,* the Institute of Medicine also included governance priority as one of its foundational elements, recommending visible and determined leadership by healthcare CEOs and board members (Cosgrove et al., 2012).

In order to meet this need for new and dynamic leadership in the healthcare industry, educational institutions will need to expand their role of developing modern leaders. Leadership, as a course of study, should be included in all health professional training programs; effective leadership skills can be taught and learned. Early exposure to leadership principles will better educate and prepare our future managers and supervisors, and teach them to conduct ongoing personal assessments and to reflect on their successes and their failures (better termed, "learning opportunities"). Health professionals have frequently been promoted into leadership positions without formal instruction in health administration. Lack of adequate training, for example, could lead a new manager to spend most of his or her time on tactical problem solving rather than strategic decision making, diminishing his or her effectiveness. With trained leaders who possess the competencies proven to promote success, the healthcare industry will be in a better position to address the challenges in this environment of reform.

LEADERSHIP VERSUS MANAGEMENT

Leadership and management aim for similar outcomes: getting people to achieve organizational goals through certain acts and behavior. A main difference though is that in management, the way this is accomplished is through processes (i.e., organizing, staffing, controlling, planning, etc.); and for leadership, this is done through influence. Another defining feature is orientation. In general, managers have more of an internal focus, concentrating on the issues associated inside the organization. Leaders have more of an external focus, concentrating on issues outside of the organization but affected by its association.

A commonly debated question in the first session of any basic leadership course is: Can good leaders be good managers, and can good managers be good leaders? And, is there a differentiation of duties between leadership and management? Yes, some leaders can be good managers, and some managers can be good leaders—depending in large part on their training and skills.

Good leaders typically rise to their position of influence through the ability to successfully lead others toward achieving a mutually agreed-upon goal. Without others willing to be led, however, there can be no leaders. "Followership" is complementary and essential to leadership (Atchison, 2003). Not everyone has the skills or inclination to be an effective leader; successful leaders need capable followers to be able to achieve their organizations' goals.

Katz (1955) conducted primary research on leadership and managerial effectiveness and determined that successful leaders and managers utilize three distinct sets of skills: conceptual, interpersonal, and technical skills. Conceptual skills include being able to work with ideas and concepts, critical to strategic planning for senior leadership. Interpersonal skills are needed by both leaders and managers. Technical skills are predominantly utilized by managers for operational functions, but can be valuable for senior leaders who are tasked with accountability data analysis. Different skills are critical to leadership versus managerial success.

Further distinctions between leadership and management foci are made by Manion (2011). Building on the original premises presented by Bennis (1989), Manion points out that those in charge must look differently at situations depending on their administrative level and position. For example, leaders are more concerned about effectiveness (*if* the task gets done), whereas managers are more concerned with efficiencies (*how* the task is done). Leaders are focused on "what" and "why," whereas managers are more focused on "how." Leaders are more concerned with people and relationships, and, even though managers are more concerned with organizational structure, people and relationships are also critical to good management. Leaders are focused on innovation and managers on "maintaining the status quo." Most importantly, whereas managers are typically eyeing "today's" bottom line, leaders look toward the horizon to help move the organization forward (see **Table 1.1**).

HISTORY OF LEADERSHIP IN THE UNITED STATES

Over the past century, leadership has been influenced by social and cultural contexts (see **Table 1.2**). From the industrial revolution to the 1920s and 1930s, the "Great Man" theorists believed that the best leaders had inherent traits such as strength, firmness, and male gender. During the 1940s and 1950s, after the devastation of World War II, leadership theories shifted toward considering relationships in addition to getting tasks

Table 1.1 Leader Versus Manager Focus

Leader Focus	Manager Focus
Effectiveness	Efficiency
What and why	How
People and relationships	Organizational structure
Innovation	Status quo
Horizon	Bottom line

Table 1.2 Leadership Theories in the United States

Period of Time	Leadership Theory	Leadership Focus
1920s and 1930s	Great Man	Having certain inherent traits
1940s and 1950s	Style Approach	Task completion and developing relationships
1960s	Situational	Needs of the subordinates
1970s	Contingency and Path–Goal	Considers style and situation
1980s	Transformational Approach	Raises consciousness and empowers followers
1990s	Team Leadership	Team development and performance
Contemporary Theories	Authentic, Servant, Spirituality and Emotional Intelligence	Leading with a purpose, serving others and being empathetic

Source: Modified from Buchbinder, S. & Shanks, N. (2012). *Introduction to health care management* (2nd ed.). Burlington, MA: Jones & Bartlett Learning.

done. In the 1960s and 1970s, the emergence of social consciousness led to situational approaches wherein the dynamic nature of relationships were examined, the needs of subordinates were considered, and the styles of leadership were assessed relative to subordinates. Path–Goal and Contingency are examples of two such theories. By the 1980s, the transformational approach became prominent, and in the 1990s, team building and leadership were heralded.

Since 2000, a number of contemporary approaches have been developed. Some specifically appeal to the "helping" mission popular in health care. Authentic leadership has people motivated by leaders who follow their internal compass of true purpose and associated values. Servant leadership rests on the principle that leaders and followers are motivated by the desire to serve others: followers to serve clients, and leaders to serve the employees that implement the organizational mission. Spiritual leadership tends to be a good fit for an industry that is often sponsored by religious organizations. Emotional intelligence, with its five dimensions of self-assessment, self-regulation, self-motivation, social skills, and social awareness, can provide healthcare leaders using any of these leadership styles with a tool kit from which to draw strategies and solutions that respect both leaders and subordinates (Rubino, 2012).

Individual Leader Perspective

In healthcare organizations, there are many opportunities for leadership. The **C-suite**, for example, especially in larger organizations such as hospitals, contains several high-level executives who are responsible for the entire entity, or multiple affiliated entities (e.g., Chief Executive Officer, Chief Operating Officer, Chief Quality Officer). Others leaders might supervise specific groups of associates (e.g., Chief Nursing Officer and Chief Medical Officer) or have critical administrative and operational responsibilities (i.e., Chief Financial Officer and Chief Information Officer). All the department leaders are expected to work together as a leadership team to ensure the alignment of action with the organization's strategic plans and mission. Smaller healthcare organizations, such as nursing homes, clinics, and home health agencies, also identify leaders for their units, but with more limited human and financial resources, may provide fewer opportunities for the development of functional leadership teams and collegial camaraderie.

Healthcare organizations tend to be hierarchical. Professionals who provide patient care are typically supervised by physicians or nurses. In hospitals, a physician is usually elected or appointed Chief of Staff and oversees the breadth of clinical operations that are organized and provided as per the hospital's Medical Staff bylaws. Subdivisions and units such as Surgery, Pediatrics, Obstetrics, and the like will usually have a physician leader who has been trained in the unit specialty to supervise the unit's specialists and advanced practice nurses. Nursing units are typically supervised by experienced senior nurses, many of whom have master's or doctorate degrees. Physicians or nurses may be elected to serve as the Chairs of Quality Improvement and/or Patient Safety Committee and monitor the quality of care provided.

There is a breadth of leaders in many other healthcare organizational units/departments/divisions (imaging supervisors, laboratory scientists, business office managers, etc.), who have similar roles and responsibilities for their various specialty. In healthcare sectors that are not provider based, such as pharmaceutical, medical supply, and insurance companies, many other leadership positions can be identified. The **leadership competencies** needed to be successful in these roles are transferable across multiple types of healthcare organizations.

THE LEADERSHIP COMPETENCIES

Competencies are a set of skills, knowledge, and abilities. An alliance of associations representing healthcare leadership groups—the American College of Healthcare Executives, the American College of Physician Executives, the American Organization of Nurse Executives, the Healthcare Information and Management Systems Society, the Healthcare Financial Management Association, and the Medical Group Management Association—collaborated to determine the set of competencies needed by successful healthcare leaders.

Leadership was identified as the central domain that intersected with four other domains: (1) communication and relationship management, (2) professionalism, (3) knowledge of the healthcare environment, and (4) business skills and knowledge. Within the area of leadership, the important competencies identified were leadership skills and behavior, organizational climate and culture, communicating vision, and managing change. The American College of Healthcare Executives (ACHE), as well as the other associations, now uses this set of competencies to help its members conduct self-assessments of their leaders' practices (ACHE, 2012).

The demands of U.S. healthcare reform for improved quality of care and cost-effectiveness have inspired a renewed examination of the competencies needed by healthcare executives who are preparing their organizations for change. A recent survey of hospital and other healthcare systems attempted to assess the promotion and adoption of these competencies in organizational leadership development programs (Awo Osei-Anto, 2011). Though leadership development programs were variable from organization to organization, the study demonstrated a correlation between leadership training in best practices and improved performance.

IHI FRAMEWORK FOR LEADERSHIP FOR IMPROVEMENT

A more specific framework for leaders to achieve better performance is provided by the Institute for Healthcare Improvement (IHI; Reinertsen, Bisognano, & Pugh, 2008). Acknowledging the pressures healthcare leaders are facing, the IHI developed a roadmap that leaders who wish to improve their organizations can follow. The core elements of this model are **Will-Ideas-Execution**. Successful leaders must develop the organizational will to achieve results, generate or identify effective ideas or strategies for improvement, and then execute those ideas. In addition, setting direction and establishing the foundation will help spread the ideas across the organization and sustain them over time. A push–pull type of response is typical in organizations implementing this model: building will and generating new ideas make the status quo uncomfortable, however, the execution of good ideas will make the future attractive. The IHI Framework for Leadership for Improvement includes 24 elements and provides a helpful perspective regarding the steps needed to achieve success in today's healthcare environment (see **Figure 1.1**)

Healthcare reform in the United States will demand a different skillset from leaders to ensure ongoing success. Bolster and Larrere (2012) present six areas in which senior leaders will need to develop expertise in this new era: having political savvy, being influential, having the ability to lead during change, being adaptable, exhibiting excellent communication, and being a true visionary. All of these areas depend on the development of successful and effective interpersonal skills.

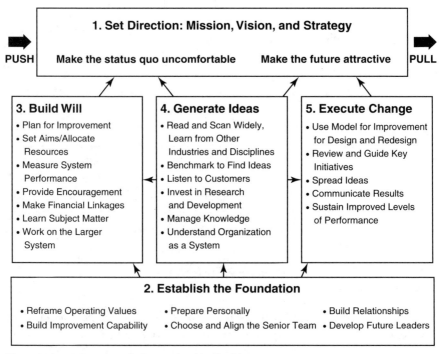

Figure 1.1 IHI Framework for Leadership for Improvement

Source: Reproduced from Reinertsen, J .L., Bisognano, M., & Pugh, M. D. (2008). *Seven leadership leverage points for organization-level improvement in health care* (2nd ed.). Cambridge, MA: Institute for Healthcare Improvement. (Available on www.ihi.org.)

Models of Leadership

As mentioned previously, a model is a construct that helps us better understand and address a situation or environment. **Leadership models** can help us understand why leaders act the way they do and which leadership actions are most likely to lead to successful outcomes. Because different situations call for different leadership approaches, leaders must avoid getting stuck using only one type of model. Two well-regarded models that address common leadership challenges are the *Managerial Grid* and the *Four Framework Approach*.

Managerial Grid

The Managerial Grid, also known as the Leadership Grid, was developed by Blake and Mouton (1985), and it is based on two dimensions or axes, each of which has a range from 0 to 9: The axes are the extent to which there is a "concern for people/relationships," and the extent to which there is a "concern for results/production."

Data or observations collected for each leader are plotted on the grid (see **Figure 1.2**). Most leaders fall somewhere in the middle of the two axes (i.e., middle of the road). When we look at the extreme quadrants of the grid, however, we find four classic types of leaders:

- Impoverished—low concern for people and results
- Country Club—high concern for people, low concern for results
- Authoritarian—low concern for people, high concern for results
- Team Leader—high concern for people and results

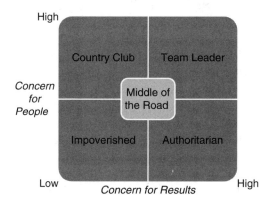

Figure 1.2 The Blake Mouton Grid

Source: Reproduced from Blake, R. R., & Mouton, J. S. (1970). The fifth achievement. *Journal of Applied Behavioral Science, 6*(4), 413–426.

Impoverished Leader

Leaders demonstrating this style detach themselves from their workforce and tend to allow their team or group members to do whatever they want. Lacking commitment to either group maintenance or task accomplishment, they generally "delegate and disappear."

Country Club Leader

Leaders demonstrating this style shy away from exerting authority or implementing disciplinary measures in the quest for improved outcomes because they fear jeopardizing the positive interpersonal relationships with their workforce. Instead, these leaders will almost exclusively use reward and recognition to encourage the team to accomplish its goals.

Authoritarian

These leaders are characterized by task orientation and a tendency to be tough with their group or team members. Authoritarian leaders will focus their energy on getting the work done at all costs and expect people to do exactly what they are told without questions. If something goes wrong, they are likely to "blame, shame, and train" in order to prevent the issue from occurring again. These types of leaders are intolerant of dissent and perceive it as disloyalty, making it difficult for their group or team members to comfortably contribute their valuable input.

Team Leader

These leaders strive to lead by example, foster a productive team environment, and encourage teams and individuals to achieve their highest potential. They constantly work at strengthening the bonds among team members and colleagues to promote successful outcomes and goal achievement.

The most desirable place to be on the grid is the Team Leader area. However, elements of the other leadership styles may sometimes be useful in specific situations.

Four Framework Approach

In the Four Framework Approach, Bolman and Deal (1991) propose that leaders frequently display leadership styles and behaviors that fit one of four types of frameworks: political, human resources, structural, or symbolic (see **Figure 1.3**).

This model suggests that leaders can be matched with one of the following four frameworks of leadership.

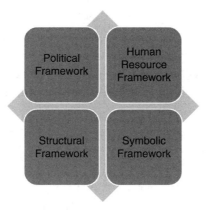

Figure 1.3 The Four Framework Approach

Source: Bolman, L., & Deal, T. (1991, Winter). Leadership and management effectiveness: A multi-frame, multi-sector analysis. *Human Resource Management, 30*(4), 509–534.

Political Framework

This leader is an advocate whose approach includes coalition building. Political leaders are clear and realistic about their goals, build connections with other stakeholders, determine distribution of power and interests, and use influence and persuasion before they resort to negotiation or coercion.

Human Resource Framework

This leader is a servant and advocate. Human resource leaders use an approach that is supportive and empowering; believes in people; is visible and accessible; shares information widely and encourages participation; and allows decisions to be made by relevant employees at all levels of the organization.

Structural Framework

This leader emphasizes analysis and design. Structural leaders serve as social architects to address issues, focusing on structure, strategy, environment, execution, and adaptation.

Symbolic Framework

This leader is inspirational and prophetic. Symbolic leaders view the organization as a theater in which they must communicate a vision to their audience. They play specific roles, use symbolism to create a setting or impression, and interpret and dynamically pitch the organization's potential future on behalf of its members.

In the healthcare industry, situations may arise in which one of the above frameworks or approaches may be more effective than another.

Successful leaders may be able to adopt aspects of a different framework to achieve a specific outcome.

UNDERSTANDING YOURSELF AND OTHERS: THE KEY TO SUCCESSFUL INTERPERSONAL SKILLS

The 6th century BCE Chinese philosopher Lao Tzu is known to have said, "He who knows others is wise. He who knows himself is enlightened." In no milieu is this adage truer than in the practice of leadership. How can one lead others if one is uninformed about, and unable to lead, oneself? The manner in which leaders engage in professional behaviors such as conversation, planning, problem solving, decision making, and a host of other leadership functions has profound effects on other individuals. Our personality and our environment influence our innate behaviors, but when behavior change is valuable in order to enhance leadership effectiveness, we are able to learn new skills and behaviors that will make us more productive and successful.

Before setting out to understand and work effectively with others, we must first strive to understand ourselves. We must become aware of our individual mental maps or models. Peter Senge (1990, p. 8) in his classic book, *The Fifth Discipline,* defined **mental models** as:

> . . . deeply ingrained assumptions, generalizations, or even pictures or images that influence how we understand the world and how we take action. Very often, we are not consciously aware of our mental models or the effect it has [*sic*] on our behavior.

Our mental model serves as a window, which frames (and sometimes distorts) the world we see (Osland, Kolb, Rubin, & Turner, 2007). We react in different ways because our "windows" show us different perspectives. One of the best ways to understand our own perspectives, reactions, and behavior is to identify our maps or models and become aware of our own beliefs, values, and expectations by using self-assessment instruments. These tools of self-discovery include instruments that assess characteristics central to leadership effectiveness such as learning style, personality, motivation, and **ethics**.

THE PSYCHOLOGICAL CONTRACT: MUTUAL EXPECTATION SETTING

When we enter into a personal or professional relationship, we aim for the relationship to have a strong foundation of trust. Trust allows us to develop integrity and credibility in our relationships. Employees joining an organization are establishing a professional relationship with their employer. This relationship starts with an implicit, unwritten **psychological**

contract. Psychological contracts are defined as a person's beliefs, formed by the organization, regarding the terms and conditions of a reciprocal agreement between people and their organization (Rousseau, 1995). The development of mutually agreed-upon expectations between the employee and employer, and stability and reciprocity in the professional relationship, promotes employee and organizational productivity.

Unfortunately, psychological contracts can be violated or broken. Broken contracts occur when one of the parties fails to meet the stated obligations or expectations. The result can be a negative impact on attitudes, behaviors, performance, and productivity.

Setting expectations can be a double-edged sword. Researchers have demonstrated a *Pygmalion Effect*—that is, "people perform in accordance with a rater's expectation of them" (Osland et al., 2007, p. 13). If a rater expects an employee to perform at a high level, the employee is likely to meet that expectation. Leaders may give highly rated employees more challenging assignments and provide the support and encouragement the individual may need to achieve the assignments successfully. On the other hand, if a rater expects poor performance, poor performance is more likely because the leader may interact negatively with the low-rated employee and not provide the support and direction necessary to succeed. Effective leaders seek to identify their perceptions, prejudices, and preconceived notions that could negatively influence interactions with their employees and take the necessary corrective actions to minimize potentially negative behaviors.

Understanding one's own theories of management and identifying one's personal leadership style is imperative in this self-development process. Effective leaders make every effort to analyze their skills, perceptions, and values; develop strategies to implement necessary changes; educate themselves in the areas and skills they need to master; practice newly learned skills; and obtain feedback about how well they are performing.

A method of managing psychological contracts is called the *Pinch Model* (see **Figure 1.4**), developed by Sherwood and Glidewell in 1972 and still in use today (Osland et al., 2007). This model describes the dynamic nature of these contracts and recommends ways to mitigate the negative consequences of changing expectations.

The Pinch Model

Osland and colleagues (2007) identify and describe the stages of this model as follows:

> *Stage 1*—The first stage of an employee/employer relationship is characterized by the sharing of information and the subsequent negotiation of expectations of one another. If the individual or

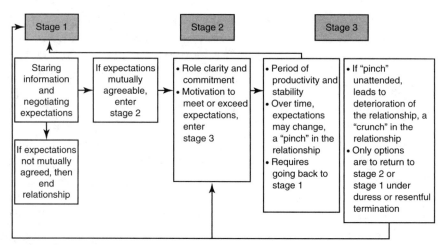

Figure 1.4 The Pinch Model

Source: Adapted from Sherwood, J. J., & Glidewell, J. C. (1972). Planned negotiation: A norm-setting OD intervention. In W. W. Burke (Ed.), *Contemporary organization development: Orientations and interventions* (pp. 35–46). Washington, DC: NTL Institute.

organization determines the expectations to be unreasonable, then they will deselect themselves from the relationship (i.e., "planned termination"). On the other hand, if both parties accept the mutually agreed-upon expectations, then they enter Stage 2.

Stage 2—The second stage allows the relationship to move to role clarity and commitment between the parties. Leaders and their employees accept and understand the roles each plays and are presumably motivated to meet or exceed those expectations. This process leads to Stage 3.

Stage 3—This stage is characterized by a period of productivity and stability in the relationship and allows for maximum energy to be dedicated to the work at hand. However, as in most relationships, with the passage of time, changes in expectations may occur due to intrinsic or extrinsic reasons. Sherwood and Glidewell (1972) call this a "pinch point" in the relationship and suggest that this is a warning sign to return to the first stages of the relationship to avoid disruption. When expectations change, one option is to renegotiate, meeting agreed-upon expectations. If renegotiation is successful, both parties will move through the stages of role clarity and stability once again. However, if renegotiation fails, one or both parties may decide to terminate the relationship.

Left unaddressed, a dissonance in shared expectations can lead to a deterioration of a professional relationship. Uncertainty or ambiguity can eventually lead to anxiety and resentment. If this occurs, the relationship may respond via three options: (1) a return to Stage 2 by attempting to return expectations to the previous contract, (2) a return to Stage 1 by renegotiating expectations (under duress), or (3) termination of the relationship either administratively or emotionally.

The key to successful leadership is to be clear about mutual expectations and to manage those expectations just like any other important operational function or process.

INDIVIDUAL AND ORGANIZATIONAL LEARNING

A **learning organization** is one that is skilled at acquiring, creating, and transferring knowledge, and modifying its behavior to reflect this new knowledge and insight (Osland et al., 2007). Members of successful learning organizations are active adult learners. Kolb (1999) has postulated that adult learning is a cyclical process composed of four primary modes:

1. *Concrete experience* or learning by experiencing. This is a feeling mode that is characterized by responses to specific experiences, relating to people, and sensitivity to feelings.
2. *Reflective observation* or learning by reflecting. This is a watching mode characterized by observation before making judgments, viewing issues from varying perspectives, and looking for meaning in functions or events.
3. *Abstract conceptualization* or learning by thinking. This mode is characterized by the logical analysis of ideas, systematic planning, and the intellectually based responses to situations.
4. *Active experimentation* or learning by doing. This mode is characterized by taking risks, demonstrating the ability to get things done, and influencing people through action.

Most adult learners tend to favor one or more of these learning modes. Organizations can benefit by having members with different learning styles involved in problem solving and decision making. Leaders who identify their learning mode can better understand how they approach work-related issues and how they can best interface with others who use a different mode or style.

Personality

Personality has been defined as a person's consistent pattern of thought, behavior, and emotions, and the psychological mechanisms that drive and support those patterns (Osland et al., 2007). Effective leaders are aware of their own personality traits and the traits of others, and understand the impact these traits may have on professional interpersonal relationships. Instruments such as the Myers-Briggs Type Indicator (MBTI) and Jung Typology are available for leaders to identify and learn about the components of their own personality as well as those of colleagues and employees. Both of these instruments suggest four components to personality:

· Extraversion/Introversion (E/I): how an individual interacts with society
· Sensing/Intuiting (S/N): how an individual collects information
· Thinking/Feeling (T/F): how an individual evaluates information
· Judging/Perceiving (J/P): how an individual prefers to make decisions

Effective leaders try to develop a robust picture of all the individuals with whom they work and attempt to understand their personalities and their "rules of engagement." They strive to analyze the causes of individual behaviors, remembering to observe specific characteristics such as motivation and skills, to be able to ensure that the "job, group, and organizational characteristics are exerting the intended consequences on behavior" (Osland et al., 2007, p. 90), and not triggering unintended negative outcomes.

Motivation

It is often heard that good leaders "motivate" others. This expression is frequently misunderstood to mean that motivation is something that is done by someone to someone else. Motivation is, in fact, an internal state, something within an individual that directs him or her toward certain goals and objectives. Motivation is facilitated by internal psychological forces that influence behavior, levels of effort, and levels of persistence (Osland et al., 2007).

It has been said that it is much better to light a fire within someone than to light a fire underneath them. The task of an effective leader is to understand, enhance, and guide the motivation employees already possess, and channel the motivation toward activities that further the goals and objectives of the organization. Effective leaders understand that the sources of motivation can be either intrinsic (e.g., the work itself) or extrinsic (e.g., economic rewards). Different people are motivated by different things; there are a variety of tools (i.e., Maslow's hierarchy of needs, McClelland's theory of motivation, Alderfer's ERG theory, etc.) available to determine people's motivators. The leader's role is to create an environment that encourages motivation by setting clear standards of performance and ensuring that there is a good "fit" between the needs of the employee and the position.

Determining what motivates an individual is not always an easy task. In addition to using the tools mentioned above, leaders can observe the individual in the work setting and discover what type of work or projects they enjoy. Face to face discussion, for example, during the performance appraisal or annual evaluation, can allow employees to provide leaders with feedback about their areas of interest for future assignments.

Ethics and Values

Healthcare leaders are frequently faced with ethical dilemmas that may challenge their decision making. These issues may include clinical challenges such as end-of-life care, queries regarding experimental research on human subjects, and operational questions about contractual and revenue-generating arrangements. Effective leaders have a responsibility to set the moral tone of an organization, should always strive to behave in an ethical manner, and should set clear expectations for subordinates and others to do the same. Standards or codes of ethical behavior have been clearly identified by professional associations such as the American College of Healthcare Executives (ACHE). Members of ACHE are accountable for adhering to codes of conduct that cover responsibilities to

- The profession of healthcare management
- Patients and others served
- The organization
- Employees
- Community and society
- Report violations of the codes

In addition, the ACHE has developed ethical policy statements that encompass such areas as leader–vendor relationships, reductions in force (layoffs), and health information confidentiality. The code of ethics and ethical policy statements can be viewed at www.ache.org/ABT_ACHE/code.cfm.

Much of a leader's behavior is rooted in his or her personal values, ethics, and moral reasoning. It is critical for effective leaders to understand their own value system and project their response to issues and situations that may arise. Values are defined as core beliefs that guide attitudes and actions. Terminal values are desired end-states or goals, either social or personal, that people would like to achieve. Instrumental values are preferable modes of behavior or means to achieving terminal values. There are two types of instrumental values: competence and moral. Osland and colleagues (2007) have identified an instrument titled the *Rokeach Values Survey*, which can identify both instrumental and terminal values for self-exploration. Individuals are placed into one of four value orientation quadrants:

1. Preference for personal competence values
2. Preference for social competence values
3. Preference for personal moral values
4. Preference for social moral values

Ethics, on the other hand, refers to standards of conduct that "indicate how a person should behave based on moral duties and virtues arising from principles about right or wrong" (Osland et al., 2007, p. 146). An ethical framework that successful healthcare leaders adopt includes:

- Respect for persons
  - Autonomy (self-governing)
  - Truth telling
  - Confidentiality
  - Fidelity (duty)
- Beneficence
  - Refraining from actions that worsen a problem or cause negative results
- Nonmaleficence
  - First, do no harm
- Justice
  - Consistently apply clear and prospectively determined criteria in decision making

Effective leaders work at identifying and understanding different perspectives on issues and then discuss the benefits, risks, and consequences of alternative actions. One way to promote positive ethical practices is through the use of the Josephson Ethical Warning System (Josephson, 2002), which includes the following elements:

- Golden Rule—Are you treating others as you would want to be treated?
- Publicity—Would you be comfortable if your reasoning and decisions were to be publicized?
- Kid on your shoulder—Would you be comfortable if your children were observing you?

Healthcare organizations are launched with mission statements that ideally define their values, beliefs, and vision, which in turn determine the responsibilities of their leaders and stakeholders. After an organization makes a decision or takes action, the consequences are scrutinized by state and federal regulatory agencies, accrediting and licensing agencies, and the public, and frequently address whether the action is ethical and legal. In order to ensure that leaders function with an optimal standard of ethical behavior, codes of conduct should be developed and used as instructions, guidelines, and/or internal organizational regulations.

Healthcare leaders can use resources such as the *American College of Healthcare Executives' Code of Ethics* for guidance regarding standards of behavior and ethical decision making. The Code can also be used as a basis for developing the organization's policies and performance metrics, and can serve as a teaching tool for colleagues, employees, and students.

Understanding yourself and others, and respecting and appreciating our differences, is key to effectiveness and success as a healthcare leader and should be a commitment that begins early in your career and continues throughout your professional life. Your efforts in this regard will ensure that your colleagues, clients, and communities will be "gifted" by your leadership.

SUMMARY

Health care in the United States is in a very exciting phase. The delivery system is rapidly changing due to a combination of government and market reform measures. These new platforms provide numerous professional opportunities for healthcare leaders with modern competencies. Use of best practices and development of skilled leaders are needed to assist the healthcare industry in meeting the challenge of improving access and establishing value through higher quality and lower costs. Today's healthcare leaders must seek to continuously improve the quality of their leadership and the quality of the services of their organizations. Critical to this process is active learning and ongoing self-assessment of one's ethics and values, and one's leadership and interpersonal styles and skills.

Discussion Questions

1. Can leadership be taught?
2. How have leadership theories changed over the last century?
3. Which competencies are most important for successful leadership during this era of healthcare reform?
4. Why is it important for leaders to "know themselves"?
5. What is the value of understanding mutual expectations?
6. When faced with an ethical dilemma, which approaches could a leader use to resolve the issue?

RELATED WEBSITES

American College of Health Care Administrators: www.achca.org

American College of Healthcare Executives: www.ache.org

American College of Physician Executives: www.acpe.org

American Organization of Nurse Executives: www.aone.org

CEO Checklist for High-Value Health Care: www.iom.edu/CEOChecklist

Complete Patient Protection and Affordable Care Act: http://docs.house.gov/energycommerce/ppacacon.pdf

Health and Human Services Summary of the ACA: www.healthcare.gov/law/provisions/index.html

Healthcare Financial Management Association: www.hfma.org

Medical Group Management Association: www.mgma.com

REFERENCES

American College of Healthcare Executives (ACHE). (2012). *Competencies assessment tool.* Chicago, IL: Healthcare Leadership Alliance and the American College of Healthcare Executives.

Atchison, T. A. (2003). *Followership: A practical guide to aligning leaders and followers.* Chicago, IL: Health Administration Press.

Awo Osei-Anto, H. (2011). Preparing hospital and system leadership for change. *Hospitals and Health Networks, 85*(9), 62.

Bennis, W. (1989). *On becoming a leader.* Reading, MA: Addison-Wesley.

Blake, R. R., & Mouton, J. S. (1985). *The managerial grid III: The key to leadership excellence.* Houston, TX: Gulf.

Bolman, L., & Deal, T. (1991). *Reframing organizations.* San Francisco, CA: Jossey-Bass.

Bolster, C. J., & Larrere, J. B. (2012). The next great explorers. *Trustee, 65*(2), 19–21.

Buchbinder, S., & Shanks, N. (2012). *Introduction to health care management* (2nd ed.). Burlington, MA: Jones & Bartlett Learning.

Cosgrove, D., Fisher, M., Gabow, P., Gottlieb, G., Halvorson, G., James, B., . . . Toussaint, J. (2012, June 5). A CEO checklist for high-value health care. *Institute of Medicine of the National Academies.* Retrieved July 19, 2012 from www.iom.edu/CEOChecklist.

Gabow, P., Halvorson, G., & Kaplan, G. (2012, June 5). Marshaling leadership for high-value health care: An institute of medicine discussion paper. *Journal of the American Medical Association.* Retrieved July 19, 2012 from http://jama.jamanetwork.com/article.aspx?articleid=1172505.

Japsen, B. (2012, June 22). *Health leaders look to 2032 for opportunities to improve the health of the nation.* Robert Wood Johnson Foundation. Retrieved July 19, 2012 from www.rwjf.org/pr/product.jsp?id=74533.

Josephson, M. S. (2002). *Making ethical decisions* (2nd ed.). Los Angeles, CA: Josephson Institute of Ethics.

Katz, R. L. (1955). Skills of an effective administrator. *Harvard Business Review, 33*(1), 33–42.

Kolb, D. A. (1999). *Learning style inventory.* Boston, MA: McBer and Company.

Manion, J. (2011). *From management to leadership: Strategies for transforming health care* (3rd ed.). San Francisco, CA: Jossey-Bass.

McDonough, J. E. (2012, July 5). The road ahead for the Affordable Care Act. *New England Journal of Medicine.* Retrieved October 7, 2012 from www.nejm.org/doi/full/10.1056/NEJMp1206845.

McLaughlin, D. B. (2011). *Responding to healthcare reform: A strategy guide for healthcare leaders.* Chicago, IL: Health Administration Press.

Osland, J. S., Kolb, D. A., Rubin, I. M., & Turner, M. E. (2007). *Organizational behavior: An experiential approach* (8th ed.). Upper Saddle River, NJ: Pearson Prentice Hall.

Reinertsen, J. L., Bisognano, M., & Pugh, M. D. (2008). *Seven leadership leverage points for organization-level improvement in health care* (2nd ed.). Cambridge, MA: Institute for Healthcare Improvement.

Rousseau, D. M. (1995). *Psychological contracts in organizations: Understanding written and unwritten agreements.* Newbury Park, CA: Sage.

Rubino, L. (2012). Leadership. In S. Buchbinder & N. Shanks (Eds.), *Introduction to health care management* (2nd ed.). Burlington, MA: Jones & Bartlett Learning.

Senge, P. M. (1990). *The fifth discipline: The art and practice of the learning organization.* New York, NY: Doubleday Currency.

Sherwood, J. J., & Glidewell, J. C. (1972). Planned negotiation: A norm-setting OD intervention. In W. W. Burke (Ed.), *Contemporary organization development: Orientations and interventions* (pp. 35–46). Washington, DC: NTL Institute.

Wachter, R. M. (2012). Why the Supreme Court's decision means a lot . . . and not so much. *The Governance Institute's E-Briefings, 9*(4), 1–2.

Chapter 2

Developing Healthcare Leaders

Brenda Freshman and Brian O. Underhill

LEARNING OBJECTIVES

By the end of this chapter, the student will be able to:

- Explain the importance of leadership development in health care.
- Discuss key components of a talent management system.
- Identify competencies critical to leadership success.
- Describe two distinct paths to healthcare leadership positions (clinical and administrative).
- Describe models and development methods used for training healthcare leaders.

KEY TERMS

360 evaluation

Accountable Care Organization (ACO)

Bench strength

Executive coaching

High potentials

Leadership pipeline

Shadowing

Stretch assignment

Succession planning

Talent management

INTRODUCTION

Healthcare organizations today are facing unprecedented challenges. The rapid evolution of technology; the constant changes in regulations, policies, and laws; and the shifting demographics of the workforce and patients placing ever-greater pressures on healthcare leaders to excel. However, there is a notable shortage of outstanding leaders who are qualified to meet and address these challenges. And the healthcare industry is not alone in this dilemma, which is exacerbated by increasing rates of retirement among Baby Boomers and earlier generations.

Development of Business Leaders

The lack of effective leaders with the necessary skills and expertise has become one of the greatest business perils in these early decades of the 21st century. Approximately 70% of the 62 companies surveyed in 2005 reported moderate to major leadership shortages (Executive Development Associates, 2005). James Bolt, author of the book *Executive Development* (1991), states, "It has become obvious that an organization's executive and leadership talent is its greatest and most sustainable source of competitive advantage . . . . Cultivating the next generation of business leaders is imperative."

A prominent McKinsey & Co. study entitled "The War for Talent" (Michaels, Handfield-Jones, & Axelrod, 2001) discovered that the highest performing companies in a breadth of industries had better **talent management** strategies (i.e., methods to identify, train, and develop leaders) than lower performing organizations. A disturbing statistic from this report is that "while 72% of all managers surveyed say that winning the war for talent is critical to their company's success, only 9% are confident that their current actions will lead to a stronger talent pool" (p. 3).

In another major study, "Increasing bench strength" and "Accelerating development of high-potentials" were listed as the #1 and #2 top workforce development priorities, respectively (Executive Development Associates, 2009). "Increasing **bench strength**" is a term commonly used in organizations today to refer to the growth of new leaders who can provide backup and eventually replace the current leaders in charge. A company is said to have a "deep bench" if several other leaders within the organization are considered fully capable of assuming the positions of key leaders who vacate their posts. General Electric was a recent well-known example of the deep bench. Following the retirement of its iconic CEO Jack Welch, GE had already groomed at least three internal leaders who could immediately take over the executive reins.

A common way to increase bench strength is to focus on the development of **high potentials**. Often called "HiPos," these are individuals who have been identified as possessing above average potential (and interest) to take on greater and greater levels of responsibility. Some organizations begin identifying these employees at entry level positions. Once identified, organizations then focus additional development efforts on these individuals early in their careers, giving them **stretch assignments**, coaching and mentoring, and even sending them to graduate school.

Leadership Development in Health Care

The leadership drought has been recently exacerbated in health care due to negative economic conditions and increases in government oversight (McAlearney, 2006). The leadership development challenge in health care is considered to be in a "state of crisis" today. Many healthcare organizations (HCO) are nonprofit operations that face crippling budget pressures. At the same time, HCO structures may include professional staff such as doctors as well as subsidiary organizations that are not directly under the authority of the parent HCO's leadership.

When compared to other business sectors, the healthcare industry has historically been slow to respond to changing trends (Beinecke, Daniels, Peters, & Silvestri, 2009; McAlearney, 2006). McAlearney (2010) sent surveys to 355 U.S. healthcare executives in July 2007 and collected 104 responses (29% of the sample). Survey results indicated that about half (53) of the respondents' healthcare systems reported having a formal leadership development program in place and that most of those programs had been established after 2003. The driving force to create these programs was HCO dissatisfaction with how prepared executives were when promoted to positions of senior leadership. Charan, Drotter, and Noel (2011) suggest addressing these challenges by developing "a framework shared by all leaders to ensure consistency of judgment and application on the human side of the business so that a cumulative leadership effect results" (p. xvi). These authors propose a structure to codify this framework, which they label the **leadership pipeline**.

This chapter uses the leadership pipeline framework to describe how leaders are selected and groomed within a healthcare organization. First, we will cover guiding principles for building bench strength—that is, the critical components of a talent management system. Second, we will identify two distinct professional career paths for leaders in health care. Third, we will describe competencies and methods used in training and development. The chapter concludes with a sample case study on how coaching can be conducted in a healthcare organization.

GUIDING PRINCIPLES FOR DEVELOPING LEADERS

Conger and Fulmer (2003) suggest five guiding principles of best practice for building an organizational leadership pipeline:

1. Actively focus on developing talent.
2. Identify key assignments and positions that move talent through the pipeline.
3. Maintain transparency.
4. Implement assessment on a regular basis.
5. Engage in continual improvement.

These five principles will be discussed with a focus on their applications in healthcare settings.

#1: A Development Focus

A focus on developing management talent involves integrating traditional activities such as workshops and seminars closely and directly with an individual's assigned roles and responsibilities. "On-the-job" learning and practice should be promoted and linked to any formal training that is offered. A common missed development opportunity occurs when an employee attends a class session to learn a new management skill but then has no opportunity to apply and practice the new skills in the workplace. The valuable time and cost of the training can be wasted. Additionally, monitoring employees for implementation of new skills and demonstration of learned behaviors as they work can show that training has been successful.

Let's take the case of Jaclyn Smith, a nurse practitioner working at a community clinic. She has demonstrated excellent clinical skills and knowledge, strong interpersonal and communications skills, and is a proactive problem solver. The clinic director has identified her as a potential leader who might fill his position in the future. However, to be effective in this new arena, Ms. Smith would need to learn additional management skills and develop a systems perspective rather than a one-on-one approach. To achieve this goal, the clinic director decides to send Jaclyn to a strategic planning training session that one of his old college classmates is facilitating. The director believes that he will be rewarding Jaclyn with an educational perk as well as supporting this friend's seminar series. He assumes Ms. Smith will be grateful for the opportunity to learn new skills at the clinic's time and expense.

Unfortunately, the outcome is just the opposite. Jaclyn's current responsibilities do not involve strategic planning, so the seminar content seems unrelated and irrelevant to her duties and responsibilities. In fact, she experiences the training as a distraction from her enjoyable "real work" of patient care and becomes stressed because her day away from the clinic has left her with a pileup of tasks and paperwork. She also worries that her patients will be disappointed that their appointments will be rescheduled and that her overburdened colleagues will need to cover her patient care duties.

The clinic director had not planned strategically for the necessary training to promote Jaclyn's leadership skills nor had he done the necessary preparation to give her the background to fully understand the relevance of the training to her professional development. As a result, the training decreased Jaclyn's morale and undermined her confidence in the director as an effective leader.

Jaclyn's story is in an example of what not to do with respect to employee development. Supervisors commonly make a variety of mistakes in talent management. Exploring the next principle suggested by Conger and Fulmer (2003), "key assignments," provides positive examples of how to effectively develop leadership talent.

#2: Identify Key Assignments and Positions That Move Talent Through the Pipeline (On-the-Job Training)

To avoid unproductive employee development efforts, a wise leader can incorporate best practices such as those proposed by Garman and Dye (2009). They suggest that an individual's ability to learn in the workplace is positively influenced by the following conditions: (1) awareness of learning needs, (2) characteristics of work assignments, and (3) attitudes about learning. In Jaclyn's case, these conditions hadn't been effectively addressed.

Garman and Dye describe the awareness of one's learning needs as a continuum, moving through a series of four phases:

- A complete lack of awareness of need to learn (unconscious development need)
- Understanding and identifying specifics for knowledge or skills that can be addressed with a learning plan (conscious development need)
- Thoughtful practice and application of a new skill, improving performance (conscious proficiency)
- Skill mastery, wherein the skill has become a natural, effective, and consistent behavior across a variety of circumstances (unconscious proficiency)

In the aforementioned example, the clinic director's plan for Jaclyn fell short in Phase 1. Jaclyn did not have awareness of the "need" to learn strategic planning. If the director had discussed her potential career path within the organization and shared his vision for her future development in advance of the seminar, Jaclyn may have had a greater awareness of need and been better able to appreciate the learning opportunity. Additionally, such a preliminary meeting and discussion would have allowed her to express her professional goals and ambitions to the director, so that they could have created a professional development plan for Jaclyn together. The director's plan also neglected to implement Phase 3, "practice." After taking the seminar, Jaclyn was not given specific on-the-job assignments to use the new skills. Without the aforementioned steps to promote effective learning, Jaclyn understandably perceived the seminar as a waste of her time.

Garman and Dye (2009) attest that characteristics of a job assignment can impact the level of engagement and professional growth of an employee. These authors cite the work of McCauley and Brutus (1998), which lists the following four types of experiences that facilitate on-the-job learning:

1. Assignment of new roles and responsibilities
2. Implementation of necessary changes
3. Granting of expanded responsibility
4. Learning from new and diverse experiences and from success and failure

Giving an employee new duties that embody one or more of these four characteristics is termed a "stretch" assignment. Organizations facilitate leadership development by tasking trainees to perform duties that will challenge, motivate, and enhance their leadership abilities. For example, such stretch assignments are a component of leadership development programs at Gundersen Lutheran Health System in La Crosse, Wisconsin. Gunderson Health is an integrated healthcare delivery system composed of a medical center with 325 beds, 41 affiliated clinics and offices, and a multispecialty medical clinic. Gunderson's successful talent management program consists of five steps (Noelke, 2009):

1. Define leadership competency
2. Identify high-potential talent
3. Assess talent
4. Develop individual plans
5. Track progress

In this model, tasking trainees with stretch assignments corresponds with Step 4, developing individual plans. Nancy Noelke, leadership coach at Gundersen, will assess the identified high-potential talent, Step 2, by compiling and analyzing employee evaluations into a summary of strengths and weaknesses. In Step 5, she collaborates with a designated review team to develop strategic interventions that will "close the gap between where the candidates are and where they would like to be from a leadership stand-point" (2009, p. 36). These strategies are then discussed with the candidates' supervisors and fine-tuned as needed. The resulting development plan will focus on meeting the needs of the organization as well as motivating the candidate to learn and grow, and will include stretch assignments and other growth activities such as coaching, mentoring, committee participation, role expansion, cross-functional duties, and job rotation.

This multistep approach to leadership development is widely used and has been shown to increase successful outcomes. Miller, Umble, Frederick, and Dinkin (2007) evaluated a multimethod program aimed at developing leaders in the public health sector. Their study compared the self-reported effectiveness of a variety of interventions such as assessment tools and coaching, learning projects, skill-building seminars, textbooks and reading, and distance-learning conference calls. And then, 6 months after graduating from the program, participants were asked to rate the utility of each of the training methods. The "learning project" received the highest rating, and the "assessment tools and coaching" gained the top scorers. The learning project required participants to tackle a community health challenge or address a public health infrastructure issue. Project components included an assessment of the problem and development of a problem statement and action plan. The assessment tools administered to the public health leaders were the Myers-Briggs Type Indicator (MBTI), Change Style Indicator (Discovery Learning, Inc. in Greensboro, NC) and a 360 (multirater) feedback survey. The 360 survey and in-depth personal coaching were facilitated by the Center for Creative Leadership (Greensboro, NC). The results were not surprising: the more specific and focused the learning methodology, the more likely the learner will find value in the activity and succeed in achieving the desired skills and outcomes.

#3: Transparency

Traditionally, succession plans had been developed behind a veil of secrecy. However, Conger and Fulmer's (2003) research on best practices in leadership development showed that transparent talent management systems produce the best results.

Two critical components of transparency are clarity of process and ease of use. The clarity of the process involves employees' ability to assess their own potential for advancement as well as managers' ability to identify a list of potential candidates for the leadership positions. However, the optimum level of information provided to an employee might vary based on operational considerations. For example, at a base level, employees simply know that they have been identified as having a high potential. A higher level of transparency would allow an employee to see exactly where he or she stands in a rank order when compared to others in the company. Whereas in some cases this knowledge could be motivating, in other cases knowing one's ranking among colleagues could have a negative impact on morale and instigate unproductive internal competition.

Another aspect of transparency, from an employee's perspective, is the availability of clear and precise information about how one can progress through the system, what potential professional opportunities can promote advancement, and what skills or expertise are needed to grow as a leader. To implement a transparent talent management system, managers should be able to obtain customizable searches of available opportunities and match them with each employee's past experience, current skill level, ability gaps, and development plans.

Therefore, to support transparency for "high potentials" as well as managers, a system that is easy to access and navigate is critical. The best practice companies in the Conger and Fulmer study (2003) make judicious use of the Internet to provide a user-friendly interface for their talent management systems. They cite Lilly's "1-click model," a web-based application tool on the desktop of employee's computers. With one click, employees can obtain access to information about their personal skills and explore potential compatible job opportunities.

Research studies indicate that a lack of information regarding one's task and responsibilities can inhibit learning (Kyndt, Dochy, Struyven, & Cascallar, 2011) and that role ambiguity and role conflict inhibit on-the-job learning effectiveness (Lin, 2010). Therefore, having a transparent talent management system with the necessary components can promote successful employee development and advancement, and prevent unfortunate and demotivating experiences such as the one that Jaclyn and her manager shared.

#4: Assessment of Quantity and Quality of the Pipeline on a Regular Basis

Transparency also requires the presence of a system that can monitor the population and strength of the leadership pipeline and succession plan on an ongoing basis at consistent intervals and in real time; this is a key component of best practices for healthcare organizations (Conger & Fulmer, 2003). For example, succession plan measurements should reveal how many qualified candidates are in the pipeline for each leadership position at any point in time. Automatic triggers should be in place that notify the HR department when the ratio of potentials to incumbents dips below a minimum threshold. Each management position should have an explicit ratio of internal employees that could be ready to step into that position in case of a vacancy. For example, a 2:1 ratio for a mid-level management position would mean that for every incumbent currently in that position, two internal employees should be capable of serving as replacements if needed.

In addition to tracking the number of individuals in the pipeline, other valuable metrics can be used to assess the quality and effectiveness of a talent management system. These include:

- The time taken to fill vacant positions
- Demographic diversity of high potentials
- Satisfaction of coworkers regarding performance of internal hires
- Self-reported satisfaction by promoted employees at 3 months and 6 months on the job
- Measures that assess the employee's performance of newly assigned duties
- Employee turnover and high potential retention rates
- Ratio of internal versus external hires (see further discussion on this issue later in this chapter)

Using technology to quickly and easily access data can promote the success of a talent management system and allows programs to be designed and administered with accuracy, transparency, and flexibility. Ongoing assessment can monitor the effectiveness of the program, suggest revisions for continuous improvement, and encourage flexibility and favorable adaptation in a changing healthcare environment.

#5: Continual Improvement—Flexibility to Adapt to Improve the Strength of the Pipeline

Conger and Fulmer's (2003) best practices underscore that talent management systems can be effective only if they are used, trusted, and flexible. A sociotechnical system, such as a leadership pipeline, must be responsive to forces of constant and rapid change in order to maintain its relevance. Elasticity to adjust to internal pressures for continuous quality improvement, as well as to external forces such as economic conditions or regulatory changes, allows the effective implementation of the principles above.

The focus on talent can be manifested by aligning development opportunities with an individual's needs and career trajectory as well as with organizational goals. Organizational goals are driven by continuous quality improvement efforts, personnel changes, and strategic planning to address impending growth or recession. An effective pipeline must adjust accordingly as different competencies become prominent and necessary.

The field of information technology (IT) is a good example of a former support function that has become an integral part of an organization's foundational structure. Health IT is now a critical element in the internal coordination and provision of care among clinician colleagues and administrators (e.g., via practice management systems and electronic health records) as well as across entities such as **Accountable Care Organizations (ACOs)**. The result is an increased need for skilled information technology workers, knowledgable and effective IT managers, and senior leaders with vision who can guide strategic planning and decision making regarding health information technology. Leaders and managers will need to stay abreast of emerging health service technologies such as radio frequency identification (RFID), global positioning systems (GPS), and nanotechnology to make informed decisions about capital investments and future service lines (McGrady, Conger, Blanke, Landry, & Zalucki, 2010).

Information technology also plays an integral role in the internal operations of healthcare organizations as well as for the provision of services and education. Multifunctional, easy to use and secure information systems can manage not only leadership pipelines, but also other human resource functions. The new role of IT has mandated adjustments in talent management focus. Key development assignments and job positions must adapt to this new environment; some former assignments will become obsolete and new roles and responsibilities will emerge, requiring different skills and revised training and assessment initiatives. These shifts will aid the organization in responding to the rapid pace of change, successfully guiding strategic planning, staff, and leadership development in effective directions.

LEADERSHIP PATHWAYS

Healthcare leaders can move into their positions from a variety of disciplines, including medicine, nursing, business, health administration, and public health. For example, the American College of Healthcare Executives (ACHE, 2010) reported a membership of just over 33,000 in January 2011. The 2011 ACHE demographic profile of Members and Fellows showed that 51% of membership held their highest degree in hospital/health administration services, 24% in business, and 13.6% in clinical/allied health administration. Approximately 21% of ACHE members either earned a doctorate or two master's degrees, 63% have one master's degree, and 15.7% have up to a bachelor's degree.

There are typically two distinct paths through which healthcare leaders can begin their careers: as clinicians trained in a healthcare delivery discipline, and as nonclinicians trained in management or another administrative discipline such as finance, marketing, economics, or information technology. Leaders on the first path start off in health care as clinically trained direct service providers (e.g., doctors, nurses, radiologic technologists) and are promoted up the organizational hierarchy into roles with increasing leadership responsibility. The second route is traveled by individuals who begin their careers in an administrative or support area (e.g., accounting, management, law, human resources, marketing, or information technology) and receive promotions in their original discipline and cross-training in relevant and related fields.

Each pathway to the executive suite provides healthcare leaders with strong skills, but also with potential gaps in expertise and blind spots in perspective. Leaders who emerge from a clinical background are usually adept at understanding patient and clinician needs, but may lack business knowledge in the areas of finance, marketing, operations, systems thinking, collaboration, and management. Leaders who emerge from a business discipline, such as finance, administration, marketing, or operations, often lack the perceptual framework to understand the needs, values, and expectations of clinicians and patients. If we accept the premise that a good leader needs to be able to relate to and engage the attention, loyalty, and motivation of a wide range of followers, then a leader in health care must be able to view any given situation from multiple perspectives and listen to and understand the various stakeholders who can provide valuable input with respect to specific issues (Freshman, 2010). Leaders must actively "learn on the job" to fill in the gaps in their training and expertise; for example, clinicians may take courses in business and management, and administrative specialists may rely on mentors, professional allies, and champions in relevant fields as well as immersion in industry professional groups to gain information and knowledge.

The following stories of Sam Kapur (clinician), and Lily Rodriquez (administrator) provide examples of each path to successful healthcare leadership.

Clinical Path to Leadership

Sam Kapur

Sam Kapur was trained as a family physician in Northern India. At the age of 32, he and his family moved to the United States so that he could accept a primary care position with a large medical group practice in Boston, Massachusetts. Dr. Kapur displayed an excellent bedside manner and developed good rapport with his practice's patients. Through referrals, his roster of patients grew rather quickly. Sam consistently demonstrated that he was an active learner; the medical group leadership noted he was proactive in making changes and adopting technology that enhanced the practice's productivity and increased quality of care. The CEO of the group took notice of Sam's outstanding performance and invited him to sit in on key meetings in which important decisions would be made. After 2 years of working in the medical group, Dr. Kapur was asked to join the Continuous Quality Improvement (CQI) Team, through which he continued to display excellent performance. Dr. Kapur realized that CQI was one of his professional strengths. Therefore, he requested, and was granted, tuition support to attend additional training in this arena. This training allowed him to become a CQI team leader in addition to his clinical duties. Dr. Kapur also embraced a high visibility role as an educator and networker, building his reputation in the local community by attending and speaking at professional association events. The medical group's executives saw him as a "high potential" employee and continued to nurture his professional development with stretch assignments. In time, the Human Resources (HR) Director offered him the opportunity to get Masters in Healthcare Administration (MHA) degree to expand his administrative competencies and refine his management and leadership skills. After Dr. Kapur had been working with the medical group for a little over 8 years, the Chief Medical Executive retired, and Dr. Kapur was offered and accepted the position. With excellent preparation, Dr. Kapur brought a strong skillset to this position and successfully continued to promote high morale and increase quality and profitability for the practice.

Administrative Path to Leadership

Lily Rodriquez

Shortly after graduating with a bachelor's degree in health services, Lily Rodriquez began her career as a receptionist and file clerk at an outpatient surgery center. This facility was part of larger health system that included two hospitals, several medical offices, and two other outpatient surgery centers in Los Angeles County. Ms. Rodriquez was noted for being outgoing, organized, and having a good rapport with the office staff and the center's clients. The office manager appreciated her work ethic and "people skills" and began to enlist Ms. Rodriquez' assistance on various HR projects. As a quick learner and hard worker, Ms. Rodriquez was promoted to assistant office manager and coordinated compensation and benefits administration for several years. The office manager identified Ms. Rodriquez as a high-potential employee and suggested she take advantage of the organization's tuition reimbursement program to obtain a master's degree in human resource management. During her graduate studies, Ms. Rodriquez volunteered to intern in the health system's HR department to further develop her skills and expand her professional network. Shortly after graduation, she accepted a position in the system's HR department as a compensation and benefits specialist.

The office manager was sad to have her high-potential employee leave the surgery center but was very proud of Lily and pleased to see her professionally advance and succeed. Lily herself was grateful to her mentor and continued to stay in touch and provide professional support when needed.

The system's HR Director also identified Ms. Rodriquez as a high-potential employee, and over the next few years provided her with stretch assignments and cross-training in other HR areas such as recruitment and leadership development and training. Subsequently, she was promoted to VP of Organization Development and developed and enhanced new initiatives and challenged herself and her staff with stretch assignments. Supported by her supervisor, she received and provided formal and informal coaching and mentoring, attended professional seminars and conferences, and lectured to others within and beyond the organization on a regular basis. When the HR Director retired, Lily Rodriquez was offered the position. Confident and well prepared, she accepted the senior leadership post.

Figure 2.1 illustrates examples of a leadership pipeline and key assignments for both clinical and administrative pathways.

FILLING AND MAINTAINING THE LEADERSHIP PIPELINE

An organization's Human Resources department performs many key functions involved in developing and maintaining a leadership pipeline. Data management, performance evaluations, and **succession planning** are all critical components of a talent management system and are typically handled by HR. Optimally, the HR Department of an organization will track each employee's work history, performance appraisals, skills strengths, weaknesses, and development plans, and provide critical input to the managers utilizing the pipeline.

Performance appraisals play a critical role in helping to identify high-potential employees and track their progress and professional development. Many performance evaluations are designed and administered by HR. An employee and his or her supervisor will fill out an annual performance

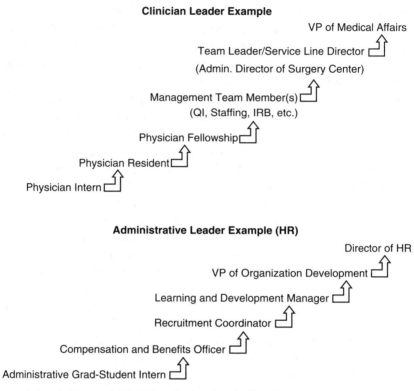

Clinician Leader Example

VP of Medical Affairs

Team Leader/Service Line Director
(Admin. Director of Surgery Center)

Management Team Member(s)
(QI, Staffing, IRB, etc.)

Physician Fellowship

Physician Resident

Physician Intern

Administrative Leader Example (HR)

Director of HR

VP of Organization Development

Learning and Development Manager

Recruitment Coordinator

Compensation and Benefits Officer

Administrative Grad-Student Intern

Figure 2.1 Clinician and Administrative Leader Pipeline Example

assessment, which will be collected and stored by HR. Broader assessments are also common, wherein other stakeholders such as peers, direct reports, patients, and vendors are asked to rate and comment on an individual employee's performance. The term, "360," as in 360 degrees, is used to describe the collection of feedback from multiple sources regarding an employee's performance and can provide insight to employees as to how others perceive their skills and function in the professional setting. These **360 evaluations** are most successful when used in a nonjudgmental fashion by coaches and employees to identify areas of strength and opportunities for improvement. The 360 process and its role in staff development and mentoring are described in more detail in the case study at the end of this chapter.

HR departments can use the collected evaluation data to help managers project the numbers and levels of potential leaders needed in a pipeline. Executives must also decide on whether specific positions can be filled by current employees of an organization (internal strategy) or by recruitment of qualified candidates from outside the organization (external strategy). Each option has its benefits and drawbacks, and both are used in healthcare organizations. The talent management system (leadership pipeline) is an internal structure and process for developing and nurturing leaders within an organization. Kathy Klock, VP of Operations and Human Resources at Gundersen Lutheran Health System, explains the value of an internal development strategy: "It ensures continuity, sends a positive message throughout the organization and provides better odds of a good cultural fit" (Noelke, 2009, p. 35). Increased motivation, higher morale, and improved retention rates are also potential benefits of internal recruitment. However, there are a few potential disadvantages associated with exclusively looking inside the organization for new talent. Internal competition could instigate resentment among those not chosen for advancement, and morale could suffer. Concerns about the influence of office politics, favoritism, and discrimination could undermine morale and productivity, and opportunities to bring fresh perspectives into an organization may be lost. These potential drawbacks to exclusive internal recruitment could damage employee relations and negatively impact quality of care.

Therefore, leadership candidates are also sought from outside the enterprise. External strategies to locate qualified applicants to fill open positions (recruitment) include advertisements in trade journals, job fairs, online job postings, social media, and employee referrals. The search for external talent can also be outsourced to employment agencies and executive search firms. The benefits of external recruitment are an increased potential for fresh perspective/new ideas, reduced training expenses if a new hire comes on board with needed expertise, and fewer risks of dysfunctional relationships and political associations within the organization. Disadvantages of external recruitment, however, can include hiring an individual who might not fit with organizational culture. Morale might also decrease among those within the organization who were passed over for the position. Furthermore, orientation training will be needed for the newly hired employee, as well as time for his or her socialization and adjustment. Ultimately, an organization's leaders and HR decision makers will weigh the risks and benefits of internal versus external recruitment and determine when external recruitment is needed. The more accurate and comprehensive their talent management system, the more informed their decision will be.

Leadership Competencies

What knowledge, skills, and behaviors do "high potentials" need to demonstrate and/or learn to be effective leaders in health care? These skillsets have been well documented thanks to professional associations such as the National Center for Healthcare Leadership (NCHL, 2012), the Healthcare Leadership Alliance (HLA, 2010), and the American College of Healthcare

Executives (2010), which have conducted collaborative research across the industry to develop competency models on which to base evaluation and training. Because the healthcare industry is constantly changing, these organizations continually review and update their models to adapt accordingly. **Figure 2.2** depicts the NCHL's version 2.1, which is composed of 3 domains and 26 competencies.

This summary version of the model provides background on the behavioral and technical competencies identified by the research. The full model contains levels for each competency that distinguish outstanding leadership at each career stage (entry, mid and advanced) and by the disciplines of administration, nursing, and medicine (National Center for Healthcare Leadership, 2005–2010).

Figure 2.2 NCHL Health Leadership Competency Model™

Source: Reprinted with permission from the National Center for Health Leadership (www.nchl .org), Chicago, IL.

Health management researchers Garman and Dye (2009) reviewed seven distinct competency models developed specifically for application to the healthcare industry. These models range in complexity and scope from the Healthcare Leadership Alliance model, which identifies 300 competencies in 5 clusters, to Dye and Garman's (2006) "Exceptional Leadership Competency Model," which lists 16 competencies across 4 clusters (cornerstones). Practitioners working in the field might find a concise model more applicable for their training purposes while researchers and academic institutions might prefer to use a more complex model that lists a greater number of specific competencies. When selecting a model, the form should fit the function. An organization could also develop its own model for talent management, adding in specific components related to its mission, goals, and demographics. Regardless of the version chosen, the strategic use of a vetted competency model can provide evidence-based direction for recruiting, training, development, and promotion in a healthcare environment.

Development Methods

Leadership skills can be nurtured and honed in a variety of ways: through degree and certificate programs, seminars, on-the-job training, mentoring, modeling, **shadowing**, and coaching. These approaches can be included in an employee's development plan and tracked through a well-designed talent management system. Many organizations will offer tuition reimbursement as a benefit to employees seeking to enhance their professional development. This perk pays off for both the organization and the employee; studies indicate that employees who are offered the opportunity to grow and learn are more satisfied with their work environments and are less likely to leave the facility for a position elsewhere (Campbell, 2001; Nelson, Sassaman, & Phillips, 2008). The organization benefits as well by supporting its rising stars and preparing those individuals to take over for retiring personnel (succession planning).

Degree and Certificate Formal Education Programs

Undergraduate programs in healthcare management and administration can prepare baccalaureate students for entry level positions in health care. Current healthcare workforce members can also enroll in a university to obtain a bachelor's or master's degree to further their career aspirations. Baccalaureate level programs offer training in the basics of management and leadership, develop skillsets and competencies, and provide students with guidance on potential career paths in the healthcare industry. According to the Association of University Programs in Health Administration (AUPHA, 2011), there are hundreds of schools advertising undergraduate healthcare management degree programs, however, only 44 are currently certified by the association. AUPHA certification is a quality assessment similar to an accreditation. Review committees are composed of program directors and faculty members from undergraduate health administration programs who are familiar with curriculum development, program management, and evaluation. Students completing a bachelor's degree program may not yet be prepared for leadership positions, but do graduate with an understanding of the healthcare industry and with skillsets that provide a solid foundation for further training and career building. For upper management positions, several years of field experience in increasingly more responsible roles is typically required.

A master's degree in healthcare management can be the next step needed to move up the career ladder to greater responsibility for professionals already in the healthcare workforce. The Commission on Accreditation of Healthcare Management Education 2009–2010 profile lists 83 accredited master's level programs at 71 universities (CAHME, 2010). Although there are many unaccredited programs in health management and related disciplines, the designation of accreditation indicates that a program has participated in a quality review and formal evaluation of adherence to high standards. Accredited programs are required to engage in continual improvement through self-studies as well as formal reviews by the Commission.

Executive Education Formats Formal educational institutions such as colleges and universities have embraced the market opportunity to train and retrain working adults. Programs available to suit the executive or the full-time employed are offered by many educational institutions in onsite, hybrid, and online formats. Campus courses are often offered at night or on the weekends to accommodate students with full-time jobs. Several years of work experience in the healthcare industry or related fields are often a prerequisite for these programs; experienced students will bring to the classroom a higher level of knowledge and skills and a greater understanding of healthcare management issues and allow the program to provide a correspondingly increased level of student engagement through discussions, interactions, and networking with seasoned peers.

Seminars, Webinars, and Conferences

Seminars, webinars, and conference retreats can also provide formal training on specific topics and broader industry challenges. Delivery formats include week-long retreats in resort locations, 2–3-hour workshops in a conference facility, or online via webinars. Healthcare professional associations frequently offer seminars, conferences, and webinars on current trends and industry challenges. Training is readily available on topics such as general management skills, including conflict resolution, employee motivation, strategic planning, and time management.

However, these stand-alone outsourced training opportunities offer many benefits as well as a few drawbacks. Many of these programs are led by external subject-matter experts who can bring fresh, up-to-date perspectives and provide greater understanding of current issues and concerns. In a setting away from their daily workplace, attendees might feel more comfortable asking questions and seeking further knowledge, allowing for a deeper "stretch" in the learning activity. Additionally, by bringing together participants from many organizations, these gatherings provide excellent networking opportunities.

However, a drawback of these stand-alone trainings are that they are often "one-shot" experiences. If the skillsets learned are not used on the job, employees may not effectively institutionalize new behaviors and approaches. Another drawback is that the vendor controls the precise content and scheduling of the training; employees will need to attend when sessions are available, not when it is most convenient for them and their organization. To promote maximum effectiveness when external training seminars are recommended as part of an employee's development plan, it is critical that managers and employees have a clear understanding of what the learning objectives are and how they relate to an individual's current and future work.

Table 2.1 provides examples of healthcare professional organizations' training programs.

On-the-Job Leadership Training

As mentioned earlier in this chapter, stretch assignments can provide excellent professional development opportunities, and should be an on-the-job assignment that is just beyond an employee's current level of confidence in that particular area and include the four types of experiences valuable to facilitating learning (McCauley & Brutus, 1998):

1. New roles and responsibilities
2. Implementing needed change
3. Expanded responsibility
4. Learning from failure and diversity

Upper-level managers should also seek out occasions in which high potentials (HiPos) can exercise skills identified in their personal development

Table 2.1 Healthcare Professional Organization Seminars, Webinars, and Conferences

Name of Organization	Organization Website	Examples of Training Programs Provided
American College of Health Executives	www.ache.org	1. Executive Workshop 2. Strategic Planning That Works: Integrating Strategy with Performance 3. Superior Productivity in Healthcare Organizations
American College of Physician Executives	www.acpe.org	1. Financial Decision Making 2. Science of High Reliability 3. Physician in Management
American Health Information Management Association	www.ahima.org	1. Interventional Cardiovascular Coding
American Society for Healthcare Human Resources Association	www.ashhra.org	1. ASHHRA Wellness Webinar: Use Stress to Your Advantage 2. The Chapter Leadership Workshop 3. ASHHRA 48th Annual Conference Call for Presentations
America's Health Insurance Plans	www.ahip.org	1. D109: ICD-10 and Administrative Simplification—Exploring the Dual Impact 2. Enabling Consumerism Through People, Process, and Technology: Best Practices for Healthcare Payers 3. Effective Strategies to Promote Influenza Vaccine Uptake Among Culturally Diverse Populations
Healthcare Financial Management Association	www.hfma.org	1. Constructing Financial Forecasting Models: Modeling for Reform 2. Creating an ICD-10 Transition Plan on the Fast Track 3. Show Me Chapter Medicare Workshops
Health Care Executives of Southern California	http://hce-socal.org	1. Managing Conflict—Avoiding the Pitfalls of Control 2. A Medicare and Medicaid Update

Table 2.1 (*continued*)

Name of Organization	Organization Website	Examples of Training Programs Provided
Medical Group Management Association	www.mgma.com	1. Mastering Business Operations and Staffing in Your Medical Practice 2. Train Your Office for Success: Mastering Patient Flow 3. Administrators in Transition: Skills for Administrators During and After Integration
National Association of Health Services Executives	www.nahse.org	1. Board Meeting 2. Educational Meeting 3. Membership Meeting
Southern California Association for Healthcare Risk Management	www.scahrm.org	1. Ostensible Agency: Tag, You're It! 2. The Circle of Innovation
Women in Health Administration of Southern California	http://whasocal.org	1. A.D.D.R.E.S.S.I.N.G. Diversity 2. Early Careerist Panel 3. Accountable Care Organizations

plan. As far as the individual development plan, before assigning a stretch goal or task, the manager and HiPos should review and discuss the HiPos' current and future goals, the benefits the new assignment can offer, and the manager's expectations for achievement. Optimally, all of these elements should be in alignment with the HiPos' individual goals as well as the organization's mission.

Mentoring

Successful people often express gratitude for the assistance they have received along their career path from valued mentors and suggest that they might not have achieved their current level of accomplishment if not for the mentors who were influential in their developing careers. A mentor is an individual who has knowledge, skills, and experience, that, when shared, can be of benefit to another. In addition, a good mentor possesses a genuine desire to be of service to others and strong interpersonal communication skills.

Mentoring relationships can be formal or informal. A formal mentor is intentionally paired with a protégé for the purpose of assisting the mentee in career advancement. In formal mentoring, the objectives, communication methods, frequency, and timeline for the relationship should be clarified, preferably in writing. A written mentor agreement can assist both parties in staying on track with their responsibilities and will allow goal achievement to be more easily assessed.

In an informal mentoring relationship, the parties involved might not even use the terms *mentor* or *mentee*. Instead, a professional relationship develops between two colleagues that includes the sharing of career advice, frank discussions, coaching, and counseling. Informal mentors often share a feeling of kinship and great respect for each other and may acknowledge the existence and quality of the professional relationship in hindsight.

Formal or informal, mentors are a valuable resource for employees, and such professional associations should be encouraged by supervisors and included in development planning discussions.

Modeling and Shadowing

Executives in every industry must remain aware that they are role models for their employees—that is, their behaviors in the workplace may inspire or facilitate the behaviors of their staff. This finding is utilized in training future leaders via two methods: modeling and shadowing. Constructive modeling occurs when people in positions of authority understand that their behavior provides an example to others and therefore act intentionally and consciously in ways that support and promote the desired organizational culture. For example, many organizations express the values of respect and integrity; their organizational leaders should demonstrate respect and integrity in all actions in the workplace. Unfortunately, destructive modeling (a negative effect) can result if leaders violate espoused values and principles. Not "walking the talk" can be damaging to employee morale and can send the wrong message to future leaders.

Shadowing is a formal technique that invites a high-potential employee to follow (or shadow) a leader for a designated period of time, witnessing and learning about his or her daily worklife. The HiPos might follow the leader around the office, sit in on meetings, listen to phone conversations, meet with clients, and observe negotiations and decision making. A conversation between the parties should occur in advance of the shadowing activity to clarify goals and expectations. At appropriate points, debriefing discussions should also take place, identifying lessons learned as well as next steps and followup that will enhance the HiPos' training.

Coaching

Executive coaching, used regularly in many industries, has gained popularity in the healthcare field in recent years. In the past, coaching was used only for those leaders who were struggling and possibly on their way out the organization's door. Today, coaching is used primarily to aid the growth of leaders in whom the organization wants to invest. Executive coaching is the "one-to-one development of an organizational leader" (Underhill, McAnally, & Koriath, 2007), a confidential set of consultations between a qualified coach and an executive, which focuses on improving the executive's leadership skills.

Coaching is considered one of the most effective methods of developing leaders because it has great "stickiness." Coaching resembles partnering with a personal trainer—not only does the employee learn proper exercises, but also has a partner to reinforce the new skills and ensure new exercises are practiced regularly. Areas that are often addressed through coaching include motivating others, treating people with respect, creating and communicating a vision, implementing accountability, and improving time management.

After a coach is selected, the process begins with an assessment of the executive's strengths and weaknesses as well as his or her personality traits that impact leadership effectiveness. The coach creates a summary of these findings and then collaborates with the executive to select an area or two for development. An action plan is created, indicating all the key steps required to improve in the selected area(s). Coaching then proceeds with ongoing meetings aimed at helping to implement the plan. After a period of time, the outcomes of the coaching are assessed, often via a 360 evaluation. Coaching usually continues for 6–9 months, but can extend from a couple of sessions to as long as a year.

Executive coaches are often former business executives themselves or come from backgrounds in business consulting or psychology. Coaches will usually possess an advanced academic degree, such as a master's in business administration or a doctorate in organizational psychology, and some may possess a certification in coaching. Coaches are experienced in the use of skill and personality assessments, such as 360 feedback tools, Myers-Briggs Indicators, Hogan Assessments, or Fundamental Interpersonal Relations Orientation (FIRO-B).

A number of studies have demonstrated the value of executive coaching. In one study, participants who had completed a training program increased their productivity by 22%. However, if coaching was paired with the same training program, productivity increased by 88% (Olivero, Bane, & Kopelman, 1997). Another study reported significant improvement in leadership effectiveness among those being coached who engaged in regular followup during the coaching process (Goldsmith & Morgan, 2004). While studies linking coaching to actual business results (e.g., increased revenue, higher stock prices) are less reliable, we do know that coaching has a demonstrable impact on leadership effectiveness.

CALL OUT BOX: CLOGS IN THE PIPELINE

Now that we have described the motivation, methodologies, and frameworks for leadership development, we might ask why some organizations develop internal leaders more effectively than others. Through their experience assisting over 100 international companies in developing leadership succession plans, Charan et al. (2011) identified four common "deep-seated, development errors" (p. ix):

1. Lack of skills required to select high-potential employees.
2. Human Resources focuses too much on "input" (identifying employees with high potential) and not enough on "output" (identifying what type of work should be done and what position level and how to measure success).
3. Lack of a consistent, integrated system for talent management by executives and/or human resources.
4. Leaders are not updating their skills rapidly enough to keep up with industry changes, requiring shifts in leadership roles and responsibilities.

SUMMARY

The Center for Creative Leadership conducted research on how successful leaders develop and report that the bulk of professional learning (70%) takes place on the job through real-world experiences, completing tasks and solving problems while at work. Feedback and observation account for 20% of workplace learning, and formal training accounts for 10% (Lombardo & Eichinger, 2000). The leadership pipeline provides a framework by which organizations can structure and track the effectiveness of these three development opportunities.

With a leadership crisis in the healthcare industry looming, organizations need to implement reliable and effective strategies to train and retain high potentials. Health care has traditionally lagged behind other industries in the area of leadership development. Healthcare organizations that embrace successful talent management strategies will not only increase their chances of survival in a changing and challenging environment, but will also be better equipped to provide cost-effective, high-quality services and products.

This chapter has provided a picture of leadership development within the healthcare environment. First, using the framework provided by Conger and Fulmer (2003), we introduced the five basic principles by which organizations can build their bench strength. The "leadership pipeline" was presented as a logical pathway for employee advancement from frontline manager to enterprise leader. The recruitment of high-potential future leaders was discussed and the key competencies expected of healthcare leaders identified. Finally, we described specific methods on how high-potential employees can be developed into outstanding leaders through training, mentoring, modeling, and coaching.

Discussion Questions

1. What are the key competencies for a successful healthcare leader?
2. What are the two primary career paths to healthcare leadership?
3. Name and discuss various methods for developing leaders.
4. List and describe the five key guiding principles for building a leadership pipeline.
5. How does a leader progress through the pipeline? What are the steps he or she must go through?
6. From the case study that follows, what were Kevin's strengths and areas needing development? What did he do to improve his knowledge and skillsets?

Case Study: Leadership in Practice

While fictitious in nature, this is a typical case study for how leadership development looks when 360 feedback and executive coaching is used to develop a healthcare leader.

Kevin is the Chief Operating Officer (COO) of a tertiary-care hospital, one of many in a large chain in the Northeastern United States. At 48 years of age, he has moved into this position much more rapidly than anyone (including he himself) expected. An unplanned vacancy had occurred in the COO position only 6 months before, and the CEO and Board of Directors chose not to recruit externally. As the director of administration for the hospital in the previous 4 years, Kevin was considered the only qualified internal candidate and was offered the position.

As COO, Kevin is responsible for all day-to-day operations of the hospital. The directors of nursing, administration, human resources, government affairs, and quality now report to him, but the doctors are part of a contracted medical group that is instead coordinated by the Medical Chief of Staff.

The CEO and the Board of Directors of the system view Kevin as a "high potential" leader who could one day become the CEO. They also recognize that Kevin's promotion might have been premature, but believe that with some further coaching and training, he could develop the needed skills to be a successful leader. To support and promote Kevin's professional development, they have hired an outside consultant to serve as a leadership coach and mentor.

The executive coach was hired to work with Kevin for 6 months. The coach first began with an assessment of Kevin's strengths and weaknesses through a 360 feedback process. A survey of approximately 75 questions was sent electronically to those who worked most closely with Kevin—his boss, his direct reports, and his peers who also worked for Kevin's boss. These raters completed the survey anonymously, and their scores were combined in the final report and analysis.

Kevin's highest and lowest scores were then identified (see **Table 2.2**). The highest score a rater can provide is 5.0, the lowest score is 1.0.

The executive coach also gave Kevin a Myers-Briggs Type Indicator (MBTI) assessment, a survey that Kevin completed himself. The result identified Kevin as fitting into 1 of 16 different personality types and helped him to better understand how he perceives, communicates, and functions in the workplace. The coach also reviewed any past performance reviews Kevin received from his supervisors, along with any other assessments he may have taken earlier in his career. Finally, the coach interviewed Kevin's boss, the hospital CEO.

Following the assessment, the coach and Kevin met for a feedback debriefing. In this confidential meeting, which lasted for several hours, the coach presented a summary report that highlighted Kevin's key strengths and areas for development.

In this meeting, Kevin learned the information laid out in **Table 2.3**.

Kevin agreed that he is a person of high integrity and of solid execution, and was pleasantly surprised that people felt he treated them with such respect. Kevin was also very surprised that people felt he did not have much of a vision, and struggled with the feedback that he was "too nice to say no to anyone." After further discussion with the coach, Kevin eventually came to terms with the less positive feedback, recognizing that this input was influenced by the perceptions of those around him, which may not be entirely on target.

In the next meeting, Kevin and his coach conducted action planning. In this session, Kevin first selected the area for development in which he planned to improve. After some thought and consideration, Kevin decided he needed to improve his ability *to create and communicate a vision* for his organization.

For his action plan, Kevin and his coach came up with a variety of action steps designed to help him create and communicate a vision. During this brainstorming session, Kevin, inspired by key questions posed by his coach, generated ideas based on his knowledge and experience with his job responsibilities. The coach also offered suggestions based on his experiences working with other leaders with similar areas needing development.

A sample action plan is provided for Kevin in **Table 2.4**.

Table 2.2 Kevin's Highest and Lowest Scores

Highest-Rated Items	Average Score (from all raters)
1. Ensures that the highest standards for ethical behavior are established and maintained (throughout the organization)	5.0
2. Genuinely listens to others	4.9
3. Demonstrates honest, ethical behavior in all personal and business transactions	4.9
4. Consistently treats people with respect and dignity	4.8
5. Is a role model for the organization's values (leads by example)	4.8
6. Appreciates the value of diversity (avoids discrimination based upon race, gender, age, or background)	4.6
7. Builds people's confidence	4.6
8. Discourages destructive comments about other people or groups	4.6
9. Consistently meets or exceeds customer expectations	4.5
10. Effectively recognizes team members for teamwork and team performance	4.4
Lowest-Rated Items	
75. Creates and communicates a clear vision for his/her organization	2.4
74. Is willing to take risks in letting others make decisions	2.5
73. Effectively anticipates future opportunities	2.5
72. Communicates a clear strategy on how to achieve the vision	2.7
71. Gives people the freedom they need to do their work	2.7
70. Effectively involves co-workers in determining how to achieve the vision	2.9
69. Looks beyond "the way we do things now" in considering future opportunities	2.9
68. Trusts people enough to "let go" (avoids overcontrolling or micromanagement)	3.2
67. Clearly identifies priorities (focuses on the "vital few")	3.3
66. Encourages active participation in strategy development and decision making	3.4

Table 2.3 Feedback Debrief Summary Report

Strengths	Supporting Data
Cares for People	360 items 2, 4, 6, 7, 8, 10: MBTI reveals he is more of a "feeler" and an "extrovert"; i.e., he is able to tune in to others and empathize with them.
High Integrity	360 items 1, 3, 5: Performance review gives him a perfect score in "Integrity."
Executes—Gets the Job Done	360 item 9: Past performance review data; Boss' interview: "It doesn't matter what you give Kevin, he will always get the job done flawlessly."

Areas of Development	Supporting Data
Lack of Vision	360 items 75, 73, 72, 70, 69, 66: MBTI reveals he is more of a "sensing" (works with immediate data, rather than thinking about future options) and "judging" (likes to move to closure, not leave things open for future possibility). Boss' interview: "Kevin has his head down working, he does not seem to have or communicate a vision of where his organization is going."
Micromanagement	360 items 74, 71, 68: Boss' interview: "Kevin's direct reports indicate he is doing their jobs rather than letting them do their jobs. His standards are so high, he feels he is the only one who can do things correctly."
Time Management	360 item 68: Past performance reviews say Kevin is such a nice guy, he never says no to any request. Boss' interview: "Kevin has difficulty figuring out what to work on first. He is so busy doing everyone's jobs, he just can't keep up. He is not working at the level of a COO, but at the level of those working under him."

Table 2.4 Action Plan Worksheet for Kevin

Area for Development:
Create and Communicate a Vision for his Organization

Action Step	Support Required	Timeline	Completed?
Create a Vision			
Meet with CEO regarding her vision	CEO meeting	Within 2 weeks	
Review industry journals for latest industry trends	Obtain journals	Within 2 weeks	
Attend industry conference for ideas	Funding for conference	April 17–20	
Draft vision statement; share with boss and others	CEO support, review of others	May 1	

Table 2.4 (*continued*)

Action Step	Support Required	Timeline	Completed?
Communicate the Vision			
Make sure vision is clear, compelling, easy to remember	Review with coach	May 14	
Host team offsite to unveil the vision	Funds for offsite expenses	May 14/15 (tentative)	
Internal website to promote vision	Marketing/Web staff to design	May 21	
Distribute t-shirts with graphic promoting new vision to all staff	Marketing/design team	June 1	
Begin each staff meeting with a review of vision		Each month	
Ensure each staff members' goals directly relate to the organization vision		During June performance reviews	
Survey everyone in 6 months to see if they can remember vision	Survey design team	December	

Preliminary Case Study Discussion Questions

1. What are Kevin's strengths as noted in the evaluation? Can you combine these strengths into a few main "themes"?
2. What are Kevin's areas of development? What themes do you identify?
3. Given your analysis of these test results, would you choose to work for Kevin?

Once the action plan was created, Kevin could begin to accomplish his objectives. His first step was to meet with his boss to gain her acceptance of the action plan and to gather her ideas and those of other stakeholders. In the ongoing coaching phase, Kevin and his coach will meet approximately every 1–2 weeks by phone, videochat, or in person. During each meeting, the coach will review the action plan to see which key steps have been accomplished and which steps still remain incomplete. As is often the case, Kevin may find himself falling behind or possibly losing focus in his areas of development. Like a personal trainer, the coach will refocus him toward his objectives and help him stay on task. Barriers and obstacles that arise are also analyzed and addressed through the coaching process.

During ongoing coaching, Kevin has informed all those who provided input about his plan so that they can be aware and supportive of his upcoming changes. He will also check in with them every other month to ask them whether or not they have noticed improvements. Research shows that the more often Kevin follows up with these key people, the more likely they are to notice improvement in his follow-up survey. The coach will also follow up with these key colleagues independently to ask if they have also noticed any improvement. The coach will also check in with Kevin's supervisor, the CEO, and Kevin's HR representative to gain their input on his improvement.

At the end of the coaching term, a results measurement, a brief follow-up survey, is sent to all the previous raters. Each person indicates whether or not he or she has observed improvement in Kevin's ability to create and communicate a vision for the organization over the past 6 months. Once again, the follow-up survey is anonymous, with the answers being combined so that individual input cannot be identified. The results are then depicted in **Table 2.5**.

A total of 12 raters working with Kevin answered the anonymous survey. In question #1, 1 rater saw no change in his overall leadership effectiveness, but 11 saw improvement on a +1, +2, +3 level. In question #2, he also showed improvement in his area of development "creates and communicates a clear vision for his/her organization." Of 12 raters, a total of 10 felt that he had improved in this area.

Table 2.5 Mini Survey for Kevin

1. Did Kevin become more (or less) effective as a leader over the past 6 months?

−3 Less Effective	−2	−1	0 No Change	+1	+2	+3 More Effective
			1	6	4	1

2. Over the past 6 months, did this leader become more (or less) effective in the following area for development: Creates and communicates a clear vision for his/her organization?

−3 Less Effective	−2	−1	0 No Change	+1	+2	+3 More Effective
			2	7	2	1

Following successful improvement as demonstrated by this survey, coaching was effectively concluded. However, Kevin continues to check in with his key raters every 6 months to see if they are still clear on his vision. He also continues to practice each of his action steps as he moves forward with his responsibilities. The CEO and Board have noticed great improvement in his leadership capabilities and are now contemplating renewing coaching for an additional 6 months to help him address one of his other two development objectives.

Concluding Case Study Discussion Questions

1. What other action steps would you recommend for Kevin to consider in creating or communicating the vision?
2. If Kevin had not followed up regularly with those working with him regarding his developmental opportunities, do you think he would have improved as much as he did? Why or why not?
3. Would you promote Kevin now to CEO of this hospital? If so, why? If not now, why not?

RELATED WEBSITES

Assessment Plus: www.assessmentplus.com/SERVICES/ots_360s.htm#LOF
Association of University Programs in Health Administration: www.aupha.org
Commission on Accreditation of Healthcare Management Education: www.cahme
   .org
Healthcare Leadership Alliance: www.healthcareleadershipalliance.org/
National Center for Healthcare Leadership: www.nchl.org/

REFERENCES

American College of Healthcare Executives. (2010). *Members and fellows profile.* Retrieved June 13, 2011 from www.ache.org/pubs/research/demographics.cfm.
Association of University Programs in Health Administration (AUPHA). (2011). Undergraduate Certification. *Association of University Programs in Health Administration.* Retrieved October 16, 2011 from www.aupha.org/i4a/pages /index.cfm?pageid=3519.
Beinecke, R., Daniels, A., Peters, J., & Silvestri, F. (2009). Guest editors' introduction: The International Initiative for Mental Health Leadership (IIMHL): A model for global knowledge exchange. *International Journal of Mental Health, 38*(1), 3–13.

Bolt, J. (1991). *Executive development: A strategy for corporate competitiveness.* New York, NY: HarperCollins.

Campbell, D. S. (2001). Training as a retention tool. *The Internal Auditor, 58*(5), 47–51.

Charan, R., Drotter, S., & Noel, J. (2011). *The leadership pipeline: How to build the leadership powered company.* San Francisco, CA: John Wiley & Sons, Jossey-Bass.

Commission on Accreditation of Healthcare Management Education (CAHME). (2010). Profile of CAHME Accredited Programs: 83 accredited programs at 71 Universities Summary of Annual Report Data 2009–2010. *Commission on Accreditation of Healthcare Management Education.* Retrieved October 16, 2011 from http://cahme.org/Resources/Profile_CAHME_AccreditedPrograms2010.pdf.

Conger, J. A., & Fulmer, R. M. (2003, December). Developing your leadership pipeline. *Harvard Business Review, 81*(12), 76–84.

Dye, C. F., & Garman, A. N. (2006). *Exceptional leadership: 16 critical competencies for healthcare executives.* Chicago, IL: Health Administration Press.

Executive Development Associates. (2005). *The leadership bench strength challenge: Building integrated talent management systems.* Oklahoma City, OK: Executive Development Associates.

Executive Development Associates. (2009). *Trends in executive development.* Oklahoma City, OK: Executive Development Associates.

Freshman, B. (2010). The forest and the trees: An organizational psychologist's perspective on collaborating across the disciplines in health. In B. Freshman, L. Rubino, & Y. Reid Chassaikos (Eds.), *Collaboration across the disciplines in healthcare.* Burlington, MA: Jones & Bartlett Learning.

Garman, A. N., & Dye, C. F. (2009). *The healthcare C-suite.* Chicago, IL: Health Administration Press.

Goldsmith, M., & Morgan, H. (2004). Leadership is a contact sport. *Strategy + Business,* 36.

Healthcare Leadership Alliance (HLA). (2010). *HLA competency directory.* Retrieved January 9, 2012 from www.healthcareleadershipalliance.org/directory.htm.

Kyndt, E., Dochy, F., Struyven, K., & Cascallar, E. (2011). The perception of workload and task complexity and its influence on students' approaches to learning: A study in higher education. *European Journal of Psychology of Education—EJPE (Springer Science & Business Media B.V.), 26*(3), 393–415. doi:10.1007/s10212-010-0053-2.

Lin, C. (2010). Understanding negative impacts of perceived cognitive load on job learning effectiveness: A social capital solution. *Human Factors, 52*(6), 627–642. doi:10.1177/0018720810386606.

Lombardo, M., & Eichinger, B. (2000). *Career architect development planner* (3rd ed.). Minneapolis, MN: Lominger Limited.

McAlearney, A. S. (2006). Leadership development in healthcare: A qualitative study. *Journal of Organizational Behavior, 27*(7), 967–967.

McAlearney, A. S. (2010). Executive leadership development in U.S. health systems. *Journal of Healthcare Management, 55*(3), 206–222.

McCauley, C. D., & Brutus, S. (1998). *Management development through job experiences: An annotated bibliography.* Greensboro, NC: Center for Creative Leadership.

McGrady, E., Conger, S., Blanke, S., Landry, B. J. L., & Zalucki, P. M., (2010). Emerging technologies in healthcare: Navigating risks, evaluating rewards/ practitioner application. *Journal of Healthcare Management, 55*(5), 353–364; discussion 364–365.

Michaels, E., Handfield-Jones, H., & Axelrod, B. (2001). *The war for talent.* Boston, MA: McKinsey & Company.

Miller, D. L., Umble, K. E., Frederick, S. L., & Dinkin, D. R. (2007). Linking learning methods to outcomes in public health leadership development. *Leadership in Health Services, 20*(2), 97–123. doi:10.1108/17511870710745439.

National Center for Healthcare Leadership. (2005–2010). *Health leadership competency model summary.* Retrieved August 31, 2012 from www.nchl.org/Documents /NavLink/Competency_Model-summary_uid31020101024281.pdf.

National Center for Healthcare Leadership. (2012). *NCHL Health Leadership Competency model.* Retrieved January 9, 2012 from www.nchl.org/static .asp?path=2852,3238.

Nelson, J., Sassaman, B., & Phillips, A. (2008). Career ladder program for registered nurses in ambulatory care. *Nursing Economics, 26*(6), 393–398.

Noelke, N. (2009). Leverage the present to build the future. *HR Magazine, 54*(3), 34–36.

Olivero, G., Bane, K. D., & Kopelman, R. (1997, Winter). Executive coaching as a transfer of training tool: Effects on productivity in a public agency. *Personnel Public Management, 26*(4), 461–469.

Underhill, B., McAnally, K., & Koriath, J. (2007). *Executive coaching for results: The definitive guide to developing organizational leaders.* San Francisco, CA: Berrett-Koehler.

Chapter 3

The Culturally Competent Leader

Carol Molinari and Laurie Shanderson

LEARNING OBJECTIVES

By the end of this chapter, the student will be able to:

· Describe the effects of changing demographics and population trends on healthcare organizations.
· Define and distinguish between diversity, diversity management, cultural competence, healthcare disparities, and health disparities.
· Discuss the value of cultural competence in healthcare organizations.
· Present leadership strategies that promote cultural competence.
· Outline steps to assess cultural competence in a healthcare organization.

KEY TERMS

Cultural competence	Diversity management
Cultural diversity	Health disparities
Cultural synergy	Limited English proficiency
Culture	Minorities

INTRODUCTION

The cultural profile and complexion of the U.S. population is changing. Migration and high birth rates among non-white groups are redefining the American racial and ethnic mix. **Table 3.1** displays projections from

Table 3.1 Projected Proportions of U.S. Population by Race and Ethnicity

Race/Ethnicity	2010		2050	
White	246,630	79.5%	324,800	74.0%
Black	39,909	12.9%	56,944	13.0%
Native American, Alaska Native	3188	1.0%	5462	1.2%
Asian	14,415	4.6%	34,399	7.8%
Native Hawaiian, Pacific Islander	592	0.2%	1222	0.3%
Two or more races	5499	1.8%	16,183	3.7%
Hispanic	49,726	16.0%	132,792	30.2%
Totals	**359,959**		**571,802**	

Note: Percentage total is greater than 100% because some responders identify "Hispanic" as an ethnicity and identify an additional race designation.

Source: Data from U.S. Census Bureau. (2008). National population projections: Released 2008. Retrieved November 29, 2012 from www.census.gov/population/projections.

the 2010 Census indicating that by 2050, over half the U.S. population will be non-white (Vincent & Velkoff, 2010).

People from diverse racial and ethnic backgrounds will make up the majority of the U.S. population by 2050 (Passel & Cohn, 2008). This increased racial and ethnic diversity will result in a more diverse workforce than in years past. Leaders of healthcare organizations will need to embrace this diversity and implement strategies that ensure that different cultural beliefs and attitudes are respected and valued by all members of the organization. Additionally, healthcare leaders must ensure that today's employees are knowledgable and skilled in communicating with and working with colleagues and clients whose backgrounds, needs, and expectations are different from their own.

Healthcare leaders can promote employee and organizational competence in this arena through training initiatives that include assessment of learned skills and performance. Successful training begins with an understanding of the common terms that refer to diversity and cultural competence.

DIVERSITY, DIVERSITY MANAGEMENT, AND CULTURAL COMPETENCE: BASIC DEFINITIONS

The definition of diversity often depends on the context of a discussion. Diversity can encompass any characteristic used to differentiate one person from another (Hubbard, 2004, p. 33). For some, diversity broadly defines people in terms of age, education, lifestyle, sexual orientation, geographic origin, personality, and education (Thomas, 1990). Others view diversity as a more focused emphasis on race, ethnicity, religion, and gender (Dickie &

Soldan, 2008). Diversity may refer to any perceived difference among people: age, functional specialty, profession, sexual orientation, geographic origin, lifestyle, position and tenure in an organization (Dobbs, 1996). **Cultural diversity** refers to attitudes, values, and behaviors that may be shared by a group of people or by an organization.

A model helpful in comprehending the dimensions of diversity displays four concentric circles, each listing factors that affect an individual's attitudes and behaviors and his or her ability to work with colleagues and to effectively provide products or services to clients (see **Figure 3.1**).

At the center of the diagram, in the inner circle, is Personality, one's unique self and style. The next circle includes intrinsic factors such as age, race, gender, ethnicity, and sexual orientation. The third circle adds external factors such as geographic location, income, religion education, and work experience. The last circle cites organizational influences such as position classification, division or department, seniority, management status, and union affiliation (Gardenswartz & Rowe, 1998). This model helps identify major factors that affect employees' behaviors and attitudes and thus influence their ability to work with others. These dimensions can be used to understand similarities and differences among employees and thus promote knowledge about personal and cultural differences between workers and clients.

Managing diverse workers and clients requires respect and sensitivity to different cultural beliefs, practices, and values. **Cultural competence** means being able to understand the organizational factors that support or obstruct cultural sensitivity. It can be defined as the ability to successfully adapt to an unfamiliar cultural setting (Moua, 2010) and to use knowledge

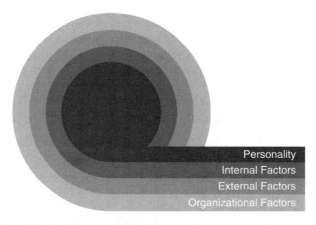

Figure 3.1 Diversity Model

about other cultures to reshape one's thinking and behavior to be more sensitive and responsive to cultural differences (Thomas & Inkson, 2009b).

Healthcare professionals practice cultural competence when they embrace and respect different cultural backgrounds, beliefs, and values, and take cultural diversity into account when providing healthcare delivery (Betancourt, 2006, p. 3). Since 2000, attention has focused on ways to address health disparities among minority populations. Cultural competence is one way to address health disparities and to promote equity in the delivery of health services. Generally, cultural competence refers to the ability and willingness to respond respectfully and effectively to people of all ethnic, cultural, and religious backgrounds (McDaniel, 2000). Cultural competence, especially at the organizational level, can be learned and developed and thus provides a significant way for management to reduce disparities among diverse patients. The following definitions help to distinguish between disparities in health status with disparities in the delivery of health services. Healthcare disparities are amenable to culturally competent management practices, and they in turn can influence health disparities.

Health disparities are health differences in individuals' or the public's (population) health that can be ascribed to social, economic, or environmental factors (National Partnership for Action, 2011). Race and ethnicity are commonly used to analyze U.S. health disparities.

Healthcare disparities are also differences in the amount and quality of health care that various groups are able to access or to receive. Racial and ethnic **minorities**, for example, comprise almost a third of the U.S. population but account for more than half of the uninsured. As a result, their access to primary care and other health services is limited (National Association of Community Health Centers, 2011). Furthermore, there is increasing evidence from the Institute of Medicine and other health policy studies that suggest underrepresented minority patients have less access to quality care and thus have poorer outcomes than nondiverse patients (Collins et al., 2002). Reports also highlight minority patient distrust that is due to perceived discrimination by providers and healthcare institutions. Shortages of culturally competent healthcare providers have had a negative impact on ethnic populations, especially for those with limited English proficiency (IOM, 2002b).

Cultural Competence in Health Care

Cultural competence in health care emerged in the 1990s as diversity in the United States continued to grow. In 1999, the Institute of Medicine (IOM) published the report "To Err Is Human," which discussed medical errors such as medication and surgical blunders that resulted in some 44,000 deaths each year (Kohn, Corrigan, & Donaldson, 2000). In 2001, the IOM released "Crossing the Quality Chasm," identifying major gaps between expected quality of care and measured quality of care, most significantly for people of color. The IOM followed with another report, "Unequal Treatment: Confronting Racial and Ethnic Disparities in Health Care" in 2002, which identified a set of root causes leading to these racial disparities (Betancourt, Green, Carrillo, & Ananeh-Firempong, 2003; Smedley, Stith, & Nelson, 2003). The identified root causes included:

- *Health system factors.* These highlight the difficulty minority patients have in accessing and navigating the complexities of the healthcare system, especially when language barriers exist.
- *Care process factors.* These causes include provider communication problems such as lack of knowledge and skills, prejudice, and discrimination, which contribute to patient mistrust.
- *Patient level factors.* These factors include patients' refusal of services, noncompliance or poor adherence to treatment, and delay in seeking needed care.

Cultural competence was initially viewed as a way to eliminate cultural and language barriers between providers and patients with **limited English proficiency** (LEP). By 2005, efforts to enhance cross-cultural health delivery had broadened beyond the acknowledgment and addressing of language differences to include an understanding of how patients from different cultures viewed health and illness. Researchers studied various cultural traditions and perspectives to develop tools for enhancing communication in clinical encounters between healthcare providers and their patients. To improve health outcomes as well as to bolster client satisfaction, healthcare organizations instituted training programs for their employees that built knowledge and skills in this arena. These programs typically included discussions of the impact of race and ethnicity on health care, the value of trust in patient–provider relationships, the role of social support systems, and the benefits of health literacy. Training helped employees to explore their own attitudes and biases, and develop tools to better communicate with colleagues and clients from different backgrounds. Providers were guided to "walk in their patients' shoes" and to view healthcare delivery "through their patients' eyes" (Beach, Saha, & Cooper, 2006).

By 2009, The Joint Commission, as part of a larger initiative to increase healthcare quality and safety through effective communication and cultural competence, approved new requirements to improve patient–provider communication for hospitals (Wilson-Stronks &

Tschurtz, 2010). New Joint Commission Standards of Practice were established in 2010 to promote culturally competent inpatient care and foster quality outcomes for diverse patients. These standards provided an additional rationale for healthcare leaders to build and evaluate cultural competence at all levels of their organizations, from the governing board to the frontline staff.

Culturally competent systems are designed to value diversity, to instill the capacity for cultural self-assessment and adaptation to diversity, and to promote knowledge about various cultures within and across institutions (Saha, Freeman, Toure, Tippens, & Weeks, 2008). Healthcare leaders responsible for cultural competence at system levels may incorporate the National Standards on Culturally and Linguistically Appropriate Services in Health Care (CLAS Standards). There are 14 standards on culturally and linguistically appropriate services (Office of Minority Health, 2001). The 14 CLAS standards include four federal requirements or mandates, nine recommended mandates or guidelines, and one voluntary adoption or recommendation, all surrounded by three themes: (1) Culturally Competent Care, (2) Language Access to Services, and (3) Organizational Supports. The CLAS standards recommend the employment of healthcare providers and staff that are ethnically similar to the patient community served and to collect and track data on quality of care for each demographic population. In 2011, the Department of Health and Human Services upgraded the CLAS standards. Revisions included professional interpreters as essential team members in the healthcare workforce and the establishment of an online national registry of certified interpreters for healthcare facilities (Koh, Graham, & Glied, 2011).

A Competitive Advantage

Corporations such as IBM have made **diversity management** a successful strategy in reaching out to diverse customers. Under Lou Gerstner's leadership, IBM "made differences matter," as the company developed products that would capture the attention and interest of this growing market (Thomas, 2004). Recent population growth and future demographic projections indicate that consumers of health care will also continue to increase in diversity. As patients become more informed and active in choosing providers and health services, healthcare organizations will be increasingly competing for consumers based on the perceived quality of customer service. Delivering services that meet the different cultural needs and preferences of diverse consumers will help a healthcare organization gain a competitive advantage.

Healthcare leaders can unfortunately face challenges when they begin implementing diversity management strategies. For example, attempts to increase diversity in a few organizations have not been successful because of employee resistance, with resulting impaired organizational performance due to heightened tension and conflicts among workers (Thomas, 2004; Thomas & Ely, 1996).

Leaders can shape the climate and **culture** of their organizations by building the capacities (i.e., the knowledge and skills) of their employees (Schein, 2006). Today's healthcare leaders need to create an environment in which diversity and culture flourish, and conflicting values can be expressed, examined, and mediated through education and dialogue (Moua, 2010). Healthcare leaders play a critical role by modeling cultural competence, by visibly and publicly supporting the value of diversity, and by providing opportunities for employees to engage in active learning that promotes acceptance of "differences." Successful leaders serve as key role models who are culturally sensitive and competent organizational representatives. In short, leaders must learn to "walk the talk" before expecting others to do so.

Leading Organizations Toward Cultural Competence

Although senior management may be less involved in the day-to-day operations that require use of cultural competence skills, their support and guidance are essential to the development of an organizational culture and climate that promotes and supports diversity and cultural competence. Leaders are critical for the successful implementation of cultural competence because they:

- Develop the mission, vision, goals, and objectives for the organization
- Set the "tone" of the organization and nurture organizational ethics and values
- Have the "big picture" of the organization in their sights
- Coordinate strategic planning efforts and initiatives, and engage in assessment of initiative effectiveness
- Have the authority to commit resources
- Deal with a broader range of constituencies

Senior management must commit to and be accountable for actions that promote individual and organizational cultural competence. Without leadership support, cultural competence efforts may flounder or fail. Dreachlin and Hobby (2008) suggest that leaders can promote cultural competence by:

1. Ensuring that their organization recruits and retains a culturally diverse workforce
2. Including culturally appropriate patient services in the organization's strategic goals
3. Routinely assessing achievement of these goals during the strategic planning and quality improvement processes
4. Assigning responsibility for promoting the organization's cultural diversity goals to a dedicated person, office, or committee
5. Annually reporting to constituents about the organization's performance in meeting the cultural and language needs of the service area

Successful promotion of organizational cultural competence is enhanced when:

- *Leaders make diversity a priority.* Leaders of healthcare organizations are tasked with identifying and implementing organizational priorities. Leaders promoting cultural competence elevate diversity to priority status and see it as a critical factor for innovation (Moua, 2010). This priority can be expressed via a statement of mission and/or vision that includes a commitment to providing culturally competent services. Leaders can advocate for the benefits of diversity with administrative and clinical employees, governing boards, and community partners.
- *Leaders get to know people and their differences.* Culturally competent healthcare leaders remain visible and engaged with organizational staff and clients, practicing and modeling cultural competence skills that can then be adopted by employees serving patients. Additionally, leaders who regularly meet and interact with employees gather cultural information that can help foster improved communications, relationships, and trust among diverse individuals and groups within the organization. Leaders who acknowledge that they are open to learning more about a culture can enrich communication by inviting intercultural dialogue with employees (Moua, 2010). Such dialogue can foster employee willingness to ask for help and to provide input.
- *Leaders create cultural synergy.* **Cultural synergy** means that we can learn from others and others can learn from us. This synergy occurs when diverse individuals work together to solve problems. Leaders

willing to create cultural synergy must draw on the diverse resources of the organization to contribute to problem solving (Adler, 2002). Cultural synergy can be facilitated by:

· *Addressing a situation or problem from the points-of-view of multiple cultures.* Different cultures may view issues and challenges from different perspectives. Soliciting the perspectives of others promotes greater understanding among participants in a problem-solving group and allows leaders and teams to get a more complete picture of relevant concerns and possible solutions.

· *Interpreting issues and concerns from a cultural perspective.* An individual may perceive his or her behavior as rational, but people from different cultures may misinterpret or misunderstand the behavior. Considering cultural factors in the interpretation of behavior can promote a more positive perception of the behavior and can identify common ground in thoughts, feelings, and actions among persons from different cultures. These help to develop new culturally-creative solutions.

Standards help workers hold themselves to high levels of performance. Standards do not necessarily prevent intercultural conflicts, but they can promote culturally competent and appropriate behavior. Clearly defining expectations for culturally competent professional behavior sets the stage for employee accountability. When employees are held accountable for culturally competent behaviors in an intercultural work environment, organizations report higher levels of respect and trust (Moua, 2010). Culturally competent behaviors can be assessed among colleagues, as well as between staff and patients. Assessing whether patients' cultural preferences are addressed in the delivery of health care should be a critical part of a healthcare organization's quality improvement program. Leaders are responsible for ensuring evaluation of these parameters to ensure that quality care is delivered in culturally appropriate ways to diverse patients.

To help leaders promote diversity and cultural competence, key steps and processes are listed in **Table 3.2**.

CREATING CULTURAL COMPETENCE IN HEALTHCARE ORGANIZATIONS: THE ROLE OF TRAINING

Thomas (2004) suggests that companies that have effectively managed diverse workers have created environments for active learning within the organization. One approach to creating and maintaining these learning environments is to provide dedicated employee training in cultural

Table 3.2 Leaders' Tool Kit

Steps	Process
Define diversity	Review definitions of diversity in healthcare organizations.
	Develop a workable definition of diversity and cultural competence that suits the needs of the organization.
Develop a business case for diversity and cultural competence	Identify organizational mission and strategic goals.
	Identify customer demographics and assess needs from a cultural perspective.
	Establish potential benefits of diversity management and cultural competence.
	Assess costs of poor or nonexistent diversity management.
	Identify areas of diversity management that the organization does well.
	Research diversity management among competitors and within market area.
	Identify strategies and opportunities for becoming an employer of choice.
	Develop a business case for diversity and cultural competence to share with stakeholders within and beyond the organization.
Sell diversity to senior management	Compile information to establish the business case for diversity management.
	Align the report with the strategic goals of the organization.
	Formally present the report to the CEO, executive team, and board of directors.
	Seek feedback on the submitted report.
Engage senior managers	Seek diversity champions in senior management as advocates.
	Form a diversity working group that includes the CEO to develop a diversity strategy with initiatives.
	Establish the commitment of senior leadership to mentor and support diversity programs.
	Enlist senior managers to serve as educators or mentors for employee training programs.
	Establish performance measures for senior leadership to monitor the effectiveness of the initiatives and to develop necessary revisions and refinements based on the periodic assessments.

Source: Courtesy of Janine O'Flynn, André Sammartino, Karen Lau, Aurora Ricciotti, & Stephen Nicholas. (2001). ATTRACT, RETAIN AND MOTIVATE: A TOOLKIT FOR DIVERSITY MANAGEMENT, Department of Immigration and Multicultural and Indigenous Affairs in Cooperation with the Australian Centre for International Business.

competence. Training objectives include the development of self-awareness and insight about personal assumptions and prejudices, of understanding of people's diverse expectations and behaviors, and of acceptance of differences.

Key training activities can help employees:

· Consider issues from a variety of perspectives
· Challenge their own assumptions and recognize the views of others as valid
· Reflect on and think about issues with an open mind and receptiveness to change
· Realize a higher awareness of our common humanity and their role as service providers

Training also requires assessment to document achievement of learning outcomes. Evaluations should be performed systematically and should assess pretraining and posttraining learning and performance. There are many different types of assessments that training programs can use, such as pre- and postsession surveys with self-reporting by attendees and participants, interviews with open-ended questions, and observations of behavioral change over time. In addition to supervisor and mentor reports, patient satisfaction surveys can contain items that allow evaluation of cultural competence performance for trainees who are delivering patient care. Assessments should also provide the opportunity for participants to suggest improvements for the training. Assessment data should be reviewed and utilized on an ongoing basis to modify and improve future training.

Individual and Group Cultural Competence Training

All diversity training programs need to have clearly stated goals and learning outcomes that will allow managers to evaluate their effectiveness. Managers and training specialists should have a clear idea of their intended objectives before launching their program. Once they know their "destination" or their goals, they can then design the educational activities needed to guide employees along the journey of change as well as the assessments needed to demonstrate employee achievements.

The process will begin with identified goals/objectives. Training will first strive to raise employee awareness about the identified issues, then move on to providing employees with the knowledge and skills to understand new perspectives, develop new attitudes, and change professional behaviors. Finally, comprehensive assessment tools will measure the extent to which employee knowledge, attitudes, and behaviors have been enhanced. Clements and Jones (2002) developed a list of measures to help assess learning goals for cultural competence training programs (see **Table 3.3**).

Table 3.4 presents an instrument that can be used to assess individual attitudes and behaviors related to cultural competence and can spur the self-examination helpful in changing professional behaviors.

Table 3.3 Learning Goals for Cultural eLearning Goal

Goals	Assessment Process
Increased knowledge	Self-report, tests, interview, group discussion
Behavior change	Role-play, group discussion; work assessment, self-report
Attitudinal change	Self-report, questionnaire, workplace assessment, group discussion

Table 3.4 Cultural Competence Instrument

Question	Strongly Agree	Agree	Not Sure	Disagree	Strongly Disagree
I try to consider the other person's point of view before giving my opinion	☐	☐	☐	☐	☐
Most of the time I am aware of my feelings	☐	☐	☐	☐	☐
I can usually explain to others how I am feeling	☐	☐	☐	☐	☐
I am tolerant when someone is argumentative	☐	☐	☐	☐	☐
I don't usually find it difficult to talk to people who do not share my views	☐	☐	☐	☐	☐
I am generally conscious of what others are feeling	☐	☐	☐	☐	☐

To help individuals manage their personal growth and relationships with others, Hemphill and Haynes (1997) developed an assessment that rates perceptions and patterns of experiencing and displaying emotions. **Table 3.5** can be used to help individuals assess their work relationships.

After filling out the self-reports, training participants can be guided in exploring their self-knowledge, beliefs, values, attitudes, and communication styles, and can learn new skills to improve professional relationships with colleagues and clients through, for example, group discussions and role-play.

After the completion of training or, in many cases, on an ongoing basis, employees should participate in assessments that can identify areas in which additional training would be helpful, as well as periodic training refreshers to promote continued active learning.

Table 3.5 Workplace Relationship Skills

Limiting Level	Me					Mastery Level
Judgmental	1	2	3	4	5	Nonjudgmental
Closed minded	1	2	3	4	5	Transformational
Insensitive	1	2	3	4	5	Empathic listener
Fear of change	1	2	3	4	5	Open to change
Discriminating	1	2	3	4	5	Open to differences
Stereotyping	1	2	3	4	5	Open minded

Organizational Cultural Competence

Both organizations and individuals are tasked with being culturally competent. Assessing the cultural competence of organizations was addressed by the Health Resources and Services Administration (HRSA) in 2002, which developed the Organizational Cultural Competence Assessment Profile to assess whether services are delivered in a culturally competent way by organizations.

This organizational assessment profile has three major parts: domains of cultural competence, focus areas within each of the domains, and indicators associated with each of the focus areas.

Within the domains of cultural competence are six areas of organizational functioning to assess:

1. Organizational Values
2. Governance
3. Planning and Monitoring/Evaluation, Communication
4. Staff Development
5. Organizational Infrastructure
6. Services/Interventions

Within each domain, key focus areas are specified along with indicators for assessment. An example can be found in the focus area of "culturally competent oral communication," as related to the new Joint Commission standards for hospital interpreters (Wilson-Stronks & Tschurtz, 2010). The indicators in **Table 3.6** can be utilized in assessment, along with potential query areas.

Once a set of indicators has been selected and the survey instrument developed, the next step is to gather information from all levels of the organization. As noted earlier, evaluative data from training obtained from surveys and interviews are common tools for collecting quantitative and

Table 3.6 Culturally Competent Oral Communication

Structure Indicators	Process Indicators	Outcome Indicators
Provide access to trained interpreters *Is there adequate access to trained interpreters?*	Provide training of interpreters *Is interpreter training provided by the institution?* *What learning outcomes have been developed?* *How effective is this training based on assessments?*	· Number of languages available at point of first contact and at all levels of interaction. *Numerical data to be benchmarked with other similar organizations.* · Use and timeliness of interpretation services. *Numerical data to be benchmarked with other similar organizations.* · Client/patient understanding of interpreted material. *Interviews or self-report surveys in the client's language.* · Low interpretation errors. *Numerical data to be benchmarked with other similar organizations.*

qualitative data related to an organization's cultural competence. These measures and indicators of cultural competence can contribute to an internal scoreboard to help monitor the effectiveness of an organization's diversity and cultural competence initiatives, as well as compare against the data from other institutions via benchmarking programs.

Leaders need to select a set of indicators that reflect the organization's mission, goals, and priorities regarding diversity and cultural competence, and develop assessments to measure progress in these areas. Indicators should also be analyzed by representatives of the various ethnic and racial groups served by the organization to help ensure that cultural competence initiatives being assessed are successfully targeting access and quality of care for their constituency. Tracking such indicators can help an organization monitor the extent to which its cultural competence initiatives are reducing disparities in health care and health status among their clientele. Findings from assessments should be reported routinely and periodically to the organization's governing board and key stakeholders. These actions demonstrate the organization's commitment and accountability to diversity and cultural competence.

Challenges and Recommendations

The culturally competent leader understands that organizational buy-in is imperative to launching and maintaining successful cultural competence initiatives. Maintaining cultural competence as a focus and priority is critical to implementation success. **Table 3.7** lists some of the key implementation challenges for healthcare leaders with regard to cultural competence.

Table 3.7 List of Challenges for Cultural Competence Implementation

Lack of organizational commitment to equity, diversity, access, and excellence	Lack of education/training about the cultures served
Absence of human resource practices and policies related to the inclusion and incorporation of racial and ethnic minority groups	Failing to recruit/retain and match the demographic of the employees with the community served
Lack of organizational resources to support diversity recruitment and retention	Failing to institute linguistic policies that conform to Culturally and Linguistically Appropriate Services (CLAS) standards for LEP patients

Healthcare leaders should be aware of these challenges and be proactive and systematic in evaluating and promoting diversity-friendly personnel as well as interpersonal and organizational practices and policies. Cultural competence remains an integral value for healthcare organizations that should be integrated into the organizational mission, vision, and goals, strategic planning, day-to-day operations, and quality assessment and improvement programs.

There is a clear and direct link between healthcare organizations' cultural competence and the quality of care provided to consumers and employees. The need for cultural competence and diversity management to help an organization achieve competitive advantage is clear. According to Dansky and colleagues (2003), "If an organizational workforce creates value, it is hard to imitate, and is rare, it will contribute to sustained competitive advantage. An organization meets these criteria with a culturally diverse workforce that performs in a supportive, enabling milieu" (p. 245).

The research evidence supporting the positive effects of cultural competence on organizational performance is slowly emerging. Today's healthcare leaders are charged with developing, implementing, and assessing cultural competence throughout their healthcare organizations. Health outcomes data that have been analyzed by ethnicity and race are important accountability measures to determine whether cultural competence activities and training are making a difference in access to care and patient safety. Diversity includes many aspects of human behavior and attributes, thus necessitating broad definitions that extent beyond race and ethnicity. By collecting and studying healthcare outcomes via diversity parameters, healthcare organizations will be able to develop evidence-based cultural competence practices that promote patient access and reduce healthcare disparities.

Healthcare leaders are being exhorted by federal regulatory agencies such as the Department of Health and Human Services and accreditation bodies such as The Joint Commission to make cultural competence an organizational strategic initiative that can help address disparities in access and quality of care for underrepresented ethnic and racial groups. If healthcare leaders accept and embrace this challenge and strive to develop culturally competent employees and organizations, they will, in turn, contribute to the equity and safety of the U.S. healthcare delivery system for our increasingly diverse population.

SUMMARY

Faced with an increasingly diverse workforce and patients, healthcare leaders are challenged to develop organizational cultures that effectively embrace, respect, and serve those from different cultures and backgrounds. This chapter provides a description of several seminal external forces (e.g., Institute of Medicine reports and census data) that identified disparities in the quality and safety of health services. This is coupled with growing evidence that supports the influence of organizational cultural competence in the delivery and management of quality health care. A practical set of tools is provided to plan and evaluate cultural competence training across all levels in an organization and thereby helps leaders create a culture committed to diversity and cultural competence.

Discussion Questions

1. How can leaders influence change regarding diversity in their organizations?
2. Explain the role of cultural competence training and education.
3. An important part of cultural competence and diversity management is assessment. Discuss a few key ways to assess knowledge, attitudes, and behaviors.
4. Discuss how a health leader can monitor the success of cultural competence activities.

Case Study: Cultural Competence

An African American woman enters a healthcare facility where she is to receive a magnetic resonance image (MRI) of her spine. She has long hair in the style known as "locks." She is greeted by the receptionist and asked to have a seat in the waiting area until the technician is ready to see her. A white, male technician arrives to escort the woman in for her procedure and briefly discuss the process of MRI with her. During his overview, he indicates that she will have to remove any metal objects (such as pins in her hair or jewelry) and that she should remove her hair for the process. The woman is appalled by his latter statement and indicates to him that her hair is her own and cannot be removed. He responds by stating that he has served a number of black women who have weaves and other "false" hair often held in by pins, so he was basically taking a precaution. The woman is highly insulted and asks to speak to the administrator on duty. A white woman, in an elegantly tapered suit, arrives, hears the concern, and explains to the African American woman that the technician meant no harm, but that it is the policy of the facility to be thorough with all patients in terms of the provision of information and that he was correct in inquiring about her hair in the manner that he did to ensure safety during the MRI process. She offers no apology and curtly responds, "I hope this resolves your concerns, as he was merely following our required protocol." The African American woman responds with a disappointed and curt thank you and leaves the building promptly, vowing never to return. She seeks her MRI at another facility.

Case Study Discussion Questions

1. What went wrong in this encounter?
2. Why was the patient offended?
3. What could be done to help patients better understand protocols in the future?
4. What role did culture play in this instance?
5. What training should be offered to the facility's employees?

References

Adler, N. (2002). *International dimensions of organizational behavior* (2nd ed.). Cincinnati, OH: Thomson Learning.

Beach, M. C., Saha, S., & Cooper, L. A. (2006). *The role and relationship of cultural competence and patient-centeredness in health care quality.* New York, NY: Commonwealth Fund.

Betancourt, J. R. (2006). *Improving quality and achieving equity: The role of cultural competence in reducing racial and ethnic disparities in health care.* New York, NY: Commonwealth Fund.

Betancourt, J., Green, A., Carrillo, J., & Ananeh-Firempong, O. (2003). Defining cultural competence: A practical framework for addressing racial/ethnic disparities in health and health care. *Public Health Reports, 118,* 293–302.

Clements, P., & Jones, J. (2002). *The diversity training handbook: A practical guide to understanding and changing attitudes.* London, UK: Kogan Page.

Collins, K., Hughes, D., Doty, M., Ives, B., Edwards, J., & Tenney, K. (2002). *Diverse communities common concerns: Assessing health care quality for minority Americans. Findings from the Commonwealth Fund 2001 Health Care Quality Survey.* New York, NY: Commonwealth Fund.

Dansky, K. H., Weech-Maldonado, R., De Souza, G., & Dreachslin, J. L. (2003). Organizational strategy and diversity management: Diversity-sensitive orientation as a moderating influence. *Health Care Management Review, 28*(3), 243–245.

Dickie, C., & Soldan, Z. (2008). *Diversity management.* Prahran, Australia: Tilde University Press.

Dobbs, M. (1996, September). Managing diversity: Lessons from the private sector. *Public Personnel Management, 25,* 351–368.

Dreachslin, J., & Hobby, F. (2008). Racial and ethnic disparaties: Why diversity leadership matters. *Journal of Healthcare Management, 53*(1), 8–13.

Gardenswartz, L., & Rowe, A. (1998). *Managing diversity: A complete desk reference and planning guide* (Rev. ed.). New York, NY: McGraw-Hill.

Hemphil, H., & Haines, R. (1997). *Discrimination, harassment, and the failure of diversity training: What to do now?* Westport, CT: Quorum.

Hubbard, E. (2004). *The diversity scoreboard: Evaluating the impact of diversity organizational performance.* Burlington, MA: Elsevier.

Institute of Medicine (IOM). (2002a). *In the nation's compelling interest: Ensuring diversity in the healthcare workforce.* Washington, DC: National Academies Press.

Institute of Medicine (IOM). (2002b). *Unequal treatment: Confronting racial and ethnic disparities in health care.* Washington, DC: National Academies Press.

Koh, H., Graham, G., & Glied, S. (2011). Reducing racial and ethnic disparities: The action plan from the Department of Health and Human Services. *Health Affairs, 30*(10), 1822–1827.

Kohn, L., Corrigan, J., & Donaldson, M. (2000). *To err is human: Building a safer health system.* Washington, DC: Institute of Medicine.

McDaniel, G. (2000). *Cultural competency: A new standard of care. Advance for medical laboratory professionals.* Retrieved January 10, 2013 from http://laboratorian .advanceweb.com/Article/Cultural-Competency-A-New-Standard-of-Care.aspx.

Moua, M. (2010). *Culturally intelligent leadership.* New York, NY: Business Expert.

National Association of Community Health Centers. (2011). *Health Centers' role in reducing racial and ethnic health disparities.* Retrieved October 8, 2012 from www .nachc.com/client/documents/research/GeneralDisparitiesFactSheet9.05.pdf.

National Partnership for Action. (2011). *National stakeholder strategy for achieving health equity.* Retrieved August 25, 2011 from www.minorityhealth.hhs.gov/npa /templates/content.aspx?lvl=1&lvlid=33&ID=286.

Office of Minority Health. (2001). *National standards for culturally and linguiestically appropriate services in health care.* U.S. Department of Health and Human Services. Retrieved October 8, 2012 from www.minorityhealth.hhs.gov/templates /browse.aspx?lvl=2&lvlID=15.

O'Flynn, J., Nicholas, S., Sammartino, A., Lau, A., & Ricciotti, A. (2001). *Attract, retain and motivate: A toolkit for diversity management.* Commonwealth of Australia, Canberra: Productive Diversity Partnership Programme, DIMIA and ACIB.

Passel, J., & Cohn, D. (2008, February). *U.S. population projections: 2005–2050.* Washington, DC: Pew Research Center. Retrieved October 24, 2012 from www .pewhispanic.org/files/reports/85.pdf.

Saha, S., Freeman, M., Toure, J., Tippens, K., & Weeks, C. I. (2008). Racial and ethnic disparities in the VA health care system: A systematic review. *Journal of General Internal Medicine, 23,* 654–671.

Schein, E. (2006). *Organizational culture and leadership.* San Francisco, CA: Jossey-Bass.

Smedley, B., Stith, A., & Nelson, A. (2003). *Unequal treatment: Confronting racial and ethnic disparities in health care.* Washington, DC: National Academies Press.

Thomas, D. (2004). Diversity as strategy. *Harvard Business Review, 82*(9), 98–108.

Thomas, D., & Ely, R. (1996). Making differences matter: A new paradigm for managing diversity. *Harvard Business Review, 74*(5), 79–90.

Thomas, D., & Inkson, K. (2009). *Cultural intelligence living and working globally* (2nd ed.). San Francisco, CA: Berrett Koehler.

Thomas, R. R. (1990). From affirmative action to affirming diversity. *Harvard Business Review, 68*(2), 107–117.

Vincent, G. K., & Velkoff, V. A. (2010). *The next four decades: The older population in the United States: 2010 to 2050* (Current Population Report P25-1138). Retrieved October 24, 2012 from www.census.gov/prod/2010pubs/p25-1138.pdf.

Wilson-Stronks, A., & Tschurtz, B. (2010, August). *Advancing effective communication, cultural competence, and patient- and family-centered care: A roadmap for hospitals.* Oakbrook Terrace, IL: The Joint Commission.

Chapter 4

Creating a Culture of Professionalism

Keith Benson and Chris Hummer

LEARNING OBJECTIVES

By the end of this chapter, the student will be able to:

- Define professional behaviors.
- Describe how leaders can create and promote a culture of professionalism within an organization.
- Compare and contrast professionalism as a healthcare leader with professionalism as a staff clinician/physician.
- Discuss the role of professional/organizational ethics or codes of conduct in building and promoting professionalism.

KEY TERMS

Character	Obligation
Codes of conduct	PIE²
Competency	Professionalism
Leadership	

INTRODUCTION

What Is Professionalism?

Healthcare executives have many different skillsets they can use in managing healthcare organizations. A key component in their management toolbox is **professionalism**; professionalism facilitates successful **leadership**.

What is professionalism and why is it so critical to executives' success? The Oxford English Dictionary defines professionalism as *"Professional quality, character, or conduct; a professional system or method."* Professionals, from accountants to physicians, can often best serve their fields by adopting a threefold approach to meeting **obligations**. The obligations are to clients (customers), to the community, and to societal needs (Medical Professionalism Project, 2002; Swick, 2000; Wyatt, 2004). Medical professionalism is a set of behaviors, attitudes, and values that serves the interests of patients and society before one's own interests (Reynolds, 1994; Wynia, Latham, Kao, & Emmanuel, 1999). All healthcare providers and managers have an ethical and professional duty to practice medical professionalism through the promotion of high-quality patient care.

The Components of Professionalism

Achieving this standard can be facilitated by understanding the three basic components of professionalism: (1) **character**, (2) conduct, and (3) quality (see **Figure 4.1**).

For example, one of the first lessons students learn in school is to not cheat. By not cheating, students are exhibiting a desired professional behavior that directly relates to both character and conduct. Many academic institutions have institutionalized this expected professional behavior through the creation and adoption of honor codes or pledges. The University of Texas Medical Branch at Galveston uses the honor pledge, *"On my honor, as a member of the UTMB community, I pledge to act with integrity, compassion, and respect in all my academic and professional endeavors"* as a statement of professionalism (Smith, Saavedra, Raeke, & O'Donell, 2007). Honor codes and pledges clearly outline expected professional behavior that sets a standard for academic leaders to promote. Similar pledges are being used in healthcare organizations to summarize behavior expectations for all members of the organization.

Examples of professionalism can be considered from two perspectives: **PIE²** or Personal (Internal & External) and Professional (Internal & External) Professionalism. The internal perspective of professionalism relates to behaviors/actions that are not always visible to others. You might be the only one who knows you are being professional. The external perspective is clearly visible to others and can be judged by them. Others usually

Figure 4.1 Components of Professionalism

rate your level of professionalism by these behaviors. **Table 4.1** lists items included in each perspective.

The Value of Professionalism

All healthcare professionals should practice medical professionalism. Modeling medical professionalism is especially critical for healthcare leaders as they interface with physicians and other clinical staff to inspire a culture of professionalism and respect. Healthcare leaders are responsible for the professional behavior of employees, many of whom work with little or no direct supervision. Ingrained medical professionalism usually allows less direct supervision and results in better patient care and improved organizational outcomes (Sergiovanni, 1992; Wojciech et al., 2006).

Healthcare organizations practicing lower levels of professional behavior (higher levels of unprofessional behavior) tend to demonstrate poor adherence to policies and procedures; lower staff morale and increased turnover; drops in patient volume; and a greater number of medical errors, adverse outcomes, and malpractice suits (Hickson, Pichert, Webb, & Gabbe, 2007). A study conducted by the Studer Group and Vanderbilt University Medical

Table 4.1 PIE^2 or Personal and Professional Professionalism

Personal Professionalism	
Internal	**External**
Being honest	Demonstrating integrity
Striving to be reliable and dependable	Being on time, meeting deadlines, keeping promises
Caring about others	Treating all people with respect
Respecting oneself	Dressing appropriately for the dress code
Professional Professionalism	
Internal	**External**
Respecting others	Dealing with sensitive issues privately
Being an active learner	Accepting criticism in a positive manner
Maintaining integrity	Ensuring honesty and accuracy in communications and other administrative tasks, avoiding real or perceived conflicts of interest
Aiming for self-control	Engaging in respectful and considerate communications
Doing your job to the best of your ability	Demonstrating that you value the privilege of caring for patients and respect others who engage in this role as well

Source: Courtesy of Keith J. Benson, PhD.

Center—Center for Patient and Professional Advocacy (CPPA) found that when policies, processes, and training for disruptive behaviors do not exist in an organization, workplace satisfaction is jeopardized. For example, 66% of survey respondents had considered leaving their job as a result of unprofessional behavior. Unprofessional behavior negatively impacts job satisfaction, workplace safety, and clinical outcomes. It is imperative for healthcare leaders to expect and promote medical professionalism and to be well prepared to intervene in cases wherein unprofessional or disruptive behaviors are reported or observed (Studer Group, 2011).

Implementing Professionalism

Successful medical professionalism requires (1) professional expertise and **competency** as a manager and/or clinician, (2) the ability to communicate and connect effectively with others such as patients and colleagues in a professional capacity, (3) the ability and commitment to achieve organizational goals through development of strong fiduciary relationships, trust, and morality (ABIM, 2002).

Mueller (2009) shares the renowned Mayo Clinic's foundation of professionalism: clinical knowledge and skills, communication skills, ethics, accountability, altruism, excellence, and humanism. The Mayo Clinic, whose primary value is "the needs of the patient come first," uses PLEASE CARE (Present, Listen, Empathize, Action, Summarize, Excite, Confidentiality, Attitude, Respect, and Emotional intelligence) to advance medical professionalism within its organization.

Reynolds (1991) stated that, in healthcare organizations, professional behaviors include a nonjudgmental and respectful approach to patients, a commitment to excellence and lifelong competency, and a collegial and cooperative approach to working with members of the healthcare team. This recipe is an excellent guide for healthcare professionals seeking to practice a high standard of medical professionalism.

Healthcare leaders play a critical role in inspiring and promoting a culture of medical professionalism. An example of this process can be observed via Carolinas Medical Center–Pineville (CMCP) initiatives. CMCP's motto, which drives the organization, is *"Uncompromising Excellence. Commitment to Care."* In the Spring of 2011, Dr. Benson worked as a faculty intern for Chris Hummer, President of Carolinas Medical Center–Pineville. During this time, Benson observed firsthand how Hummer and his leadership team promoted professionalism by modeling these guidelines and mentoring staff in their implementation. **Table 4.2** illustrates the CMC-Pineville Way or the professional behaviors the senior leadership team exhibited.

Table 4.2 The CMC-Pineville Way

- Set the best example of the desired behavior.
- Listen to everyone—patients, patient families, employees, physicians, providers.
- Get to know your employees so they can see you as a role model. A great way to do this is to frequently take walks throughout the facility.
- Hold people accountable—congratulate them on a job well done. Coach them if they need to improve to meet a standard.
- Smile—it makes others feel better and inspires them to act professionally.
- Finally, and perhaps the most important—CARE! Care for your patients, care for your employees, care your providers, care for your organization, and care for your community.

Source: Courtesy of Carolinas Medical Center–Pineville.

Sources of Professionalism

Leaders of healthcare organizations can develop resources and tools to help promote professionalism from internal (within the organization) or external (outside the organization) sources. A source of professionalism can be an organization's mission, vision, and value statements. These statements prescribe why the organization exists, what the organization believes in, and what is important to the organization.

The Carolinas HealthCare System (2012), one of the nation's largest integrated delivery systems and owner/operator of CMC-Pineville, provides the following example:[1]

Our Mission

The mission of Carolinas HealthCare System is to create and operate a comprehensive system to provide healthcare and related services, including education and research opportunities, for the benefit of the people we serve.

Our Vision

Carolinas HealthCare System wants to be chosen by consumers and physicians as the Carolinas premier healthcare provider for high quality and cost-effective health services.

Our Values

Carolinas HealthCare System recognizes our employees are our most valuable asset. We have identified four core values successful employees need to strive for in order for us to accomplish our mission.

- **Caring:** We treat our customers with dignity, giving them the courtesy and gentleness they need. We are helpful; we listen; we communicate; we respond to patient needs.
- **Commitment:** We are dedicated to Carolinas HealthCare System, taking pride in our organization and our jobs, projecting a professional image and striving to be the best in all we do.
- **Integrity:** We honor and uphold confidentiality, are honest and ethical, keep our commitments, accept responsibility for our actions, and respect the rights of patients, families and each other.
- **Teamwork:** Linked by our common mission, we respect the professionalism and contributions of our coworkers, understand that physicians are an integral part of the team, value diversity in all its forms, and recognize that people are our greatest assets.

Each of the statements from Carolinas HealthCare contains guidance for acting professionally. The mission statement directs all of the organization's

---

1. Courtesy of Carolinas Medical Center–Pineville.

activities to benefit the people they serve, a charge that embodies the core of medical professionalism. The vision statement acknowledges that Carolinas HealthCare strives to be the premier healthcare provider for high-quality, cost-effective care. The organization's vision once again taps into the requirements of competency and quality cited by the ABIM. And finally, Carolinas HealthCare values include specific guides to professional behavior.

DEVELOPING AND PROMOTING PROFESSIONALISM THROUGHOUT AN ORGANIZATION

Healthcare leaders have many tools at their disposal that can help develop professionalism throughout an organization. One of the most effective methods for leaders to mentor employees is to serve as exemplary role models and demonstrate the desired professional behaviors themselves. The tools below afford opportunities for executives to "lead by example."

Meetings

When leading a meeting, conduct it in a professional manner. Have an agenda and then follow it. Keep people focused on the meeting topics and limit tangential discussions. And most importantly, respect people's time. Time is a valuable commodity and needs to be guarded and not wasted. One sign of an effective professional is his or her ability to run a professional/effective meeting.

Communications

Effective communication facilitates professionalism. Leaders should use clear, precise, and concise statements; avoid jargon and acronyms whenever possible; listen with empathy; interpret nonverbal communications such as body language and gestures; and ask pertinent questions. Managers also need to turn their focus beyond conversations. In addition to demonstrating clarity and articulateness with the written word, leaders in today's media-rich environments need to be effective communicators and display professionalism in presentations and when using email and social media.

Organizational Culture

Leaders must monitor and evaluate the organization's culture in order to ensure the promotion of professionalism. Fortunately, there are leadership models available for leaders to help create, shape, and influence professionalism within an organization.

There are several sources for executives to mine that focus on leader roles. One source that addresses organizational culture that promotes professionalism is *The Leadership Challenge* by Kouzes and Posner (2003). Its *First Five Practices* are outlined as follows:

· *Model the way.* Leaders create principles concerning the way people should be treated and the way goals should be pursued. They develop standards of excellence and then set an example for others to follow.
· *Inspire a shared vision.* Leaders believe that they can make a difference. Through their persuasion, leaders get people to see exciting possibilities for the future.
· *Challenge the process.* Leaders look for opportunities to change the status quo and are willing to experiment and take risks.
· *Enable others to act.* Leaders foster collaboration and actively involve others. They understand mutual respect and work to create an atmosphere of trust and human dignity.
· *Encourage the heart.* Leaders recognize contributions that individuals make, celebrate accomplishments, and make people feel like they are making a difference.

Another leadership expert in health care, Quint Studer, discusses *Straight A Leadership* (2009), based on his teams' work with organizations. Studer notes, "If everyone in the organization doesn't truly understand the behavior that's needed to be successful, the organization won't achieve its goals" (p. xvi). This statement demonstrates that leaders must not only understand and model necessary professional behaviors themselves, they must educate, train, and mentor staff in understanding and practicing these behaviors.

To help leaders realize this objective, Studer developed the Straight A Leadership model for delivering consistency in a professional organization: Alignment, Action, and Accountability. Studer states that all senior leaders need to be aligned (i.e., on the same page) and should expect accountability from employees. Leaders should assess employee professionalism and performance and reward high performers, help advance midrange performers, and intervene to assist those not performing up to standards (Studer, 2009).

Hiring/Performance Management

One of the best ways to support professionalism within an organization is to begin with the hiring process. Mueller (2009) and Reynolds (1991) recommend a team approach to evaluating, interviewing, and hiring applicants who are able to practice the expected behaviors and conduct. Professionalism should be included in the job description and addressed in employee performance evaluations. Once employees are hired, ongoing staff assessment and development can help underperformers meet the organization standards and expectations. Methods for assessing compliance include (Mueller, 2009):

- Direct observation
- Tests that measure specific skill (e.g., communication skills, conflict resolution, ethical judgment)
- 360 reviews
- Clinical evaluations and peer reviews
- Patient feedback
- Critical incident reports

Coaching/Mentoring

Developing a culture of professionalism does not happen overnight. A critical step in developing and maintaining a culture of professionalism within an organization is a viable and active coaching/mentoring program, strongly and openly supported by the senior management. Mentors, including senior leaders, can serve as role models for employees, and provide advice, guidance, and coaching when needed (Wells, 2002). Sadly, failure of senior management to uphold the organization's standards of professionalism can have a profound negative impact on employees and should be avoided at all cost.

CODES OF CONDUCT, PROFESSIONAL OATHS, AND CODES OF ETHICS

Most occupations embrace a definition of professionalism, which is often embedded in their **codes of conduct**. The code of conduct dictates duties and responsibilities, and typically shares the following common elements (Gawande, 2009):

1. An expectation of selflessness
2. An expectation of skill
3. An expectation of trustworthiness
4. An expectation of discipline

Codes of conduct may relate to a specific occupation within an organization or to the entire organization. One example of an organizational code of conduct is from the Wissota Health and Vent Center in Chippewa Falls, Wisconsin:[2]

> **We are proud of the leadership and reputation that Wissota Health has in the Chippewa Falls community.** In order to meet and exceed our mission, as well as create a positive working culture, each of our employees is personally committed to continually enforcing and adopting the following attitudes and behaviors:
>   · I will take personal responsibility for my actions and behaviors.
>   · I will work at developing a culture of trust and respect.
>   · I will be an active participant at team meetings.
>   · I will be genuinely concerned about each team member's personal welfare.
>   · I will communicate in a manner so others will know they can believe, depend, and count on what I say.
>   · My behaviors will be proactive, not reactive.
>   · I will demonstrate pride and a sense of ownership in my role at Wissota Health and Regional Vent Center.
>   · I will work as part of a holistic team

These eight behaviors, when followed by each organizational member, help ensure the practice of professionalism within Wissota Health.

The American College of Healthcare Executives (ACHE) is an international professional society of over 35,000 healthcare executives. ACHE developed a code of ethics to guide healthcare executives in their professional duties and obligations. This code of ethics and conduct includes:

I.   The healthcare executive's responsibilities to the profession of healthcare management
II.   The healthcare executive's responsibilities to patients or others served
III. The healthcare executive's responsibilities to the organization
IV.   The healthcare executive's responsibilities to employees
V.   The healthcare executive's responsibilities to community and society
VI.   The healthcare executive's responsibility to report violations of the ACHE code

The complete ACHE code of ethics is available at www.ache.org/abt_ache /code.cfm. Other professional associations for healthcare executives such as the Medical Group Management Association (MGMA), the American Health Information Management Association (AHIMA), and the American

---

2. Courtesy of Wissota Health and Regional Vent Center.

Health Care Association (AHCA) also have codes of ethics to help guide their members' professional behavior.

Professional oaths reflect a binding promise. One of the earliest professional oaths is from Hippocrates, a 5th century BC physician, who prescribed that physicians should treat the sick to the best of their ability, preserve patient privacy, teach the secrets of medicine to the next generation, and above all, "abstain from doing harm" (see **Figure 4.2**).

Physician professionalism emerged directly from the Hippocratic Oath (Harms, 2004). Clinical professionals must not only care for and about the patient, but also deliver necessary medical care in a high quality, cost-effective, compassionate manner. Each member of a clinical care team is guided by the professional oath that relates to their clinical profession. Understanding the elements of each profession's oath and the promises that each clinical professional has made can help healthcare leaders use common elements to advance medical professionalism in the organization as a whole.

Chris Hummer came to CMC-Pineville in 2006 as its President. When Hummer arrived, there was growing friction between the physician staff and the administrative team. In just 5 years, Hummer and his leadership team forged strong relationships with the physicians. Together they joined to build a professional medical center delivering high-quality care. During this engagement process, physician satisfaction scores with CMCP increased dramatically. The case study at the end of this chapter describes Hummer's experience maintaining professionalism in a healthcare organization during a period of growth and change.

© Maximus256/ShutterStock, Inc.

Do Not Harm

Figure 4.2 Hippocratic Oath

SUMMARY

Healthcare leadership best serves its organization, mission, employees, and clients when promoting professionalism. An organization practicing a high level of professionalism delivers better care, encourages improved employee satisfaction and productivity, and sees greater achievement of organizational goals. It is up to healthcare managers to lead by example and set the expectations for professionalism to flourish and thrive within our healthcare organizations.

This chapter discusses the relationship between professionalism and leadership. The concept of professionalism spans the entire range of interactions between a healthcare manager and patients, physicians, nurses, allied health professionals, payers, employees, and other stakeholders. To help managers better understand the concept of professionalism and the relations between leadership and professionalism, we present the PIE^2 model. This model provides guidance and gives examples of professional behaviors.

Discussion Questions

1. What is professionalism?
2. Relate your academic training to the three basic components of professionalism.
3. How can professionalism help improve patient care?
4. How can professionalism improve relationships with physicians, nurses, and other medical staff professionals?
5. What are examples of "good" and "bad" professional behavior you have encountered in your life? What leadership lessons can be learned from these examples?

Case Study: Leadership in Practice

Working with Physicians to Create a Culture of Professionalism: A CEO's Perspective

Carolinas Medical Center–Pineville (CMCP) is a 120-bed community hospital located in Pineville, NC, a town located in the south end of Charlotte, NC. The hospital was built in 1987 as a satellite of Mercy Hospital, was acquired by Carolinas HealthCare System (CHS) in 1995, and was renamed CMC-Pineville in 2000.

In 2007, CMCP launched an ambitious multiphase expansion in an effort to transform the facility from a community hospital to a tertiary medical center by 2012. The cost of the expansion is nearly $300 million and includes a new energy plant, a parking deck, a medical office building, 86 additional inpatient beds (25 of which are intensive care), four operating rooms, 10 ED bays, and 10 private neonatal intensive care rooms. The new construction will increase the facility from 175,000 to 515,000 square feet. Tertiary services in the new facility will include inpatient dialysis, medical and surgical intensive care, interventional and vascular cardiology, cardiothoracic surgery, and surgical oncology with emphases on breast and lung cancer.

CMCP's current reputation is very good in all operational areas, resulting in market share gains. For example, CMCP excels in quality (e.g., top 10% in mortality, multiple Joint Commission disease specific certifications), patient satisfaction (e.g., top quartile or higher as rated by Professional Research Corporation, multiple JD Powers awards), physician satisfaction (top 10% as rated by Healthstream), and employee satisfaction (top 15% as rated by Morehouse and Associates).

CMCP's medical staff today is highly engaged in working with the administration team to deliver high-quality care. The medical staff includes several veteran physicians who were affiliated with Mercy, along with physicians hired more recently by Carolinas HealthCare System, its parent organization. CMCP physicians are generally accepting of technology, collaborative and reasonable in their approach to problem solving, and value the contributions and professionalism of their colleagues, holding them accountable for their actions both clinically and behaviorally. Most importantly, the physicians understand that the medical staff's role and contributions as a whole are more significant than those of its individual practitioners alone.

Since the launch of the first expansion, CMCP's medical staff has grown by 75 active staff, with an additional 40 to 50 physicians looking to redirect their practices from other hospitals to CMCP as a result of the expansion. Though the physical and programmatic growth at CMCP have improved the facilities and increased access for patients, there were concerns that the influx of new physicians could erode the positive and collegial culture of CMCP's medical staff. Efforts over the past 5 years were implemented to ensure that the professionalism of CMCP's medical staff not only weathered the transformation, but also excelled in this new environment.[3]

---

3. Since the time of construction, the hospital has increased its full-time equivalents (FTEs) from 535 to 940 in 2011, adding another 191 in 2012. Several efforts are underway to ensure that CMC's employee development and support (e.g., peer interviewing, more robust orientation, expanded training and education, reward and recognition, etc.) continues to strengthen.

Rebuilding Engagement

Efforts to maintain the atmosphere of professionalism are guided by CMCP's history. In 2005, the relationship between administration and CMCP's medical staff was strained. In its first physician satisfaction survey of Carolinas HealthCare System's Metro Group, Healthstream ranked CMCP last in "Overall Satisfaction," with a mean score of 2.90 out of 4, in the bottom quartile nationally.[4]

In 2006, a leadership change at CMCP, along with a renewed Carolina HealthCare System focus on physician satisfaction, led to changes that reversed the hospital's position from last to first, with a 3.32 mean score, equal to 83rd percentile nationally. This level of engagement continues to the present.[5]

CMCP's administration used a variety of tactics to promote physician engagement by inviting input and participation in strategic planning and decision making. Supporting the medical staff's professionalism resulted in improved physician satisfaction and productivity.

For example, CMCP's administration chose to work closely with its medical staff leadership in two areas. The first: developing ways to obtain internal and external input about the proposed expansion via an annual event. The second: addressing the growing separation between physicians who practiced at the hospital; in other words, hospital-based physicians (i.e., emergency physicians, hospitalists, anesthesiologists, and radiologists), proceduralists, and surgeons, and the growing number of primary care physicians who no longer came to the hospital.

After the addition of hospitalists at CMCP in 2003, family practice and internal medicine doctors began using the hospital less and less, if at all. The result: (1) Medical staff responsibilities fell on fewer individuals, (2) the medical staff developed a high and disproportionate concentration of specialty physicians and hospital-based physicians, and (3) the interaction

---

4. Carolinas HealthCare System's Metro Group includes the following facilities: CMC, CMC-Mercy, CMC-Pineville, CMC-University, CMC-Randolph, CMC-Northeast, CMC-Lincoln, CMC-Rehabilitation, CMC-Union, CMC-Anson, Levine Children's Hospital, Jeff Gordon Children's Hospital.
5. CMC-Pineville's mean scores and percentile rankings: "Overall Satisfaction"
- 2005: 2.90/23rd
- 2007: 3.32/83rd
- 2008: 3.37/86th
- 2009: 3.51/93rd
- 2010: 3.46/87th
- 2011: 3.55/90th

and communication between referring primary care physicians and specialists was sharply reduced.

To bridge this separation, CMCP leaders launched an event in October of 2006, known as "State of the Hospital Address," to bring together community and hospital physicians. The invitation list included physicians who had privileges but no longer used the hospital. After welcoming the guests and allowing a period for networking and fellowship among the attendees, the leaders offered a formal program that included medical staff business (e.g., election of officers), departmental updates, awards and recognitions, and even a humorous video that offered a parody of modern medicine. This event helped rebuild CMCP connections with community physicians and continues as the annual medical staff meeting today.

Additionally, the economics of health care placed a premium on productivity, which drove physicians to try to save time as they cared for their patients. When orders were placed or questions about a referred patient arose, busy doctors would opt to communicate with office personnel, nurses, or midlevels and turn away from physician-to-physician communication. This practice eroded collegiality and risked increasing conflict and negative patient outcomes. Failure to communicate directly with physician colleagues became an important issue that needed to be addressed by the CMCP Medical Executive Committee (MEC). The MEC is composed of physician leaders selected by the physicians with staff privileges. In 2007, the bylaws were reworked requiring doctor-to-doctor communication.

Finally, the recognition of practice and time demands on physicians, which limited physician participation in committee activities, led the MEC to reorganize committee structure and function so that it became a meaningful use of physicians' time. Departmental Committees instituted operational subcommittees to deal with routine items, allowing a more substantive agenda for the large-group meetings that addressed quality of care. One tool for improved use of physician time was the implementation of consent agendas. A consent agenda allows routine matters that do not need explanation to be bundled and voted on as one package. Consent agendas took care of less critical matters and allowed time at meetings for meaningful debate of hospital-wide issues of concern to the medical staff. To encourage retention of physician leaders and recruitment of new champions, the organizational structure of the medical staff was updated and revised, and an annual MEC orientation and retreat was scheduled at the beginning of each year to prepare new and existing leaders for the year ahead.

Physician Oath

CMCP's medical staff has long valued and promoted both clinical competence and professionalism among its members. To underscore this commitment in the atmosphere of rapid growth and expansion, the MEC developed a physician oath in late 2010 with two objectives in mind: to remind current medical staff of its professional culture and its responsibility to foster it for the next generation, and to provide an explicit description of the professional culture and its expectations for the newest members. The complete oath is reproduced as follows:[6]

Carolinas Medical Center–Pineville Physician Oath

We the physicians of Carolinas Medical Center–Pineville have taken and follow the Hippocratic Oath. In all our relationships with our patients and their families, all hospital staff and other physicians, we promise to the best of our ability and judgment with all humility to always:

- Seek the healing and comfort of those who are sick, treating them with respect and dignity, protecting them from harm and injustice.
- Guard our professional moral integrity.
- Seek the counsel of those with appropriate special skills for the benefit of our patients.
- Hold in strict confidence whatever we may see or hear about our patients.
- Engage, listen to and clearly communicate with patients, their families and all team members to enhance the patient's quality of care.
- Respect the professionalism and contributions of all team members.
- Value diversity in all its forms, recognizing that people are our greatest asset.
- Recognize that all life is sacred and should be cherished, protected and valued.

Health care has undergone a seismic evolution in recent years that has driven physician practice from independent autonomy to team function. CMCP recognized that the groundbreaking changes in its institution, as well as the healthcare industry as a whole, have had a significant impact on physicians and could negatively impact professionalism. By acknowledging that physicians, just like other professionals, value being respected, empowered, recognized and rewarded, and included in strategic planning and decision making that affects their practice, CMCP enlisted and enhanced physician engagement and support and promoted and encouraged ongoing physician professionalism.

---

6. Courtesy of Carolinas Medical Center–Pineville Medical Executive Committee.

Case Study Discussion Questions

1. From your perspective, what are the strengths of the CMC-Pineville's CEO to create a culture of professionalism?

2. Why are physician and employee satisfaction signs of a professional organizational culture?

3. If you had to create an organizational oath similar to the CMC-Pineville physician oath, what concepts and components would you ensure are in the oath?

4. What lessons from the case study are applicable to long-term care facilities, physician practices, and other healthcare organizations?

RELATED WEBSITES

American Health Care Association: www.ahcancal.org/Pages/Default.aspx

American Health Information Management Association: www.ahima.org/

Carolinas HealthCare System: www.carolinashealthcare.org

Medical Group Management Association: www.mgma.com/

Studer Group: www.studergroup.com/DB

The Leadership Challenge: www.leadershipchallenge.com/WileyCDA/Section /id-131055.html

Wissota Health and Regional Vent Center: www.wissotahealth.com/about_us /code_of_conduct.phtml

REFERENCES

ABIM Foundation. American Board of Internal Medicine; ACP–ASIM Foundation. American College of Physicians–American Society of Internal Medicine; European Federation of Internal Medicine. (2002). Medical professionalism in the new millennium: A physician charter. *Annuals of Internal Medicine, 136*, 243–246.

Carolinas HealthCare System. (2012). *Mission and value statement.* Retrieved November 29, 2012 from www.carolinashealthcare.org/chs-mission-and-values.

Gawande, A. (2009) *The checklist manifesto.* New York, NY: McMillian.

Harms, R. (2004). Physicians, professionalism, and organizational efforts to improve quality—A systems perspective. *Wisconsin Medical Journal, 103*(3), 63–64.

Hickson, G. B., Pichert, J. W., Webb, L. E., & Gabbe, S. G. (2007). A complementary approach to promoting professionalism: Identifying, measuring, and addressing unprofessional behaviors. *Academic Medicine, 82*, 1040–1048.

Kouzes, J. M., & Posner, B. Z. (2003). *The leadership challenge* (3rd ed.). Hoboken, NJ: Jossey-Bass. Retrieved August 31, 2012 from www.leadershipchallenge.com /WileyCDA/Section/id-131055.html.

Medical Professionalism Project. (2002). Medical professionalism in the new millennium: A physician charter. *Lancet, 359*, 520–522.

Mueller, P. (2009, September). Incorporating professionalism into medical education: The Mayo Clinic experience. *Keio Journal of Medicine, 58*(3), 133–143.

Reynolds, P. P. (1991). Professionalism in residency [editorial]. *Annual Internal Medicine, 91,* 91–92.

Reynolds, P. P. (1994). Reaffirming professionalism through the education community. *Annual Internal Medicine, 20*(10), 609–614.

Sergiovanni, T. J. (1992). Why we should seek substitutes for leadership. *Educational Leadership, 49*(5), 41–45.

Smith, K. L., Saavedra, R., Raeke, J. L., & O'Donell, A. A. (2007). The journey to creating a campus-wide culture of professionalism. *Academic Medicine, 82,* 1015–1021.

Studer Group. (2011). *Disruptive behaviors in healthcare.* Retrieved October 24, 2012 from www.studergroup.com/DB.

Studer, Q. (2009). *Straight A leadership.* Gulf Breeze, FL: Fire Starter.

Swick, H. M. (2000). Toward a normative definition of medical professionalism. *Academic Medicine, 75,* 612–616.

Wells, B. G. (2002). Leadership for reaffirmation of professionalism. *American Journal of Pharmaceutical Education, 66,* 334–335.

Wissota Health and Reginal Vent Center. *Code of conduct.* Retrieved October 24, 2012 from www.wissotahealth.com/about_us/code_of_conduct.phtml.

Wojciech, P., Hromanik, M. J., Milanese, T. R., Dierkhising, R., Viggiano, T. R., & Carmichael, S. W. (2006). Leadership and professionalism curriculum in the gross anatomy course. *Annuals Academic Medicine Singapore, 35,* 609–614.

Wyatt, A. R. (2004). Accounting professionalism, they just don't get it! *Accounting Horizons, 18*(1), 45–53.

Wynia, M. K., Latham, S. R., Kao, A. C., & Emmanuel, L. L. (1999). Medical professionalism in society. *New England Journal of Medicine, 341,* 1612–1616.

Chapter 5

Human Resource Considerations at the Top

Mary Helen McSweeney-Feld and Nancy Rubin

LEARNING OBJECTIVES

By the end of this chapter, the student will be able to:

- Define the functions and responsibilities of human resources in a healthcare organization.
- Describe the concept of strategic management of healthcare human resources and its importance in delivering cost-effective healthcare services with outstanding patient outcomes.
- Identify key human resources metrics that are indicators of successful human resources management in a healthcare organization.
- Define and describe talent management and succession planning strategies for healthcare organizations.
- Describe the role of change management and its connection to strategic human resources management in health care.
- Identify opportunities for improvement of healthcare human resources management in light of global economic trends and a changing regulatory environment for healthcare organizations.

KEY TERMS

Human resources metrics

Performance evaluation

Recruitment

Retention

Selection

Total rewards model

Training and development

Workforce planning

INTRODUCTION

People are key inputs in the provision of services and care for any healthcare organization. Healthcare organizations would not exist without a well-trained, highly motivated workforce that works together to produce the best quality care for its patients or residents. However, the healthcare world is complex and requires extensive amounts of specialized training for its professionals who utilize evolving amounts of technology in the provision of these services. Consequently, it is important to look at the concept of strategic human resources management, or the comprehensive set of managerial activities and tasks related to developing and maintaining a qualified workforce that can contribute to an organization's effectiveness as defined by their strategic goals (Fottler, 2008).

In this chapter, we will outline the components of human resources management, their application to healthcare organizations, and how these concepts translate to the strategic management of any healthcare workforce. We will also introduce the concept of **human resources metrics**, or how a healthcare organization can measure how effective it is in the management of its highly skilled workers. An overview of new developments in the management of human resources will be discussed, as well as future directions for healthcare providers in light of global economic trends and an evolving regulatory environment.

HUMAN RESOURCES MANAGEMENT IN HEALTH CARE: THE BASICS

Human Resources Activities

Human resources management is typically defined as the process of planning, recruitment, selection, rewarding, training, and development of an organization's workforce. It is a system of activities and strategies that focus on successfully managing employees at all levels of an organization to achieve organizational goals (Byars & Rue, 2007). To be a high-performing healthcare entity, its overall strategic plan should be matched with its workforce plan. A strategic plan will include a mission and vision statement, performance objectives, a plan for achieving these objectives, and a method for evaluating and correcting the actions of the organization based on its evaluation of outcomes from its performance. Departments, in turn, may create their own mission, vision, and performance goals in light of the organization's overall objectives to guide their activities; and a human resources department can create its strategic workforce plan as part of this process. This process is somewhat different from standard human resources planning in that it emphasizes the need to have employees whose knowledge, skills, and abilities help the healthcare organization achieve its specific mission, vision, and goals. An example of these activities would be a healthcare facility that recently adopted an enterprise-wide electronic medical record system (EMR). Employees within this facility must be willing to understand the knowledge and skills required to use the EMR, thus acquiring and utilizing these skills effectively so patient services and outcomes can benefit from use of the EMR.

Legal and Regulatory Environment

Surrounding all human resources functions is a complex system of laws and regulations that guide the implementation of these activities. Federal, state, and local laws determine the outcomes of hiring processes, compensation, **performance evaluation**, and work conditions for virtually all individuals in the healthcare field. **Table 5.1** provides a summary of key Federal legislation that every healthcare manager should know if he or she engages in any aspect of strategic management of the healthcare workforce. These laws guide the employment of individuals, including regulations for specific groups of individuals, the provision of compensation and employee benefits programs, the ability of workers to join unions and collectively bargain for pay, benefits or work conditions, and workplace environment and safety.

Employment regulations include the landmark Title VII of the Civil Rights Act of 1964, prohibiting discrimination in employment on the grounds of gender, race, color, religion, and national origin, which is enforced by the Equal Employment Opportunity Commission (EEOC). This Act laid the groundwork for legislation covering specific groups such as individuals over the age of 40, people with disabilities, pregnant women, and individuals performing military duty. The Employee Retirement Income Security Act of 1974 was the seminal piece of legislation creating regulations for pensions and employee benefits such as life and health insurance, and the Patient Protection and Affordable Care Act of 2010 seeks to extend these provisions through requiring the purchase of health insurance for all employees by 2014. Concerns with a safe and healthy work environment led to the passage of the Occupational Safety and Health Act of 1970, which provides guidelines for maintaining a safe workplace, including provisions on training workers to maintain safe work conditions, and the Worker Adjustment

Table 5.1 Major Human Resources Legislation

Employment Laws	Fair Labor Standards Act of 1935	Established minimum wages, overtime pay, and standard work hours; enforced by the Department of Labor DOL
	Title VII, Civil Rights Act of 1964	Prohibits discrimination based on gender, race, color, religion, and national origin; enforced by the EEOC
	Age Discrimination in Employment Act of 1967 (ADEA)	Protects employees and job applicants 40 years and older from discrimination in hiring, firing, promotion, layoffs, training, benefits, and assignments
	Pregnancy Discrimination Act of 1978	Protects employees who are pregnant against discrimination
	Americans with Disabilities Act of 1990 (ADA)	Protects individuals with disabilities from employment discrimination
	Lilly Ledbetter Fair Pay Act of 2009	An amendment to Title VII of the Civil Rights Act of 1964 that addresses unlawful employment practices related to compensation discrimination; enforced by the EEOC
Compensation and Benefits Laws	Employee Retirement Income Security Act of 1974 (ERISA)	Regulates pension and benefit plans for employees; enforced by the DOL
	Consolidated Omnibus Budget Reconciliation Act of 1986 (COBRA)	Allows employees who change jobs to obtain health insurance; enforced by the DOL
	Older Workers Benefit Protection Act of 1990	Amended ADEA to provide benefits to younger and older workers; enforced by the EEOC
	Family Medical Leave Act of 1993 (FMLA)	Requires employers with 50 or more employees working more than 1250 hours annually to provide up to 12 weeks of unpaid leave to any employee in a 12-month period for care of a family member or themselves; enforced by the DOL

Compensation and Benefits Laws (continued)	Uniformed Services Employment and Reemployment Rights Act of 1994 (USSERA)	Employees serving in the military have job protection and benefits extended during this period; enforced by the DOL
	Health Insurance Portability and Accountability Act of 1996 (HIPAA)	Protects the privacy and confidentiality of patient information; enforced by the Department of Health and Human Services
	Pension Protection Act of 2006	Strengthens employer funding requirements for pensions and pension insurance; enforced by the DOL
	National Defense Authorization Act of 2008	Extends FMLA to include the families of employees in military service
	Genetic Information Nondiscrimination Act of 2008	Prohibits insurance companies and employers from discriminating in areas of compensation and benefits based on results from genetic testing; enforced by the EEOC
	Patient Protection and Affordable Care Act of 2010 (ACA)	Requires individuals to obtain health insurance by 2014 and allows children of employees to remain on their parents' health insurance up to age 26
Safety and Work Environment Laws	Occupational Safety and Health Act of 1970	Requires employers to provide a safe and healthy work environment for their employees; enforced by the Occupational Safety and Health Administration (OSHA)
	Worker Adjustment and Retraining Notification Act of 1989	Employers with 100 or more employees must give their employees 60 days notice of layoffs and closings

and Retraining Notification (WARN) Act of 1989 made notification of major layoffs or plant closings mandatory for work places with 100 or more employees. Strategic management of the healthcare workforce requires administrators to be keenly aware of these laws, as well as any amendments or changes in provisions that impact employees or their families.

Recruitment, Selection, and Retention

The **recruitment** and **selection** processes in a healthcare entity utilizing strategic human resources management principles also have a specific purpose and direction. Recruitment activities determine how many employees are needed, what kinds of individuals are needed, how many are new, and how many need to be replaced. The goal of recruitment activities is to address areas in which an organization has skill deficits. Recruitment activities cast a wide net and encompass a process with internal and external elements. For example, you may have an internal recruitment and referral program to encourage existing employees to recommend individuals who would be a good fit for the organization's culture and help it achieve its strategic goals. At the same time, you may engage in online recruitment activities, participate in job banks, and speed interviewing processes. Another key change in the recruitment process is that you may bank the résumés of candidates for the future and hold them in abeyance in case they are a good fit for future job needs. The selection process also has a broader objective, given that many healthcare organizations have a mature workforce and valuable, long-service employees. Human resources managers may look at a candidate's ability to perform certain functions and have specific skills, but they may also be looking at the individual's fit with the organization with an eye to succession planning for more senior members of their workforce. A study by the National Center for Healthcare Leadership (NCHL) identified succession planning—establishing a process for identifying and training individuals who could perform senior management roles in the future—as an important tool for high-performing healthcare organizations seeking to accomplish their organization's strategy, achieve their projected priorities, and fulfill their staffing needs (NCHL, 2010, p. 1). The development of a set of leadership competencies for each organization, the ongoing assessment of candidates with strong leadership potential, and the creation of new job opportunities to "stretch" the capabilities of candidates while ensuring their **retention** with the organization were also identified as key components of the succession planning process (NHCL, 2010, p. 2).

Once a candidate accepts an offer from a healthcare organization, an orientation period typically occurs, which is referred to as "onboarding." This shift in language is also important, as it goes beyond presenting the new employee with the company's history, an organization chart, and information on health insurance and retirement plan options. It may encompass a multiday process wherein the individual still obtains the standard orientation program information, but starts the process of immersing him- or herself in the culture, vision, and values of the organization.

Retention of employees in healthcare settings has become a major concern in recent years. The natural stressors of the healthcare clinical workplace environment, long work hours, and continual pressures of performance in light of reduced financial reimbursement for healthcare services have led many younger workers to leave the field for other career opportunities. In addition, continued immigration of foreign nationals for healthcare education and training, and older workers staying longer in employment, has led to a more multicultural healthcare workforce, with generational differences in work attitudes, including those seeking greater balance of work schedules and family responsibilities. Many healthcare organizations have hired retention specialists in their human resources departments to create specialized career development and training programs.

New ways of configuring human resources work output have also become an outgrowth of strategic human resources management. These developments include a move to interdisciplinary care teams—that is, teams of clinical and administrative professionals across healthcare disciplines providing care to patients and residents, which has become the norm. Greater focus on patient and resident outcomes as individuals are transitioned from inpatient or residential settings to home and community-based settings has produced other innovations such as the growth of community-based medical homes in which a care team continues to provide and monitor patient services through the use of sophisticated technology. All of these developments necessitate a human resources staff that is willing to assist its workforce with implementing and managing these workplace developments and ensure that outcomes from these new care models result in a high level of reimbursement as well as continued linkages to the original mission, vision, and goals of the organization.

Workforce Rewards

In healthcare organizations, workers may include the clinical workforce that provides hands-on patient or resident care and the administrative workforce that ensures the provision of management services such as admission and discharge of patients/residents, housekeeping, and dietary services, as well as marketing the organization and payment for services provided. Determining a process of rewards for these individuals is a critical component of the processes of recruitment and retention of these workers due to their specialized education, and skills that are high in demand by competing healthcare providers. A **total rewards model** (see **Figure 5.1**) encompasses compensation such as salaries and bonuses or incentive payments, benefits such as health and life insurance, retirement plans and wellness programs, work–life programs, and policies that allow the worker to balance job responsibilities and family/community obligations, as well as nonmonetary rewards such as acknowledgement and recognition in the workplace, and promotion and advancement opportunities (Christofferson & King, 2006).

The total rewards model encompasses the monetary and nonmonetary return provided to employees in exchange for their time, talent, efforts and results. This type of integrated model also helps organizations providing health care to attract and retain high-performing employees, and motivates them to produce results consistent with their organization's strategic plan. Rewarding workers through the provision of market-rate salaries and benefits such as insurance and retirement plans can also play a role in retaining workers, as well as providing them with opportunities for continued training and refinement of their clinical and/or managerial skills (Kabene, Orchard, Howard, Soriano, & Leduc, 2006).

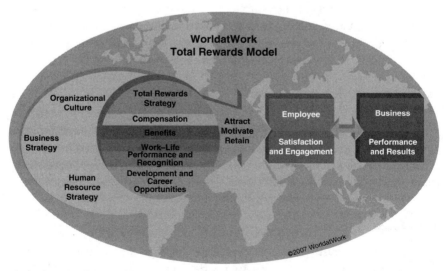

Figure 5.1 Total Rewards Model

Source: Courtesy of WorldatWork

Physicians and the medical staff in a healthcare organization are good examples of the need for human resources professionals to develop specialized reward programs. Physicians' performance is controlled by professional norms and culture that arise from outside a healthcare organization, and they expect more autonomy and less managerial oversight than they would receive in a traditional bureaucracy (Olden, 2011, p. 75). However, healthcare organizations need to ensure that the medical staff is aligned with their strategic plan and goals and are aware of the importance of quality outcomes for their patients. As a result, more physicians are moving away from being in independent private practice in the community with fee-for-service reward relationships toward institutional ownership of their practice and the use of bundled payments and incentive compensation plans based on quality, production, and utilization metrics (Darves, 2011). These trends may continue to evolve if regulatory reforms continue to emphasize quality and value in patient outcomes.

Performance Evaluation

Once employees are hired in a healthcare organization, their performance within their position needs to be evaluated. Performance appraisal is a formal, systematic assessment of how well employees are performing in their jobs in relation to established standards (French, 2007, p. 359). A performance appraisal process typically consists of (1) giving employees feedback about their performance and identifying individual training needs; (2) providing a basis for directing employee efforts over the next time period; (3) providing the line managers with a basis for recommending promotions, raises, and future assignments; (4) clarifying and reinforcing lines of authority; and (5) providing a basis and record for disciplinary action when necessary (McSweeney-Feld, 2010). Appraisals are typically conducted on an annual basis, but in some instances, the review cycle could be as frequent as quarterly or twice a year. Many healthcare organizations use a 360 feedback evaluation process, in which input from workers at the same level or grade above and below the worker is obtained. If the individual interacts with entities outside the organization, such as patients, business partners, and community organizations, feedback from these stakeholders may also be solicited as part of the employee's professional development process.

Training and Development

Employees in health care are in need of continual **training and development** to keep their skills consistent with changes in technologies used in the delivery of healthcare services. Training also helps to provide services to an increasingly diverse workforce and patient population, and to keep a workforce engaged and focused on strategic goals. Training may consist of on-the-job programs specific to the needs of the healthcare organization and may be conducted with a facilitator or delivered through self-study or online methods. Programs may include tuition remission for external degree programs or specialized certificate training. In addition to specialized training programs, many organizations provide new employees and managers with a mentor for their first year wherein they can ask questions safely. Training programs frequently include professional development and leadership programs that cultivate workers for more senior positions by introducing them to new modalities, which in turn helps the organization to become resilient in the face of external and internal environmental change. All of these specialized internal training programs have a large payoff in retaining specialized workers within an organization.

Labor Unions

Unions are membership organizations that can negotiate for workers in healthcare settings on issues of pay, benefits, and work conditions. The right of workers to unionize was created under the Workforce Planning Act (Wagner Act), as was the right of the union to engage in **workforce planning** on behalf of its members with management. Labor unions and their organizing activities have increased in healthcare organizations in recent years due to the increasing work responsibilities of the healthcare workforce, with greater pressures to improve performance and achieve outcomes. Consequently, workers at entry levels as well as management professionals have turned to labor unions.

Unionization continues to be a significant human resource and operational issue for healthcare organizations. Some organizations have adopted a strategy of union avoidance. When a union targets these organizations' employees for unionization, senior management may spend a significant amount of time and resources launching a campaign to maintain a union-free environment. These organizations believe that employees are better served by having a direct relationship with leadership, and that a third party is not necessary to bargain for employees. Other organizations believe that unionization is going to occur despite efforts to avoid union recruitment, and choose not to launch a campaign against the union. A benefit of having a collective bargaining agreement with a union is that organizations can predict labor costs for the segment of their employees that are covered by collective bargaining. Most organizations have significant strategies to address interactions with unions, and there are definite pros and cons for both unionization and nonunionization. Human Resource professionals are usually tasked with helping to negotiate union contracts and attending to grievances and arbitrations.

THE ROLE OF STRATEGIC HUMAN RESOURCES MANAGEMENT

How are these basic human resources management functions transformed by the notion of strategic human resources management? The healthcare industry in the United States has experienced recent regulatory changes that cause organizations to focus on issues of providing quality care for patients and residents and tying outcomes from healthcare services to payment for these services. In this world, good outcomes are rewarded with high levels of reimbursement for services, and services with medical errors run the risk of zero payment for the organization. In turn, healthcare organizations need to make their workforce keenly aware of their mission and vision, as well as any short-term or long-term goals of the organization, which can affect their ability to obtain good clinical outcomes, high levels of customer service, and ultimately, payment for services at the highest prevailing rates. This is a profound shift in the notion of healthcare human resources management, as it ties employees' performance to levels of service reimbursement and necessitates a new way of thinking about service delivery and work models. It also makes human resources professionals responsible for providing clear linkages between the larger world of the healthcare organization's business strategy and the willingness of workers to be motivated to perform at outstanding levels of service performance.

Human Resources Metrics: How to Gauge Your Workforce Performance

Many healthcare organizations have their doors open for business 24 hours a day, 7 days a week. Consequently, it can become challenging to measure the optimal number of employees that any department needs in order to provide high-quality healthcare services. A typical measure used by healthcare organizations to determine the number of employees needed by any department is called a full-time equivalent, or FTE. This measure provides an organization with their best estimate of the number of full-time employees needed given the number of encounters or services that they typically provide, and it helps them to develop appropriate staffing numbers for departmental budgets. It also allows for development and comparison of workloads across different types of work settings. One FTE is equal to 2080 hours per year (based on an

8 hour day, 40 hour workweek, with 52 weeks in a year), and can be adjusted for days of vacation, sick time, or other measures of leave.

Other important measures of workforce performance critical for healthcare organizations are staff turnover rates and vacancy rates. Turnover can be determined by the number of employees who leave an organization per year divided by the total number of employees; if this number (converted to a percentage) is a double-digit number, we can say that the organization has high turnover of its employees. Similarly, vacancy rates are measured by the ratio of open, unfilled positions divided by the total number of positions within an organization; if vacancy rates are at double-digit levels, this may affect the optimal performance of any healthcare facility.

Healthcare organizations also use a strategic planning process wherein their mission, vision, and goals are translated into measures of financial and operating performance that appear on a "dashboard"—a management tool specific to the needs of that organization. In turn, many healthcare human resources organizations are developing and using specific measures of their contribution to productivity and performance, known as human resources metrics. These measures can be developed for any healthcare organization and compared to industry benchmarks for performance.

The American Society for Healthcare Human Resources Administration (ASHHRA) has developed a human resources metrics tool that provides healthcare organizations with six categories of performance measurement: (1) retention and separations (measures of staff turnover and years of service); (2) workforce productivity and profitability (labor costs and overtime pay); (3) staffing and hiring (cost of hiring and time to accept a job); (4) workforce diversity (diverse personnel headcount); (5) human resources cost and structure (human resources cost and training costs); and (6) compensation and benefits (benefits cost and healthcare costs per employee) (ASHHRA, 2011). Other metrics may include measures of unionization activities and risk management information such as numbers of injuries and numbers of workers' compensation cases (Hospital Association of Southern California, 2011).

Specific examples of key metrics that can be applied to a variety of healthcare work settings are (ASHHRA, 2011):

- Staffing and Hiring
  - Vacancy rates
  - Cost per hire
- Workforce Diversity
  - Ethnically diverse headcount/percentage
  - Ethnically diverse external hiring percentage

- Retention and Separations
  - Turnover rate
  - Nurse voluntary separation rate
- Compensation and Benefits
  - Average hourly rate by job class
  - Average benefits cost per employee
- Workforce Productivity and Profitability
  - Labor cost per full-time equivalent
  - Labor cost expense percentage
- Human Resource Cost and Structure
  - HR cost per employee
  - Learning and development investment per employee

NEW DIRECTIONS IN STRATEGIC HUMAN RESOURCES MANAGEMENT

Strategic human resources management can target all types of healthcare workers, as well as specific groups of employees. There is a plethora of research on the best strategies for attracting and retaining clinical employees such as physicians and nurses. However, the issues affecting the healthcare industry in the future go far beyond basic human resources strategies for hiring the right person for an open position. Population dynamics will affect the global healthcare industry in the 21st century, as growth in the Boomer segment of the global population (those born between 1945 and 1960) will create unprecedented demand for healthcare services (Institute of Medicine, 2008). As the demand for healthcare workers increases, the existing healthcare workforce in the United States is also aging, and it is predicted that many seasoned workers will retire over the next decade (Center for Health Workforce Studies, 2005). Increasing focus on quality due to new regulatory and compliance requirements, and evolving approaches to national healthcare reform will also place pressure on healthcare organizations to compete for a smaller number of trained professionals. Consequently, talent management in healthcare organizations—attracting the best members of a trained healthcare workforce while continuing to engage and develop existing employees—is a new theme in strategic human resources management.

What types of strategies should healthcare organizations use to effectively manage their talent? Getting the right person for a job may result in a shorter hire process if it includes preemployment assessments and skills testing (Aberdeen Group, 2010, p. 6). Many organizations also encourage the use of an internal referral system wherein current employees are paid a small stipend if they refer a friend who is consequently hired for a position.

Healthcare organizations are also facing a variety of forces requiring them to become more nimble players in an increasingly competitive industry. Increasing use of healthcare information technology in the form of electronic medical records, new medical devices, and the growing use of simulations and web-based applications require healthcare workers to obtain new skillsets and be open to working in new situations and applications. The use of change management strategies—planned or spontaneous responses to external or internal developments requiring organizations to respond to consumers and/or external stakeholders in new ways—requires new and creative uses of an organization's healthcare workforce. Changes in job descriptions and specifications, specialized interdisciplinary work teams, and work groups that may exist on a temporary or permanent basis are examples of responses to organizational change strategies. Training human resources professionals to act as internal consultants to facilitate change within healthcare organizations and having a Chief Learning Officer (CLO) to lead the change management and organizational development processes are new responses taken by healthcare human resources organizations.

Growing attention is being paid to the challenges of providing care for chronically ill individuals by healthcare organizations. These patients have ongoing needs for care that exist beyond the walls of a hospital or nursing home. The development of medical homes to improve care after discharge is a new attempt to engage primary care physicians and medical group practices in community-based care services. Another interesting approach to health workforce planning for delivery of primary and community care was conducted by Segal and Leach in South Australia. The authors developed a workforce evidence-based (WEB) planning model for delivery of best practice care for chronic disease, in this instance, diabetes. A needs-based model was developed for estimating a health workforce team to serve patients with diabetes. The first step was to conduct a needs assessment. This was accomplished by describing the status of the population through a review of the literature, meeting with a panel of experts, and having discussions with cross-disciplinary teams. From this activity came four themes/levels: (1) promotion, prevention, and screening; (2) type or stage of disease; (3) complications; and (4) threats to self-care (Segal & Leach, 2011, p. 4). Level 1 concerns involve the workforce delivering health promotion and prevention services for "at-risk" populations. Levels 2 to 4 concern healthcare needs for persons diagnosed with diabetes. A unique set of attributes were established based on the type of diabetes, whether the patient had experienced any complications and if there was a threat to his or her ability to care for themselves. After this step, 13 databases were studied to determine the population's health status. Best practice care was translated into care protocols. These guidelines came from a variety of diabetes and chronic care associations in Canada and the United States. When there was a gap and a best practice was needed, a consensus of expert opinions based on the interdisciplinary team interviews was developed to meet the need. The best practices were then translated into care protocols again using the interdisciplinary care teams. Mapping took place based on care protocols and the diabetes services needed by the populations. Because the care protocols also took into account the competency needed by the workforce to deliver service and the occupation level best able to provide these services, it was possible to map out who needed service, who should provide the service, and how many services were needed. This model is also robust enough to account for millions of people if there became a need to do so.

SUMMARY

Strategic human resources management in healthcare organizations requires rethinking and redeployment of the healthcare workforce in new ways, with openness to changing strategies based on the evolving needs of the healthcare industry. As the demand for healthcare services increases globally, leaders of healthcare organizations need to examine their strategies for managing their clinical and administrative talent in light of these changes. These developments also require a metrics system for evaluating the performance of those workers in new settings. Identification of these management strategies will assist healthcare organizations in maintaining high performance and outcomes, and remaining flexible enough to be proactive if faced with future challenges.

Discussion Questions

1. Define the concept of strategic human resources management and why it is important for healthcare organizations in the 21st century to incorporate this concept into their management of a high-performing workforce.

2. What is the total rewards approach to rewarding employees in the workplace, and how could this be a useful approach to attract and retain key healthcare workers?

3. What are interdisciplinary care teams? What impact do they have on healthcare human resources? Why are healthcare organizations utilizing this model of providing patient or resident healthcare services?

4. Define two human resources metrics that can be used to assess the performance of healthcare professionals, and discuss a way in which each metric can be applied in a workforce setting.

5. Define and discuss two types of talent management strategies for a healthcare workforce.

6. How can human resources professionals be used to facilitate organizational change in a healthcare organization?

Case Study: In Search of Optimal FTEs—The Post-Acute Care Unit at Sunnyside Hospital

The question many healthcare leaders grapple with is: "How many staff members (measured as full-time equivalents, or FTEs) do I need to cover my daily census?" This introduces us to a discussion of units of service and what are the determinants of adequate staffing. Consequently, we have developed a case study of a nursing home taking residents for rehabilitation and therapy wherein accurate calculation of FTEs made an enormous difference.

A community hospital, Sunnyside Health Center, provided surgical services on an inpatient and outpatient basis, and was the only surgical center in the city of Sunnyside. The nurse manager of the surgical services department traditionally measured its volume by counting the total number of surgical cases. About 80% of all its rehabilitation cases were transferred to its post-acute care unit, where the manager counted their volume of work in a similar fashion. In February, a new retirement community opened, and its administrator hired a marketing manager who actively recruited rehabilitation cases from Sunnyside, claiming that they could provide the same quality of therapy services at a significantly lower cost. It was estimated that half of all the rehabilitation cases would transfer to the new therapy unit at the nursing home. The staff in the post-acute care unit at Sunnyside was reduced to account for this reduction in outpatient volume. When the nursing home opened, the hospital could not retain sufficient staff to handle the number of cases that remained in the hospital therapy unit, as they did lose rehabilitation cases. However, a different problem arose: the remaining hospital post-acute care staff were working overtime, there was never enough staff for the daytime shift, and existing rehabilitation cases experienced long delays for therapy services. Where had Sunnyside gone wrong?

The majority of the rehabilitation cases that had been transferred to the nursing home were short-stay cases that required minimal therapy services. The cases that remained at Sunnyside were therapy cases that were clinically complex and longer in duration, requiring more rehabilitation services and ongoing nursing care. It became clear that, when it came to measuring the work involved in servicing patients needing rehabilitation care, a case is not a case. A new approach to measuring the workload of the unit had to be devised.

The care team in Sunnyside's post-acute care unit decided to look at each patient's functional assessment and need for rehabilitation care, as these assessments would more accurately reflect the measurement of work. When the team leader did a retrospective review of the 6 months prior to the opening of the nursing home and compared it with the 6 months after the nursing home opening, the department had lost cases and found that, on average, each case kept by the hospital required 30% more services than the average rehabilitation case in the past. This demonstrated the need to measure the units of service that are used for calculating a department's volume to accurately determine workload.

The post-acute care unit team leader also compared the average number of staff needed prior to the nursing home rehabilitation unit opening with the average number of staff needed after the nursing home unit opening. This staff number increased from an average of 4.0 staff per room to 4.5 staff per room. This information was instrumental in helping the unit justify its additional staffing needs.

With its new rehabilitation unit open on the other side of town, the nursing home owners began actively recruiting the best staff from the post-acute care unit at Sunnyside with offers of better shifts, an enhanced benefits package, and onsite childcare. Three key therapists in Sunnyside's unit started to call in sick and take their vacation days earlier than in the past. The unit's team leader asked human resources for assistance but was told that Sunnyside had already negotiated union contracts for the next 2 years and that HR had no flexibility in the pay and benefits that could be offered to the therapists.

Case Study Discussion Questions

1. Why is the calculation of FTEs important for Sunnyside's post-acute care unit?

2. How could Sunnyside have better planned for the opening of the nursing home's rehabilitation care unit?

3. What initiatives could be taken by Sunnyside's human resources unit to retain their seasoned therapists in the post-acute care unit?

REFERENCES

Aberdeen Group. (2010). *Talent management in healthcare: Post-hire strategies to build from within.* Boston, MA: Author.

American Society for Healthcare Human Resources Administration (ASHHRA). (2011). *Human resources metrics tool.* Retrieved July 7, 2012 from www.ashhra .org/products/metrics.shtml.

Byars, L., & Rue, L. (2007). *Human resources management* (9th ed.). New York, NY: McGraw-Hill.

Center for Health Workforce Studies. (2005). *The impact of the aging population on the health workforce in the United States.* Albany, NY: State University of New York at Albany.

Christofferson, J., & King, B. (2006). The "IT" factor: A new total rewards model leads the way. *Workspan, 49*(4), 2–5.

Darves, B. (2011, January). Physician compensation models: Big changes ahead. *NEJM Career Center.* Retrieved October 24, 2012 from www.nejmcareercenter .org/article/92/physician-compensation-models-big-changes-ahead/.

French, W. L. (2007). *Human resources management* (6th ed.). Boston, MA: Houghton Mifflin.

Fottler, M. D. (2008). Strategic human resources. In B. Fried & M. D. Fottler (Eds.), *Human resources in healthcare: Managing for success* (3rd ed.). Chicago, IL: Health Administration Press.

Hospital Association of Southern California. (2011). *2011 HR metrics report.* Los Angeles, CA: Author.

Institute of Medicine. (2008). *Retooling for an aging America: Building the health care workforce.* Washington, DC: National Academies Press.

Kabene, S. M., Orchard, C., Howard, J. M., Soriano, M. A., & Leduc, R. (2006). The importance of human resources management in health care: A global context. *Human Resources for Health, 4*(20). doi:10.1186/1478-4491-4-20.

McSweeney-Feld, M. H. (2010). Human resources. In *NAB nursing home administrators examination study guide* (5th ed.). Washington, DC: National Association of Long-Term Care Administrator Boards.

National Center for Healthcare Leadership (NCHL). (2010). *Best practices in healthcare talent management and succession planning: Case studies.* Chicago, IL: National Center for Healthcare Leadership.

Olden, P. C. (2011). *Management of healthcare organizations: An introduction.* Chicago, IL: Health Administration Press.

Segal, L., & Leach, M. J. (2011). An evidence-based workforce model for primary and community care. *Implementation Science, 6*(93). doi:10.1186/1748-5908-6-93.

Chapter 6

Strategic Thinking Leaders

Thomas F. McIlwain and Michael Ugwueke

LEARNING OBJECTIVES

By the end of this chapter, the student will be able to:

- Explain the importance of strategic management in health care.
- Identify the nature of strategic management and concepts of thinking strategically.
- Describe the characteristics of strategic thinkers.
- Discuss methods for leading strategically in today's complex healthcare organizations.
- Identify ways to help think creatively.

KEY TERMS

Creative thinking

External environment

Mission, vision, and values

Situation analysis

Strategic management

Strategic planning

Strategic thinking

Strategy formulation

Strategy implementation

INTRODUCTION

Leaders of complex healthcare organizations are faced on a daily basis with unique and urgent problems and issues that demand enormous amounts of time and energy. Attention to these immediate problems can leave less time for leaders to think about the future of the organization and the decisions that must be made today to ensure future success. Leaders must carve out time to consider the future and envision a strategy for the organization, and then articulate and communicate it to their staff. Thinking strategically begins as an individual intellectual process, facilitated by experience, perspective, and skills; and utilizes methods of intellectual analysis to provide a pathway for the organization's future success. This chapter focuses on identifying why it is important to think strategically, how one goes about thinking strategically, and how this orientation enables the organization to meet the future needs of its stakeholders.

What Is Strategic Thinking?

Strategic thinking is a mental process of synthesizing and analyzing information to envision the strategies and tactics needed to achieve an ultimate goal. The process can be likened to learning a game in which winning is the objective. Imagine the first time you learned a new board, card, or backyard game. One of the first questions you likely asked yourself was, "How do you win this game?" After you clarified what was considered a victory, you formulated your ideas of what you needed to do to win and then put those strategies into practice. Unfortunately, despite your efforts, you probably did not always succeed. However, many times, the greatest excitement and fun of the game hinged on your "chance" of winning; that is, even though you played by the rules of the game, there was always some part of victory that was left to chance. Strategic thinking very much echoes this process.

Strategic thinking is a prerequisite to **strategic planning** and management. As Mintzberg (1994) pointed out, "Strategic planning is not strategic thinking. One is analysis, the other is synthesis." Strategic planning is used to define the tasks and operationalize activities that must be accomplished to reach an identified or agreed-upon goal. **Strategic management** is how we assign authority and responsibility to implement and monitor the activities that must be accomplished to reach the goal. This entire process begins with strategic thinking. Importantly, as Liedtka (1998a) points out, *individuals* think strategically, not organizations. The following are elements of strategic thinking (Liedtka, 1998a):

1. A systems perspective—strategic thinking requires analyzing the organization as part of an interdependent and interactive **external environment**, with inputs, processes, outputs, and feedback.

This perspective provides the opportunity to see how the world interacts and impacts the internal parts of the organization and the outputs the organization can in turn provide.

2. **Mission, vision, and values** driven—strategic thinking implies that there is an intention of the organization to accomplish something of value for its clients, customers, and stakeholders. This element provides a unique perspective about the goals of the organization and its relationship with the environment, and at the same time, provides intention. These three drivers—client, staff, and stakeholders—provide a focus and energy that motivate individuals, groups, and the organization to accomplish its goals.

3. Sense of opportunity—strategic thinking requires being willing to see and take advantage of opportunities. Not only does it require a level of knowledge, experience, and skill to understand when an opportunity presents itself, but it also requires an emotion of willingness to take a risk or advantage of the situation.

4. Sense of time—strategic thinking requires "seeing" in time, a concept of strategic thinking Mintzberg, Ahlstrand, and Lampel (1998) adapted from Nasi (1991). Mintzberg describes "seeing" as looking ahead in time, but underscores that seeing ahead also means being grounded in the past. Additionally, strategic thinking asks leaders to see the big picture by contemplating issues from above, below, beside, and beyond, and understand that strategies developed, when implemented, will change the future. All of these perspectives are necessary for productive strategic thinking.

5. Connection of cause and effect—strategic thinking requires the ability to hypothesize if A happens, it will cause B. Although causation is very hard to prove, strategic thinking requires skills in predicting outcome B from action A. Creative hypothesis testing then becomes critical. Asking "what if" questions is creative, and testing "if . . . then" is critical assessment. This hypothesis-driven thinking clarifies which actions should be undertaken to take advantage of a possible future. By believing there is a way to affect the future, leaders are motivated to think strategically.

In summary, strategic thinking is an individual intellectual process of considering the organization from a systems perspective, and creatively and critically assessing the future within the context of the past. This intellectual process implies the intent to take advantage of opportunities that sometimes involve risk but may positively change the way the organization competes (how the game is played). To return to the game analogy, one thinks strategically in a new board game when one creatively and critically assesses the game, remembers how it was played the last time and uses that experience to help predict the future, and monitors and takes advantage of opportunities that might lead to victory. However, if other players observe that your strategy worked, they may attempt it in another cycle of the game, thereby changing the game and triggering the necessity of a new cycle of strategic thinking and action on your part. Heracleous (1998) states that thinking strategically is discovering "novel, imaginative strategies which can re-write the rules of the competitive game; and to envision potential futures significantly different from the present" (p. 485).

It should be noted that strategy literacy is a prerequisite of strategic thinking. This means that the strategic thinking leader must understand the concepts associated with strategic management and the way organizations analyze, formulate, and implement strategies. In later sections, we will discuss the strategy process and the understanding and skills a leader needs in order to think strategically.

Why Focus on Thinking Strategically in Health Care?

Strategic management requires a future orientation that takes into consideration the external and internal environments of the organization. Leaders of healthcare organizations must think and act strategically because the environment around the organization is ever-changing. From customers, competitors, technology, social systems, the economy, and such, significant trends are occurring that will have an impact on the organization. To be successful and remain viable, strategic thinkers and their organizations need to embrace these changes.

Leaders of healthcare organizations make decisions, major and minor, on a daily basis. Major decisions likely carry a great deal of risk and require an investment of significant funding and resources, but may not always provide the returns projected or expected. The organization may keep doing what it is doing, stop doing what it is doing, modify what it is doing, or do new and different things altogether, in addition to choosing to do a combination of these. With so many options, it is important to develop a mission that guides and helps direct the decisions of the leader of the organization. Thinking strategically involves not only deciding the best course of action and weighing its risks and benefits, but also making decisions that are consistent, congruent, and in line with the overall mission of the organization.

The Rapidly Changing Healthcare Environment

There is little doubt that rapid changes are occurring in the healthcare industry, many of which are the result of changes in social, regulatory, technology, and political arenas. These changes may seem to be of little consequence to an organization; however, they may have huge implications.

One of the most active areas of environmental change is the area of healthcare reform. Healthcare reform is both political and social, but has been set in motion through political debate and action. Healthcare reform is the topic of political conversation on a daily basis in the media, with discussions of what is good and what is bad about the system. Most lay individuals are not aware that what we call a "healthcare" system is really a "sick care" system. Rather than focusing on preventing illness and injury and maximizing individual and public health, our healthcare system is largely reactive, treating diseases and conditions after they appear. Additionally, the variety of healthcare options in place today can be described as an "unsystematic" system of care that includes diverse groups and constituencies of professionals, technicians, organizations, financiers, and patients. Healthcare reform advocates have been challenged to address the needs of the healthcare industry and our population, but continue to use legislative mechanisms to improve service provision. With each change motivated by political venues, organizations will need to respond by identifying and acknowledging the change, understanding its impact, and modifying its strategies in order to survive and prosper.

This political issue of reform has an impact on the regulatory environment also. Tendencies to increase or decrease government regulation is a tide that ebbs and flows depending on the ruling political party. Healthcare leaders must stay abreast of these trends in the political process and, in some cases, become actively involved in shaping health care's political future.

And finally, there are evolutions in social communications in today's environment that may have a major impact on the organization. The impact of social media on the healthcare system and organizations may be significant as growing numbers of clients desire to interact with healthcare organizations and their providers through online digital and social media outlets.

All of these changes are drivers for leaders to engage in active strategic thinking to allow their organizations to adapt and survive in an evolving healthcare environment.

The Expected Organizational and System Benefits

Although strategic planning and management are touted as the "be all, end all" method of managing in today's volatile business world, they are not panaceas that cure and solve all organizational ills. Studies on the effectiveness of strategic planning have provided mixed results regarding strategic management and financial and organizational performance (Boyd, 1991). Simply because an organization attempts to manage strategically does not mean the organization will be successful. There are many potential obstacles in traveling from point A to point B. Though the road to organizational performance is paved with good intentions, the choice of a particular strategy does not mean the organization will be able to effectively carry out the strategy. On the whole, if an organization understands the business it is in, who its customers are, and opts to focus on its best practices, it will more likely be successful. However, the organization must remain responsive in a timely manner to environmental changes in its industry and be able to realign its strategies as needed. Of course, not all changes can be predicted in either type or magnitude; therefore, no matter how well an organization plans and implements its strategic plans, unforeseen factors can negatively influence its ability to reach its intended goals.

We look to strategic management to help the organization be financially successful, but there are many other benefits that accrue from the process. Those benefits include the organizational development of a concept and vision for the future, and an identity (i.e., what the organization is and what it wants [or needs] to become in the future). This process should involve leadership at all levels of the organization, enhancing vertical and horizontal communication, and facilitating buy-in to implement strategies for success. As employees at all levels understand the business they are in, learn about the environmental issues that impact the organization, and provide input regarding solutions to meet identified challenges, they become more innovative and more willing to change themselves. Through this process, the organization may experience greater productivity and profitability.

WHAT IS THE NATURE OF STRATEGIC MANAGEMENT? WHY IS IT DIFFERENT FROM TRADITIONAL MANAGEMENT? HOW DOES ONE THINK AND MANAGE STRATEGICALLY?

Strategy Definitions

Strategy can be defined in many different ways. Most authors agree that it is a set of related actions that leadership makes to increase the organization's performance on agreed-upon and significant outcomes and benchmarks. In some industries, these measures of performance may be obvious; but in healthcare organizations, many of which are not-for-profits, the objectives and outcomes may not be initially obvious. Strategic leadership is how leaders guide the organization through the strategy process, including decisions in formulating and implementing a set of strategies that should provide the organization with achievable outcomes and a competitive advantage. The method of developing or selecting a strategy is termed **strategy formulation**, and putting those decisions into effect is called **strategy implementation**. Some argue that strategic management follows the 20–80 rule: that success is 20% strategy formulation and 80% strategy implementation. Unfortunately, if the strategy formulated is wrong, the implementation is likely to be unsuccessful from the start. Therefore, it behooves the strategic leader to weigh strategic decisions carefully. This chapter is about how leaders can do so.

The Process and Schools of Strategic Management Thought

There is no one "best" definition or approach for strategic management. Henri Mintzberg and his associates, in an effort to shed light on this issue, wrote in *Strategy Safari* (1998) that there are as many as 10 schools of strategic management. These approaches, or schools, are excellent examples of the similarities and dissimilarities in how strategic management can be carried out. But the authors contend that these schools of thought are all part of one overarching process. Though each school and its approaches to strategy differ, they all are important in the overall scheme of strategic formulation and implementation.

As discussed earlier, strategic thinking requires one to be "strategy competent." This competency means that one has an understanding and conceptualization of the strategic development and management process. Based on Mintzberg's discussion, **Figure 6.1** serves as an overview of what constitutes a general strategic management process. Mintzberg and colleagues (1998) provide an extremely well-conceived discussion of the many perspectives of strategic management.

In describing strategic management, the authors use the story of the blind men and the elephant, wherein blind individuals attempt to describe an elephant by touching only one part of the animal. The result is that each individual believed the elephant to be entirely composed in likeness to the part he touched; for example, the man who felt the legs believed it to be round and solid like a tree; the trunk created an image of a snake-like beast, and so forth. None of the participants had a clear picture of the elephant as a whole.

Strategic planning can evolve very similarly. Depending on which element one chooses to focus (or with which one has experience), one may tend to describe the strategic process from only one meaningful but limited viewpoint. So if one sees strategic management as mostly planning, then that is not necessarily an incorrect description. If one sees strategic management as

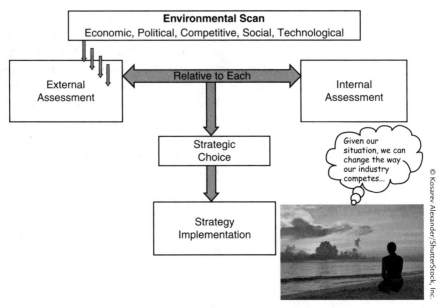

Figure 6.1 General Strategic Management Process

putting decisions into action, then that too is a component of the process. If one is entrepreneurial and uses insight rather than data analysis to drive decisions, then that too is strategic management. Even if an organization rejects planning to avoid being tied to one specific strategy, that omission becomes a method of strategically managing.

The multiple perspectives and schools of thought described by Mintzberg for strategic planning are presented in **Table 6.1**. Mintzberg and colleagues (1998, p. 72) imply that strategy implementation is required to help formulate strategies (strategic thinking), and likewise, formulation of strategies (strategic thinking) is needed for strategy implementation. This idea is noteworthy in that no matter what the approach, strategic thinking is required. Mintzberg and colleagues have critiqued many less successful formal strategic planning approaches, noting that "formal systems could certainly process more information, at least hard information, consolidate it, aggregate it, move it about. But they could never *internalize* it, *comprehend* it, *synthesize* it" (Mintzberg et al., 1998, p. 73).

To internalize, comprehend, and synthesize requires more than just collecting data and information. Information needs to be discussed, analyzed, and mulled over. But most of all it needs to be synthesized—through *thinking*.

Table 6.1 Mintzberg's Schools of Strategic Thought

School of Thought	Characteristics: Strategy Formation as a Process of
Design	Conception—seeks to attain a match between internal capabilities and external possibilities
Planning	Formal—strategy can be developed in a structured, formalized process
Positioning	Analytical—matching the right strategy to the conditions at hand; generic strategies match generic conditions; use of analysis to identify the right relationships
Entrepreneurial	Visionary—much of strategic thinking takes place in the mind of the founder or leader; strategy comes from the intuition, judgment, wisdom, and insight of the leader
Cognitive	Mental process—in the mind of the leader, strategies emerge as a map or scheme
Learning	Emergent process—strategy comes from lessons learned and involves others in the organization besides the leader
Power	Negotiation—strategy comes from negotiating between leaders (power holders) in the organization
Cultural	Collective—strategies are decided through a collective and cooperative process and reflect the culture of the organization
Environmental	Reactive—strategy is the result of responding to the challenges of the external environment
Configuration	Transformation—strategies are stable but eventually changes in the environment and business require transforming the organization through changing its decision-making structure

Source: Adapted from Mintzberg, H., Ahlstrand, B., & Lampel, J. (1998). *Strategy Safari: A guided tour through the wilds of strategic management.* New York, NY: Free Press.

Strategic Decisions

The strategic management process is only a starting point for understanding how organizations decide to and then act on their strategic initiatives.

It is also necessary to recognize the typology of strategic choices (see Swayne, Duncan, & Ginter, 2008, for a useful hierarchy of strategic decisions and alternatives). Having a vocabulary of strategies is very helpful when formulating, evaluating, and choosing the best strategies for an organization.

At the most basic level, an organization can choose to grow, stay the same, or get smaller. These strategies can be classified as growth, maintenance, or contraction. In most cases, organizations are driven to grow. Growth can be measured in many ways, including sales and profits. Growth strategies include mergers, acquisitions, and product and market development strategies. Organizations can vertically (both upstream and downstream) and horizontally integrate or diversify (both related and unrelated).

Most individuals want to be part of a vibrant, growing organization; however, in times of economic and environmental uncertainty, an organization may be forced to maintain its size or even contract. Contraction means the divesting of assets, both capital and labor, in an effort to survive. Strategies such as liquidation and harvesting are contraction strategies. In order to determine the best strategy, leaders must be aware of what potential actions are possible. There are numerous sources or texts available describing organizational strategic choices.

There is also much written about financial performance of organizations that the reader is encouraged to study. Many strategy evaluation methods use market share and market growth as dimensions of the market that help guide strategic choices of the organization.

WHAT ARE THE CHARACTERISTICS OF A STRATEGIC THINKING LEADER?

A useful way to develop both creative and critical thinking abilities is to study the characteristics of strategic thinking leaders. A list of important characteristics mentioned throughout the literature when discussing successful leaders includes:

- *Having a vision*—As discussed earlier in the definition of strategic thinking, the leader must develop and champion the vision of the organization. Although the leader may involve individuals from all levels in the organization in the strategy process, the top leadership is responsible for carrying forward the vision of the future. Visioning is both a thinking process and a communication process. The vision must be articulated in understandable terms and be shared with the entire organization.
- *Understanding the business and your clients*—Leaders must have a complete understanding of the business of the organization in all its facets. The mission, also known as a directional strategy, defines the business you are in and the customers that you serve, and should manifest the uniqueness of your organization. Examples of mission statements are found on websites and annual reports of organizations. A typical mission statement articulates the following: target customers, principal services delivered, geographical area served, the organization's philosophy and values, the distinctive services provided, and other items that express the uniqueness of the organization (Swayne et al., 2008).

- *External orientation*—As discussed throughout this chapter, strategic thinking requires systems thinking; that is, envisioning an open system interacting with its environment. The environment writes the script of change, and its issues and trends must be monitored and analyzed to predict the impact they will have on the organization.
- *Penchant for analyzing data*—Strategic thinkers need data to review and analyze to provide the foundation for creative generation. Little synthesis can occur without data or information to analyze. The strategic thinker's formidable task is to sift through today's enormous amounts of data, convert the data to meaningful information, and synthesize or bring meaning to bear from this synthesis to the organization's decision-making processes.
- *Creatively generating new ideas*—A leader is responsible for keeping the organization on course while generating new ways of meeting the challenges ahead. Much is gained from the entrepreneurial spirit of creatively identifying new ways to compete in the marketplace. Strategic leaders need to develop their own ways of engaging others as well in helping to generate new ideas.
- *Propensity for questioning assumptions*—Leaders have to develop skill in knowing when and how to question assumptions. The creative process requires thinking "outside the box"; concurrently, the critical assessment process requires logical assessment of assumptions. Both creative and critical thinking are required of leaders.
- *Understanding the score of the game*—Strategic thinkers should be well aware of how the game they are "playing" is "scored." For most organizations, the scoring occurs through the reporting of market share. Market share can sometimes be difficult to measure and assess, but it is an essential benchmark within and among organizations that measures whether implemented strategies are successful.
- *Knowing that change is inevitable*—Strategic leaders know that change is inevitable and that nothing remains constant. Leaders cannot rest on the laurels of recent successes, but must embrace this evolution. Leaders should track major trends or issues that could have a negative impact on the organization and utilize strategic thinking to develop innovative strategies for the future. The strategic leader's mantra is that "change means opportunity."
- *Knowing strategic choices must have focus and force*—Leaders must be very aware that their organization cannot be all things to all people and that there are tradeoffs among various choices. Although in health care most community hospitals are "general acute care" hospitals, they cannot all be on the top-100 hospitals list. For example, the

hospital may aim to develop an open heart or a regional cancer treatment center, but may not be able to do both at a level of excellence. The leader must choose which project to focus on and guide the hospital's implementation team toward the goal that will most likely ensure success.

- *Understanding the business they are in*—Leaders have the responsibility to know the breadth and the nuances of how their business works—to have "business sense." They should be knowledgable about the firm's operations, market, staff, and clients. Leaders should be aware of the stage of the life cycle of their services and how the business is categorized in a portfolio of services and markets. Each stage of the life cycle or each category of the portfolio represents a given phase of sales and profit.

- *Knowing the competition*—Strategic thinking leaders are fully aware of their competition. This awareness is paired with an understanding that the competition is also searching for a way to provide improved services to the marketplace. This reality should motivate leaders to continuously improve their strategic thinking and development to "stay one step ahead." This motivational driver is what Liedtka (1998b) describes as "intent focused."

- *Knowing their customers*—Strategic thinking leaders consider the customer the number one priority for the organization. Even so, healthcare leaders must serve a multitude of other stakeholders such as staff, stockholders, trustees, and the like. It is necessary to effectively and diplomatically manage these stakeholder relationships while at the same time understanding that customer preferences drive the strategic decisions of the organization.

WHAT ARE SOME TOOLS FOR THINKING STRATEGICALLY?

As Liedtka (1998b) noted, strategic thinking involves five elements. These elements are:

- Having a systems perspective
- Being intent focused
- Having a propensity for intelligent opportunism
- Thinking in time
- Being hypothesis driven

So how do strategic leaders invoke these five elements in the thinking process? The literature is replete with examples of how to analyze the environment and evaluate, formulate, and implement strategic choices. As discussed by Allio (2006), every day a consultant comes up with a new method or technique designed to be the "latest and greatest." Many of these are helpful, but many are only a reinvention of the ones that have proven to be useful over time (i.e., tried and true). These include:

- *Scenario writing*—seeing the big picture and the major trend in a changing environment and documenting possible scenarios for the future.
- *Situation or SWOT analysis*—analyzing the current situation by evaluating the Strengths and Weaknesses internal to the organization and the Opportunities and Threats in the external environment.
- *Competitor analysis*—learning about the competition and its impact on the marketplace is important to the survival and growth of the organization.
- *Evaluation of strategic alternatives*—using techniques such as the Boston Consulting Group (BCG) portfolio matrix approach, product life cycle (PLC), or strategic position and action evaluation (SPACE) analysis to encourage strategic thinking by providing an understanding and evaluation of the strategic options.

Scenario Writing

Scenario writing is a process of describing the likely future of the environment with regard to one or more variables or issues. These environmental issues are usually organized within broad categories: economic, political, technological, social, and regulatory. A scenario is a short story that describes the future as projected by the analysis and judgment of the management and leadership team. Scenarios based on only one issue may be easier to write, but they do not provide the richness and depth needed to stimulate strategic thinking. Scenarios containing too many variables may be more realistic, but risk developing many inaccuracies as time goes by.

For example, consider the following scenario: The healthcare environment will witness rapid change, including political pressures demanding free-market reform and decreased regulation; breakthrough IT and pharmaceutical advances in the treatment of major illnesses; expectations by a growing population of older patients for increased decision-making influence and authority in determining services and treatments; and a robust, booming economy fueled by decreasing unemployment and low interest rates. It's possible, perhaps even likely, that the team has "guessed wrong" on one or more issues in the projection above. Strategies based on wrong assumptions of the future can lead to huge financial problems for an organization and its leaders. Therefore, it is equally important to continue to monitor the variables incorporated into the scenario and to "rewrite the story" if the projections are no longer accurate or valid.

Situation Analysis

In the television series *Star Trek*, after the Starship Enterprise had been hit with a photon torpedo from the unfriendly Romulan Bird of Prey, Captain Kirk would invariably ask his Chief Engineer Scotty a question: "What's the situation, Scotty?" Scotty would report to the bridge an assessment of the structural integrity of the ship and its ability to ward off the next attack. In other words, Scotty conducted a **situation analysis**. In strategy analysis, leadership must evaluate the organization's current and expected future situation, and be able to incorporate that assessment into the strategic planning. A SWOT analysis can be very valuable in this regard.

SWOT is an acronym for Strengths, Weaknesses, Opportunities, and Threats. Strengths and weaknesses are factors that are internal to the organization, and opportunities and threats are factors and issues that are external (i.e., from the outside environment). For example, finances, human resources, organizational structures, and information systems are internal to the organization and can manifest both strengths and weaknesses. Factors in the external environment can include the local and national economy, technological advances, consumer needs and advocacies, and the presence and effectiveness of competitors; and can represent either opportunities or threats to the organization.

SWOT analyses can be presented in a TOWS matrix, wherein each environmental factor is matched with each internal factor (Weihrich, 1982). This process helps the leader think through how to:

1. Use strengths to take advantage of matched opportunities
2. Utilize strengths to address challenges and threats in the environment
3. Overcome weaknesses that make the organization vulnerable to threats
4. Overcome weaknesses that inhibit the organization from taking advantage of opportunities as they arise

Table 6.2 presents an example of a typical TOWS analysis. Note that each quadrant in the matrix provides options for how the organization might react.

Competitor Analysis

Many strategic leaders admit to having disconcerting feelings that there may be better ways to meet their patients' needs, which "the competition" will develop first. The anxiety that the competition is "on our heels" spurs

Table 6.2 Example TOWS (Applied SWOT) Analysis for a Typical Healthcare Organization

	Opportunities 1. Growing number of young married professionals 2. Increase in insured population 3. Growing economy	Threats 1. Increased competition 2. Alternative treatments 3. Decrease in population 65+
Strengths 1. Financials 2. New data systems 3. Good employee morale	Develop new labor and delivery services. Develop a new app for patients to access their own information.	Use financial strength to establish physical presence in areas that are threatened with increased competition.
Weaknesses 1. Location 2. Aging facility 3. Increasing physician retirements	Assess the viability of building a replacement facility. Increase physician recruitment in areas of projected market growth.	Develop services that cater to young professionals such as orthopedics, labor and delivery, plastic surgery.

strategic leaders to communicate the urgency of continuous improvement so that their organizations can "stay ahead in the game."

To realistically assess the threat from competition, a thorough competitor analysis should be conducted. Most competitor analyses include these basic steps:

1. Define the services to be assessed.
   - For example, a family medicine physician begins a competitor analysis. She defines her services as "ambulatory primary care services" and will compare her services to competitors' in this arena.
2. Define the service area—primary and secondary.
   - Our physician's family practice walk-in clinic sees most of its patients from which geographical area? She studies her patient population and identifies that 80% of her patients come mainly from the surrounding county. The rest come from other surrounding counties.
3. Identify the competition in all its forms.
   - She investigates not only family care practices but also minute clinics, pharmacies, alternative care providers, internal medicine and OB/GYN specialists, and other providers who provide primary care services.

4. Analyze the strengths, weaknesses, opportunities, and threats of each competitor.
   - The information gained from a thorough analysis of each competitor gives the family physician insight and direction on how best to compete in the marketplace.
5. Synthesize the information from the analysis.
   - Questions she asks include: How are the competitors similar to my practice? How are they different? How does the competition threaten my clinic? Are there any needs in my market that are not being fully met? If I implement initiatives to address these needs, such as adding after-hours and weekend appointments, how will my competitors react?

Leaders engaging in competitor analyses should avoid the pitfalls of misjudging the service area, or of too narrowly defining the competition and thereby missing important competitors. Careful attention to the steps above will allow for a more accurate and helpful analysis.

Evaluation of Strategic Alternatives

With so many potential strategic choices available, it is sometimes difficult to identify and select the best options. The TOWS matrix in Table 6.2 helps to organize and clarify the strategic choices. Additional frequently used methods for evaluation of strategic alternatives are the Product Life Cycle (PLC), Boston Consulting Group (BCG) Portfolio Matrix (Barksdale & Harris, 1982), and the Strategic Position and Action Evaluation (SPACE) (Rowe, Mason, Dickel, & Snyder, 1989). The following example demonstrates how a BCG Portfolio analysis can help stimulate strategic thinking.

The Boston Consulting Group Portfolio Matrix has its supporters and detractors; however, it is a good example of an analysis technique that generates information to spark creative strategic thinking. A strategic business unit is defined as a unit of an organization that produces a product or service—that is, an individual operating unit of business within the larger organization. For strategic business units, BCG Portfolio analyses compare the relative growth of the market and the share of the market for each of their products or services. **Figure 6.2** illustrates an example of BCG Portfolio Analysis.

The first step in this method is to decide which services within an organization may be considered strategic business units (SBUs). SBUs are in most cases easy to identify because they generate revenue and often have identified competitors. After the SBUs have been designated, the next step is to

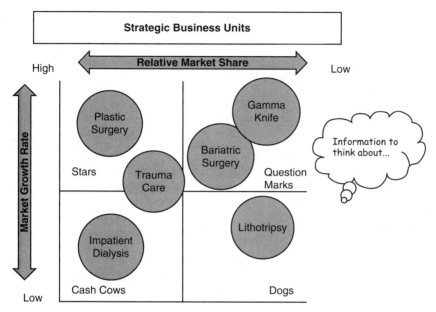

Figure 6.2 Boston Consulting Group Portfolio Analysis

Source: Adapted from "The Product Portfolio" (1970) by Bruce D. Henderson, in The Boston Consulting Group on Strategy, edited by Carl W. Stern and Michael S. Deimler. Copyright © 2006 by The Boston Consulting Group, Inc.

identify each unit's market share (i.e., the score of the competitive game). In addition to accessing internal organizational data for this purpose, leaders may need to access sources of data from state agencies, hospital alliances, or Medicare or Medicaid for an accurate assessment. Sometimes, the market data have to be assumed, based on the expected disease rates and available services in the service area. The basic formula for market share is:

$$\text{Market Share} = \frac{\text{Units Delivered by SBU}}{\text{Total Units Delivered in Service Area}} \times 100$$

The result is usually reported as a percentage of total market. Data from the same time frame and service area should be used for the denominator and the numerator.

The strategic choice for each SBU depends on the market share and the market growth rate. The BCG matrix provides a picture of how well each service or product is competing in its relative market. Organizations that structure their costs competitively and capture a large share of a growing market will be successful. Services or products that occupy a small share in a slow-growing or contracting market should, depending on the mission of the organization, be downsized or restructured (i.e., divested, liquidated, or closed).

THINKING CREATIVELY

An examination of strategic thinking would not be complete without discussing the process of **creative thinking** and identifying some techniques for improving creative thought. As Jonah Lehrer points out in his book, *Imagine: How Creativity Works* (2012), the subject of creativity has intrigued man for ages. Humans solve problems not only by logic, but also by inspiration, those sudden "aha" moments when a vision or idea becomes clear. Strategic thinking involves both. What techniques can be used to promote creative solutions to our problems and situations?

Research shows that many inspirational ideas come when one is relaxed and not necessarily focused on an issue. Scientific studies have demonstrated that certain specific parts of the brain are involved when logic is used to solve a problem, but when an impasse is encountered, a brief relaxing and distracting activity often brings on the solution. Of course, answers to difficult problems do not appear out of thin air, but the mind that has addressed and understands a problem may benefit from a spell of relaxed, unforced thinking. Some observations from the research literature suggest the following techniques to promote innovative problem solving:

1. Be inspired and guided by the work of others. Strategic thinking involves choosing the right strategy for the right situation, and usually your situation is not totally new to the universe. It is perfectly acceptable to borrow a successful idea or best practice to develop a new strategy and give it your own twist.

2. Create a culture of innovation by encouraging collaboration. The best ideas for complicated solutions will most likely emerge from a group effort. People can bring diverse skills and expertise to the table to collaborate and create synergy. Design buildings to encourage and push employees to mingle.

3. The strategic team should develop a strong working relationship to promote successful exchange of ideas. Be careful to avoid the pitfall of overfamiliarity, however, in which a group may become less receptive to the generation of new ideas and to the examination of issues in new and different ways.

4. Collect and analyze useful and meaningful data. Analyze the data and use the data as the foundation of your strategic thinking. Make assumptions when necessary, but periodically question those assumptions. Then put your planning efforts aside and do

something else; if you generate additional creative strategies, jot them down on your tablet or notepad for your next meeting.

5. The strategic solutions that develop will not be perfect, so rely on the planning group to help develop and improve them. Encourage constructive criticism in the thinking and planning meetings, and be receptive to it as a strategic leader yourself.

WHAT ARE SOME FINAL THOUGHTS FOR THE STRATEGIC THINKING LEADER?

Strategic thinking is a key to successful leadership in healthcare organizations, especially in the current environment of regulatory changes and economic challenges. The process can aid healthcare leaders in developing a mission, vision, goals, and objectives, and in developing strategies and initiatives that will promote successful and high-quality operation of their organizations in today's competitive marketplace.

Strategic management promotes the implementation of the leader's creative vision through (Goldman, Cahill, & Filho, 2009):

· Developing and effectively communicating the vision
· Defining goals and objectives
· Assigning and delegating tasks and responsibilities
· Expecting accountability (practice makes perfect)
· Assessing, evaluating, and revising the strategic process

Mintzberg (1994) noted that the process of strategic management requires interactive participation by both formulators and implementers. He argues that the term *strategic planning* should be dropped altogether, and we should "talk instead about strategic thinking connected to acting" (p. 72). The corporation 3M is famous for requiring all scientists a portion of their time to pursue new projects of personal interest (Lehrer, 2012; Liedtke, 1998). Organizations that wish to promote innovative strategic thinking at all levels may need to provide "slack" time for leaders and managers, during which they can think creatively and proactively about their businesses (Liedtke, 1998).

SUMMARY

This chapter discussed the definition of strategic thinking and how it is a critical part of the strategic management process of an organization. Leaders of healthcare organizations can be extremely busy handling day-to-day operational challenges, often leaving little time to consider the future of the organization and to make the necessary decisions to ensure ongoing success. Time has to be scheduled to think about the organization's future, envision and develop effective strategies, and articulate and communicate these strategies to managers and employees. Thinking strategically begins as an individual intellectual process but should evolve into a group activity, facilitated by group members' diverse expertise, perspective, and skills. This chapter focused on identifying why strategic thinking is important, the skills necessary for successful strategic thinking, and how a strategic thinking orientation enables a healthcare organization to meet the future needs of its stakeholders and succeed in an ever-changing healthcare environment.

Discussion Questions

1. Define the difference between strategic management, strategic planning, strategy, and strategic thinking. How are they similar and how are they different?

2. Why is knowing one's market share important? How is market share determined?

3. Define a strategic business unit (SBU). How is it used in the Boston Consulting Group Matrix?

4. List the characteristics of strategic thinkers and describe why these characteristics are important to successful strategic management.

5. What are some major categories of external environmental issues? Which issues do you think are more important in this healthcare environment and why?

Case Study: A Strategic Dilemma

You just hung up the phone after a conversation with the Chairman of the Board of Directors of the St. Michaels Medical Center, a not-for-profit, acute care, community hospital that is part of a 10-hospital healthcare system located in the southern part of the United States. You accepted the offer to become their new CEO. You are a little unsure if you're ready for such a big step, but you know it will be an exciting challenge. With 300 beds and a wound-care center, St. Michaels serves a service area population of 250,000 people and provides cardiac, general medicine, OB/GYN, emergency, and outpatient services.

The hospital was built about 30 years ago in what was a thriving urban community and had no significant healthcare competition. Over time, a worsening economy has led to changing demographics in the service area, and the community is now populated mostly by underrepresented groups with limited financial resources. With the community's growing economic challenges, the hospital has continued to experience significant losses in market share and a negative operating margin.

Over the last 8 years, the hospital has struggled to return to a sustainable model, but these efforts have been frustrated by a lack of capital, low patient census, departures of physicians, perceived poor quality and low morale among the employees, and lack of community support. As the hospital's condition has continued to deteriorate, the need for a complete overhaul of the hospital operation has become imperative.

During its heyday, the hospital had been very profitable and renowned for its high-quality care as well as its high level of patient satisfaction. In an attempt to improve the operations of the hospital, the board has offered you this opportunity with a mandate to "turn things around." You pride yourself on being a strategic thinking leader, but you are worried about what options to consider in developing your turnaround plan for the hospital.

As you ponder the issues before you, you realize that improving St. Michaels will demand significant critical thinking and ingenuity. You will have to financially stabilize the hospital and improve its quality of care and patient satisfaction. You begin making notes and identify the steps that you will consider for your turnaround plan. This plan will include your action steps for the next 90 days, 6 months, and 1 year after you have been on the job. The following are key statistical attributes that were used to help generate your plan.

Key Statistical Attributes of the Hospital 2010
Capacity

Licensed Beds	300
Operated Beds	200
Medical Staff	80

Key Services

Cardiac Services

Emergency Services

Maternity/Women's Services

General Medicine

Patient Statistics

Admissions	6254
Total Surgeries	2444
Outpatient Visits	17,453
Emergency Room	39,362
Deliveries	1252
Total Patient Days	27,863

Revenue/Expenses

Key Financials 2007	(000)
Total Gross Revenue	$236,129
Total Deduct from Revenue	$156,938
Net Patient Revenue	$79,191
Total Operating Expenses	
Contribution Margin	$(1251)
Total Capital Expense	$3640
Operating Margin	$(4891)

Case Study Discussion Questions

1. What can you do to foster strategic thinking in this situation?
2. How will you involve your team and encourage them to think strategically?
3. List the items in your action plan for the next 90 days, 6 months, and 1 year after you have been on board.
4. What are the various strategic options that you have considered and the reasons for your preferred choices?
5. What metrics would you use to measure your progress? Show a sample TOWS matrix.
6. Which individuals, organizations, and structures might present obstacles or challenges for successful implementation of your plans? Which individuals, organizations, and structures could be supportive for your actions? Why?

REFERENCES

Allio, R. J. (2006). Strategic thinking: The ten big ideas. *Strategy & Leadership, 34*(4), 4–13.

Barksdale, H. C., & Harris, C. E., Jr. (1982). Portfolio analysis and the product life cycle. *Long Range Planning, 15*(6), 74–83

Boyd, B. K. (1991). Strategic planning and financial performance: A meta-analytic review. *Journal of Management Studies, 28*(4), 353–374.

Goldman, E., Cahill, T., & Filho, R. P. (2009). Experiences that develop the ability to think strategically. *Journal of Healthcare Management, 54*(6), 403–417.

Heracleous, L. (1998). Strategic thinking or strategic planning? *Long Range Planning, 31*(3), 481–487.

Lehrer, J. (2012). *Imagine: How creativity works*. New York, NY: Houghton Mifflin Harcourt.

Liedtka, J. M. (1998a). Linking strategic thinking with strategic planning. *Strategy and Leadership, 26*(4), 30–35.

Liedtka, J. M. (1998b). Strategic thinking: Can it be taught? *Long Range Planning, 31*(1), 120–129.

Mintzberg, H. (1994). Fall and rise of strategic planning. *Harvard Business Review, 72*(1), 107–114.

Mintzberg, H., Ahlstrand, B., & Lampel, J. (1998). *Strategy safari: A guided tour through the wilds of strategic management*. New York, NY: Free Press.

Nasi, J. (1991). *Arenas of strategic thinking*. Helsinki, Finland: Foundation for Economic Education.

Rowe, A. J., Mason, R. O., Dickel, K. E., & Snyder, N. H. (1989). *Strategic management: A methodological approach* (3rd ed.). Reading, MA: Addison Wesley.

Swayne, L., Duncan, J., & Ginter, P. (2008). *Strategic management of healthcare organizations*. Hoboken, NJ: John Wiley & Sons.

Weihrich, H. (1982). The TOWS matrix—A tool for situational analysis. *Long Range Planning, 15*(2), 54–66.

Chapter 7

Building a Successful Leadership Team

John Shiver and Craig Nesta

LEARNING OBJECTIVES

By the end of this chapter, the student will be able to:

- Explain the importance of team composition.
- Identify models and methods of team member selection.
- Describe the characteristics of successful teams in health care.
- Discuss the traits of effective team management.

KEY TERMS

Agenda	Multidisciplinary team
Consensus	Process improvement
Group think	Team charter
Healthcare teams	Virtual team

INTRODUCTION

The healthcare industry in the United States is undergoing a revolutionary transformation that will likely continue and accelerate in the foreseeable future. The demand for healthcare services is increasing as life expectancy has extended and the Baby Boomer cohort continues to age. These demographic trends, coupled with the economic impact of shifting health plans from traditional employer sponsorship to government payers, require a new system of coordinated healthcare delivery. Both clinical and administrative teams are essential for the successful delivery of health care in a high quality, cost-effective, accountable, and transparent manner.

Teams in Health Care

In this era of growing client demands and shrinking human and financial resources, healthcare leaders have turned to collaboration and teamwork as possible solutions for the multiple challenges arising in our changing healthcare landscape. Collaboration, within and among departments and institutions, promotes synergy and can increase the cost-effectiveness and quality of healthcare services delivered.

Teams in health care are essential for the successful management of a healthcare organization and for the delivery of high-quality patient care. Teams may be large and complex, or composed of only a few relevant members. For example, a team performing a surgical procedure is composed of individuals with varying but equally important clinical skills. The surgeon is typically the team leader, but works closely with the anesthesiologist and the nurses who coordinate operating room function and hand off the necessary instruments during the surgery. Other members of the surgical team include the orderlies who transport the patients in and out of the OR suite, the housekeeping staff that disinfect the operating theaters, and the nurses in the recovery rooms where patients awaken from surgery. Each individual brings a unique skillset to the team. Each knows his or her role and how it relates to the others. Without the invaluable contribution of every one of these team members, the patient would suffer. In a similar manner, the management of a large healthcare organization such as a hospital requires teams in order to function successfully. In the pages that follow, you will learn how teams are created and utilized to promote the successful operation of a healthcare organization.

Healthcare entities may develop several teams, perhaps even hundreds of teams; it is important that each team have an organizational purpose. Examples of organizational purposes that can lead to the formation of teams or task forces are finding ways to reduce the infection rate, determining ways to reduce days in accounts receivable (DAR), and improving patient satisfaction. Each of these team purposes aligns with organizational goals that are beneficial to the operating entity.

Teams are integral to the management structure of a healthcare organization. Two teams commonly observed in hospitals are an Executive Team,

EXECUTIVE TEAM
Chief Executive
Chief Operating Officer
Chief Nursing Officer
Chief Information Officer
Chief Financial Officer

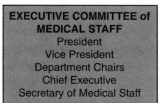

Figure 7.1 Executive Team

EXECUTIVE COMMITTEE of MEDICAL STAFF
President
Vice President
Department Chairs
Chief Executive
Secretary of Medical Staff

Figure 7.2 Executive Committee of Medical Staff

which typically consists of the senior executive and his or her direct reports (see **Figure 7.1**) and the Executive Committee of the Medical Staff, with the President of the Medical Staff at the helm and key officers making up the rest of the team (see **Figure 7.2**).

The terms *committee* and *team* are sometimes used interchangeably, but they have distinct definitions. Committees are typically permanent and integrated into the organizational structure. Membership is defined by the participants' positions within the organization rather than by their skillsets or expertise. Teams are often created with a defined lifespan to address a specific goal or organizational purpose and enlist members who can contribute to the solution or resolution of the specific task at hand.

Why Teams?

No single individual can possess all the skills necessary to manage a complex healthcare organization such as a hospital. Hospitals employ people with many specialized skills, diverse degrees, and varied training and expertise. Walking through a hospital's halls, one would encounter a breadth of employees: those who clean the facility, build and repair it, perform surgery, prepare food for the patients, diagnose diseases, treat maladies, manage finances, operate sophisticated and dangerous equipment, maintain security, and many other interesting and exciting professions. In some ways, a hospital is not dissimilar to a local community, and, in fact, hospitals often provide a source of employment for many diverse individuals who reside in nearby neighborhoods.

To best utilize these varied skills and specialties, hospitals develop inter-disciplinary teams that allow for smoother collaboration and synergy. In a team setting, employees can work together to create strategies, guide the organization and its leaders, serve as coordinators and communicators, address unusual situations, solve problems, and contribute to the successful management of a complex organization.

Teams do not routinely form of their own volition. Teams are created by management for a specific organizational purpose. In fact, one of the most important tasks of management is the successful creation and management of teams. Leaders must determine what functions of the organization are best handled by teams, create the teams, develop team charters and guide-lines, facilitate their performance, and manage the process.

It is important that there is no single rule relative to creating teams, and there is no formula for developing the correct mix of skills, stakeholders, interpersonal skills, or other characteristics. Every team is, in the end, situation specific (Shuffler, DiazGranados, & Salas, 2011).

DEFINING TEAM FUNCTIONS

Management's role is to articulate those functions of the organization that are best served by creating teams. These functions can include general managerial duties, clinical care delivery, problem solving, **process improvement**, and organizational governance. Once an organizational purpose is clearly articulated, the function(s) of the team can be determined.

Charter

Teams must exist for a purpose. The purpose and function of the team may be delineated in the group or **team charter**. The team charter may include:

- *The team name or title.* The team should have a name that broadly represents the team's goals and functions. The name provides an identity for the team and its members and informs the greater organization of the team's role.
- *The team purpose.* Team purpose should be delineated in a clear and concise manner to express why the group was convened. The mission statement of the team, often aligned with the organization's mission, defines the team's purpose and guides the team members to work

together to achieve the defined outcomes. Teams may also express a vision that is linked to the group mission and serves to communicate the team's aspirations and goals and inspire its members.

· *The goals and objectives of a team frame the purpose of why the team is necessary.* It is important when convening a group to identify specific goals and objectives for the group as well as define the scope of activity. Whenever possible, goals should be objective and measurable. Goals that have a clear desired outcome provide the group with the guidance necessary to pursue the goal.

- For example, one goal in a healthcare delivery setting may be to reduce the hospital acquired-infection rate from a specified baseline level. In this case, it would be clearer and more measurable to state "how much" of a reduction in the infection rate is desired. Therefore, the goal may be stated as "reduce the hospital acquired infection rate by 50% from the baseline within 6 months." This goal is clear and concise, and can be assessed to determine improvement and ultimate success.

- It may also be helpful to state two goals for a desired outcome. In this particular scenario, the 50% reduction from baseline would be the "base" goal, and a second goal, known as a "stretch" goal, is set for a 75% reduction from the baseline. This provides the group with additional opportunity and incentive not only to meet the stated goal, but to strive to achieve an even better outcome.

Team Membership

A team is a group of individuals who act collectively to make a contribution or achievement that could not be made individually. Team members may have to defer their personal goals to focus on the larger mission of the group.

The team membership should be determined based on the ability of the individuals to contribute to the overall purpose of the team. Membership on a team may be defined by the position of a member within the organization (as is seen in executive teams in which senior administrators are appointed to a team by virtue of their position). Other teams might be composed of members selected because of their professional expertise or education, their professional interests, their diligence, or their collaboration and communications skills. Qualities or attributes to be considered when recruiting team members include the ability to work within a group, subject knowledge, stature and credibility, and formal and informal roles within the organization.

Deliverables/Milestones

Each team member should know and understand what is expected of the team. The team deliverables (the measurable outcomes of the team's work) should be quantified, listed, and accompanied by anticipated milestones. Although the eventual outcomes may not be predictable with specificity, the general deliverables/milestones should be clarified so that the membership can understand the expected time frame and results. Recent research suggests that just as there is no formula for creating the right team and there is no specific set of metrics for measuring the effectiveness of a team (Mathieu, Maynard, Rapp, & Gilson, 2008).

It is often difficult to discern between goals/objectives and deliverables. For example, a key goal may be to implement a new electronic health record (EHR) system in a physician group practice within the next 9 months. The ultimate goal is the implementation of the system, but the process of implementation may include several key deliverables such as purchasing the necessary hardware to meet software specifications, transferring of patient medical records from the legacy system to the new system, and training for all medical and administrative staff in the new system's operation and function. The goal is the "big picture," and the deliverables are the steps and processes that must take place to achieve the goal.

Scope

It is important for team leaders to define the scope (the boundaries and limits) of the team's efforts, to aid the group with focus, and help minimize unnecessary distractions from the designated tasks. However, in more formal or official settings or for committees required by law or regulation, voting is generally expected. If a vote is taken, the results should be recorded in the minutes.

Meeting Schedule and Agenda

Team leaders should outline the meeting schedule for the group and define how the meetings will be conducted (e.g., in person or remotely by conference call). Clear and concise **agendas** should be crafted and provided to group members in advance of each meeting for review.

Duration/Time Commitment

Different groups have different purposes and expectations, depending on the tasks at hand. Team members should be informed in advance as to the anticipated duration of the assignment, as well as the time commitment necessary to complete the given task(s).

Decision Making

Teams, especially with larger membership, need to define how decision making and group **consensus** will be achieved. Team leaders should outline the procedures in advance and ensure the group's understanding whether or not there will be formal votes or tallies versus informal consensus building. For most teams, an informal consensus is a good option.

Group Progress Reports

Teams should determine and implement a reporting "schedule" of their progress and report their findings regularly to the larger organization. Depending upon the purpose of the group and the issue(s), reporting may be performed daily, weekly, monthly, or quarterly. In order to avoid confusion, the timing of these reports should be specified in the team charter.

TYPE OF TEAMS

The healthcare industry is heavily reliant on teams to fulfill its mission. There are several different types of teams; some are permanent in nature and others are temporary, depending on the mission and the targeted goals and objectives. Teams of varying functionality, purpose, and duration can be developed to accomplish specific tasks. Some examples of common **healthcare teams** include the following.

Executive Leadership Team

The executive leadership team is critical to a healthcare organization. The executive leadership of both for-profit and not-for-profit healthcare organizations, including the Chief Executive Officer (CEO), the Vice Presidents, and other senior executives, take direction and execute strategic plans on behalf of the governing board or Board of Directors. The executive leadership team serve as fiduciaries to the organization and are held to the highest standard of ethical behavior and personal conduct. A fiduciary must act in the best interests of the organization, not solely in his or her personal interest. Executive decisions should be made with high integrity and ethics and should reflect the priority of organizational interests.

The executive leadership team has the day-to-day management responsibilities of an organization, directs and drives the performance of the organization and its employees, and ultimately is accountable for that performance. The executive leadership is responsible for implementing strategies and tactics in pursuit of goals and objectives set by the organization's Board of Directors. The leadership team's performance is measured by the achievement of specific targets and anticipated outcomes.

Problem-Solving Team

A problem-solving team is assembled to address a specific problem or a set of related problems. Organizations rely on problem-solving teams to tackle organizational issues and concerns. Employees selected for these teams have the background and experience to work collaboratively to address issues and propose resolutions. Depending on the breadth of the problem, employees might be recruited for a departmental team to work on a micro-issue or could be summoned from across an organization to address a macro-issue. Problem-solving teams of all sizes and types function collaboratively in healthcare organizations and also contribute to strategic planning and decision-making efforts.

Self-Managed Work Team

Self-managed work teams function without direct management supervision and are responsible for the given deliverable(s). This delegation of responsibility by management to self-management teams serves to empower the team and to provide its members with a sense of ownership. Affording employees the ability to work in self-managed teams can also serve to improve morale, create a stronger sense of participation, and positively impact organizational performance.

Cross-Functional Team

Cross-functional teams are another important organizational tool to address a relevant task by bringing together employees from diverse work areas to collaborate. The task at hand will help determine the configuration of the team among individuals from across the organization. Each member adds different but complementary value to the team by contributing specific expertise that may be based on education, experience, and/or work history.

Virtual Team

With the proliferation of technology, especially in the area of communications, **virtual teams** are increasingly becoming an option for organizations. Virtual teams are especially prevalent and helpful in healthcare organizations that have employees working various nonoverlapping shifts. Virtual teams are also valuable for healthcare organizations that have multiple points of service/geographic locations and allow additional interaction and communication that may not be possible with traditional face-to-face meetings. Virtual teams may be physically separated in diverse locations but communicate electronically via modern technology.

If circumstances allow, virtual teams benefit from an initial face-to-face kickoff meeting to introduce team members to one another, to discuss the team charter, and to review and train the members in using the technology needed to complete the team's work. Technological tools to communicate and complete given tasks include email, video conferencing, and social media. The virtual team should select tools that work best for their members and most effectively facilitate the achievement of goals and objectives.

THE IMPORTANCE OF TEAM COMPOSITION

- *Team Formation*: A key factor for a team's success is team formation (i.e., team composition). Regardless of its type and mission, each team needs to be carefully crafted with team members who will add value to the team. Merely establishing a team and providing a task does not translate into success. Leaders should be able to analyze what will be needed to accomplish the task and use that understanding to guide the selection process of the team members. The assessment of candidates' skillsets, technical competencies, and professional behaviors and styles will help leaders determine the make-up of a team (Buchbinder & Shanks, 2012).
- *Skillset Evaluation*: The first step is to determine the various skillsets that will be necessary for the team to achieve its goals. Depending on the task, these skillsets may vary substantially. Leaders should match the needed skillsets with the expertise of potential team members and consider the candidates' strengths and weaknesses. The skillset should be the baseline for participation and can then be supplemented by the consideration of professional styles of communications and function that would benefit the group.
- *Technical Competence*: The purpose of the team may dictate that team members have technical competence in a particular area. For example, a healthcare organization is seeking to purchase and install a new electronic health records system and develops a team to address this objective. The determination of which system/vendor to choose will require substantial analysis of available information systems and their compatibility with legacy systems from other vendors in the organization. To perform this analysis, team members will not only need to have expertise in health information management, but also technical competence in electronic practice management systems to evaluate how well the software options being considered would serve the needs of the organization.

· *Interpersonal Skills*: A critical component of team formation and composition is the assembly of a group that will be able to work together as a team. Beyond the basic skillsets and necessary technical competence, team members should have the skills and expertise to collaborate with others smoothly and to work efficiently toward a common goal. Although disagreements may occur, the ability to transition and gain consensus from respectful and productive dialogue allows the team to proceed with its mission. Understanding and valuing individual roles and contributions helps facilitate an environment that is positive and productive, and creates an *esprit de corps* that promotes achievement of team goals and objectives.

TEAM EVOLUTION

Team development generally follows a common path from formation to full functionality and productivity. When first created, many teams may consist of members who are unfamiliar with each other or have not worked together in the past. In other cases, the selected team members must assume new or different roles within the context of the team. Therefore, team leaders should introduce team members to each other within the framework of the purpose and objective of the team, creating a common understanding of overall goals and mission, as well as outlining individual roles. To be most effective, the team members will need to begin "singing from the same sheet of music."

Teams generally evolve through a cycle of development toward a more mature stage through the following four phases (Tuckman, 1965):

1. Forming
2. Storming
3. Norming
4. Performing

A **multidisciplinary team** is displayed in **Figure 7.3**, and **Figure 7.4** features a work team in the storming phase.

The time it takes a team to advance through each phase varies with the group; not every member progresses at the same speed. However, the team as a whole cannot move forward until all members are "in sync."

· *Forming*: During the initial stage of creation, a team is said to be forming. This phase is generally dominated by the team leader and includes the introduction of members as well as of the team's purpose/charter, timelines, and anticipated meeting dates. During this phase, it is not unusual to have nonmembers speak to the

Figure 7.3 Multidisciplinary Team

Figure 7.4 Phase Two of Teaming—Storming

team or distribute reading material relevant to the issues the team will need to address.

· *Storming*: During the initial phase of team creation, forming, controversy is unusual. Members are learning about their mission and roles and not sufficiently informed to create conflict. However, once a team is established and informed, it enters the storming phase, characterized by questions and disagreement as members begin to internalize the information provided and take on the mantle of their roles. Information is interpreted differently by each individual and filtered through personal beliefs, background, perspectives, and biases. The storming phase is a period of adjustment during which team members ask questions, present opinions, and work toward a group understanding and balance or stasis. The role of the team leader during this phase of team growth is quite different than it was during formation. During the storming period, the leader needs to give the members as much freedom as possible to ask questions and debate within an atmosphere of decorum. The leader may also become the servant to the team by providing answers to questions and supplying additional research material for review.

· *Norming*: As team members better understand themselves, each other, and their roles on the team, they approach a normalized state of understanding and tolerance of each other's personalities and perspectives, and will no longer need to question each other or the team mission in the manner observed during storming. Relationships will begin to normalize. During the norming phase, a committee or team may not produce discernible results, but will be actively learning. During this phase, members discuss matters in more detail and with a productive focus, and team leaders may assume a more proactive role in steering the agenda and conversations.

· *Performing*: Finally, the team enters its mature phase, sufficiently developed to begin producing definitive results. Teams can remain in this phase for very long periods. Every time a new member is introduced to the team or a new task is provided, however, the team regresses to a prior stage to absorb the changes, then returns to the mature phase more quickly.

A recent addition to the phases of a team's life span has been discovered: "Adjourning." Science fiction writer Robert Heinlein is credited with saying, "A motion to adjourn is always in order." (Heinlein, 1973). Every team should have a defined objective; once reached, the team should be permanently adjourned. Allowing a team to continue to function once it has outlived its original charter or after its stated objective has been met can be a disservice to an organization.

TEAM DYNAMICS

Teams can be considered "living beings." They are born, learn, evolve, and develop personalities. Successful teams are complex organisms. They may act like 2 year olds or mature and sensible adults. As with rearing children, nurture and nature both play a role in a team's success or failure. How teams behave and perform speaks more about their leadership and development than their structural constitutional makeup.

Successful team function is a product of a mix of factors, including effective leadership, capable management, productive communications, mentoring and guidance, a clearly defined pathway, facilitated decision making, and successful closure. The following components are critical to team success.

Leadership

Team leadership is critical to the ultimate success or failure of a team; therefore, selection of leaders must be approached seriously. Depending on the team's purpose and structure, its leader may be appointed or may be elected by the membership. An Executive Committee consisting of an organization's top leadership, for example, will probably be led by the most senior executive on the committee, who is, in essence, appointed by virtue of position. An ad hoc committee, on the other hand, may be asked to select its leader from among the members. Each member then carries responsibility for choosing the best leader who will set the tone for the group and serve as an effective guide and mentor. In the latter scenario, team members must delicately balance their personal desires and the good of the group.

Management of a Committee Is a Serious Business

Good management will support the team leader and the members by keeping the process organized, moving forward, informed, and disciplined. The responsibilities of the management function include duties such as developing a schedule of meetings, keeping members advised of meeting dates and times, documenting attendance, maintaining accurate minutes, ensuring the minutes are distributed and reviewed, reminding members of assignments, and other administrative functions. Without proper and effective management, a committee may stall and not achieve its purpose.

Research has shown that the interaction among team members can play a very significant role in the success or failure of a meeting. Teams that showed more functional interaction, such as problem-solving interaction and action planning, were significantly more satisfied with their meetings. Better meetings were associated with higher team productivity. Moreover, constructive meeting interaction processes were related to organizational success 2.5 years after the meeting. Dysfunctional communication, such as criticizing others or complaining, resulted in significant negative relationships and outcomes. These negative effects were even more pronounced than the positive effects of functional team meeting interaction. The results suggest that team meeting processes shape both team and organizational outcomes. The critical meeting behaviors identified here provide hints for group researchers and practitioners alike who aim to improve meeting success (Kauffield & Lehmann-Willenbrock, 2012).

Protocols

Most people function best when there is a sense of purpose and order in their lives. So do committees and teams. Knowing the purpose of bringing the group together and focusing on that purpose via specific procedures contribute to the success of the committee. Some components of team rules and guidelines are presented as follows.

Participation

Participation in committee activities is the first responsibility of every member. Attendance at meetings is the only way a member can actively participate and interact with the other members and engage fully in the business of the committee. Each individual has been assigned to the committee for a reason. Members are responsible for contributing their relevant expertise, experience, knowledge, and energy to the activities of the team. Members do not need to have an opinion or voice their thoughts on every topic, but they should consider all agenda items seriously and participate when they can make a positive contribution. The progress of a team is hindered if members do not attend meetings or activities, do not contribute actively to committee work, or act in ways that are detrimental to the achievement of the team purpose and goals. If such a situation does occur, the team leader should intervene to correct negative behavior via counseling or removing the team member.

Respect

As in all aspects of life, including teams, respect for others is the socially acceptable norm. Respectful behavior among team members is necessary in building a cohesive team, whereas lack of respect can destroy a team very quickly. Respect includes understanding and tolerance of the professional, ethnic, and cultural differences among diverse groups of people. At its core, respect demands that all team members treat others with consideration, show common courtesy, listen, avoid open conflict, and maintain focus on the goals and objectives of the team.

Meeting Schedule

Team leaders need to create a schedule for team meetings and abide by it. As the saying goes, "time is money." Time is limited and should not be wasted, especially between committees and teams. Wasting time is disrespectful and unprofessional, and hampers progress toward the team's ultimate goals.

Meeting Agenda

A meeting without an agenda often turns into a gathering for chitchat. Routine meetings or briefings held to update staff or other attendees may not require a written agenda, but a meeting that is not routine needs an agenda to wisely utilize the attendees' time and produce valuable results. Creating an agenda gives the team leader an opportunity to think through the purpose and objectives of the meeting and the important issues to be addressed and gives the participants a chance to prepare for the meeting and "hit the ground running." Without an agenda, there should not be a meeting.

Minutes

Every worthy meeting should be documented by accurate records. Minutes of meetings record the important issues addressed, the discussions held, the findings discovered, the decisions reached, and the action plans designed. A specific individual should be assigned responsibility for recording meeting proceedings and producing minutes for the committee to review and revise if necessary. These minutes should be distributed to the meeting attendees within a reasonable time after the meeting so that the participants' memory of the proceedings is still fresh. Meeting minutes should include the following information:

- Attendees
- Date and location of the meeting
- A copy of the agenda
- Summary of key issues addressed, relevant facts or data presented, and the essence of the team discussions at the meeting
- The results of any votes and, if appropriate, how each member voted
- Decisions, recommendations, and conclusions from the meeting
- Action plans developed and assigned responsibility for tasks to be performed

Communication

Throughout history, great thinkers and great leaders have been observed to be great communicators. Outstanding leaders must be adept at the sophisticated art of communication to be able to inspire and motivate others. Effective team leadership demands that communications be very well thought out, simple, clear, succinct, and directed toward the team's mandate or purpose. Communications that are not focused on the goal of the team are distracting at best and may misdirect team members and harm the committee's efforts.

Decision Making

One value of teams is that they can positively impact the quality of decision making, either by providing reasoned input and feedback to decision makers or by developing a consensus of recommendations based on committee expertise, research, and discussion. Sometimes, however, teams are unable to reach a conclusion, decision, or recommendation. This lack of closure can be harmful to the team and the organization and indicates the need for leadership to intervene and facilitate resolution of the team's function. Some reasons for the stalling of teams' progress include:

- Lack of diverse opinions, or "**group think**"—Group think occurs when a team's participants find themselves agreeing on almost everything but don't move forward. In these cases, the team leader should intervene and redirect the members back onto the path toward the team goal. Warning: Commonality of opinion can sometimes be due to a leader dominating the team with his or her agenda and opinions. Teams and their leaders should be on guard to recognize this trait and change tactics if needed.
- Open hostility/open attacks—Common courtesy is a bulwark of civilization and is mandatory for team members. Open hostility or personal attacks are to be avoided at all costs and if they occur, should be addressed immediately by the team leader.
- Change aversion—One of the most common roles of a team or committee is to evaluate and suggest change. Humankind is well known for an aversion to change; facilitating change is not easy and must be handled well. Anytime change is recommended it should include consideration of the impact upon others and upon the overall organization. How will people respond to the recommendations for change and the change itself? Whom will it impact? How can the change be implemented, and what must be done to assure the most success? Are there alternatives to this process? What is the exit strategy if the change

does not accomplish its intended objective? If all these questions can be answered, yet the team members are still averse to the change, then the leader must explore the reasons for the aversion. Why are members not in favor of the changes? Can the issue be looked at differently? Might there be influences outside the purview of the committee, team, or organization that are not being considered? Understanding the reasons for aversion to change can help leaders and teams develop tactics to help ease transitions through the change process.

- Intractable issues—It is not uncommon for a team to find itself in a stalemate with no obvious solutions. If time and other constraints allow, the following steps may help resolve the impasse.
    i.   Table the issue for future consideration to give the team members time to gather additional information, think through their opinions, and "sleep on it."
    ii. Assign the issue to a subgroup to further analyze it and report back to the team at a future meeting. Some issues can be better addressed by small groups tasked with returning specific recommendations to the larger committee.
    iii. Sidebar. Have the team leader take the conflicting parties aside and discuss the issue privately "in chambers." In particularly sensitive situations, it may be best for the team leader to exercise executive authority and take personal ownership for finding a resolution. This tactic, however, runs the risk of the team leader taking over the team process and alienating team members; therefore it should be used rarely.
    iv. Remove the issue from team responsibility. This tactic is more heavy-handed and, if implemented without the consent of the team members, may be perceived as a rebuke of the team participants.
    v.   Disband the team. This tactic is the most serious and should be used only as a last resort. Not only will the team purpose remain unfulfilled, but the action may negatively impact the morale, enthusiasm, and reputation of the team members and leadership.

SUMMARY

Teams are an important and integral component of health care. Healthcare systems are among the most complex organizational entities in existence, multidisciplinary and multilayered. There is no one individual or professional capable of delivering health care alone; teams help healthcare organizations more effectively provide both clinical and administrative functions. Healthcare managers must become adept at successfully creating, managing, and utilizing teams to ensure cost-effective, high-quality services and operations in today's challenging healthcare marketplace.

Discussion Questions

1. Discuss if health care is unique as an industry in its use of teams.
2. What are the benefits associated with working in teams? What are the detriments?
3. How should a leader manage a team without controlling it?
4. Will healthcare reform change the way we use teams in the healthcare industry?

Case Study #1: The Quality Improvement (QI) Team Kick-Off?

(Courtesy of Victoria Parker, Program Director Department of Health Policy and Management Boston University School of Public Health)

Jeff looked at his watch again, sighed, and glanced around the room. It was already 5 minutes past the hour. His first quality improvement (QI) project at Suburban Hospital, and only 3 of the 15 people he had invited to the kick-off team meeting had appeared.

Disappointed, Jeff proceeded to talk through the slide presentation he had carefully prepared, which outlined the targeted problems and the structured quality improvement methods that would be used to tackle the concerns. The three people in attendance asked few questions and seemed eager for the meeting to end. After a short and awkward discussion, Jeff watched them hurry out of the room.

Back in his cubicle in the Quality Improvement department, Jeff struggled to sort through the mixture of anger, embarrassment, and frustration that he was feeling about his effort to launch this QI team. As the quality director had suggested, Jeff had invited stakeholders from all the clinical and administrative areas involved in these issues to join this team. Using the hospital's email system, he had created and sent an electronic meeting invitation, and at least 10 of the 15 stakeholders recruited had accepted the invitation. Jeff had not wanted to make the e-vite message too long; the invitation had stated that each recipient had been named to a "new QI team." Yet, only three had bothered to show up! And even those who attended did not seem very interested or engaged in what Jeff had to say.

Prior to the meeting, Jeff had been anxious to implement all of the great ideas about self-managing teams and group facilitation that he had learned in his healthcare management courses at State University. Now, based on today's attendance, he found himself feeling desperate about how he would even get the project off the ground, never mind make it self-managing. As a quality analyst, Jeff realized that he had no formal authority over any of the people he had invited. How could his director expect him to get them actively involved?

Case Study Discussion Questions

1. What factors related to team formation do you think contributed to the poor attendance at Jeff's kick-off meeting?
2. Based on what you've learned, what advice would you give Jeff about how to manage the formation of a new team?
3. Assuming the team does get started, are there any steps Jeff can take to keep members engaged and involved in its efforts?
4. What do you think Jeff should do next in his effort to get this team underway?

Case Study #2: Equal Workload?

(Courtesy of Victoria Parker, Program Director Department of Health Policy and Management Boston University School of Public Health)

With a huge sigh, Marianna deleted the latest email from one of the members of her fellow clinic reorganization committee. Picking up her phone and dialing her fiancé, she mulled over the events of the last 2 months with a growing sense of unease.

"Hey," she started, "you won't believe what that clinic reorganization committee is doing now. I've told them over and over again that our wedding and honeymoon fall in the last 3 weeks before the report is due, and I've repeatedly offered to get started on different parts of the report, but they just keep telling me to 'chill out,' and that there's still plenty of time to get our work done. In fact, I just got an email suggesting that we go back and rerun a whole bunch of the predicted patient volume analyses that I know are already complete. Sure, maybe the rest of them have plenty of time, but not me! I'm worried that I'm going to end up having to work all night the whole week before the wedding and walk down the aisle with giant bags under my eyes. It's just not fair. I've been trying to plan ahead, and they are just not working with me on this." After venting a while longer, she hung up and returned to working on other clinic projects needing attention before her planned 3-week absence for the nuptials.

[Four weeks later]

"Marianna! What do you mean "today's your last day in the office until 3 weeks from now"? We have a ton left to do on this clinic reorganization report, and you're supposed to be part of this committee! I hope you're not expecting us to put your name on this report, given how little you've contributed!" shouted Kyle, the committee chair.

"Kyle, I really don't know what to say. I've been telling you all since the first few committee meetings that I had plans for this time off! I've been offering to work ahead on anything that could be done ahead of time, and you just kept telling me not to get worked up about it. Did you think I was going to reschedule my wedding and honeymoon because the rest of you were determined to wait until the last minute?"

"Well, excuse me for not keeping track of the details of your life. I assumed that if you wanted to be on this committee, you were committed to getting its work done, no matter what it takes. Clearly, I was mistaken about your commitment to organizing the clinic in a better way."

Marianna walked away, muttering, and wondering if she'd still have a job after her "big day." She decided then and there that signing up for an important cross-departmental committee was something she was not going to do again.

Case Study Discussion Questions

1. Do you think this committee could have prevented this conflict over getting its work done by the deadline? If so, how? If not, why not?

2. What could the committee chair have done early in the committee's life to ensure that its members were in agreement about its workplan?

3. Should the team include Marianna's name on its report? Why or why not?

4. If you were coaching the committee chair, what advice would you give Kyle about dealing with this situation?

RELATED WEBSITES

Agency for Healthcare Research and Quality, TeamSTEPPS: http://teamstepps
.ahrq.gov/

Institute for Healthcare Improvement: www.ihi.org/knowledge/Pages/HowtoImprove
/ScienceofImprovementFormingtheTeam.aspx

Learning Center: www.learningcenter.net/library/health.shtml

Mind Tools: www.mindtools.com/pages/article/newTMM_30.htm

OTHER SUGGESTED READING

Kovner, A., & Neuhauser, D. (2004). *Health services management, readings, cases and commentary.* Chicago, IL: Health Administration Press.

Liebler, J. G., & McConnell, C. R. (2008). *Management principles for health professionals* (5th ed.). Sudbury, MA: Jones & Bartlett.

White, K. R., & Griffith, J. R. (2010). *The well-managed healthcare organization* (7th ed.). Chicago: IL: Health Administration Press.

Wolper, L. F. (2011). *Health care administration* (5th ed.). Sudbury, MA: Jones & Bartlett.

REFERENCES

Buchbinder, S. B., & Shanks, N. H. (2012). *Introduction to health care management* (2nd ed.). Burlington, MA: Jones & Bartlett Learning.

Heinlein, R. (1973). *Time enough for love.* New York, NY: Putnam Publishing Group.

Kauffeld, S., & Lehmann-Willenbrock, N. (2012, April). Meetings matter: Effects of team meetings on team and organizational success. *Small Group Research, 43*(2), 130–158.

Mathieu, J., Maynard, M. T., Rapp, T., & Gilson, L. (2008). Team effectiveness 1997–2007: A review of recent advancements and a glimpse into the future. *Journal of Management, 34,* 410–476.

Shuffler, M. L., DiazGranados, D., & Salas, E. (2011, December). There's a science for that: Team development interventions in organizations. *Current Directions in Psychological Science, 20*(6), 365–372.

Tuckman, B. (1965). Developmental Sequence in Small Groups. *Psychological Bulletin, 63*(6), 384–399.

Chapter 8

Leading Quality Initiatives

Marsha Chan and Louis Rubino

LEARNING OBJECTIVES

By the end of this chapter, the student will be able to:

· Describe the importance of leadership to create a quality driven organizational culture.
· Identify the stakeholders and drivers of quality and patient safety.
· Explain the strategies a leader can use to achieve and sustain high performance levels.
· Understand the influence of public and private agencies in setting the national quality agenda.

KEY TERMS

Aims for Improvement	Organizational culture
Balanced scorecard	Six Sigma
Baldrige National Quality Award	Transparency
Leadership leverage points	Value-based purchasing
Lean	
Nursing Magnet Recognition Program	

INTRODUCTION

Quality initiatives have become essential in today's healthcare industry to promote high standards of care and protect patient safety. In the past, administrators often relied upon a healthcare organization's internal clinical staff to oversee and ensure the quality of the services provided. This self-monitoring is no longer sufficient. Quality of care must now be evaluated by healthcare leaders through quantitative, objective, and reproducible assessments that address external requirements and standards. Under the U.S. Affordable Care Act, healthcare entities designated as Accountable Care Organizations will be rewarded for meeting specific standards of performance related to quality of care. These measures of success will be linked directly to an Accountable Care Organization's rates of reimbursement, and in many cases, to that healthcare organization's executive compensation. For example, the Center for Medicare and Medicaid Services' **value-based purchasing** is providing reimbursement incentives to accountable providers who produce high-quality outcomes, and disincentives for the provision of poor-quality outcomes. Other third-party payers are following suit; healthcare leaders will need to focus on demonstrating achievement of high-quality standards to ensure not only the operational excellence but also the fiscal stability of their organizations.

SETTING THE QUALITY AGENDA

At the turn of the 21st century, new campaigns were led by respected government and voluntary agencies to identify and address the significant and widespread deficiencies identified in U.S. healthcare quality. The latest research reveals that, over a decade later, some progress (but not nearly enough) has been made in improving quality of care (Chassin & Loeb, 2011).

The Institute of Medicine (IOM) has defined high-quality care as being safe, effective, patient-centered, timely, efficient, and equitable. The IOM has recommended that quality improvements be addressed on four levels: that of the patient, of health-delivery microsystems (teams or units), of organizations that house such systems (hospitals, clinics, health systems, etc.), and of the regulatory and financial environment in which those systems operate (IOM, 2001). Effective leadership is needed on all four levels to meet these aims and support a quality-driven healthcare system (see **Figure 8.1**).

Quality-Driven Leadership

Quality initiatives do not successfully progress through an organization without effective leadership. Executives must visibly lead efforts to change the culture of a healthcare organization toward a quality-driven model.

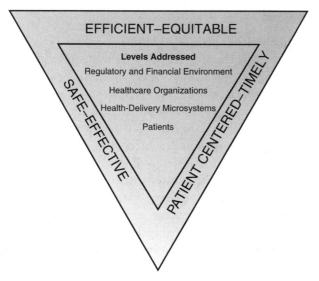

Figure 8.1 IOM's Six Aims and Four Levels Addressed

Leaders must also identify areas in which quality improvement is indicated and decide on the strategic directions the organization must follow to achieve positive outcomes. They must be able to facilitate the development and implementation of initiatives to promote and ensure quality of care and to serve as role models and influence others to strive for quality improvements throughout the delivery system.

Through their research, Taylor and Rutherford (2010) have identified challenges and opportunities for executive leaders to establish patient- and family-centeredness in the healthcare setting; their advice also applies to leaders' efforts to improve quality of health care in general. Leaders must inspire a vision for a healthcare organization's future and advocate for the goal that the entity becomes a quality-driven organization. Leaders must lead by example and speak openly about quality and patient safety. Leaders must show that they are dissatisfied with "resting on their laurels," and are continuously challenging the organization's processes and procedures to improve patient care. They must enable and empower an organization's employees to work collaboratively to address quality improvement. Finally, leaders must "encourage the heart"—as passion fuels achievement. A leader should inspire and bolster the enthusiasm of an organization's employees and partners, and celebrate the positive contributions individuals and teams make to the organization's quality-enhancement efforts.

Governing Boards

Governing boards of healthcare organizations have traditionally been legally accountable for the quality of care their individual facilities provide; but in the modern healthcare environment, boards in a variety of sectors such as hospitals, clinics, and long-term care facilities are being tasked with the responsibility of monitoring collaborative patient care as well. Under the Affordable Care Act of 2010, a systemwide emphasis for quality of care is being promoted, which integrates previously separate components of healthcare delivery and demands group responsibility for patient care. These new integrated entities will need to assess quality of care rendered by all components because they will be compensated through a shared bundled payment rather than individual payments for member components. Governing boards will need to develop and implement effective quality oversight processes on a systemwide basis (Belmont et al., 2011).

A proactive, comprehensive approach must be taken by the governing board to guide and support senior leadership in promoting excellence in this new environment. For hospitals and other large healthcare organizations, a commissioned subcommittee to address quality of care and patient safety is recommended to ensure adequate oversight (Rubino & Chan, 2008). A survey of hospital and system leaders demonstrated that the following engagement measures were also effective in enhancing quality oversight: establishing strategic goals for quality improvement, using quality dashboards to track performance, and following up on corrective actions related to adverse events (Jiang, Lockee, Bass, & Fraser, 2008). More recent research reveals better performance on benchmarks of quality care and on mortality rates when organizations implement practices such as soliciting both their governing board and their medical staff to collaborate with management in setting the agenda for discussion and development of quality improvement initiatives; requiring new clinical programs to meet quality-related criteria; setting selected quality outcome targets at ideal levels; and requiring the issuance of public quality/safety performance reports (Jiang, Lockee, & Fraser, 2012).

Executive and Senior Leaders

Quality issues impact every area of a healthcare leader's responsibility, including patient morbidity, client satisfaction, and financial metrics. Leaders must be able to measure and evaluate the quality of services and care their units or divisions provide and to compare their performance with other units within the organization. They must also be able to assess and understand how their units' quality outcomes affect the performance of the organization as a whole.

Successful leaders develop formal bylaws, policies, and procedures that address quality issues critical to daily operation. For example, medical staff bylaws and nursing policies should include policies and procedures on the performance of credentialing, privileging, peer evaluation, continuing education, skills assessment, and quality improvement studies and audits. Procedures for identifying areas for quality improvement, implementing positive changes, and reassessing performance should be outlined. All clinical staff should be formally encouraged to report or intervene if they become aware of work-related activities that may endanger patient safety and quality of care. Additionally, nonclinical areas also require guidelines for maintaining and improving quality. For example, Health Information Management department leaders must ensure that coding of medical records is being done appropriately to prevent errors in documentation that could negatively impact patient care or organizational reimbursement.

Healthcare leaders' efforts to improve quality not only profoundly improve patient outcomes and satisfaction, but can also result in additional benefits for their organizations such as reduced costs and increased profits. These benefits have encouraged leaders from among a broad range of healthcare sectors to identify quality of care and patient safety as their top priority (HealthLeaders Media Industry Survey, 2011a), and to model and facilitate culture shifts promoting quality of care for their organizations (see **Table 8.1**).

Table 8.1 Healthcare Leaders Priorities

Priority	% Leaders Selected
1. Quality/Patient safety	37%
2. Cost reduction	36%
3. Patient experience/Patient satisfaction	33%
4. Reimbursement	26%
5. Developing Accountable Care Organizations	22%

Source: Data from HealthLeaders Media Industry Survey. (2011). Overall Cross-Sector Report. Retrieved November 29, 2012 from www.healthleadersmedia.com/pdf/survey_project/2011 /Overall_Cross_Sector_press.pdf.

Quality Initiatives

Professional associations from a breadth of healthcare sectors are also promoting the importance of dynamic leadership for successful quality management (AHA & HRET, 2011). These professional associations provide resources and guidance about successful research and evidence-based processes that can inform leaders' strategic planning and initiative development in this arena. The associations promote new best practices and recommendations through their written and online communications with members as well as through meetings, educational programs, seminars, and conferences. The Joint Commission, for example, has begun annual reporting on high-quality performers and their successful initiatives in their *Improving America's Hospitals Report* (The Joint Commission, 2011).

Several other organizations have launched outreach initiatives to disseminate best practices to their stakeholders. Some recent examples are:

- The Comprehensive Unit-Based Safety Program, which aims to reduce central-line associated bloodstream infections (CLABSI)
- The Institute for Healthcare Improvement's standardized processes (bundles), which strive to prevent ventilator-associated pneumonia
- Patient Safety First, California Partnership for Health, with the goals of eliminating hospital-acquired infections and improving patient care

Stakeholders and Drivers

Unlike monolithic industries, the healthcare industry can include and involve many parties with divergent agendas and interests. Each party, or stakeholder, shares the common goals of supporting the mission of a healthcare organization or system, but also brings its individual objectives to the partnership or collaboration. Stakeholders will seek to assess not only how well the system or organization is performing, but also whether their individual objectives are being met. Executive healthcare leaders need to identify leaders and champions within each stakeholder unit who can ensure that the units' initiatives are not only advancing system improvement as a whole, but also achieving the individual units' specific objectives. Selection of effective leaders of stakeholder groups is especially critical for Accountable Care Organizations, for which the success of quality initiatives depends on stakeholders' collaboration and alignment (Kocher & Sahni, 2010). An organization's stakeholders, both internal and external, can be effective drivers of quality initiatives. Internal drivers of quality can include an organization's Board of Directors, its executive and senior leaders, the

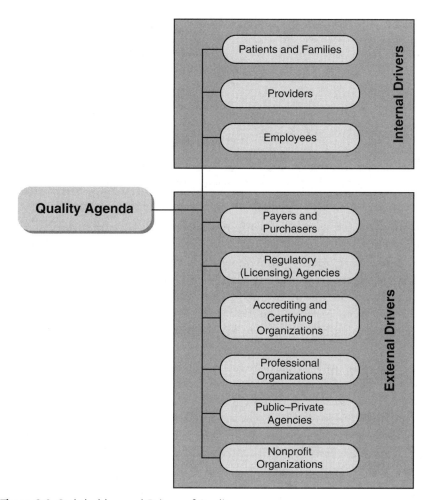

Figure 8.2 Stakeholders and Drivers of Quality

medical staff, the employees, and the patients/clients and their families. Externally, the quality agenda can be driven by payers, purchasers, regulators, accrediting and certifying bodies, professional organizations, public–private agencies, as well as nonprofit agencies whose mission is to improve health care (see **Figure 8.2**).

Physicians and Other Providers

The selection and retention of excellent and cost-effective providers is a key to success in quality improvement; enlisting and empowering providers to embrace quality-improvement initiatives is critical for healthcare

Table 8.2 Physician Survey on Important Issues

Issue	Strongly Positive/Positive
1. Patient experience, patient-centered care	80%
2. Quality-improvement initiatives	76%
3. Electronic health record adoption	67%
4. Increase insured patients	60%
5. Accountable Care Organizations	49%

Source: Data from HealthLeaders Media Industry Survey. (2011). Physician Leaders Report. Retrieved November 29, 2012 from www.healthleadersmedia.com/pdf/survey_project/2011 /Physician_press.pdf.

organizations and systems. For example, physicians have traditionally aimed for high quality in the individual services they provide to each patient, but now realize that quality improvement on a broader scale is vital for their practices and for their affiliated healthcare organizations to be successful in today's healthcare environment. Success can be measured in many ways, including client outcomes, patient safety, revenue generation, and most importantly, customer satisfaction. A physician anticipates that not only will her patients be satisfied by her efforts and care, but also by the care provided by her affiliated healthcare organization and the colleagues to whom she refers. Doctors surveyed predicted that by 2014, quality improvement initiatives and enhancement of the patient-care experience will have the greatest positive impact, surpassing other expected advances such as expanded healthcare insurance for the population and the widespread adoption of electronic health records (HealthLeaders Media Industry Survey, 2011b) (see **Table 8.2**).

Payers

In 2009, the U.S. National Health Expenditure (NHE) reached $2.5 trillion and accounted for 17.5% of Gross Domestic Product (GDP), with Medicare accounting for $502.3 billion (20% of NHE), Medicaid, $373.9 billion (15% of NHE), and private health insurers, $801.2 billion (32% of NHE). The agencies that pay for health care exert a significant influence on the oversight of care provided with their dollars. For example, the Center for Medicare and Medicaid Services (CMS) has launched a number of quality initiatives aimed at improving the quality of care provided through its programs. These quality initiatives and measures are aligned with the IOM **Aims for Improvement** and are disseminated publicly to promote **transparency** and accountability. They affect a breadth of stakeholders in the healthcare system, including nursing homes, home health agencies, hospitals, kidney dialysis facilities, physicians and mid-level providers, and Accountable Care Organizations. The initiatives have evolved since 2001; among the changes are moving from voluntary to mandatory reporting; from payment for simple reporting to payment based on the outcomes in reported results (i.e., pay for performance); and to utilizing the collected data to determine value for CMS in purchasing healthcare services. The CMS initiatives are summarized in **Table 8.3**.

Other significant healthcare payers, such as commercial and nonprofit insurance companies, have followed the lead set by CMS by establishing incentives for performance and disincentives for undesired outcomes such as hospital-acquired conditions and readmissions. Contracts are negotiated by the insurance companies' contract managers, who seek out healthcare providers and organizations in the areas needed by their clientele and negotiate the best quality and price for these purchased or contracted services.

Purchasers

Purchasers of healthcare include employers who purchase or subsidize healthcare benefits for their employees. In the past, business leaders focused on finding the best price for their employee health insurance plans. Today, they are also concerned about the quality rankings for their approved providers. Healthcare performance data are more transparent, allowing business leaders to consider performance and quality measures and select the providers and affiliated institutions that can most effectively keep the business' employees healthy and productive.

One heralded approach was developed by the Leapfrog Group, which represents 65 employers and agencies that purchase health care for over 34 million individuals. In 2000, with a mission to "trigger a giant leap forward in quality, customer service, and affordability of healthcare," the Leapfrog Group developed its Leapfrog Hospital Survey. The survey collects hospital performance data in order to provide an assessment of conformity and compliance with standards of safety, quality, and efficiency. The Leapfrog survey has now expanded to include an extensive review of patient safety measures, which are released annually to the public at www.leapfroggroup .org. By recognizing and rewarding top performers in its survey, Leapfrog leverages its purchasing influence and motivates lower performers and nonparticipants to meet the Leapfrog safety standards. The overall impact of Leapfrog, however, has been attenuated by limited survey participation and adoption of its standards by healthcare organizations; but the Leapfrog approach is credited with serving as an early catalyst for transparency of quality and safety measures (Galvin, Delbanco, Milstein, & Belden, 2005; Pronovost, Thompson, Holzmueller, Domran, & Morlock, 2007).

Table 8.3 Transition of CMS Quality Focused Programs

CMS Program	Approach	Participants	Description
Home Health Quality Initiatives (1999-OASIS; 2010-OASIS-C)	Mandatory reporting	Home health agencies	Outcome and Assessment Information Set (OASIS) intended to guide quality improvement; modified dataset launched in 2010 supports evidence based care (OASIS-C). Results publicly reported on Medicare.gov/homehealthcompare.
Nursing Home Quality Initiative (2002)	Mandatory reporting (informational)	Nursing homes, skilled nursing facilities/centers	Minimum Dataset (MDS) Some MDS measures and certification survey findings are publicly reported data for consumers on CMSNursingHomeCompare.gov.
Reporting Hospital Quality Data for Annual Payment Update (RHQDAPU) (2003–2011 name changed to Hospital Inpatient Quality Reporting Program)	Pay for reporting	Any hospital	Through an increase in the annual market basket for reporting (or a reduction for not reporting). Initially a 0.4% reduction, 2% by 2005.
CMS-Premier Hospital Quality Improvement Demonstration (HQID) Project (2003–2009)	Pay for performance	Premier member hospitals	Financial incentives based on threshold attainment, top performance, and significant improvement. Over the 6 years of the HQID, CMS awarded $60 million to the top performers.
Hospital Outpatient Quality Reporting Program (Hospital OQR) (2006– ongoing)	Pay for reporting	Hospitals—outpatient services	Two percentage point reduction in their annual payment update (APU) under the Outpatient Prospective Payment System (OPPS). Includes radiology and emergency department measures.

Program	Type	Applies to	Description
Physician Quality Reporting Initiative (2006) (2011: name changed to Physician Quality Reporting System)	Pay for reporting	Physicians	Data on quality measures for covered professional services furnished to Medicare beneficiaries.
Hospital Consumer Assessment of Healthcare Providers and Systems (HCAHPS) (2006)	Mandatory reporting	Patients discharged from a hospital (not restricted to Medicare patients)	Hospital–patient experience survey. Results are publicly reported under the Hospital Compare website.
Hospital Acquired Conditions (HACs) (2008)	Disincentive for hospital-acquired conditions	All hospitals	Beginning in 2007, conditions present on admission (POA) must be identified. Beginning in 2008, specific conditions no longer resulted in higher reimbursement for Medicare patients if acquired during hospitalization.
Electronic Prescribing (e-Rx) Incentive Project (2009)	Incentive program	Physicians	A 2% incentive payment; an individual eligible professional must report the e-Rx measure in at least 50% of the cases in which the measure is reportable.
Nursing Home Value-Based Purchasing (NHVBP) demonstration project (2009)	Pay for performance	Nursing homes in New York, Wisconsin, and Arizona	Domains: staffing, appropriate hospitalizations, outcome measures from the minimum dataset (MDS), and inspection survey deficiencies.
Medicare and Medicaid Electronic Health Records (EHR) Incentive Programs (2011)	Meaningful use incentive program	Eligible professionals, eligible hospitals, critical access hospitals	Incentive for those eligible providers that adopt, implement, upgrade, or demonstrate meaningful use of certified EHR technology, followed by Medicare payment adjustments for failure to meet meaningful use.

(continues)

Table 8.3 (*continued*)

CMS Program	Approach	Participants	Description
End-stage Renal Disease Quality Incentive Program (ESRD QIP) (2012)	Pay for performance	Dialysis facilities	To enhance the quality of care received by end-stage renal disease patients. Quality measures are publicly available on the CMS Dialysis Facility Compare website.
Value-Based Purchasing (2012)	Purchaser of value (value = quality/cost)	All hospitals	No longer payment for reporting. Quality incentive payment program based upon performance in quality (70%) and patient experience (30%) measures (HCAHPS). 2012: Hospital 1% contribution "at risk," 0.25% increase each year until 2% in 2017.
Accountable Care Organizations (ACO) Quality Measures (2012)	Pay for reporting and pay for performance	Accountable care organizations	Requires reporting of 33 individual measures of quality performance that will be used to determine if an ACO qualifies for shared savings. These 33 measures span four quality domains: patient experience of care, care coordination/patient safety, preventive health, and at-risk population.
LTCH-IRF-Hospice Quality Reporting (2014)	Mandatory reporting	Long-term care hospitals (LTCHs), inpatient rehabilitation facilities (IRFs), and hospice programs	CMS required measures published by October 2012; failure to report results in a 2% reduction in the annual payment.

Patients and Families

Before 2008, the end users of health care had not been empowered to advance quality improvement efforts. Spurred by the onset of mandatory performance reporting and public dissemination of patient-experience survey results in the *Hospital Consumer Assessment of Healthcare Providers and Systems* (HCAHPS), healthcare leaders are increasingly implementing patient- and family-centered care, developing patient–family advisory councils, and integrating patient and/or family representatives into key committees.

Former and current patients and their family members are becoming involved in leadership positions on such councils and committees to ensure their voices are heard. The Institute for Patient- and Family-Centered Care (2010) has recommended that their constituents (i.e., patients and families) act as co-leaders on quality improvement teams in healthcare organizations. Depending on their experience, skills, and expertise, these representatives can serve as facilitators of meetings, content experts, evaluators, faculty on educational seminars, and authors of disseminated work that supports the movement. Even sharing the customer experience provided by having been a patient in its facilities can be of great value to a healthcare organization seeking to improve its quality of care and services.

Regulators, Accrediting and Certifying Organizations

Regulatory agencies and accrediting and certifying organizations play a very important role in ensuring high-quality and safe patient care by periodically inspecting and reviewing healthcare organizations and facilities for compliance with designated standards and requirements for licensure, accreditation, and certification. Failure to comply with standards and regulations could lead to significant negative consequences for an organization, such as loss of accreditation, loss of licensure, and criminal or civil liability.

CMS has driven the accreditation process through its development and oversight of the Federal Conditions of Participation. Accreditation organizations, such as The Joint Commission, the Accreditation Association for Ambulatory Health Care (AAAHC), Det Norske Veritas (DNV), and the American Osteopathic Association, have been granted "deeming" authority (i.e., the authority to appraise and judge that a healthcare organization meets the Medicare and Medicaid certification requirements). The Conditions of Participation as well as the accreditation organizations' standards, establish the requirements that healthcare organizations must meet in order to become accredited and thus be eligible to treat Medicare and Medicaid patients and to receive federal reimbursement for the care provided. Achieving accredited status serves a dual purpose for healthcare organizations: it allows them to care for and be reimbursed for treating Medicare and Medicaid patients, and it establishes that the organization has met the various performance improvement, quality, and patient safety standards of the accrediting body.

Though certification status may not be a requirement for the provision of specialized services such as stroke care, palliative care, or other disease-specific care, many healthcare organizations seek additional certification for such services as a sign of distinction and excellence. Disease-specific care certification can serve to differentiate an organization from its competitors and may assist in providing leverage in recruiting outstanding physicians and other healthcare professionals, in negotiating favorable or enhanced contracts and in promoting business development. **Table 8.4** identifies some of the most commonly utilized certification organizations.

Federal and state regulators, licensing agencies, and accreditation organizations also maintain and enforce requirements regarding significant adverse and sentinel events to which organizations must adhere. In many states, hospitals are required to notify the state department of public health within a specific time frame of discovery if certain types of negative events occur. As of 2011, a total of 28 states have some form of mandatory reporting requirements. For example, since 2007, California hospitals have been required to report certain serious or sentinel "never events" that are considered preventable. Some examples of "never events" are surgery performed on the wrong body part, an infant discharged to the wrong person, a patient death or serious disability associated with a medication error, and a sexual assault on a patient (California Department of Public Health, 2007). The Joint Commission (TJC) does not mandate (but encourages) reporting by its accredited organizations. TJC will require a report and a follow-up action plan should it become aware of an organization's sentinel event or adverse outcomes as a result of a regulatory agency report, media reports, and/or complaints from patients, families, or other individuals. Failure to demonstrate an effective improvement plan may jeopardize an organization's accreditation status.

Professional Organizations/Public–Private Agencies/ Nonprofit Organizations

A number of other entities help to drive the quality agenda. For example, the American Nurses Association (ANA) has established the National Database for Nursing Quality Indicators (NDNQI). The NDNQI collects and reports data that assess and reflect nursing-focused processes of care and outcome measures. These metrics allow hospitals to compare patients-per-nurse

Table 8.4 Examples of Accreditation and Certification Organizations

Accreditation Organization	Accreditation Services (deemed status)	Certification(s) Offered
The Joint Commission (TJC)	Ambulatory health care	*Disease-Specific Care*
www.jointcommission.org	Behavioral health care	(Orthopedic joint replacement, stroke rehabilitation, acute
/accreditation/accreditation_main	Critical access hospital	myocardial infarction, wound care, spinal surgery programs)
.aspx	Home care	*Advanced Disease-Specific Care*
	Hospitals	(Chronic kidney disease, chronic obstructive pulmonary disease,
	Laboratory services	heart failure, inpatient diabetes, lung volume reduction, palliative
	Long-term care	care, ventricular assist device)
		Healthcare Staffing Services
Accreditation Association for Ambulatory Health Care	Ambulatory health care	Medicare-deemed status for ASCs
www.aaahc.org/	Ambulatory surgical centers	
	Federally qualified community health centers	
	Managed care organizations	
Det Norske Veritas	Hospitals	Primary stroke certification
Offers national integrated accreditation for healthcare organizations (NIAHO)	Critical access hospitals	
http://dnvaccreditation.com/pr/dnv /default.aspx		
American Osteopathic Association's	Acute care	Primary stroke center
Healthcare Facilities Accreditation Program (HFAP)	Critical access hospitals	
www.hfap.org/	Ambulatory surgical centers	
	Clinical laboratory	
	Behavioral/mental health	
	Ambulatory care/office-based surgery	

staffing ratios and other factors that may correlate with quality outcomes, as well as to identify benchmarks for performance improvement.

The Agency for Healthcare Research and Quality (AHRQ), an agency in the U.S. Department of Health and Human Services, supports health services research aimed at improving the quality, safety, efficiency, effectiveness, and cost-effectiveness of health care. The results of research funded through the AHRQ are used by policymakers, providers, payers, consumers, health systems, and health plans to evaluate and improve services, as well as to enhance informed decisions regarding health care.

The National Quality Forum (NQF) is a not-for-profit entity whose vision is to become a force in establishing national healthcare priorities and improvement goals by reporting on the quality and efficiency of health services as measured against NQF-endorsed standards. For examples of public/private organizations that influence quality and patient safety policy, see **Table 8.5**.

Employees

A quality agenda may be launched from the executive offices of a healthcare organization, but its successful implementation depends on the contributions and commitment of employees at all levels of the organization. To develop and promote a culture of quality and safety, leaders need to provide opportunities for employee education and training in professionally relevant regulations and standards, and to encourage employees to actively participate in planning and implementation of quality initiatives. Healthcare professionals and support staff serving within an organization are likely to be positively motivated by enhancement of the organization's reputation. Leaders can embrace their employees' enthusiasm for excellence and leverage the diligence and expertise of their workforce to build morale and engagement and to drive the quality agenda.

Patient Safety

Patient safety is an essential component of a comprehensive quality program in all healthcare organizations; administrative and clinical alignment is necessary for performance improvement in this arena. As research provides new findings about patient safety and the causes for procedural errors and policy breakdowns, senior leaders' responsibilities in this regard will continue to increase. Successful healthcare executives embrace their roles as safety change agents who are leading an organization's dynamic patient safety team (Birk, 2011). Among the groundbreaking initiatives to

Table 8.5 Public/Private Organizations That Influence Quality and Patient Safety Policy

Organization	Type	Mission/Focus
Agency for Healthcare Research and Quality (AHRQ)	One of 12 agencies in the U.S. Department of Health and Human Services.	Awards funds to support research to improve the quality, safety, efficiency, and effectiveness of health care for all Americans.
Institute for Healthcare Improvement (IHI)	Independent, not-for-profit organization.	Motivating and "building the will for change"; identifying and testing new models of care in partnership with both patients and healthcare professionals, and ensuring the broadest possible adoption of best practices and effective innovations.
Institute for Safe Medication Practices (ISMP)	Independent nonprofit, established in 1975.	Devoted entirely to medication error prevention and safe medication use.
Institute of Medicine (IOM)	Independent nonprofit, established in 1970.	Works outside of government to provide unbiased and authoritative advice to improve health to decision makers and the public.
Medicare Quality Improvement Organizations (QIOs)	Network of 53 organizations contracted with CMS. Responsible for each U.S. state, territory, and the District of Columbia.	Work with consumers, physicians, hospitals, and other caregivers to refine care delivery systems to ensure patients, particularly from underserved populations, receive "the right care at the right time."
National Quality Forum (NQF)	Independent, not-for-profit organization, founded in 1997. Collects funding from public and private sources.	Works to improve the safety of care provided to patients by building consensus on and partnering to promote and achieve national priorities and goals for performance improvement, endorsing national consensus standards for performance to be assessed and publicly reported, and promoting the attainment of national goals through education and outreach programs.

promote patient safety recently advanced by healthcare leaders are improving infection control practices, focusing on identifying and preventing medical errors, sharing knowledge about patient safety best practices with staff, implementing programs to reduce falls and injuries, and introducing information-technology-based safety checks (Cantlupe, 2011).

Organizational Culture

Organizational culture is defined by Hill and Jones (2012), as "the specific collection of values and norms that are shared by people and groups in an organization, and that control the way they interact with each other and with stakeholders outside the organization." Organizational cultures evolve over time and reflect the organization's mission, vision, and values and inform ways of communicating and behaving in the workplace. Quality is a critical value, as well as a goal, that should urgently infuse all aspects of an organization's culture. Successful leaders take dynamic action to promote quality as a key driver in their organizational cultures and to inspire a commitment to quality among their organizations' stakeholders.

The Joint Commission requires that healthcare leaders create and maintain a culture of safety and quality throughout their accredited hospitals (The Joint Commission, 2012). The accreditation agency understands that quality-focused leadership provides the foundation for effective performance and has identified specific standards associated with this expected leadership role.

- Leaders regularly evaluate the culture of safety and quality using valid and reliable tools.
- Leaders prioritize and implement necessary changes identified and indicated by the evaluation.
- Leaders provide opportunities for all individuals who work in the hospital to participate in safety and quality initiatives.
- Leaders develop a code of conduct that defines acceptable, disruptive, and inappropriate behaviors.
- Leaders create and implement a process for managing disruptive and inappropriate behaviors.
- Leaders provide education that focuses on safety and quality for all individuals.
- Leaders establish a team approach among all staff at all levels.
- All individuals who work in the hospital are able to openly discuss issues of safety and quality.
- Literature and advisories relevant to patient safety are available to all individuals who work in the hospital.
- Leaders define how members of the population served can help identify and manage issues of safety and quality within the hospital.

Organizational Framework

Competencies are a set of professional and personal skills, knowledge, values, and traits that guide a leader's performance, behavior, interaction, and decisions (Dye & Garman, 2006). They can be utilized to give developing leaders a means to identify the critical elements of effective leadership and to adopt the necessary skills and practices to achieve success. The National Association for Healthcare Quality (NAHQ) has developed a model to provide healthcare leaders with the knowledge and skills to lead successful quality improvement initiatives in their healthcare organizations (Garman & Scribner, 2011). This Quality Leadership Developmental Competency Model has analyzed and distinguished the skillsets and processes necessary at each level of leadership within an organization.

Leaders at all levels are tasked with maintaining *professionalism* and demonstrating outstanding *values, integrity, and performance.* Among the additional competencies necessary for entry-level leaders in the healthcare setting are vision, a focus on the future, engagement in lifelong learning, and effective consumer advocacy. When leaders move into mid-level roles, three other domains emerge as crucial for quality leadership. The first is *performance improvement*, which includes collecting and managing data, implementing analytical thinking and evidence-based decision making, and developing and promoting a knowledge-rich environment. The second is *communication and education*, which includes demonstrating excellent verbal, written, listening, and educating skills. The third is *self-management*, which includes maintaining a high standard of professional ethics, managing personal limits, and demonstrating resilience and self-restraint. Finally, for leaders who move to the senior levels of the organization, two additional domains are recommended. The first is *organizational awareness*, which includes utilizing and demonstrating systems thinking, strategic thinking and planning, and financial acumen. The second domain, *fostering positive change*, includes competencies such as advocating for and adapting to change, partnering for change, cultivating a quality-supportive climate, and driving results.

These six domains and their associated competencies can guide healthcare leaders to be more effective in their roles and develop capacity in the area of quality leadership (see **Figure 8.3**). The Quality Leadership Developmental Competency Model provides a basic framework for successful quality leadership, but additional factors such as a collaborative culture also contribute to quality leadership success.

Leverage Points

The Institute for Healthcare Improvement (IHI) recognizes that healthcare leaders need further guidance in developing and implementing their quality initiatives. They have outlined leverage points for leaders to consider how a small change can bring about substantial system-level positive results. These seven **leadership leverage points** can be used by healthcare

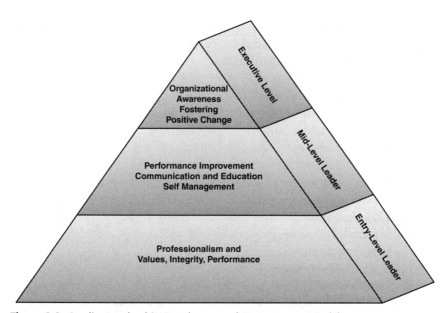

Figure 8.3 Quality Leadership Developmental Competency Model

Source: Adapted from National Association for Healthcare Quality Leadership Development Model. Retrieved November 30, 2012 from www.nahq.org/membership/leadership/devmodel.html.

executives to get maximum returns from their investments of time and effort (Reinertsen, Bisognano, & Pugh, 2008).

Leverage Point One: Establish and Oversee Specific System-Level Aims at the Highest Governance Level

An organization's mission statement may include a broad quality aim or goal. Additionally, senior executives should outline quality goals and objectives that apply to the entire organization. These goals could change or evolve, depending on the organization's needs and the healthcare environment. For example, for a hospital, a quality aim could be to reduce mortality; or for a clinic, to decrease the number of nonemergent visits to an Emergency Room. The organization's leader needs to commit personally and publicly to the stated aims and to communicate them effectively to all stakeholders.

Leverage Point Two: Develop an Executable Strategy to Achieve the System-Level Aims and Oversee Their Execution at the Highest Governance Level

Executive leaders must develop an achievable action plan for their quality initiatives. These key initiatives should be coordinated and monitored by senior executives as well as by lower-level leaders who can capably execute the necessary strategies to achieve the intended outcomes. Executives should not simply delegate quality initiatives to "the quality team" without continuing to provide oversight.

Leverage Point Three: Channel Leadership Attention to System-Level Improvement—Personal Leadership, Leadership Systems, and Transparency

If leaders call attention to specific initiatives, their organizations' employees are more likely to focus on these initiatives as well. Leaders need to demonstrate their commitment to an improvement strategy through their actions, including spending time informing and educating staff about the quality goals the strategy will serve. Systems that facilitate and support necessary changes at all levels of the organization need to be implemented, and reports of progress toward achievement of quality aims should be available to employees throughout the improvement process.

Leverage Point Four: Put Patients and Families on Improvement Teams

Engaging patients and families is critical to the success of quality improvement initiatives. Several ways to involve patients and families include asking these constituents to join quality improvement teams or to serve on permanent committees. Leaders and their designees can seek feedback and input from patients through surveys, personal communications and "rounds," and through comment solicitations. Patient input should be reported formally to managers and executives so that leaders can identify and address concerns as well as develop strategies to improve patient care.

Leverage Point Five: Make the Chief Financial Officer (CFO) a Quality Champion

Quality and financial performance are interrelated; high-quality services are likely to improve an organization's financial status through increased reimbursements, expanded business volume, partnership growth, and such. The CFO is integral to this process, as he or she controls the allocation of resources that can make or break an improvement strategy or initiative. Improvements that enhance value-based purchasing would also be under the CFO's purview and positively affect the company's bottom line; a CFO's enlistment and inclusion in quality improvement programs is therefore imperative.

Leverage Point Six: Engage Physicians

For quality initiatives to succeed, physicians must be actively involved in the quality improvement process. Aligned incentives are becoming more prevalent through Accountable Care Organizations, and healthcare leaders should educate and inform physicians about the benefits of quality improvement not only for the organization as a whole, but also for the doctors themselves. Additionally, many external stakeholders and agencies view physicians as business partners of healthcare organizations rather than as contracted "clients" and expect that physicians' responsibilities in the quality arena should equal those of hospital administrators. Some physicians may find this new healthcare landscape challenging and resist changing their perspectives and embracing quality improvement partnerships; providing physicians with an understanding of the advantages of participation and opportunities to contribute as early as possible is likely to promote engagement.

Leverage Point Seven: Build Improvement Capability

Executive healthcare leaders can originate a quality improvement program, but the program's development and implementation is best served by including capable leaders from every level of the organization. Additionally, enlistment of employees and clients is critical to the success of initiatives. Therefore, education, training, and information dissemination are critical for system-level improvement, as is recognition of achievement of outcomes and aims. Healthcare leaders must devote resources to establish skilled champions of improvement throughout the organization.

Move to Reliability

Leverage points have been identified that can improve quality in a healthcare system, but the industry is still challenged by the frequent inability of organizations to reliably maintain performance excellence over time. Some doubt that 100% reliability can be achieved, and others suggest its eventual attainment would be dependent on a combination of leadership commitment, fully implemented culture change, and adoption of robust process-improvement tools and methods (Chassin & Loeb, 2011). Health care is moving in the right direction, however, with its increased focus on developing new, improved, and more reliable quality improvement practices. Leadership's role in this evolution will be critical to a successful outcome (see **Table 8.6**).

Barriers

As healthcare organizations strive to improve their performance and quality outcomes, they often encounter barriers that may impair progress or derail the effort altogether. One of the key responsibilities of healthcare leaders in driving performance improvement is to identify and then remove these barriers (see **Table 8.7**).

Table 8.6 Leadership's Evolving Role in a Healthcare Organization's Path to Reliability

Early Minimal Stage	Developing Stage	Approaching Stage
Focus is on regulations and laws	CEO leads proactive quality agenda	Full organizational commitment
Strategic importance not recognized	Board reviews adverse events	Aim toward near zero failure rates
Quality metrics not utilized properly	Few measurable quality aims	Reward system for staff
Little support from information tech (IT)	IT supports some initiatives	IT integral to sustain initiatives
Physicians not actively engaged	Some physician champions	Physicians routinely lead efforts

Source: Adapted from Chassin, M. R., & Loeb, J. M. (2011). The ongoing quality improvement journey: Next stop, high reliability. *Health Affairs, 30*(4), 566. Exhibit 1.

Table 8.7 Barriers to Quality Improvement

Barriers	Description
Conflicting priorities	Lack of alignment of goals across the organization
Lack of commitment, complacency	Lack of urgency, motivation, engagement Rationale not compelling, lack of understanding
Lack of expertise, skepticism	Team composition issues and dysfunctionality Respected, persuasive leader needed
Organizational culture	Organization resists change; not a learning-focused culture
Physician buy-in and support	Lack of agreement with the need and/or plan Insufficient evidence to warrant action
Resistance to change	Perception that costs of change outweigh benefits Lacking organizational readiness or change-management skills
Resource constraints	Real or perceived limitations in: · Time to devote to the project · Quantity or quality of human resources · Funds and resources to support the project · Access to required information or materials
Technology	Lack of technology to support the changes

Strategies and Methods

The IOM publications, *To Err Is Human* and *Crossing the Quality Chasm* (2000), advanced the emphasis on quality and patient safety to the top of the healthcare agenda over a decade ago. The promotion of transparency through the public reporting of clinical performance metrics and significant patient harm events are additional factors that are providing motivation for providers and healthcare organizations to demonstrate outstanding results. As the champions of quality and patient safety, healthcare leaders must determine which strategies may be most effective in creating sustainable high performance. Some of the most frequently used strategies are summarized as follows.

Collaborative Learning and Improvement

In 1995, the IHI created a model for breakthrough improvement supported through collaborative learning. The model relies upon a short-term (usually 6–18 months) collaboration among a number of teams from various organizations seeking to improve care or services within a specific focused area. Together, the teams learn key principles of performance improvement as well as best practices, and have the opportunity to brainstorm and create innovative solutions for quality concerns. As the teams work on improvements at their organizations, they share their strategies, performance, progress and results across the collaborative (IHI, 2003). Regional and state trade associations, nonprofit disease-focused associations, quality and patient safety foundations/groups, and healthcare systems regularly conduct collaborative efforts modeled after the IHI's breakthrough series.

Lean

Lean methodology is based upon the Toyota Production System (TPS). It focuses on efficiency, removing waste (*muda*—anything unnecessary to produce the product or service) and on creating value. The seven types of waste identified are (1) overproduction, (2) waiting, time in queue, (3) transportation, (4) non-value-adding processes, (5) inventory, (6) motion, and (7) costs of quality: scrap, rework, and inspection.

Lean promotes "the customer first" by recommending the following steps: (1) define value as determined by the customer, (2) identify the value stream (set of actions required to bring a specific product or service from concept to completion), (3) make value-added steps flow from beginning to end, (4) let the customer pull the product from the supplier rather than push products, and (5) pursue perfection of the process (Ransom, Joshi, Nash, & Ransom, 2008).

Six Sigma

Motorola is largely credited with successfully developing and launching **Six Sigma**, which stemmed from the recognition that producing a high-quality product resulted in fewer repairs and improved customer satisfaction. After implementing Six Sigma in 1988, Motorola was among the first recipients of the Malcolm **Baldrige National Quality Award**. Six Sigma uses DMAIC (Define-Measure-Analyze-Improve-Control) as a framework for improvement and is supported by analytical and statistical tools (Kubiak & Benbow, 2009). Traditionally, Six Sigma focuses on eliminating defects, measured as defects per million opportunities (DPMO), in key business processes. Six Sigma is implemented by an infrastructure of trained leaders: "champions," "master black belts," "black belts," and "green belts," who attain certification after demonstrating expertise in the program methodology and completing black-belt projects.

Baldrige Performance Excellence

The Malcolm Baldrige National Quality Award was developed in 1987 by the U.S. Government to encourage American companies to adopt best practices and to make the changes necessary to become high performing and more competitive in the global market. In 1999, Congress passed an amendment that allowed additional sectors to apply for the award, such as nonprofits and healthcare industries. In 2002, the first healthcare organization received the Baldrige Award; today, the number of healthcare applicants for the Award exceeds all other sectors combined. Many healthcare organizations striving to achieve high performance have applied the Baldrige Framework and Criteria to their quality-improvement programs. The Baldrige Criteria for Performance Excellence include a set of questions within seven categories: (1) Leadership; (2) Strategic Planning; (3) Customer Focus; (4) Measurement, Analysis, and Knowledge Management; (5) Workforce Focus; (6) Operations Focus; and (7) Results (NIST, 2011).

Nursing Magnet Recognition Program

The **Nursing Magnet Recognition Program** is a credentialing program of the American Nurses Credentialing Center, which recognizes healthcare organizations that provide outstanding nursing care. The Magnet Recognition Program is considered to be the highest recognition for nursing excellence; fewer than 7% of hospitals have attained Magnet status (AHA, 2011). Obtaining this recognition is a strategy by which hospitals can position themselves more competitively, particularly in the areas of nursing recruitment and retention, improved patient care, safety, satisfaction and experience, and physician recruitment.

Tools for Alignment and Sustainability

To aid them in their quality journey, healthcare leaders can draw on a number of tools. Most valuable are tools to collect and analyze data and information to be used to assess performance of the organization's key processes, systems, and services. These tools allow leaders to evaluate their organizations' progress toward quality goals and to create effective

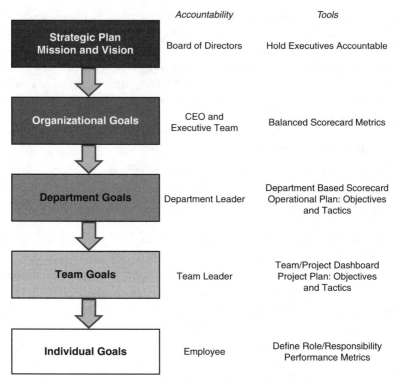

Figure 8.4 Cascading Organizational Goals

strategic decisions and action plans. Leaders can align goals and objectives throughout an organization and promote common understanding and complementary efforts by multiple units through building a cascade of strategic goals and key processes that begins at the organization-wide level and flows to the department level, and then to the team and individual levels (see **Figure 8.4**).

Balanced Scorecard

One approach utilized by businesses and healthcare organizations to draw organizational focus toward its strategic objectives is a **balanced scorecard**, which depicts the organization's key metrics as they relate to the organization's strategic goals. The origins of the balanced scorecard approach are attributed to Kaplan and Norton, authors of "The Balanced Scorecard— Measures that Drive Performance," in the January/February 1992 issue of the *Harvard Business Review*. The balanced scorecard management system aligns unit goals and metrics with organizational goals and provides an organizational and unit "dashboard" through which managers and leaders can monitor and evaluate progress toward quality goals.

Four key categories of balanced scorecard indicators have been identified: financial measures, customer measures, internal business (process) measures, and innovation and learning measures. Leaders can identify operational objectives within each of the four key categories for their units, which provide "balance" to the organization. This management system creates awareness and directionality throughout the organization toward common goals via a balanced, linked set of performance metrics and allows leaders to supervise the linkages and maintain organizational focus on achieving the desired results.

Many healthcare organizations have adopted a modified balanced scorecard approach, which identifies key result categories (also referred to as "pillars") such as finance, quality, service, people, and growth (Studer, 2003). As described previously, objectives can be established within each pillar category at all levels of the organization; then through a cascade, objectives at the organizational level, the departmental level, the team level, and the individual employee level can be linked. Employees are able to see how their contributions "fit into the big picture," and managers are able to supervise performance through metrics at each level and determine progress toward the organization's strategic aims.

Operational Plans

Operational plans are used as a roadmap of the various strategies and tactics a leader will deploy and implement in order to achieve his/her operational targets. By establishing operational targets at the department or unit level that support and link to the organization's strategic goals and objectives, the leaders create the "cascading" effect that communicates and demonstrates alignment across the organization. Designed and implemented effectively, these operational plans can assist employees at all levels of an organization in understanding their specific roles and duties that support the institutional goals and mission.

Performance Management Plan

Today's healthcare leaders are expected to facilitate an organizational culture of accountability. An effective performance management plan should be developed to establish a mechanism for ongoing formal and informal feedback between employees and their supervisors, and to guide and support managers and employees in developing and setting career goals and creating an individual development plan. Employees who achieve their individual developmental goals may then be further incentivized to achieve department/unit-based goals. These opportunities create an employee-employer win-win situation, which, if designed correctly, promotes departmental and organizational goals as well as those of the unit and the individual.

SUMMARY

A national strategy has been launched to improve healthcare quality by addressing the needs of patients, families, and communities; easing administrative burdens on care providers; and encouraging collaboration and communication among and between providers and their patients (U.S. Department of Health and Human Services, 2011). Improvements to the healthcare system will not be fully successful without dynamic healthcare leadership to set the course and steer the healthcare industry. This new landscape will demand skilled, knowledgeable, and creative leaders who can lead beyond their own organizations; leaders who will take an active role in collaborating with healthcare partners to promote quality improvement across the healthcare system.

Discussion Questions

1. How is healthcare reform influencing the creation of a quality-driven culture in organizations?
2. What style of leadership might be best suited for advancing a quality agenda?
3. How can leaders move their organizations to a state of continual performance reliability?
4. Would different healthcare sectors (i.e., acute, ambulatory, long-term care, etc.) have the same or different challenges associated with leading quality initiatives?
5. What can we learn from other industries to improve healthcare quality and patient safety?

Case Study: A Leadership Approach to Quality and Patient Safety

In response to the IHI's campaign to protect five million patients from harm and to a recommendation from the Daughters of Charity Health System's Task Force on Quality, the St. Francis Medical Center's Board of Directors created the Quality and Patient Safety Committee (QPS) in 2006. The QPS launched its efforts to enhance Board accountability for quality and patient safety by calling for improved performance in clinical quality, as reflected in the core measures; by aiming to reduce mortality (its "Big Dot," or overarching goal) through the adoption of best practices; by improving accountability across the organization and its units; by improving the comprehensiveness and timeliness of the peer review process; and by improving patient satisfaction and fostering a culture of patient safety. One of the first steps taken by the Board's QPS Committee was to educate itself about key quality and patient-safety initiatives and metrics, about the medical staff credentialing and reappointment process, and about patient satisfaction. To enhance Board and QPS member competency, the QPS Committee made a commitment to continuous learning, and sought knowledge about best practices and the principles of quality improvement and patient safety. Several members, physicians, and executive leaders made a site visit to a best practice facility and met with the facility's leaders to learn about their hospital's keys to achieving top performing results. Additionally, Board members attended IHI and Leapfrog Group conferences, which focused on the role of governing boards in driving quality outcomes. For example, an ongoing commitment to education is demonstrated not only through conference attendance but also through the regular provision and discussion of pertinent literature at each committee meeting.

The QPS explored and supported the adoption of several innovative strategies to foster a culture of quality and safety. These included crew resource management, QPS rounds, and the "Just Culture" approach[1] to errors. The crew resource management model was adapted from the techniques used by aerospace cockpit crews to promote effective teamwork and structured communication for enhanced patient safety. The QPS also began conducting rounds throughout the medical center prior to its monthly meetings. The rounds are used to create greater visibility for leadership's commitment to quality and safety, and provide an opportunity for QPS members to assess and validate the deployment of effective, patient/family-centered and evidence-based care practices at the bedside. Rounds have been made to various St. Francis units and clinics to interact with frontline staff, physicians and managers, and evaluate progress using tracer methodology.[2] Some areas assessed during rounds were core measure processes, pressure ulcer prevention, emergency department and hospital throughput, the case management process, and spiritual care. At its monthly meetings, the QPS reviews a dashboard of metrics that reflect clinical quality, patient

---

1. "Just Culture" is a model used to analyze errors, which allows healthcare leaders to consider the contributions of both human behavioral choices along with system design in determining the appropriate follow up. The Just Culture approach emphasizes individual accountability as part of the duty to prevent harm, to follow procedural rules, and to produce an outcome. For more information, go to www.justculture.org/.
2. Patient "tracers" are a technique developed by The Joint Commission that is used to evaluate a patient's care across a continuum of care in order to evaluate compliance to the standards. Surveyors and others use this approach to follow a care scenario, to determine if appropriate steps such as patient assessment, care, intervention, and education are provided at the various points of care for a particular patient. For more information go to www.jointcommission.org/facts_about_the_tracer_methodology/.

safety, and patient satisfaction/experience. The dashboard includes data to identify trends over time, actual performance as compared to organization targets, as well as benchmarks with top-performing healthcare institutions. The committee receives reports about significant untoward events, performance improvement initiatives, and patient complaints, as well as about medical staff peer review, credentialing, appointments, and reappointments.

In the years since its inception, the QPS has led efforts to engage physicians by creating aligned incentives such as the incorporation of performance goals in physician administrative contracts and the referral of core measure fall-outs for peer review. The QPS has supported physician leadership in their oversight of medical staff credentialing, proctoring, and tracking of medical staff performance data as part of their ongoing professional practice evaluation process. To ensure a continued focus on the patient and family experience, a family member representative was added to the committee as a voting member. To reinforce leadership accountability across the organization, the QPS invited department managers and directors to the QPS meetings to communicate their plans for improving their area's performance if their results were falling short of target.

As a result of these efforts, the St. Francis Medical Center has demonstrated significant improvements, including a 25% reduction in mortality, improved core-measure perfect-care scores, emergency department and hospital throughput improvement, a shift to performance-based medical staff reappointment, and the sharing of their best practices with others through publications in peer reviewed journals. As a founding member of the Premier QUEST program (focused on Quality, patient Experience, Safety, and Transparency), the St. Francis Medical Center achieved top performer status in mortality, core-measure perfect care, and cost per case.

Case Study Discussion Questions

1. Identify the stakeholders and drivers discussed in this case study who are involved with the improvement in quality and safety. Are there others who should be mentioned?
2. Which of the key strategies adopted by the St. Francis Quality and Patient Safety Committee do you think are the most effective for ongoing quality improvement?
3. What additional rounds can you suggest for the QPS team besides the ones already mentioned?
4. What other measures can be used to assess the quality and patient safety at St. Francis Medical Center?

RELATED WEBSITES

Agency for Healthcare Research and Quality (AHRQ): www.ahrq.gov/

American Nurses Credentialing Center (ANCC): www.nursecredentialing.org /Magnet.aspx

American Society for Quality (ASQ): http://asq.org

Baldrige Performance Excellence Program: www.nist.gov/baldrige/enter/health _care.cfm

Center for Medicare & Medicaid Services (CMS): www.cms.gov

Det Norske Veritas Healthcare (DNV): www.dnvhealthcare.com/

Institute for Healthcare Improvement (IHI): www.ihi.org/about/pages/default.aspx

Institute of Medicine (IOM): www.iom.edu/

Institute for Patient- and Family-Centered Care (IPFCC): www.ipfcc.org

The Joint Commission: www.jointcommission.org/

The Leapfrog Group: www.leapfroggroup.org/home

National Association for Healthcare Quality (NAHQ): www.nahq.org/membership /leadership/devmodel.html

National Database of Nursing Quality Indicators (NDNQI): www.nursingquality .org/

National Quality Forum (NQF): www.qualityforum.org/Home.aspx

Premier, Inc.: www.premierinc.com/safety/

REFERENCES

American Hospital Association (AHA) and Health Research & Educational Trust (HRET). (2011, July). *Allied Hospital Association Leadership for Quality—2011.* Chicago, IL: Author.

American Hospital Association (AHA) Resource Center Blog. (2011, March). Retrieved October 22, 2012 from http://aharesourcecenter.wordpress.com /2011/03/22/magnet-status-is-it-worth-it/.

Belmont, E., Haltom, C. C., Hastings, D. A., Homchick, R. G., Morris, L., Taitsman, J., . . . Peisert, K. C. (2011). A new quality compass: Hospital boards' increased role under the Affordable Care Act. *Health Affairs, 30*(7), 1282–1289.

Birk, S. (2011). The patient safety team: Healthcare executives embrace their role. *Healthcare Executive, 26*(5), 13–22.

California Department of Public Health. (2007). *Reporting of adverse events AFL 07-10.* Retrieved on October 14, 2012 from www.cdph.ca.gov/certlic/facilities /Documents/LNC-AFL-07-10.pdf.

Cantlupe, J. (2011). Who "owns" patient safety? *HealthLeaders, 14*(5), 3–40.

Chassin, M. R., & Loeb, J. M. (2011). The ongoing quality improvement journey: Next stop, high reliability. *Health Affairs, 30*(4), 559–568.

Dye, C. F., & Garman, A. N. (2006). *Exceptional leadership: 16 critical competencies for healthcare executives.* Chicago, IL: Health Administration Press.

Galvin, R. S., Delbanco, S., Milstein, A., & Belden, G. (2005). Has the Leapfrog Group had an impact on the health care market? *Health Affairs, 24*(1), 228-233.

Garman, A., & Scribner, L. (2011). Leading for quality in healthcare: Development and validation of a competency model. *Journal of Healthcare Management, 56*(6), 373-382.

HealthLeaders Media Industry Survey. (2011a). *Overall cross-sector survey.* Retrieved October 14, 2012 from www.healthleadersmedia.com/pdf/survey _project/2011/Overall_Cross_Sector_press.pdf.

HealthLeaders Media Industry Survey. (2011b). *Physicians leaders.* Retrieved October 14, 2012 from www.healthleadersmedia.com/pdf/survey_project/2011 /Physician_press.pdf.

Hill, C. W., & Jones, G. R. (2012). *Strategic management theory* (10th ed.). Boston, MA: South-Western College Publishing.

Institute for Healthcare Improvement (IHI). (2003). *The Breakthrough series: IHI's collaborative model for achieving breakthrough improvement.* IHI Innovation Series white paper. Boston, MA: Institute for Healthcare Improvement. Retrieved October 14, 2012 from www.doh.wa.gov/Portals/1/Documents/1000/PMC -IHI-BreakthoughSeries2003.pdf.

Institute for Patient- and Family-Centered Care. (2010, October). *Framework for patient and family involvement in quality improvement.* Bethesda, MD: Institute for Patient- and Family-Centered Care.

Institute of Medicine (IOM). (2000). *To err Is human: Building a safer health system.* L. T. Kohn, J. M. Corrigan, M. S. Donaldson, eds. Washington, DC: National Academies Press.

Institute of Medicine (IOM). (2001). *Crossing the quality chasm: A new health system for the 21st century.* Washington, DC: National Academies Press.

Jiang, H., Lockee, C., Bass, K., & Fraser, I. (2008). Board engagement in quality: Findings of a survey of hospital and system leaders. *Journal of Healthcare Management, 53*(2), 121-133.

Jiang, H., Lockee, C., & Fraser, I. (2012). Enhancing board oversight on quality of hospital care: An agency theory perspective. *Health Care Management Review, 37*(2), 144-153.

The Joint Commission. (2011). *Improving America's hospitals: The Joint Commission's annual report on quality and safety 2011.* Retrieved October 14, 2012 from www .jointcommission.org/2011_annual_report/.

The Joint Commission. (2012). *Hospital accreditation standards.* Oakbrook Terrace, IL: Joint Commission Resources.

Kaplan, R. S., & Norton, D. P. (1992, January/February). The balanced scorecard—Measures that drive performance. *Harvard Business Review, 70*(1), 71-79.

Kocher, R., & Sahni, N. R. (2010). Physicians versus hospitals as leaders of account-able care organizations. *New England Journal of Medicine, 363*(26), 2579-2582.

Kubiak, T. M. & Benbow, D. (2009). *The certified Six Sigma black belt handbook* (2nd ed.). Milwaukee, WI: American Society for Quality, Quality Press.

National Institute of Standards and Technology (NIST). (2011). *Baldrige 2020: An executive's guide to the criteria for performance excellence.* Retrieved October 14, 2012 from www.nist.gov/baldrige/publications/upload/Baldrige_20_20.pdf.

Pronovost, P., Thompson, D. A., Holzmueller, C. G, Domran, T., & Morlock, L. L. (2007). Impact of the Leapfrog Group's intensive care unit physician staffing standard. *Journal of Critical Care, 22*(2), 89–96.

Ransom, E. R, Joshi, M. S., Nash, D. B., & Ransom, S. B. (2008). *The healthcare quality book: Vision, strategy, and tools* (2nd ed.). Chicago, IL: Health Administration Press.

Reinertsen, J. L., Bisognano, M., & Pugh, M. D. (2008). *Seven leadership leverage points for organization-level improvement in health care* (2nd ed.). IHI Innovation Series white paper. Cambridge, MA: Institute for Healthcare Improvement.

Rubino, L., & Chan, M. (2008). Quality and patient safety from the top: A case study of St. Francis Medical Center governing board's call to action. *Patient Safety and Health Care Management Advances in Health Care Management, 7,* 99–122.

Studer, Q. (2003) *Hardwiring excellence.* Gulf Breeze, FL: Fire Starter.

Taylor, J., & Rutherford, P. (2010). The pursuit of genuine partnerships with patients and family members: The challenge and opportunity for executive leaders. *Frontiers, 26*(4), 3–14.

U.S. Department of Health and Human Services. (2011). *Report to Congress: National Strategy for Quality Improvement in Health Care.* Retrieved October 14, 2012 from www.ahrq.gov/workingforquality/nqs/nqsplans.pdf.

Chapter 9

Collaborative Leadership

Nancy Borkowski and Barbara Perez Deppman

LEARNING OBJECTIVES

By the end of this chapter, the student will be able to:

- Define collaborative leadership.
- Identify the characteristics, skills, and behaviors of a collaborative leader.
- Define and explain how collaborative leadership strategies are interrelated.
- Describe different ways to build collaborative leadership skills.

KEY TERMS

Collaborative alliances

Collaborative leadership

Community collaborators

Emotional intelligence

Healthcare Executive Competencies Assessment Tool

Healthcare Leadership Alliance

Servant leadership

Transformational leaders

Turning Point Leadership Development National Excellence Collaborative

INTRODUCTION

After the publication of Rosabeth Moss Kanter's 1994 article on the advantages of collaboration, the term **collaborative leadership** was coined to describe the leadership skills and attributes needed to successfully develop and manage interorganizational strategic alliances and other forms of partnership. Archer and Cameron (2008) stated that a collaborative leader's basic task is to achieve positive outcomes for common objectives among different organizations. For example, a collaborative manager of a county's department of disaster/emergency management must effectively lead and coordinate the emergency responses of multiple organizations, government agencies, and community resources before, during, and after an emergency or disaster. Given the different cultures and goals among organizations, promoting effective collaboration can be a challenging task!

Traditionally, leadership is described as one's ability to move an organization toward its strategic goals by influencing other organizational members to participate in a collaborative effort to achieve corporate success and economic sustainability (Borkowski, 2011). Collaborative leadership is more complex because it requires a leader to achieve success by motivating individuals in multiple organizations, in addition to bringing together and aligning the goals of many stakeholders. However, in many circumstances, these stakeholders may be engaged in adversarial relationships because they hold different perspectives of their mission, vision, objectives, and concerns. As such, leaders need to overcome common challenges when facilitating collaborative endeavors. These challenges include disagreement among stakeholders regarding the definition of the problem, varying interests, resources and knowledge bases, and past history of unsuccessful collaborative attempts (see **Table 9.1**).

In today's complex and competitive healthcare environment, collaborative relationships allow organizations to achieve better outcomes by obtaining knowledge, skills, technology, or other essential resources that a single organization cannot provide on its own (Kanter, 1994). Collaborative

Table 9.1 Common Challenges Encountered by Collaborative Leaders

Conflict	Disagreement among stakeholders about how the problems/issues should be defined. For example, issues may be multifaceted, technically complex, or under scientific debate.
Lack of coordination	Lack of systematic organization among stakeholders with common, vested interests in specific issues/problems.
Varying resources among stakeholders	Stakeholders have different skills, tools, and resources to deal with issues and problems. For example, differences in levels of authority and influence, different knowledge bases, and disparities in human and financial resources.
Prior relationships	A history of unsuccessful efforts by stakeholders to address these problems/issues, perhaps due to insufficient processes or resources available independently.

Source: Courtesy of London, S. (1995). *Collaboration and community*. A report prepared for the Pew Partnership for Civic Change. Retrieved November 9, 2012 from www.scottlondon.com/reports/collaboration.pdf.

partnerships bring together individuals with very different knowledge bases, attitudes, and assumptions. Each partner possesses unique knowledge and skills that can benefit the others. As partners organize, plan strategies, and move forward, they create learning opportunities for themselves and each other (North Central Regional Educational Laboratory, n.d.).

Rubin (2009, p. 2) states that a "collaboration is a purposeful relationship in which all parties strategically choose to cooperate in order to accomplish a shared outcome." The newly established New York Genome Center (NYGC, 2012) is an example of how, under highly effective collaborative leadership, an ecosystem from previously fragmented and competitive healthcare sectors can be formed with the goals of improved patient outcomes and the delivery of personalized medicine. NYGC, a public–private coalition of competitors—universities, medical centers, technology firms, and pharmaceutical companies—have joined together in a cooperative effort to transform medical research and clinical care. Under NYGC's efforts, stakeholders such as healthcare managers, scientists, clinicians, policymakers, payers, and patients are engaged in information-enabled common projects for therapeutic and diagnostic product development.

Collaborative leadership was first identified with the growth of strategic alliances among private corporations as well as with the formation of social partnerships (i.e., alliances between independent organizations in the public and private sectors). As healthcare reform moves the industry from segment-based delivery models to integrated systems such as accountable care organizations (ACOs), collaborative leadership becomes critical to organizational success. The leader of an ACO is expected to integrate and coordinate the various component parts of health care, such as primary care, specialty services, hospitals, and home health care; and to ensure that all "parts function well together" to deliver efficient, high quality, and cost-effective patient-centered care. Managers of 21st-century healthcare organizations must be able to lead diverse groups of people and facilitate their professional efforts and problem solving both within an organization as well as across formal organizational boundaries.

CHARACTERISTICS OF A COLLABORATIVE LEADER

In today's complex and ever-changing healthcare environment, **collaborative alliances** are emerging as the preferred model for complex problem solving or "getting the job done," especially when diverse stakeholders address issues that affect broad segments of an organization or community. To promote collaborative problem solving among stakeholders, the healthcare manager should demonstrate specific behaviors, including:

1. Confidence that the goals and objectives are achievable.
2. The skills to clearly communicate with the stakeholders regarding the issues needing to be addressed and the potential approaches to problem solving.
3. The ability to serve as an active listener.
4. The ability to share knowledge and authority with the collaborators.
5. The ability to assess and handle varying levels of risk in decision making and implementation (Carter, 2006).

Through their extensive research, Chrislip and Larson (1994, pp. 138–146) discovered that certain principles were displayed by leaders who excelled as **community collaborators**. For example, these leaders influence diverse groups to work together, assist with the group's problem solving process, and provide the necessary resources for the group to achieve its goals (see **Table 9.2**).

Building on Chrislip and Larson's (1994) work, as well as Van Wart's (2005) research in public administrators' competencies, Morse (2008) developed a comprehensive set of traits and skills necessary for successful collaborative leadership (see **Table 9.3**).

Table 9.2 Principles Displayed by Community Collaborative Leaders

Inspire commitment and action	Collaborative leaders bring people together when incremental or unilateral efforts are not working. They are action oriented, but much of the action they drive involves influencing others to achieve a specific goal rather than telling others what needs to be done or doing the work themselves.
Lead as peer problem solvers	Collaborative leaders guide others so the entire group can work as team to problem solve. They avoid engaging in autocratic management behaviors.
Build broad-based involvement	Collaborative leaders make a conscious and disciplined effort to identify and bring together all relevant stakeholders.
Sustain hope and participation	Collaborative leaders communicate that each participant brings value and strengths to the group effort, assist in developing short-term and long-term goals, and celebrate the group's achievements throughout the problem solving process.
Lead as "servants"	Collaborative leaders serve the group members by providing the resources necessary to meet the participants' internal and external needs.
View leadership as a process	Collaborative leaders safeguard the collaborative process that facilitates productive and rewarding working relationships among the participants and stakeholders.

Source: Reproduced from Chrislip, D. D., & Larson, C. E. (1994). *Collaborative leadership: How citizens and civic leaders can make a difference.* San Francisco, CA: Jossey-Bass.

Table 9.3 Traits and Skills of Collaborative Leaders

Traits	Skills
Self-confidence	Communication
Decisiveness	Social
Resilience	Influence
Energy	Analytic
Need for achievement	Technical
Willingness to assume responsibility	Continual learning
Flexibility	Self-management
Service mentality	Strategic thinking
Personal integrity	Facilitation
Emotional maturity	
Collaborative mindset	
Passion toward outcomes	
Systems thinking	
Openness	
Risk-taking	
Sense of mutuality and connectedness	
Humility	

Source: Adapted from Morse, R. S. (2007). *Developing public leaders in an age of collaborative governance*. University of Delaware, Institute for Public Administration. Retrieved November 9, 2012 from www.ipa.udel.edu/3tad/papers/workshop4/Morse.pdf.

There are many similarities among the behaviors, traits, and skills observed in various organizational leadership styles. Many equate collaborative leadership with transformational and **servant leadership** styles because of the various characteristics displayed by these leaders. As examples, **transformational leaders** provide followers with a vision and motivate them to go beyond self-interest for the good of the organization (Osland, Kolb, & Rubin, 2001). Transformational style leadership is about value-driven change, innovation, improvement, and entrepreneurship through vision and inspiration. Transformational leadership incorporates both direct and indirect influence through a variety of mechanisms, which affect the intellectual, emotional, and behavioral processes of the followers. Servant leadership is an approach to managing people that "begins with a clear and compelling vision that excites passion in the leader and commitment in those who follow" (Blanchard & Hodges, 2003). A servant leader values others' strengths and talents and encourages the use of these strengths and talents for the betterment of the organization.

Although collaborative leadership has much in common with both transformational and servant leadership theories, there are also many differences. One of the main differences is that collaborative leaders must be able to achieve success through alliances with people and resources beyond their direct reporting control. As Lindon (2003, p. 42) points out, "By definition, collaborative leaders have no formal authority over their peers. They must use persuasion, technical competence, relationship skills, and political smarts to get and keep the coalition together and produce the desired goal." As an example, in 1961, President Kennedy announced his famous goal to place a 'man on the moon' by the end of the decade. He motivated and unified the public, inspiring Americans to set aside their own agendas and ideologies to achieve a successful moon landing in 1969 (Hansen, 2009).

Emotional Intelligence

Emotional intelligence (EI) is a leadership attribute that is viewed as increasingly critical to an individual's social effectiveness. When an individual is more socially effective, he or she is more adept at achieving successful collaborative outcomes (Cox, 2011).

Emotional intelligence involves the self-assessment of one's own feelings and the interpretation of others' feelings, which help to guide one's thinking and action. EI has five distinct competencies:

1. Self-awareness
2. Self-management or regulation
3. Self-motivation
4. Empathy or social awareness
5. Social skills

Goleman (1998, p. 318) identified that *self-awareness* involves having knowledge and understanding of one's true feelings at any given moment. *Self-management* requires that managers control their emotions so they can focus on problem solving and assist with necessary processes and tasks. *Self-motivation* allows the manager to stay focused on the specified goals and desired outcomes and to overcome negative emotional stimuli and accept delayed gratification. *Empathy* is the ability to perceive what others feel and want, expressing sensitivity to their needs and perspectives. Finally, *social skills* relate to one's ability to "read" others and interact effectively in social situations, guiding and influencing others' perspectives and behaviors.

Using the Myers-Briggs personality preference profile, Goldman and Kahnweiler (2000) discovered that successful collaborative leaders are more likely to have high scores on the "feeling" index rather than the "thinking" index. The researchers noted that "the essential ingredients for collaborative leaders' success were flexibility, patience, understanding of others' viewpoints, sensitivity to diversity, and a cooperative spirit" (p. 449).

STRATEGIES FOR A COLLABORATIVE LEADER

The **Turning Point Leadership Development National Excellence Collaborative** (2006) identified six key practices or strategies that are unique to leading a collaborative process:

1. Assess the environment for collaboration
2. Create clarity
3. Build trust and create safety
4. Share power and influence
5. Develop people
6. Self-reflection

Each of the six strategies is a key element in the collaborative process, but the strategies are also interrelated and provide a comprehensive overview of the necessary steps for leaders to guide successful collaborations (see **Table 9.4**).

BUILDING COLLABORATIVE LEADER SKILLS

With the value of collaborative leadership having been demonstrated, the good news is that collaborative leadership skills can be learned by dedicated leaders who commit the necessary time and effort. Leadership skill development for healthcare managers has been widely implemented over the past decade. Beginning in 2003, the **Healthcare Leadership Alliance** (HLA), a consortium of six major professional membership organizations, identified competencies that support excellence in healthcare management across diverse professional roles. Through job analyses and research, HLA identified 300 competencies (skills or areas of knowledge) within five major categories:

1. Leadership
2. Communications and relationship management
3. Professionalism, structure, and functions
4. Business knowledge and skills
5. Knowledge of the healthcare environment

Drawing upon this HLA framework, the American College of Healthcare Executives (ACHE) developed a **Healthcare Executive Competencies**

Table 9.4 Necessary Steps for Leaders to Guide Successful Collaborations

Strategies	Action
1. Assess the Environment	A collaborative leader should be able to recognize common interests and understand others' perspectives. Collaboration promotes goal attainment around shared visions, purposes, and value. When different points of view on or regarding an issue or problem are addressed, a collaborative leader facilitates connections and encourages group thinking, which identifies clear, positive change for all participants. The first priority is to set goals. The second priority is to identify the barriers and obstacles to achieving the goals.
2. Create Clarity	Having and communicating the "clarity of purpose" (i.e., shared vision) is a quality that characterizes collaborative leaders. Clarity allows the group members to focus so their energy can be directed toward problem solving. Visioning in relation to clarity involves making a commitment to a process or a way of doing things. Mobilizing refers to helping people develop the confidence to take action and sustain their energies through difficult times.
3. Build Trust	The collaborative leader must have the ability to promote and sustain trust between and among the participants for the sharing of innovative approaches. If a collaborative leader fails to engender trust and openness among participants, best ideas and innovative approaches for problem solving will not be developed or shared by the group.
4. Share Power and Influence	The collaborative leader must allow the participants to be empowered to fully contribute in the decision-making process. Rather than being concerned about losing power through collaboration, the leader needs to recognize that sharing power actually generates strength.
5. Develop People	The collaborative leader needs to bring out the best in others, maximize the use of other people's talents and resources, build power through sharing power, and cede authoritarian ownership or control. By doing so, the leader increases others' leadership capacities by encouraging experimentation, goal setting, and performance feedback.
6. Self-Reflection	Successful collaborative leaders demonstrate high levels of EI or maturity. Through self-reflection, leaders can examine and understand their values and assess whether their behaviors are congruent with their values. In addition, successful leaders critically consider the impact their actions and words have on the group's progress toward achieving its goals and adjust their behaviors if necessary.

Source: From Turning Point, a national program of the Robert Wood Johnson Foundation from 1996–2006. Used with permission from the Robert Wood Johnson Foundation in Princeton, New Jersey.

Assessment Tool to assist managers in identifying areas of strength as well as areas in which they may wish to improve their performance.

To begin the process of leadership skill development, managers need to identify personal developmental needs, gain a better understanding of how their own and others' behavioral styles influence leadership style, and develop their own leadership philosophy.

To identify personal developmental needs, leaders can engage in a self-reflection process by completing a personal SWOT matrix. In the SWOT matrix, leaders list their:

1. **Strengths** and positive characteristics
2. **Weaknesses** and negative characteristics
3. Dreams, wishes, or goals (**opportunities**);
4. Barriers preventing the advancement toward personal goals (**threats**); see **Figure 9.1**.

In this self-assessment process, there are no right or wrong answers, but honest answers are necessary in order to guide leadership development.

Your strengths and positive characteristics	Your areas needing development
1.	1.
2.	2.
3.	3.
4.	4.
5.	5.
Dreams, wishes or goals you have for yourself (growth opportunities)	**The barriers that are preventing you from reaching your dreams or achieving your goals (e.g., threats or factors that cause a resistance to change)**
1.	1.
2.	2.
3.	3.
4.	4.
5.	5.

Figure 9.1 Personal SWOT Matrix

To complete the SWOT Matrix and to obtain a better understanding of how behavioral patterns influence one's leadership style, leaders are encouraged to obtain anonymous multirater feedback from peers and colleagues, subordinates, and supervisors from current and previous positions. Multirater feedback is a valuable method for individuals to gain insight into their strengths and weaknesses as perceived by others.

Additional leadership development tools include self-assessments of one's professional relationships and interactions with others and provide awareness of how one's own behavioral patterns influence one's leadership style. Many instruments are used in the workplace to assess behavioral patterns that can impact leadership styles. For example, the Myers-Briggs Type Indicator (MBTI) is an instrument that assesses personality types and identifies individual preferences across the spectrums of four dimensions (extraversion/introversion, sensate/intuitive, thinking/feeling, and judging/perceiving). These self-reported preferences and characteristics are useful in assessing leadership strengths and styles and can be utilized to support and enhance managers' training and skills development (Borkowski, 2011).

Through self-assessments and self-reflection, individuals develop their own leadership philosophy. A leadership philosophy is a guiding set of principles that incorporate an individual's values and vision as to personal and professional development. One's philosophy helps an individual "stay on track" as he or she grows as a professional and provides the framework to guide one's actions when interacting with others and making decisions throughout one's career.

POTENTIAL PITFALLS IN COLLABORATIVE LEADERSHIP

The Work Group for Community Health and Development at the University of Kansas notes that despite the many advantages of collaborative leadership, disadvantages also exist. Some of the challenges associated with collaborative leadership are:

1. Collaboration may be a slow and time-consuming process
2. There may be a high degree of conflict requiring management and mediation
3. Collaborative leaders may need to cede some of their power and authority to the partnership and credit the group rather than themselves for the positive outcomes achieved

Collaborative decision making may take longer because large groups of participants and stakeholders may proceed slowly and bring multiple "private" agendas to the table, which can lead to significant conflicts. Collaborative leaders can help mediate when conflicts arise and refocus the group toward achieving the agreed-upon objectives. Of course, collaborative leaders must always remain alert to not force their own biases and demands into the problem-solving process, but instead promote an open and inclusive process that guides the group to achieve its goals, strategies, and implementation plans.

SUMMARY

Collaborative leadership is a valuable tool to promote synergy and successful outcomes in today's complex healthcare environment. Though collaboration can be challenging, the advantages of collaborative management within an organization and across entities can outweigh the potential difficulties. The movement toward accountable care organizations will require that leaders add managing collaboration to their skill set for the benefit of their organizations, patients, and communities. As such, tomorrow's healthcare collaborative leaders will need to demonstrate a vision-based, systems-thinking, power-sharing leadership style.

Discussion Questions

1. Explain the increasing importance of collaborative leadership in today's complex and changing healthcare industry.
2. Discuss the interrelatedness of the six key practices/strategies for guiding a successful collaboration. Is one practice/strategy more important than another? If yes, why? If no, why not?
3. Which segment of the health industry do you think would benefit most from using a collaborative leadership style? Why? Explain by using examples.
4. Why is a high degree of emotional intelligence (EI) essential for an individual to be a successful collaborative leader?
5. Why does self-assessment play such an important role in the practice of collaborative leadership?

Case Study #1: Barnabas Medical Center

Barnabas Medical Center (BMC) is a tertiary-care academic medical center with a Level One trauma center and serves not only as the community's safety net, but also as a training center for the U.S. Armed Forces. BMC is renowned for its excellence in care for acutely ill or injured patients. The organization's emergency department (ED) treats over 120,000 adults and children annually, but has the reputation within the local community of imposing very long wait times.

Dr. Antonio "Tony" Mornan, BMC's new Associate Chief Medical Officer, was challenged to reduce the time a patient is in the ED from 24 hours to 6 hours, calculated from initial intake to either admission or discharge. Dr. Tony was aware that patients' ED experiences included services from many different departments and stakeholders, such as registration, radiology, laboratory, the hospitalist service, and the university medical teams. These services were being delivered through a fragmented system; that is, each service was providing health care to patients independently. Despite hearing his staff report that "that's the way it's always been," Dr. Tony knew that systemic change was necessary to deliver more efficient and effective care to the patient. However, as none of these departments directly reported to him, Dr. Tony did not have the authority to mandate such changes.

Dr. Tony opted to use collaborative leadership to address the challenge. Initially, he set up several workshops in which individuals from the relevant departments could discuss their issues and difficulties with regard to achieving the shared goal—efficient patient-centered care. This sharing of information resulted in the development of a workflow chart identifying inefficiencies, slow communication channels, underutilization of the system's technology, and other problems contributing to the patient care delays. Participants were encouraged to contribute suggested solutions to these concerns.

Dr. Tony's next step was to lead a series of meetings in which the various department managers were brought together to discuss how each department's services impacted other departments, as well as how each department might provide its services more efficiently. For example, the radiology department was tasked with reducing the time from a clinician's order to the start of an imaging study. However, the workflow analysis showed that there were a number of intermediate steps, such as nurse staffing and availability as well as insurance authorization, that slowed the process and were out of the radiology department's control. Under Dr. Tony's guidance, discussions and workshops continued among the clinicians and the managers of the relevant departments with the shared goal of reducing the span between the radiology procedures' order and the imaging start times.

Within 2 months, through this collaborative problem-solving effort, patients' ED times were significantly reduced and patient satisfaction scores improved.

Case Study Discussion Questions

1. What were the driving forces behind the success of this collaborative effort?

2. What were the "boundaries" that posed challenges to this collaborative effort?

3. Who were/are the leaders? What characteristics do you think were displayed by the leader(s) of this collaborative effort that led to its success?

4. Discuss the factors that contributed to the success of this collaborative effort.

Case #2: Willow Springs Memorial Hospital[1]

Dr. Solomon Till has just recently been appointed the new president of Willow Springs Memorial, the only hospital in Willow Springs. Dr. Till has lived in Willow Springs for the past 5 years and has been an active member of the community. Prior to being appointed hospital president, he served as the director of development. Dr. Till is excited about his new appointment and has come to think of Willow Springs as home. He is eager for the opportunity to help his residents achieve the best health possible.

During his first week as president, the state announced a budget shortfall and a plan to reduce Medicaid expenditures by 22%. Because almost one-third of the revenue at Willow Springs Memorial is from Medicaid, this change could result in a significant "setback" for the hospital.

Additionally, Dr. Till is aware that the hospital board and many physicians on staff are concerned that Willow Springs Memorial does not have the ability to perform some of the latest procedures in medicine. They want Willow Springs Memorial to be as "technologically advanced" as any hospital in the state. He was hired to "fix these problems" quickly.

Dr. Till has decided that one of the first things on his agenda as the new president of Willow Springs Memorial is to reach out and listen to the residents of Willow Springs about what they need and want from a hospital. He has arranged to attend a series of six events in town, such as church meetings, Rotary Club meetings, senior center lunches, and the like, where he can engage directly with the residents. He has invited a hospital board member and a medical staff member to join him at each of these meetings to listen to the community input. Dr. Till has also asked the county health department director to collaborate on this project by providing additional

---

1. From Turning Point, a national program of the Robert Wood Johnson Foundation from 1996–2006. Used with permission from the Robert Wood Johnson Foundation in Princeton, New Jersey.

assessment information, participating in the outreach events, and to implement community assessment and documentation and analysis of findings.

Through this broad collaborative process, Dr. Till is optimistic that he can facilitate the development of a shared vision of health in Willow Springs and promote Willow Springs Memorial's role in maintaining a healthy community.

Case Study Discussion Questions

1. What were the "boundaries" that posed challenges to this collaborative effort?
2. Who were/are the leaders? What characteristics do you think were displayed by the leader(s) of this collaborative effort that led to its success?
3. Discuss the various stakeholders who can contribute to or create barriers for the success of this collaborative effort.

RELATED WEBSITES

American College of Healthcare Executives: www.ache.org

Healthcare Leadership Alliance: www.healthcareleadershipalliance.org

New York Genome Center: http://nygenome.org/

Turning Point Leadership Development National Excellence Collaborative: www.collaborativeleadership.org/

Work Group for Community Health and Development: www.communityhealth.ku.edu/

OTHER SUGGESTED READINGS

Ferren, A. S., & Stanton, W. W. (2004). *Leadership through collaboration*. Westport, CT: Praeger.

Freshman, B., Rubino, L., & Chassiakos, Y. R. (2010). *Collaboration across the disciplines in healthcare care*. Sudbury, MA: Jones & Bartlett Learning.

Goleman, D. (1995). *Emotional intelligence: Why it can matter more than IQ*. New York, NY: Bantam.

Hambrick, D. C., Nadler, D. A., & Tushamn, M. L. (1998). *Navigating change*. Boston, MA: Harvard Business School Press.

Hesselbein, F., Goldsmith, M., & Beckhard, R. (1997). *The organization of the future*. San Francisco, CA: Jossey-Bass.

Lank, E. (2006). *Collaborative advantage*. New York, NY. Palgrave MacMillan.

Lyman, L. L., Ashby, D. E., & Tripses, J. S. (2005). *Leaders who dare: Pushing the boundaries.* Lanham, MD: Rowman & Littlefield Education.

Maccoby, M. (2007). *The leaders we need and what makes us follow.* Boston, MA: Harvard Business School Press.

Marshall, E. (1995). *Transforming the way we work: The power of the collaborative workplace.* New York, NY: AMACOM.

Seifter, H., & Economy, P. (2001). *Leadership ensemble: Lessons in collaborative management from the world's only conductorless orchestra.* New York, NY: Henry Holt.

REFERENCES

Archer, D., & Cameron, A. (2008). *Collaborative leadership: How to succeed in an interconnected world.* Maryland Heights, MO: Butterworth Heinemann.

Blanchard, K., & Hodges, P. (2003, May 12). The journey to servant leadership in work, life. *San Diego Business Journal,* p. A2.

Borkowski, N. (2011). *Organizational behavior in healthcare.* Burlington, MA: Jones & Bartlett Learning.

Carter, M. (2006). The importance of collaborative leadership in achieving effective criminal justice outcomes. *Center for Effective Public Policy.* Retrieved November 6, 2012 from http://nicic.gov/Library/021201.

Chrislip, D. D., & Larson, C. E. (1994). *Collaborative leadership: How citizens and civic leaders can make a difference.* San Francisco, CA: Jossey-Bass.

Cox, J. D. (2011, February). *Emotional intelligence and its role in collaboration.* Proceedings of the American Society of Business and Behavioral Sciences (ASBBS) annual meeting, 18(1), Las Vegas, NV. Retrieved November 6, 2012 from http://asbbs .org/files/2011/ASBBS2011v1/PDF/C/CoxJ.pdf.

Goldman, S., & Kahnweiler, W. (2000). A collaborator profile for executives of nonprofit organizations. *Nonprofit Management & Leadership, 10,* 435–450.

Goleman, D. (1998). *Working with emotional intelligence.* New York, NY: Bantam.

Hansen, M. T. (2009). *Collaboration: How leaders avoid the traps, create unity, and reap big results.* Boston, MA: Harvard Business School Press.

Kanter, R. M. (1994, July/August). Collaborative advantage: Successful partnerships manage the relationship, not just the deal. *Harvard Business Review,* 96–108.

Lindon, R. (2003). The discipline of collaboration. *Leader to Leader Journal, 29,* 41–47.

London, S. (1995). *Collaboration and community.* Retrieved November 6, 2012 from www.scottlondon.com/reports/collaboration.pdf.

Morse, R. S. (2008). Developing public leaders in an age of collaborative governance. In R. S. Morse & T. F. Buss (Eds.), *Innovations in Public Leadership Development* (pp. 79–100). Armonk, NY: M.E. Sharpe, Inc.

New York Genome Center. (2012). *Making the technology work: A collaborative ecosystem for improved patient outcomes.* Retrieved November 6, 2012 from http://nygenome.org/.

North Central Regional Educational Laboratory. (n.d.). *Putting the pieces together: Comprehensive school-linked strategies for children and families.* Retrieved November 6, 2012 from www.ncrel.org/sdrs/areas/issues/envrnmnt/css/ppt/putting.htm.

Osland, J., Kolb, D., & Rubin, I. (2001). *Organizational behavior: An experiential approach* (7th ed.). Upper Saddle River, NJ: Prentice Hall.

Rubin, H. (2009). *Collaborative leadership: Developing effective partnerships for communities and schools.* Thousand Oaks, CA: Corwin.

Turning Point Leadership Development National Excellence Collaborative. (2006). Retrieved November 6, 2012 from www.turningpointprogram.org and www.collaborativeleadership.org.

Van Wart, M. (2005). *Dynamics of leadership in public service: Theory and practice.* Armonk, NY: M.E. Sharpe.

Chapter **10**

Transformational Leadership

Ethel Elkins, Jeanne Melton, and Mellisa Hall

LEARNING OBJECTIVES

By the end of this chapter, the student will be able to:

· Explain the differences between a transactional and transformational leader.
· Discuss the history of leadership theories and the movement toward transformational leadership.
· Identify and explain strategies for transformational leadership.
· Understand personal strategies that can be used for change in the workplace.

KEY TERMS

Core values	Theory X
Empowerment	Theory Y
Rounding	Transactional leader

INTRODUCTION

The importance of effective leadership has never been greater given the changes and challenges that currently characterize the U.S. healthcare system. The importance of defining effective leadership is attested to by the tremendous amount of research into the issue. The number of books, articles, and dissertations on the topic is sometimes overwhelming. What good leadership means and how it is best practiced have changed over time.

The relationship between a leader and his or her employees can be thought of as a *quid pro quo* arrangement. This means that something is given with the expectation that something will be received in return. For example, some people give their work in exchange for an anticipated paycheck. Others offer their experience and expertise in anticipation of a promotion or new title. Still others give their talents in order to feel valued and to gain a sense of worth from doing their jobs well. Seen from this perspective, the relationship between leader and employee is a transaction.

In his book, *The Human Side of Enterprise* (1960), Douglas McGregor introduced the **Theory X** and **Theory Y** concept of motivation based on the views and preconceptions of leaders (see **Figure 10.1**). Those who subscribe to Theory X hold the fundamental belief that people do not really enjoy work and would not engage in it if they did not have to in order to make a living. Because they lack a sense of loyalty or other motivation to perform, they have to be carefully supervised, controlled, and rewarded to their satisfaction.

This approach to management was common in the past. For example, in the early years of the American industrial period, the economy was newly forming and work was scarce. People (many of whom were immigrants) were desperate for jobs and would do virtually anything to provide for themselves and their families. For many jobs, few if any skills were required, and workers were replaced with relative ease. There was no need for managers to be

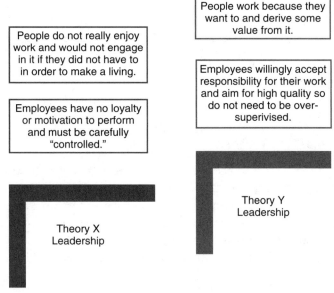

Figure 10.1 Theory X Versus Theory Y Leadership

concerned about motivating workers who willingly would work incredibly long hours in unsafe conditions for minimal pay.

As the American economy improved, there was a mandate for managers to adopt alternative approaches for motivating employees. As the workforce became better educated and organized, and as skilled workers became more essential and valuable, new strategies were developed to motivate employees to be productive and loyal. (This discussion leaves aside the issue of the relative moral values that were ignored under previous leadership models.)

Leaders who operated according to Theory Y believed differently from those who thought that employees were not personally invested in their work and would abstain from working if they could. Theory Y leaders lead out of the conviction that people work because they want to, believing employees derive satisfaction and joy from doing a job and doing it well. As a result, according to Theory Y, employees do not require a significant amount of direction and, if supported by their leaders, willingly accept responsibility for their work as well as its quality.

This chapter will provide an overview of the ways in which effective leaders can provide the motivation necessary to engage employees and encourage their dedication to the work at hand. This is especially important to consider in health care because the workforce is so diverse, change is constant, and the cost of error can be devastating.

Leaders who transform the nature of patient care, and the culture in which it is accomplished, improve employee commitment and motivation. The differences between transactional leadership and transformational leadership will be discussed. This will be accomplished from both the perspective of the leader and the clinician.

THE PATH TO TRANSFORMATIONAL LEADERSHIP

Early management models were generally based on the previously mentioned foundational elements of McGregor's (1960) Theory X. Leaders assumed that employees were driven by the singular motivation of making money or receiving something else of value in exchange for their work. This concept provided the basis for the development of James MacGregor Burns' theories of transactional and transformational leadership. In his book, *Leadership* (1978), Burns proposed that exchanges are made by the **transactional leader** in the furtherance of his or her personal interests. At the same time, followers comply because they realize that their own interests will be best served if they do what the leader wants. These leaders make broad generalizations that ignore the differences between individual workers and apply strategies that do not address potential differences that make employees more invested in their jobs (Kuhnert & Lewis, 1987). For example, using transactional leadership theory, pay raises would be an effective way to motivate employees to come to work on time, do their jobs efficiently and effectively, work harder, and increase productivity. Is this a realistic way to view the healthcare workforce?

Many people who work in health care have advanced degrees and have devoted a great deal of time and money in order to be able to do the work they do. They are professionals who are passionate about providing the best possible care, giving accurate diagnoses, maximizing patient comfort and functioning, and assuring the safety of their patients. While healthcare employees are interested in making a living, their motivations go far beyond that. The transactional leader, with her assumption that all workers are motivated by the same thing, misses a tremendous opportunity to capitalize on the dedication and loyalty of these employees to their patients and ultimately to the organization in which they practice. While transactional leadership might be effective in other industries such as sales or marketing, it has less relevance in the healthcare workplace. Employees are intensely driven to practice in their profession by factors that are personal and can be motivated by leaders who allow them to feel valued and to find fulfillment in their work.

TRANSFORMATIONAL LEADERSHIP DEFINED

Burns expounded on transactional and transformational leadership in his 2003 book *Transforming Leadership*. In this work, he examined the ways in which world leaders and other lesser known but no less important people influenced history with their transforming leadership styles. Yet, it is important to note that all leaders at all levels have an impact, either in a positive or a negative manner.

Hopefully, most of us can point to a person (or several people) who provided support, mentoring, and motivation that transformed our lives. It might have been a family member, a coach, or a teacher. There are people whom we naturally want to please because we value their opinion of us. We are not driven to do things out of a desire to "get something" from them other than their respect and approval. These are our personal transformational leaders.

Randy Dobbs is an acknowledged business leader who is the former CEO of General Electric and a champion of transformational leadership. He suggests that without it, good workers are often worried about their futures, frightened of their supervisors, and simply "punch the clock." Effective leaders transform the work and the workplace so that people feel energized about what they do and where they do it. The exchange for their work is a sense of self-worth and a realization that they are contributing to an organization they value (Dobbs, 2010).

Bernard Bass (1985) expanded on Burns' work by shifting the focus from the behaviors and beliefs of leaders to the importance of the needs and expectations of followers. In his model of transformational leadership, the focus is not on an exchange or transaction between leaders and employees, but on ways to develop and invest in workers in order to motivate them to perform. As a result, these employees develop a sense of loyalty to their work and their organizations. Again, the healthcare leader might be at a bit of an advantage given the nature of the workforce. People enter the field of health care out of a sense of caring about the welfare of others. They are generally passionate about their work and genuinely want to continue doing it. This provides leaders with many opportunities to make the most on the investment that workers bring in their larger commitment—one that extends beyond financial gain.

Davis Taylor wrote an interesting and engaging book about transformational leadership called *The Imperfect Leader* (2007). Taylor spent 23 years working in leadership positions in small companies as well as Fortune 500 corporations prior to his work with TAI (see http://taiinc.com), which is a consulting firm focused on value-based leadership. In his book, Taylor looks at lessons learned from both effective leaders and leaders who were not as transformational. He summarizes several "truths" for transformational leaders. Among them, he proposes that transformational leadership must focus on employees, it must be mission focused, and it must be driven by a leader who possesses vision, character, humility, and **core values**.

The National Park Service (2011) defines core values not as the description of the work we do or the processes we use to do it, but rather the underlying foundation of our relationships with one another and which strategies we use to accomplish what needs to be done: "They are the practices we use (or should be using) every day in everything we do." Our core values define who we are and what we stand for. They guide us in the practice of our profession and explain why we do what we do.

The importance of core values in the development of a transformational leadership style is noted throughout the literature. Not only is it essential that leaders and employees have a well-developed and defined set of core values, but also that these values are shared. Jo Manion, whose background is in nursing, has become a recognized expert on effective leadership in health care. She proposes that these values lead to a shared sense of mission and vision that create the foundation for organizational commitment (Manion, 2011). In uniting everyone in the organization, there is greater opportunity for improving patient services at all levels.

Unlike the transactional leader, the transformational leader does just that; he transforms people and the work culture so that motivation is based on the individual needs and aspirations of employees. His or her own personal and professional aspirations must be subjugated to those of employees. This type of leader understands that different people need different things out of their work, yet recognizes that there are common themes. Among these themes are a sense of being valued and treated as an individual and not just a cog in the production wheel. Transformational leaders understand the importance of relationships and personal interaction.

Another important distinction between the transactional and transformational leader was made by Peter Northouse (2011). He suggests that the traditional notion of the leader as the driver of change is short-sighted and incorrect. While the role of the leader is indeed important, transformational leadership can be incorporated only when employees and leaders work closely together. In this model, the traditional notions of power and hierarchy are challenged, and the essential involvement of workers in decision making and acclimation to change is acknowledged.

TRANSFORMATIONAL LEADERSHIP AND MOTIVATION

A recent study of the factors that motivate workers to stay in their jobs and work to increase their productivity was conducted—with surprising findings. The respondents reported that pay and benefits were much less important to them than personal fulfillment, i.e., having the sense that they were valued and being involved in decisions that impacted their work (Atchinson, 2003). This is good news for healthcare administrators who work for organizations that generally have very low profit margins. Yet, it also presents a challenge to these leaders: How do we identify the specific things that individual employees value and how do we enhance those experiences and opportunities?

How do we learn about employee values? We return to a discussion on the importance of developing relationships. For example, it is relatively safe to assume that asking employees to take on additional tasks outside of those in their job description would have a demotivating effect. However, given the limited resources available to many healthcare organizations, working across departments and cross-training are becoming increasingly common. For example, John in Human Resources is already having a hard time balancing his job and his family obligations. Such a request would hardly serve as a motivation. But Jane in Accounting might value the opportunity to gain skills that are outside of her expertise. She might have hopes of advancing to a position that requires supervising staff, so the experience would be valuable to her.

Clearly, becoming familiar with the interests, priorities, and aspirations of all of the people in a department would be tremendously time consuming in a larger organization. Benefits have been found by some who have invested the time and effort. Quint Studer practices "**rounding**." Mr. Studer was an administrator in a number of different industries, with the majority of his leadership roles having been in healthcare organizations. He does not use the term *rounding* in the traditional, clinical sense. As an administrator, he rounds on staff in the same manner that doctors round on patients. He spends several minutes each day visiting various departments and talking to those who work there. Simply put, he gets to know his employees. He reports that the activity more than pays off as staff come to realize that he has a personal interest in what matters to them. In that way, he is able to assist them in their professional development (Studer, 2004).

This approach has the added benefit of lending an air of humility to leaders. It communicates the notion that "I am not better than you; we are peers." By taking the time to understand what motivates employees, the leader acknowledges staff members as "whole persons," who are much more than their job title. An additional payoff is that as leaders identify the values and aspirations of their staff members, they can devise ways to help them actualize and achieve their goals. The result is an employee who has an increased sense of loyalty along with additional skills that will benefit the organization and culture (see **Figure 10.2**).

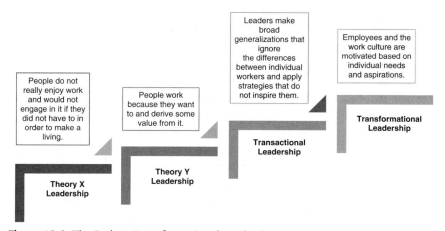

Figure 10.2 The Path to Transformational Leadership

TRANSFORMATIONAL LEADERSHIP STRATEGIES

There are many suggested models for transformational leadership that focus on differing characteristics of the leader. All of these are important and informative. The following strategies are suggested for the transformational leader:

1. *Integrity above all else.* While it was noted that different things motivate different people, it is clear that dishonesty and inconsistency on the part of a leader will destroy the trust and confidence that followers need in order to invest themselves in their work and the organization. Transformational leaders are always true to their values and honest in their interactions.

2. *Get down in "the trenches."* Transformational leaders will not ask a follower to do anything that they would not do themselves (if they have the training and expertise). They will put in more hours than they ask of followers. They are the first to pitch in when necessary. They "get their hands dirty."

3. *Communicate, communicate, and communicate.* Transformational leaders will maintain a clear and open line of communication. Gone are the days of "the boss" who maintains a "closed door" policy. The proprietary treatment of information undermines a sense of community, commonality, and shared goals. Granted, there might be times when it is not in the best interest of the organization to share all information immediately, but these must be seriously considered, and such information should be withheld only when it is absolutely necessary.

4. *Have a meeting.* Involving followers in all matters and decisions relative to their work is essential. This is especially important given the constantly changing nature of health care. Authoritative leaders who feel as though their followers are not equipped or qualified to provide input forfeit valuable information and perspectives. Staff members who believe that their perspectives were communicated and seriously considered are more likely to accept changes that are made, even if they do not necessarily agree with them.

5. *Keep the mission of the organization in mind.* When discussing business and potential change with employees, keep the mission of the organization in mind. Reinforce your appreciation of the job being performed, whether it is done by the secretary greeting patients as they register in the waiting room or the neurosurgeon who has been in the operating suite 16 hours straight. All levels of services are vital to provide high-quality, safe, and accurate patient care. Everyone in an organization is valuable, but no one is indispensable.

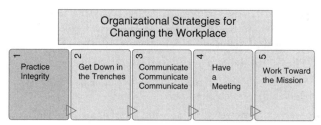

Figure 10.3 Organizational Strategies for Changing the Workplace

Figure 10.3 lays out the steps toward making positive changes in the workplace.

LEADING THROUGH CHANGE

Change can be threatening to all of us, especially in situations in which we do not feel we have the power or authority to respond to or prepare for it. Yet, arguably, the healthcare industry is subject to more change than any other. These changes very often come from external sources over which leaders charged with its implementation have little control.

Some examples of such changes can be drawn from the not-so-distant past. In 1965, Congress amended the Social Security Act of 1935 and established the Medicare and Medicaid programs to subsidize health care for the poor, elderly, and disabled (Banaszak-Holl, Levitsky, & Zald, 2010). The repercussions for the healthcare industry were significant. Droves of new patients acquired access to care. Limits on reimbursement were put in place. Significant regulatory and legal requirements were enacted (Banaszak-Holl et al., 2010). As a result of the passage of the legislation, 20 million Americans enrolled in the 3 years following enactment. Basic hospitalization coverage and some assistance paying for the costs of physicians became available, greatly increasing access to care.

In 1996, the Health Insurance Portability and Accountability Act (HIPAA) was enacted. Among other things, it contained extensive provisions for the protection of personal health information and regulations governing the continuation of some employer-sponsored insurance when patients changed jobs. In addition, it mandated national standards for the electronic transfer of patient information. Implementation of the provisions of the Act is ongoing, with deadlines reaching into 2016 (Centers for Medicare and Medicaid Services, 2012). See **Table 10.1** for a summary of changes in the U.S. healthcare system over the past 150 years.

The Medicare Part D Prescription Drug Program was enacted in 2003 and implemented in 2006. It represented the largest change to and expansion of the original Medicare program since its inception. By providing subsidies

Table 10.1 Significant Changes in the U.S. Healthcare System

1847	American Medical Association founded; largest medical lobby in the U.S.
1930s	Birth of health insurance plans (Blue Cross/Blue Shield)
1935	Social Security Act: Federal aid to states for public health assistance, maternal and child health, and children with disabilities
1960	Development of biomedical equipment; surge of advanced life-supporting equipment into market
1963	Health Professions Educational Assistance Act: Direct federal aid to medical, dental, nursing, and other healthcare discipline programs
1965	Public Health Service Act: Regional medical programs to address leading causes of death
1965	Medicare and Medicaid legislation expanded from original Social Security Act
1966	Comprehensive Health Planning Act: Regional medical resources to improve clinical and educational health services
1970s	Growth of medical specialties
1973	Health Maintenance Organization Act: Health services for prepaid fees
1974	National Health Planning and Resources Development Act (combination of the 1965 and 1966 programs)
1982	Diagnosis Related Groups (DRGs): Limits to federal reimbursement (Medicare) to health organizations based on patient diagnoses
1994	Death with Dignity Act: Oregon first state to enact
2001	Growth of Preferred Provider Organizations
2010	Patient Protection and Affordable Care Act

Source: Data from Sultz, H. A., & Young, K. M. (2011). *Health care USA: Understanding its organization and delivery* (7th ed.). Burlington, MA: Jones & Bartlett Learning.

to the elderly and disabled for the purchase of prescription medications, it had the effect of forcing providers to accept reimbursement at federally mandated or negotiated levels.

With the passage of the Patient Protection and Affordable Care Act in 2010, America's healthcare system is once again facing change. It is unknown exactly how some of these changes will affect our healthcare facilities and the individuals who work or seek treatment within their walls. There is no doubt that this is a time of transformation as the Act is implemented over the next several years, providing opportunities for leaders to step forward and embrace what lies ahead.

Additional new changes face healthcare leaders. These include the aging of the population, the aging of the healthcare workforce, retention problems, and rapid technological advances. All of these will have a direct impact on providers of care; some of them positive, some negative. The results will depend on the ability of the leader to positively transform workers and their workplaces.

BECOME A GAME CHANGER

A transformational healthcare leader should promote positive dynamics in the workplace and be ahead of change mandated by healthcare legislation. To implement positive change, consider what has been tried in the past and is known to be successful. Develop a personal and organizational action plan (see **Figure 10.4**). Try:

1. *Continuously working to motivate employees to higher levels of personal achievement.* This means the leader knows employees well enough to make suggestions for their personal growth. The employees should also feel enough comfort with their leader to discuss disagreements with organizational decisions. The leader should demonstrate respect for employee conversations and recognize a job well done. The leader should display confidence, act as a mentor and a teacher, and help to promote a shared sense of mission for the organization (Grant, Gino, & Hofmann, 2011; Swartz, Spencer, Wilson, & Wood, 2011).

2. *Staying happy!* Emotions are contagious and boost employee and team performance. Significant improvements have been shown in team helping behaviors, team goal commitment, and team satisfaction when leaders maintain positive moods (Chi, Chung, & Tsai, 2011).

3. *Considering employees' health and wellbeing through empowerment.* Transformational leaders should encourage their employees to problem solve and take responsibility, especially when dealing with changes in patient status. Given that healthcare employees often have the daunting responsibility for a patient's continued health and are the first to recognize worsening conditions, all levels of staff performing direct patient care should feel they have access to their leadership to make positive changes in their workplace. With this feeling of **empowerment**, employees actually have better sleep quality, which is associated with fewer chronic illnesses (Munir & Nielsen, 2009).

4. *Considering safety promotion.* Transformational leaders who specifically work to promote and develop a safe work environment make a difference for their patients as well as their employees. The devastating consequences of a patient or employee injury can be prevented by leaders who promote safety awareness through

Occupational Safety and Health Administration (OSHA) compliance, staff education, and posting reminders in the workplace (Mullen & Kelloway, 2009).

5. *Recognizing the ability to move even the most difficult employee personalities toward team goals.* When dealing with individuals who could possibly be more motivated toward self-interests instead of the interests of the organization, transformational leaders can inspire individuals toward a team concept for the betterment of the organization (Arthur, Woodman, Ong, Hardy, & Ntoumanis, 2011).

6. *Staying a step ahead of the game.* Transformational leaders should embrace change and new policy, greeting it with a positive approach. Looking to develop ways to do things differently and more efficiently is key in improving productivity and providing higher quality patient services. Waiting until the budget drops to the point of cutting staff or resources would not be a positive example of transformational leadership. Transformational leaders encourage employees to suggest and develop improved methods that are innovative and promote organizational solvency (Botting, 2011).

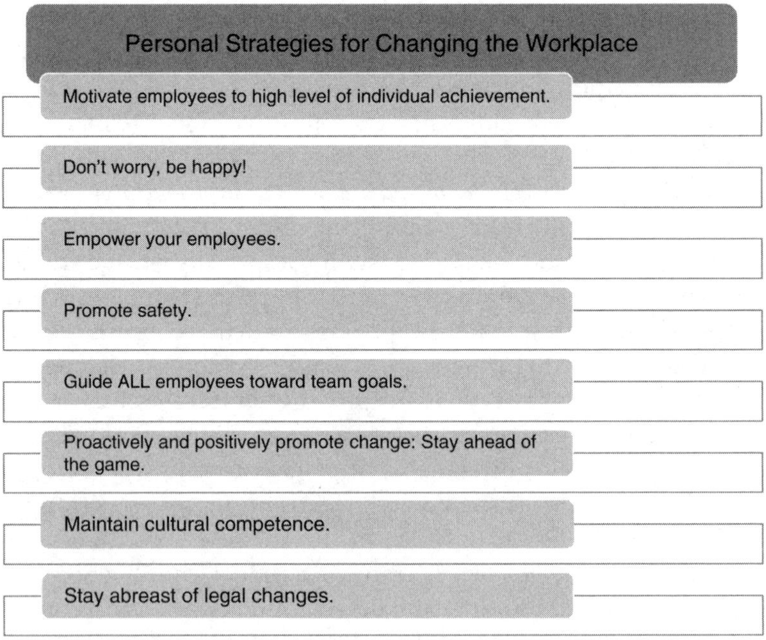

Personal Strategies for Changing the Workplace

Motivate employees to high level of individual achievement.

Don't worry, be happy!

Empower your employees.

Promote safety.

Guide ALL employees toward team goals.

Proactively and positively promote change: Stay ahead of the game.

Maintain cultural competence.

Stay abreast of legal changes.

Figure 10.4 Personal Strategies for Changing the Workplace

7. *Recognizing the importance of a culturally competent organization.* Because of the changing demographics of the United States, both the workforce and patients served will need a leader who recognizes the importance of cultural competence. Cultural competency is defined as "the ability of systems to provide care to patients with diverse values, beliefs, and behaviors, including tailoring delivery of care to meet patients' social, cultural, and linguistic needs" (Betancourt, Green, Carrillo, & Ananeh-Firempong, 2003, p. 293). Leaders need to recognize the importance of cultural competency for their workforce as well. Cultural proficiency increases not only patient and employee satisfaction, but is important in the reduction of medical errors (Gertner, Deitrick, & Geiger, 2010).

8. *Keeping at least one finger on legislative action.* The transformational leader has to remain aware of new legislation in order to stay in front of change that will impact payer sources, professional staff, potential for new/or elimination of previous grant funding, and state and federal statutes that affect the organization. A leader who looks ahead will maintain a strong, effective organization (Greer & Jacobson, 2010).

SUMMARY

Transformational leadership is essential to the development of employee commitment and successful resolution of the challenges facing healthcare organizations. Leadership must understand that employees are vital to accommodating change while at the same time assuring quality of care and patient safety. A healthcare workforce that is motivated by inclusion, respectful treatment, and the opportunity to grow and develop rather than to suffer from these challenges will help leaders to lead effectively.

Finally, it must be noted that the most threatening type of change is change that we do not fully understand. There is much uncertainty surrounding the Affordable Care Act that was signed into law in 2010. The proposed changes are sweeping, and the majority of them will be put in place by 2014. Yet, there are many unknowns. Even now that the Supreme Court has upheld the Affordable Care Act, there are many challenges yet to be faced as our state and federal governments work out their differences and details. Many of the elements of the Act have already been implemented, though, and are difficult to "unravel." For example, it will be hard to undo the spending caps or coverage extensions (insurance coverage for student dependents until age 26) that have already been put into place.

This presents what is arguably the greatest challenge and greatest opportunity for transformational healthcare leaders; effectively managing change in times of chaos and uncertainty. Old-school models of top-down management and authoritarians will not work. Today's healthcare professionals are engaged and invested. They will not be excluded from the change process, nor should they be. Transformational leaders will treat employees with individual respect and consideration. They will involve them in planning and discussion. They will function as a peer instead of as a superior. They will have a clear set of values and hold to them consistently. With these attributes, they will lead the way for the development of a culture that does not shrink from change but embraces and prospers from it.

Discussion Questions

1. How do environmental conditions influence a healthcare leader's chosen style?

2. What are the barriers that prevent a healthcare leader from being transformational?

3. What were some of the changes to hospitals, clinics, pharmacies, and insurance companies brought on by the United States healthcare developments since the 1960s? How might these have been perceived as threatening by workers?

4. How might the recent healthcare reform measures influence change over these sectors?

Case Study: The Honeysuckle Clinic

Honeysuckle

Family Health Care Clinic

The Honeysuckle Clinic is a community, rural health clinic, which is open 6 days a week and currently manages nearly 4000 patient visits annually. The staff includes one full-time administrator, one full-time nurse practitioner, two part-time nurse practitioners, one full-time intake specialist, one full-time receptionist, and one part-time medical coder/biller. Mental health services, physical therapy, and some complementary and alternative medicine therapies are done by contract providers. Lab services are available 3 days a week. The dental program costs are covered by a grant that covers the cost of a dentist, hygienist, and dental assistant, all of whom work part-time. The clinic is a Medicare/Medicaid provider and accepts most insurance plans. Patients are encouraged to pay in cash rather than with debit and credit cards due to the fees incurred by both the clinic and the patient with card use. This is just one more attempt by clinic administrators to keep patient costs as low as possible.

Patients receive assistance in accessing pharmaceutical benevolent programs. The practitioners work diligently to prescribe generic medications that can be purchased at low cost through a number of large retailers. The clinic does keep on hand some emergency and sample brand name products.

Nola Salem is the clinic's director. She has been on the job approximately 3 years, arriving after a period of financial difficulty and declining grant monies nearly closed the clinic. Ms. Salem reports to an independent Board of Directors consisting of 12 area citizens and community leaders. Of the 12 members, 4 are patients of the clinic as required by state law for facilities receiving state grant monies. The Board meets bimonthly at the clinic.

Since Ms. Salem arrived, Honeysuckle has been awarded numerous grants and is currently financially stable. The annual budget for this thriving clinic runs approximately a half million dollars.

Ms. Salem was asked to describe her leadership style. Some of her self-descriptions include the following:

- "I am not a micromanager. Each clinician or staff member was hired to do a job. If someone is not doing his or her job, then that person needs to go."
- "I like to stay organized and insist that employees make an appointment if they need to discuss something in private. It helps us all to stay on track."
- "I want to hear their ideas. None of us is comprehensively trained in all fields. Each employee contributes to the team that makes up Honeysuckle."
- "We brainstorm a lot."
- "There are no big people here, only small puzzle pieces that make up the whole. We each need the other and his or her ideas and skills to complete the picture."
- "Everybody's responsible for a piece of that puzzle."
- "I make it a point to walk through the clinic every day so if any employee needs to talk with me, I'm available."

· "After I make a decision, my employees are expected to 'get on the band wagon' and get it implemented."

Ms. Salem does have a regularly scheduled staff meeting with the full-time employees, with part-time employees attending when possible. Most staff meetings are held with 5 minutes notice, while all employees are on the run. She notes the luxury of having a small practice. "We can move fast," she remarks. "If we need a new form created or need to make a policy decision, we do not need committees. We do not work in a slow, cumbersome process like in a larger healthcare system. We can decide something at 10 A.M. and put it in place at noon."

The clinic's Medical Director, Dr. Seymor, has the final approval on clinical changes. Nurse practitioners feel that they are routinely ignored when they present requests for more information. They feel like they are given no choice about patient flow and documentation, when they are the ones in actual practice with patients. Per policy, Dr. Seymor reviews 100% of the clinical records, but is not present on-site. While the nurse practitioners were willing to talk candidly about the clinic, other employees were reluctant to discuss their leader. All of them declined, citing the constant fear that they might lose their jobs at a moment's notice.

Case Study Discussion Questions

1. Nola Salem, through her business background, has brought many improvements to the Honeysuckle Clinic in the past 3 years. However, there are no strategic plans yet in place. The Board of Directors is pleased at the influx of grant funding, but the staff members worry when the new budgets are announced. Staff reveal that they cannot anticipate if they will have employment on a long-term basis—and morale plunges. Is Ms. Salem a transformational leader? Justify your position. If not, how might a true transformational leader handle some of these issues?

2. Ms. Salem has just tendered her resignation to take another position. The Board of Directors hired a consultant who has recommended that the clinic seek a transformational leader to lead Honeysuckle into the next decade. Relative to what you know about the clinic's structure, financial status, and patient base, what traits should this new leader embody? What questions might you ask the candidate you are interviewing to determine his or her leadership philosophy?

3. You are a community leader in an area similar to the region served by the Honeysuckle Clinic. One of the area's largest employers has just closed its doors, leaving many of your community's "breadwinners"

unemployed and uninsured. Your locality seeks a healthcare provider to offer locally-based, reduced-fee medical care to its population and turns to you to coordinate the recruitment of this practice or organization. The medium-sized state university 50 miles away has a large nursing school, and nurse practitioners from its faculty have agreed to staff an outpatient clinic on a volunteer basis until a new practice is fully established. As you begin planning for the new low-cost services you plan to launch, you and your team make a site visit to Honeysuckle to observe and learn from their experiences. You have questions about recruitment and retention of qualified medical staff, about the aging of the healthcare workforce, and about how changing technology and healthcare reform demands for accountability and quality may impact your proposed clinic. Please prepare a list of topics/concerns to be discussed.

RELATED WEBSITES

American College of Healthcare Executives: www.ache.org/
American Recovery and Reinvestment Act of 2009: www.recovery.gov
Healthcare Leadership Alliance: www.healthcareleadershipalliance.org/
Health Reform Information: www.healthcare.gov/
Leadership Health Care: www.healthcarecouncil.com/leadership_health_care.aspx
National Association of Community Health Centers: http://nachc.com/
Additionally, every state has its own association
National Center for Healthcare Leadership: http://nchl.org/
Primary Health Care Associations are identified by state; for example:

- Illinois at www.iphca.org
- Wisconsin at www.wphca.org
- Mississippi at www.mphca.org

Studer Group: http://studergroup.com/
U.S. Dept. of Health and Human Services, Health Resources and Services Administration: http://bhpr.hrsa.gov/shortage/

REFERENCES

Arthur, C. A., Woodman, T., Ong, C. W., Hardy, L., & Ntoumanis, N. (2011). The role of athlete narcissism in moderating the relationship between coaches' transformational leader behaviors and athlete motivation. *Journal of Sport & Exercise Psychology, 33*(1), 3–19.
Atchinson, T. (2003). Exposing the myth of employee satisfaction. *Healthcare Executive, 17*(3), 20.

Banaszak-Holl, J., Levitsky, S., & Zald, M. N. (2010). *Social movements and the transformation of American health care.* New York, NY: Oxford University Press.

Bass, B. (1985). *Leadership and performance beyond expectations.* New York, NY: Free Press.

Betancourt, J. R., Green, A. R., Carrillo, J. E., & Ananeh-Firenpong, O. (2003). Defining cultural competence: A practical framework for addressing racial /ethnic disparities in health and health care. *National Institute of Health Public Health Report, 118*(4) 293–302.

Botting, L. (2011). Transformational change in action. *Nursing Management, 17*(9), 14–19.

Burns, J. (1978). *Leadership.* New York, NY: Harper & Row.

Burns, J. (2003) *Transforming leadership.* New York, NY: Grove.

Centers for Medicare and Medicaid Services. (2012). *HIPAA general information.* Retrieved November 6, 2012 from www.cms.gov/Regulations-and-Guidance /HIPAA-Administrative-Simplification/HIPAAGenInfo/index.html.

Chi, N., Chung, Y., & Tsai, W. (2011). How do happy leaders enhance team success? The mediating roles of transformational leadership, group affective tone, and team processes. *Journal of Applied Social Psychology, 41*(6), 1421–1454.

Dobbs, R. (2010). *Transformational leadership: A blueprint for real organizational change.* Little Rock, AR: Parkhurst Brothers.

Gertner, E. J., Deitrick, L. M., & Geiger, J. F. (2010). Developing a culturally competent health network: A planning framework and guide. *Journal of Healthcare Management, 55*(3), 190–203.

Grant, A. M., Gino, F., & Hofmann, D. A. (2011). Reversing the extroverted leadership advantage: The role of employee proactivity. *Academy of Management Journal, 54*(3), 528–550.

Greer, S. L. & Jacobson, P. D. (2010). Health care reform and federalism. *Journal of Health Politics, Policy, and Law, 35*(2) 203–226.

Kuhnert, K., & Lewis, P. (1987). Transactional and transformational leadership: A constructive/developmental analysis. *Academy of Management Review, 12*(4), 648–657.

Manion, J. (2011). *From management to leadership: Practical strategies for health care leaders* (3rd ed.). San Francisco, CA: Jossey-Bass.

McGregor, D. (1960). *The human side of enterprise.* New York, NY: McGraw-Hill.

Mullen, J. E. & Kelloway, E. K. (2009). Safety leadership: A longitudinal study of the effects of transformational leadership on safety outcomes. *Journal of Occupational and Organizational Psychology, 82,* 253–272.

Munir, F., & Nielsen, K. (2009). Does self-efficacy mediate the relationship between transformational leadership behaviours and healthcare workers' sleep quality? A longitudinal study. *Journal of Advanced Nursing, 65*(9),1833–1843.

National Park Service. (2011). *What are core values?* Retrieved December 17, 2012 from www.nps.gov/training/uc/whcv.htm.

Northouse, P. (2011). *Leadership: Theory and practice* (5th ed.). Thousand Oaks, CA: Sage.

Studer, Q. (2004). *Hardwiring excellence.* Gulf Breeze, FL: Fire Starter.

Sultz, H. A., & Young, K. M. (2011). *Health care USA: Understanding its organization and delivery* (7th ed.). Burlington, MA: Jones & Bartlett Learning.

Swartz, D. B., Spencer, T., Wilson, B., & Wood, K. (2011). Transformational leadership: Implications for nursing leaders in facilities seeking magnet designation. *American Operating Room Nurses Journal, 93*(6) 737–748.

Taylor, D. (2007). *The imperfect leader: A story about discovering the not-so-secret secrets of transformational leadership.* Bloomington, IN: AuthorHouse.

Chapter 11

Patient- and Family-Centered Leadership

Mary Lynne Knighten and Beverly Quaye

LEARNING OBJECTIVES

By the end of this chapter, the student will be able to:

- Describe core concepts of patient- and family-centered care and values-based professional practice.
- Define servant leadership and patient- and family-centered leadership.
- Differentiate between the roles of patient- and family-centered leadership and management.
- Articulate how to transform a traditional healthcare organizational culture to one that is patient and family centered.
- Describe the role of patient–family advisors play in hospital leadership, safety, and quality.

KEY TERMS

Care delivery model

Patient- and family-centered care

Patient- and family-centered leadership

Patient and family partnerships

Professional practice model

Top box achievement

INTRODUCTION

Patient- and family-centered care (PFCC) can enhance the patient experience and improve a healthcare organization's operational performance metrics. Effectiveness of PFCC is demonstrated via an example of an urban, community, faith-based hospital, which adopted a PFCC delivery model, forming new partnerships with families, physicians, and internal and external stakeholders, and developing an organizational culture based on interdependence, mutual learning, and collaboration. The result was improved service, quality, and cost per adjusted discharge outcomes.

DEFINITION OF PATIENT- AND FAMILY-CENTERED CARE

There are several approaches to healthcare delivery that center around patients and their individual, specific health and wellness needs. Among them are *patient- and family-centered care,* and *family-centered care*. Though the terms are used interchangeably, each approach contains separate and distinct philosophies and care concepts. To better understand **patient- and family-centered leadership**, it is important to understand the basics of common patient-centric philosophies and care models.

The *patient* is the person who needs and seeks care. *Family* refers to two or more persons who are related in any way—biologically, legally, or emotionally. *Patient-centered care* implies that the focus is only on the patient. Of course, the patient *is* central to the delivery of care. In patient-centered care, family members may be, and often are, included; however, the concept of partnership with patients and families is not well developed.

Patient- and family-centered care is an approach to the planning, delivery, and assessment of health care grounded in mutually beneficial partnerships among healthcare providers, patients, and families (IPFCC, 2010). It is this partnership that defines patient- and family-centered leadership.

In the **patient- and family-centered care** (PFCC) approach, the definition of family, as well as the degree of the family's involvement in health care, is determined by the patient, provided that he or she is developmentally mature and competent to do so. The term *family-centered* is in no way intended to remove control from patients who are competent to make decisions concerning their own health care (IPFCC, 2010).

CORE CONCEPTS

Four core concepts comprise patient- and family-centered care (**Table 11.1**). These concepts provide the foundation for patient- and family-centered leaders to transform their organizations' cultures.

Table 11.1 Core Concepts of Patient- and Family-Centered Care

Dignity and Respect: Healthcare practitioners listen to and honor patient and family perspectives and choices. Patient and family knowledge, values, beliefs, and cultural backgrounds are incorporated into the planning and delivery of care.

Information Sharing: Healthcare practitioners communicate and share complete and unbiased information with patients and families in ways that are affirming and useful. Patients and families receive timely, complete, and accurate information in order to effectively participate in care and decision making.

Participation: Patients and families are encouraged and supported in participating in care and decision making at the level they choose.

Collaboration: Patients and families are also included on an institution-wide basis. Healthcare leaders collaborate with patients and families in policy and program development, implementation, and evaluation; in healthcare facility design; and in professional education, as well as in the delivery of care.

Source: Reprinted with permission from the Institute for Patient- and Family-Centered Care: www.ipfcc.org.

Rationale

Leaders and providers who are patient- and family-centered recognize the vital role that families play in ensuring the health and wellness of patients of all ages. They listen to and value the individual and collective voice of patients and families and empower patients and their families to take charge of their own health and welfare. There are numerous examples in the literature showing that improved health outcomes, better allocation of resources, and greater satisfaction with the healthcare experience for the patient and family are achieved with PFCC. Patient- and family-centered leaders astutely recognize that **patient and family partnerships** inform and shape their healthcare organization's operational policies, staff interactions, facilities, services, and programs. Health systems, hospitals, ambulatory services, and other healthcare institutions committed to patient- and family-centered care proactively collaborate with patients and families, advocate for family presence, and facilitate participation in patient care.

INFLUENCES AT THE HEALTH POLICY LEVEL

The term *patient-centered medicine* was introduced in psychiatry by Balint and colleagues in 1969. *Patient-centered care* was coined by the Picker Commonwealth Program for Patient-Centered Care, currently the Picker Institute, in 1988. The Picker Commonwealth Program researched and documented patients' needs and preferences in order to understand patients' and families' definitions of high-quality care and to explore models of care to better address those needs. This qualitative research ultimately resulted in the production of survey instruments that measured patients' experience in eight dimensions of care (see **Table 11.2**). In addition to safe and technically excellent care, these eight dimensions of care had been identified by patients and their families to be the most critical aspects of the care experience (Conway et al., 2006, p. 5).

In the 1980s, after 2 decades of childbearing, women and families helped drive family-centered changes within maternity care. U.S. Surgeon General C. Everett Koop, the Maternal and Child Health Bureau of the U.S. Department of Health and Human Services, the Association for the Care of Children's Health, and other organizations collaborated with families in defining and providing leadership to advance the practice of *patient-centered care* (Conway et al., 2006, p. 6).

Today, the Institute for Patient- and Family-Centered Care (formerly the Institute for Family-Centered Care) is one of the foremost authorities on the PFCC concept in the United States. According to the Institute's website, its work in the early 1990s focused primarily on family-centered approaches to pediatric care. Within this framework, it was consistently envisioned that as patients matured, they should be encouraged to become more involved as decision makers in their own health care along with their families. In the past decade, the Institute has become more involved in adult and geriatric care and believes it is important to acknowledge the patient's role more explicitly. Thus, the Institute began using the term *patient- and family-centered care.*

This integration of patient- and family-centered care reflects our social framework. The original definition of patient-centered care in the literature of the late 1980s and early 1990s did not include the concept of patients and families as advisors and essential partners in improving care practices and systems of care. Families have been shown to positively influence patients' health and wellness, and social isolation is a risk factor in today's

Table 11.2 Eight Dimensions of Care Measurement (Picker Institute)

Access
Respect for patients' values and preferences
Coordination of care
Information, communication, and education
Physical comfort (including help with activities of daily living)
Emotional support
Involvement of friends and family
Preparation for discharge and transitions in care

Source: Reprinted with permission from the Institute for Patient- and Family-Centered Care: www.ipfcc.org.

society. Most patients have families or are affiliated with a support system or network and benefit when healthcare organizations encourage continuing linkage to these natural supports. Additionally, individuals, (such as the very young, the elderly, and those with chronic conditions and disabilities) who are most dependent on hospital care and the broader healthcare system, are typically also dependent on and receive invaluable support from families and social networks.

In 2001, the Institute of Medicine (IOM) released a highly influential report entitled *Crossing the Quality Chasm: A New Health System for the 21st Century,* which analyzed problems facing the U.S. healthcare system and presented recommendations for its improvement. Patient- and family-centered care—partnerships among professionals, patients, and families—offers the framework and strategies to enhance the quality and safety of health care. In its "Six Quality Aims for Improving Care," the IOM report defines patient-centered care as "care that is respectful of and responsive to individual patient preferences, needs and values, and ensuring [*sic*] that patient values guide all clinical decisions" (IOM, 2001, p. 40).

The *Quality Chasm* report also offers "10 Rules to Redesign and Improve Care." All 10 rules are consistent with patient- and family-centered approaches; the 5 most relevant are listed in **Table 11.3**.

Organizations such as The Joint Commission (TJC) (formerly the Joint Commission on Accreditation of Healthcare Organizations, or JCAHO), the National Committee for Quality Assurance (NCQA), the Institute for Healthcare Improvement (IHI), the Centers for Medicare and Medicaid Services (CMS), and the American Hospital Association (AHA) are making patient- and family-centered care a priority in their long-term strategic agendas, validating the essential role these core concepts play in healthcare design and improvement. For example, Conway and colleagues (2006) cite the influence of four prominent organizations (AHA, JCAHO, IHI, and NCQA) in this area:

- In 2004, the AHA collaborated with the Institute for Family- Centered Care to produce and disseminate a *Toolkit on Patient- and Family-Centered Care* to the chief executive officer of every hospital in the United States.
- In 2006, the JCAHO convened its first Patient and Family Advisory Committee and published a book, *Patients as Partners: How to Involve Patients and Families in Their Own Care.*
- The IHI, under the guidance of Donald Berwick, MD, made patient- and family-centered care an area of innovation and research for 2006 and ensured its inclusion in all the Institute's major

Table 11.3 Patient- and Family-Centered Rules to Redesign and Improve Care

Care based in continuous healing relationships. Patients should receive care whenever they need it and in many forms.	The health care system should be responsive . . . 24 hours a day, every day . . . Access to care should be provided over the Internet, by telephone, and by other means in addition to face-to-face visits.
Customization based on patient needs and values.	The system of care should be designed to meet the most common types of needs but have the capability to respond to individual patient choices and preferences.
The patient as the source of control. Patients should be given the necessary information and the opportunity to exercise the degree of control they choose over healthcare decisions.	The health system should . . . accommodate differences in patient preferences and encourage shared decision making.
Shared knowledge and the free flow of information. Patients should have unfettered access to their own medical information and to clinical knowledge.	Clinicians and patients should communicate effectively and share information.
The need for transparency.	The healthcare system should make information available to patients and their families that allows them to make informed decisions when selecting a health plan, hospital, or clinical practice or choosing among alternative treatments. This should include information describing the system's performance on safety, evidence-based practice, and patient satisfaction.

Source: Data from Institute of Medicine. (2001). *Crossing the quality chasm: A new health system for the 21st Century*. Washington, DC: Author.

programs, including the 100,000 Lives Campaign, Quality Allies, and Transforming Care at the Bedside initiatives.

· The NCQA is creating a patient- and family-centered physician practice recognition program that will reward medical groups for developing and implementing patient- and family-centered practice designs and interventions.

Patient-centered initiatives have become integral to federal and national standards for high-quality healthcare delivery. For example:

· In 2005, the Agency for Healthcare Research and Quality (AHRQ) and the Centers for Medicare and Medicaid Services (CMS) supported the development of the Consumer Assessment of Healthcare Providers and Systems (CAHPS) surveys, which measure the patient and consumer experience across a continuum of care. The CMS publicly reports data from many of the CAHPS surveys on its website, www.hospitalcompare.hhs.gov (HCAHPS, 2005).

- In 2010, to improve the safety and quality of care provided by hospitals, TJC released *Advancing Effective Communication, Cultural Competence, and Patient- and Family-Centered Care; A Roadmap for Hospitals.* This guidance document encourages healthcare leaders to aspire to meet the unique needs of each of their patients and address patients' demographic and personal characteristics as well as the clinical aspect of care.
- CMS released the Final Rule on changes to the hospital and critical access hospital Conditions of Participation to ensure visitation rights for all patients, which became effective January 1, 2011 (CMS, 2010).
- In 2011, Health and Human Services Secretary Kathleen Sebelius announced the Partnership for Patients, which requires collaboration between hospitals, physicians, nurses, patient advocates, and others to reduce hospital-acquired conditions and prevent readmissions (HHS, 2011).
- The IHI published an innovation series white paper entitled, "Achieving Exceptional Patient and Family Experience of Inpatient Hospital Care," which can serve as a guidance document for hospitals wishing to transform the culture from being provider-centric to achieving patient and family centeredness (Balik, Conway, Zipperer, & Watson, 2011).
- The Robert Wood Johnson Foundation produced a new policy paper in August 2011 regarding patient-centered medical homes and predicted their potential to positively transform health care (RWJF, 2010).

This brief synopsis of organizations, agencies, and individuals influencing the advancement of patient- and family-centered care is by no means all-inclusive. For more information, the work of patient- and family-centered leaders in the United States such as Donald Berwick, MD; Beverly Johnson; Jim Conway; Patricia Sodomka; and Polly Arango should be referenced, as well as information from Planetree, Family Voices, the Agency for Healthcare Quality and Research (AHRQ), the National Quality Forum (NHQ), the American College of Physicians and American Board of Medical Specialties (ABMS), the Society of Pediatric Nurses, and the American Nurses Association (SPN/ANA). Internationally, patient- and family-centered resources may be accessed from the World Health Organization (WHO), National Health Service (NHS) in the United Kingdom, the Australian Commission on Safety and Quality in Healthcare and Clinical Excellence Commission, and the Picker Institute Europe. Patient- and family-centered care is influencing many of the policies included in the healthcare reform initiatives slated for the United States in the coming decade and is incentivized with payment for performance (P4P) by governmental agencies. Healthcare leaders are challenged with designing PFCC models to deliver care that will improve and optimize patient quality, safety, and clinical outcomes, which will ultimately result in enhanced operational efficiency, organizational effectiveness, and sustainability.

LEADERSHIP AND ORGANIZATIONAL CULTURE

Assessment

The transition from traditional provider-centric healthcare models to transformational models that are patient- and family-centric is challenging and demands that leaders adopt a new global perspective on health care.

The process begins with the assessment of leadership readiness for the patient- and family-centered care approach. There are a few excellent assessment tools available from the Institute for Patient- and Family-Centered Care, the American Hospital Association, and Family Voices that can be used for this purpose. Healthcare executives and managers aspiring to be patient- and family-centered will then need to research best practices; identify leadership role models; and initiate open, evidence-based dialogue regarding PFCC with employees, colleagues, and patients and their families. Dialogue about PFCC planning and focus, benefits and barriers, and strengths and challenges, can be facilitated via tools such as the World Café, fishbowl exercises, brainstorming, nominal group technique, and swim-lane flow charts. Engaged parties involved in this dialogue frequently become transformed, and many voluntarily agree to assist with PFCC design and implementation.

Along with an assessment of leadership readiness, an assessment of organizational culture for embedded patient- and family-centered approaches should be conducted. Among key areas to evaluate are the organization's mission, vision, values, and philosophy of care statements; the language in the organization's policies; and the tone of the communications and signage. The *Patient- and Family-Centered Care: A Hospital Self-Assessment Inventory* (IPFCC, 2010) is a robust tool healthcare leaders can use to obtain a comprehensive assessment of an organization's current practices, generate a gap analysis, and develop action plans for transformational change to a PFCC model.

Managing Systemic Change

Since change is inherent in moving from a traditional organizational culture to one that is patient and family centered, PFCC leaders must be adept at managing change. Change will occur even if it is not managed, but successful culture transformation often depends on how well change was managed. There are several change management and transition models that can be useful at key intervals at macro-, meso-, and microsystem levels, including the improvement model.

According to Donald Nelson, a physician and expert on quality, an organization will transform the culture only when it moves from improvement projects to improving systems (Nelson, Batalden, & Godfrey, 2007, p. 201). **Figure 11.1** depicts the progression from improvement projects to systems improvements.

The first phase of improvement involves improvement projects that focus on areas of high interest, with a clear beginning and clear end. An example of a PFCC improvement project was to recruit a patient–family advisor to the Quality and Patient Safety Committee. The second phase of improvement focuses on microsystems, building the habit for improvement into frontline systems. Individual microsystems (units, departments, teams) are encouraged to plan and make changes as part of their regular work routines (Nelson et al., 2007). Examples of PFCC microsystems changes include encouraging PFCC practices in the Neonatal Intensive Care Unit (NICU). This resulted in family presence guidelines, family participation in multidisciplinary treatment rounds, as well as seeking family advice and embedding PFCC projects in the NICU unit council goals.

The third phase focuses on the mesosystem, in which the best practice that was designed and implemented in one microsystem is spread to other microsystems. The family presence guidelines at SFMC were shared, and subsequently the Radiology Department implemented family presence guidelines for children undergoing radiologic procedures and a policy revision for family presence in the Intensive Care Unit was facilitated.

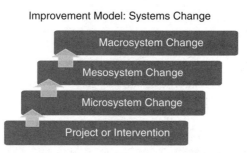

Improvement Model: Systems Change

Figure 11.1 Improvement Model: Systems Change

Source: Adapted from Nelson, E. C., Batalden, P. B., & Godfrey, M. M. (2007). *Quality by design: A clinical microsystems approach.* San Francisco, CA: Jossey-Bass.

The fourth phase of improvement focuses on the entire system as all parts of the system become aligned with the goal of organization-wide improvement (Nelson et al., 2007). The example of macrosystems improvement was the design of a PFCC family and visitor guidelines policy applicable to the entire organization to replace the traditional "restrictive" visitor policy.

Organizational culture includes not only the internal policies and functioning of the organization itself, but also the composition and culture of the community the organization serves. Many healthcare institutions, teaching hospitals, and health systems with vast resources have been successful in implementing PFCC, but organizations with limited resources, serving vulnerable and underserved populations, may face significant challenges. A study conducted by the Economic and Social Research Institute for the W. K. Kellogg Foundation found that certain populations, such as low-income individuals, uninsured persons, immigrants, racial and ethnic minorities, and the elderly, face greater barriers to patient- and family-centered care; and organizations that serve these populations face numerous barriers in pursuing patient- and family-centered care (Silow-Carroll, Alteras, & Stepnick, 2006, p. 4). Some organizational barriers are listed in **Table 11.4**.

To help overcome these potential barriers to PFCC, Silow-Carroll and colleagues (2006) suggested a set of recommendations (outlined in **Table 11.5**) for implementing PFCC with underserved populations.

Table 11.5 depicts core components recommended by Silow-Carroll and colleagues (2006) for a comprehensive patient- and family-centered approach, which can serve as a blueprint for leaders to successfully implement PFCC in underserved populations.

Table 11.4 Organizational Barriers to Patient-Centered Care

Difficulty recruiting and retaining physicians (and culturally competent professionals) from underrepresented groups/minorities.

Lack of defined "boundaries" for outreach staff, who may be overwhelmed dealing with interrelated health, social, cultural, and economic issues of patients.

Fatigue and burnout.

Competing priorities.

Strict hiring requirements that pose obstacles to hiring neighborhood residents.

Lack of tools to gauge and reward patient-centered performance.

Financial constraints.

Traditional attitudes among staff unwilling to change the "old school" provider/patient relationship or acknowledge and address cultural and socioeconomic issues.

Source: Data from Silow-Carroll, S., Alteras, T., & Stepnick, L. (2006, January). *Patient-centered care for underserved populations: Definition and best practices* (White Paper, p. 6). Washington, DC: Economic and Social Research Institute.

Table 11.5 Core Components for PFCC in Underserved Populations

Welcoming environment	Provide physical space and initial interactions that are familiar and not intimidating
Respect for patients' values and expressed needs	· Inquire about patient's care preferences and priorities · Inform and involve patients/families/caregivers in decision making · Individualize care · Promote consistent, mutually respectful patient–provider relationships
Patient empowerment or "activation"	Educate and encourage patients to expand health-related behaviors, self-management, and decision-making roles
Sociocultural competence	· Understand and consider culture, economic and educational status, health literacy level, family patterns/situation, and traditions (including alternative or folk remedies) · Communicate in language and at levels patients understand
Coordination and integration of care	· Assess need for formal/informal services that impact health or treatment · Provide team-based care/care management · Advocate for patients and families · Make appropriate referrals · Ensure smooth transitions between providers and phases of care
Comfort and support	Emphasize physical comfort, privacy, emotional support, and family/friends' involvement
Access and navigation skills	· Provide what patients consider a "medical home" · Minimize waiting times · Provide convenient service hours · Promote access and patient flow · Help patients attain better healthcare system navigation skills
Community outreach	Make demonstrable, proactive efforts to understand and reach out to local communities

Source: Data from Silow-Carroll, S., Alteras, T., & Stepnick, L. (2006, January). *Patient-centered care for underserved populations: Definition and best practices* (White Paper, p. 6). Washington, DC: Economic and Social Research Institute.

Clinician Engagement and Integration

Prior to implementation of PFCC, the clinical staff leadership must be engaged and begin orienting and integrating physicians and other healthcare professionals into the patient- and family-centered care approach. Alignment between clinicians and hospital leaders is critical to the success of patient- and family-centered care. Collaboration between providers and administration is essential when engaging in any assessment, planning (short-, long-, or midterm), implementation, or evaluation of the key components of PFCC.

Among the items that should be included in the orientation is the idea that all aspects of communication and decision making should include the patient and, with the patient's approval, the family; be transparent; and be guided by clear expectations informed by mutual goals for improved patient care. PFCC leaders must value and keep open the lines of communication with clinicians' offices and clinics, provide education and knowledge to help clinicians achieve the mutual goal of enhancing the patient and family experience, and reward and recognize clinicians who adopt PFCC practices.

Hospital leadership and providers can also promote PFCC by collaborating with patient–family advisors as they develop policies and procedures, and engage in healthcare organization operational decision making and planning. Advisors can counsel healthcare leaders on options for equipment, supplies, electronic health records, forms, educational materials, interior design, and signage, which will enhance patient- and family-centered care.

PFCC implementation challenges for clinicians may include:

- The shift from pay-for-service to pay-for-performance
- The inability to make necessary changes due to declining reimbursement and dwindling net revenue with fewer liquid resources available to hire staff, fund marketing, and maintain practice operations
- Higher reliance on evidence-based care and regulatory and healthcare reform requirements for patient- and family-centered care, including the Joint Commission, Centers for Medicare and Medicaid Services, and the federal government, to name a few

However, healthcare reform expectations affirm the value of clinician and hospital leadership interdependence when both stakeholders share common goals and objectives to improve the quality and the cost-effectiveness of care. The development of contracts and healthcare frameworks that can address current and future demands of ongoing healthcare reform can be a win-win for both clinicians and hospitals.

In a successful PFCC model, hospitals and clinicians are aligned on the approach to the provision of patient care, and patient perception of care is thereby improved. Good alignment between clinicians and hospital leaders results in more effective decision making, less competition, improved patient and family loyalty and satisfaction, and a higher-quality patient experience.

PARTNERSHIP WITH PATIENTS AND FAMILIES

Atlas, Grant, Ferris, Chang, and Barry (2009) determined that patients' satisfaction with their health care was not tied to the technical quality of their care, but rather to the quality of communication with their provider, a critical component of the PFCC model. A key driver of overall patient (and family) satisfaction is effective physician communication, with 61% of the variability in patient (and family) satisfaction tied to physician behaviors (Resnick et al., 2008). More than any other group, physicians most influence patients' perception of care. Information exchange between providers and patients can be enhanced by partnering with family members to ensure accurate patient interpretation of information and education, obtain customer feedback, promote patient adherence to treatment recommendations, and such, which are instrumental to the patient's healing and recovery.

One of the essential precepts in patient- and family-centered care is the tenet that patients and families (as the patient determines) are true partners in care, decision making, and setting policy at the individual *and* organizational level, as delineated in the Four Concepts of Patient- and Family-Centered Care featured in Table 11.1. Healthcare leaders must serve as role models to inspire healthcare professionals to engage patients and listen to the individual and collective voice of patients and families. These patient and family partnerships may take the form of:

- Partnership in the processes of patient assessment and in planning patient care and treatment
- Partnership in organizational advisory roles
- Partnership in hiring, educating, and evaluating clinicians (see **Table 11.6**)

Table 11.6 Form of Partnership and Strategies for Partnership with Patient and Families

Form of Partnership	Strategies for Partnership
Partnership in the processes of patient assessment and in planning patient care and treatment	The family provides input into patient assessment and, together with clinicians, plans care with the patient.
	The patient and family attend care-planning conferences (more commonly seen in LTC, behavioral health, and rehabilitation programs, but becoming more common in critical care and the medical/surgical areas).
	Family members participate in physician and multidisciplinary rounds with the patient.
	A family support person (family caregiver and/or family spokesperson) is identified on admission and actively participates throughout the care episode.
	The patient and family have access to information in the patient's medical record and can contribute their own observations and documentation.
	Family members participate with the patient during nursing bedside shift report.
	The family interfaces with all of the patient's providers during transitions of care.
Partnership in organizational advisory roles	Patients and families provide feedback on the care experience through a variety of mechanisms (during executive and other leader rounds on patients and families, in postdischarge patient surveys, in family feedback sessions, in focus groups, etc.).
	Patients and family members are placed in the formal role of Patient Family Advisors (PFAs) (paid or unpaid).
	Patients and family members participate on Patient Family Advisory Councils at the departmental and organizational level.
	Patients and family members serve as designers, editors, and advisors for educational materials in which patient health literacy is involved.
	Patients and family members participate in creative supportive roles such as compassionate listener, peer advocate, peer navigator.
	Patients and family members provide input on the environment and architectural design of healthcare facilities (e.g., informally, by completing a "noise at night" feedback survey during hospitalization or, formally, by serving on facility design teams).
	Patients and family members provide input into the development and revision of patient care and administrative policies and processes; policies are written from the perspective that patients and families are partners.
	Patients and family members fully participate as equal members of key organizational committees, teams or councils at the departmental, organizational, and governing board levels (e.g., quality and patient safety committees).

Table 11.6 (*continued*)

Form of Partnership	Strategies for Partnership
Partnership in hiring, educating, and evaluating clinicians	Patients and family members provide input into the design of behavioral interviewing questions and participate in the interview process for recruiting and hiring new clinicians and PFAs, to ensure individuals with patient- and family-centered attributes are hired.
	Patients and family members act as Adjunct Faculty to teach physicians and clinical staff about patient- and family-centered care, and participate in curriculum design for hospital-associated nursing and medical schools.
	Patients and family members provide feedback on important aspects of care, and leaders actively seek feedback about the effectiveness and patient- and family-centeredness of the care provided. This feedback informs the criteria for clinician position descriptions and performance evaluations.

SUMMARY

Transforming an organization from a provider-centric and hospital-convenient care delivery approach to a patient- and family-centered care model requires leaders to form new partnerships with patients, families, clinicians, and other staff, as well as internal and external stakeholders. Patient- and family-centered healthcare leaders create and promote a culture based on collaboration between health professionals and organizations and patients and their families that promotes mutual learning and shared accountability to achieve key outcomes for quality of care.

Discussion Questions

1. What are the implications of shifting care delivery strategies for the workforce from provider-centric to patient- and family-centered care?

2. What are ways to effectively prepare a workforce to operate in a changing care delivery context?

3. What does a partnership between healthcare leaders, providers, patients, and families look like?

4. In what ways might PFCC introduce additional internal dynamics and support requirements that need to be met?

5. How do we as healthcare leaders model collaboration with patients and their families?

Case Study: A Values-Based Approach

As a result of changing local, state, and national economic and societal circumstances, leaders of acute care hospitals face complex concerns. Although financial and quality outcomes are critical benchmarks for successful leaders, leaders must also focus on how to empower patients and families to make personal healthcare decisions, better prepare them to prevent illness, and to manage chronic conditions and diseases. For this reason, St. Francis Medical Center (SFMC), the urban, faith-based (Catholic) organization used as an example in this chapter, elected to use patient- and family-centered care as its **care delivery model** in 2008. SFMC's goal is, over time, to improve the health of the general population in its economically depressed and underserved community.

As a component of its healthcare reform strategy, SFMC is participating in the formation of *accountable care organization (ACO)* structures and incentive-generated healthcare reform programs. An ACO is defined as an entity in which healthcare providers are jointly held accountable for achieving measured quality improvements and reductions in the rate of spending growth for services. While caring for a defined patient population, the ACO should achieve overall cost and quality improvements per capita. ACOs may involve a variety of provider configurations—that is, integrated delivery systems, primary care medical groups, hospital-based systems, and virtual networks such as integrated practice associations. All ACOs, however, have a strong basis in primary care, and hospitals are encouraged to participate in ACOs to provide a breadth of healthcare options for patients (McClellan, McKethan, Lewis, Roski, & Fisher, 2010). Partnerships with patients, families, and community healthcare providers are essential for a hospital to be able to provide a full range of care to its clients.

SFMC's parent organization sponsored a patient-experience planning workshop, at which a PFCC transition team was developed. The PFCC model was so aligned with the goals of the system that the organization's leaders decided to strategically focus on developing the structure and processes to build out and implement the concept.

SFMC, founded on the values of Saint Vincent de Paul, Saint Louise de Marillac, and Saint Elizabeth Ann Seton, had already begun to create a **professional practice model** based on the Vincentian values: simplicity, respect, compassionate care, advocacy for the poor, and inventiveness to infinity. This professional practice model (i.e., a practice system that included specific structures, processes, and values) supported registered nurse control over the delivery of nursing care and the environment in which the nursing care was delivered (Hoffart & Woods, 1996). This model was named VVOOM, an acronym for "Vincentian Values Optimizing Our Mission" (**Figure 11.2**).

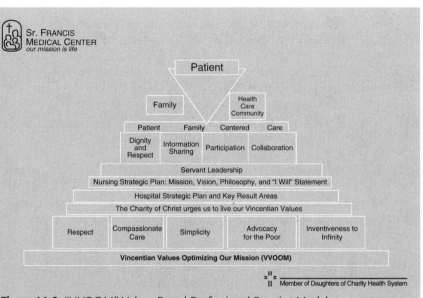

Sr. FRANCIS
MEDICAL CENTER
our mission is life

Patient

Family

Health
Care
Community

| Patient | Family | Centered | Care |

| Dignity and Respect | Information Sharing | Participation | Collaboration |

Servant Leadership

Nursing Strategic Plan: Mission, Vision, Philosophy, and "I Will" Statement

Hospital Strategic Plan and Key Result Areas

The Charity of Christ urges us to live our Vincentian Values

| Respect | Compassionate Care | Simplicity | Advocacy for the Poor | Inventiveness to Infinity |

Vincentian Values Optimizing Our Mission (VVOOM)

= ‖ = Member of Daughters of Charity Health System

Figure 11.2 "VVOOM" Values Based Professional Practice Model

Source: Reproduced from the St. Francis Medical Center. (2010). *Strategic plan.* Lynwood, CA.

Servant Leadership

SFMC is a Catholic hospital that defines itself as a "ministry," promotes health care as a "calling," and expects its leaders to commit to the mission for the Daughters of Charity (DOC). The concept of being a servant first for the better good of the patients/families served as well as being stewards of the ministry has been reinforced by the sisters who have served the hospital's patients. According to the model's founder, Robert K. Greenleaf (1976, p. 9):

> Caring for persons, the more able and the less able serving each other, is the rock upon which a good society is built . . . if a better society is to be built, one that is more just and more loving, that provides greater creative opportunity for its people, then the most open course is to raise both the capacity to serve and the very performance as servant of leaders and existing major institutions.

Vincentian institutions carry a responsibility for the greater good of society by promoting the Vincentian character and mission. However, the declining number of religious practitioners participating in faith-based institutions has driven a need for greater numbers of laity leaders to carry this mission forward. Laity leaders, like the nuns before them, are motivated and inspired to commit to the culture, values, and mission of their Vincentian institution and practice elements of this ministry via the model of servant leadership.

Servant leadership is a model that is conducive to PFCC and complements the four key components of dignity and respect, information sharing, participation, and collaboration, that are at the foundation of the WOOM model's structure. By serving all clients and customers, the associates of SFMC place the patient and family at the heart of the plan of care and humbly provide support and assistance with the recuperation and/or management of their healthcare needs.

Values Congruency

SFMC leaders believed it important to assess whether the internal/personal values of those entrusted to promote and model Vincentian culture were congruent with those of the organization. Nursing research was conducted, and congruency of nursing personal values with Vincentian values was evaluated.

Using the concept of managing by values can enhance organizational effectiveness for organizations that face increasing complexity, competitive challenge, and a high rate of change (Blanchard & O'Connor, 1997). However, SFMC needed a professional practice model based on "caring by values" versus "managing by values." According to Covey (1990), one cannot transform an organization into a total quality culture unless and until basic habits of personal character and interpersonal relations based on principles (values) are built within the workforce.

Building the foundation to make a culture change was dependent on first creating WOOM to support patient- and family-centered care delivery. Then, leadership and management at all organizational levels, including the governing board, executive leadership, department directors, unit managers, and clinicians, participated in the planning, design, and implementation of both the professional practice model and the care delivery model. Shortly after the initial system patient experience planning workshop, the leaders added PFCC to the hospital's strategic plan and the nursing strategic plan. PFCC became the fundamental approach for a key area of the SFMC strategic plan: "Excellence, Consistency & Sustainability," defined as consistent and sustainable top performance, top 10% performance, and **top box achievement** across the areas of patient safety, quality, service (patient experience), and financial indicators through a balance of systematic approaches and innovation (SFMC, 2010).

Simultaneously with the Patient Care Service Division's defining and designing the professional and care delivery models, SFMC also participated in Premier healthcare alliance's national collaborative: "QUEST," a program for quality, evidence-based medicine, cost efficiency, and mortality reduction (May, 2011). SFMC met or exceeded clinical quality and cost benchmarks for mortality, CMS core measures, and cost per adjusted discharge, and was designated a top performer in 2010 among 157 nonprofit hospitals.

Many patient and family approaches became a part of the SFMC initiatives to improve outcomes. Among them were patient- and family-initiated rapid-response teams. Specific interventions and standardized bundles of care were implemented, and patients and families were encouraged to partner and participate with SFMC healthcare professionals. As utilization of evidence-based care increased, mortality rates declined. Education and communication were also key drivers among the patients, families, and multidisciplinary team to ensure an appropriate level of care and length of stay in preparation for the transition to home/community.

In fiscal year 2010, the management team was tasked to identify key departmental/hospital policies and procedures that needed revision in order to support the goals of PFCC as well as to design department-specific tactics that would improve the patient experience. The chief nursing officer (CNO) used the PFCC approach to uphold the mission of the Daughters of Charity, the sponsoring religious organization for SFMC. To transform the Daughters of Charity, the CNO took on the responsibility of motivating stakeholders, effectively communicating the WOOM/PFCC model, defining strategies, and prioritizing tactics (**Figure 11.3**).

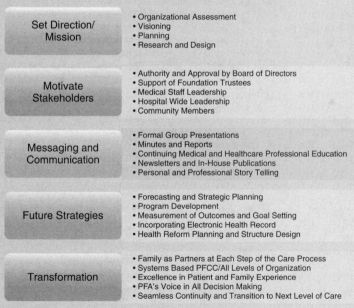

Figure 11.3 PFCC Leadership Competencies

The directors and managers at the point of service were charged with specific tasks and actions, such as coordinating staffing, coordinating and supervising internal and client/family communications, and holding personnel accountable to perform in alignment with leadership's vision and the DOC mission (**Figure 11.4**).

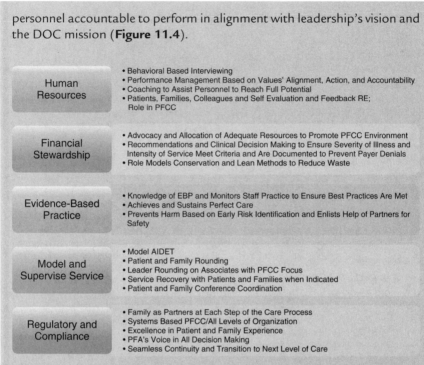

Human Resources
- Behavioral Based Interviewing
- Performance Management Based on Values' Alignment, Action, and Accountability
- Coaching to Assist Personnel to Reach Full Potential
- Patients, Families, Colleagues and Self Evaluation and Feedback RE; Role in PFCC

Financial Stewardship
- Advocacy and Allocation of Adequate Resources to Promote PFCC Environment
- Recommendations and Clinical Decision Making to Ensure Severity of Illness and Intensity of Service Meet Criteria and Are Documented to Prevent Payer Denials
- Role Models Conservation and Lean Methods to Reduce Waste

Evidence-Based Practice
- Knowledge of EBP and Monitors Staff Practice to Ensure Best Practices Are Met
- Achieves and Sustains Perfect Care
- Prevents Harm Based on Early Risk Identification and Enlists Help of Partners for Safety

Model and Supervise Service
- Model AIDET
- Patient and Family Rounding
- Leader Rounding on Associates with PFCC Focus
- Service Recovery with Patients and Families when Indicated
- Patient and Family Conference Coordination

Regulatory and Compliance
- Family as Partners at Each Step of the Care Process
- Systems Based PFCC/All Levels of Organization
- Excellence in Patient and Family Experience
- PFA's Voice in All Decision Making
- Seamless Continuity and Transition to Next Level of Care

Figure 11.4 PFCC Management Competencies

Demonstrated outcomes for the SFMC PFCC process during the specified interval include the following:

- The establishment of the role of patient–family advisor on high-level quality and patient safety committees and task groups
- Input on hospital design, signage, and brochures
- Planning for the Patient and Family Advisory Council

These outcomes achieved 75% of the goals set in the original strategic plan for this interval.

Case Study Discussion Questions

1. How can SFMC obtain input or feedback from patients and their families?
2. How can employees at all levels of SFMC be guided and facilitated to engage in constructive, open dialogue regarding necessary capabilities and skills to partner with patients and families in health care?

3. In what ways does a PFCC model help to mitigate the current healthcare reform pressures facing SFMC?

4. Given the changing nature of healthcare delivery in hospitals, what are the training and workforce development implications for an organization such as SFMC that have adopted a servant leadership approach?

RELATED WEBSITES

Agency for Healthcare Research and Quality: www.ahrq.gov

Family Voices: www.familyvoices.org

Institute for Healthcare Improvement: www.ihi.org

Institute for Patient- and Family-Centered Care: www.ipfcc.org

The Joint Commission: http://jointcommission.org

PFCC Partners: www.PFCCpartners.com

Planetree: www.planetree.org

Picker Institute: www.pickerinstitute.org

The Schwartz Center for Compassionate Healthcare: www.theschwartzcenter.org

Resource Guides and Toolkits

Advancing Effective Communication, Cultural Competence and Patient- and Family-Centered Care: A Roadmap for Hospitals Advancing the Practice of Patient- and Family-Centered Care: How to Get Started: www.ipfcc.org

Patient-Centered Care Improvement Guide: www.patient-centeredcare.org

Strategies for Leadership: Patient- and Family-Centered Care: www.aha.org

The Family as Patient Care Partner: Leveraging Family Involvement to Improve Quality, Safety and Satisfaction: www.advisory.com/Research/Nursing-Executive -Center/Studies/2006/The-Family-as-Patient-Care-Partner

REFERENCES

Atlas, S. J., Grant, R. W., Ferris, T. G., Chang, Y., & Barry, M. J. (2009, March 3). Patient-physician connectedness and quality of primary care. *Annals of Internal Medicine, 150*(5), 325–335.

Balik, B., Conway, J., Zipperer, L., & Watson, J. (2011). *Achieving and exceptional patient and family experience of inpatient hospital care* [IHI Innovation Series White Paper]. Retrieved November 7, 2012 from www.ihi.org/knowledge/Pages /IHIWhitePapers/chievingExceptionalPatientFamilyExperienceInpatient HospitalCareWhitePaper.aspx.

Blanchard, K., & O'Connor, M. (1997). *Managing by values*. San Francisco, CA: Berrett-Koehler.

Centers for Medicare and Medicaid Services (CMS). (2010, November 19). *Federal register rules and regulations, final rule. Medicare and Medicaid programs: Changes to the hospital and critical access hospital Conditions of Participation to ensure visitation rights for all patients* (Federal Register/Vol. 75, No. 223). Washington, DC: U.S. Government Printing Office.

Conway, J., Johnson, B., Edgman-Levitan, S., Schlucter, J., Ford, D., Sodomka, P., & Simmons, L. (2006). Partnering with patients and families to design a patient- and family-centered health care system: A roadmap for the future: A work in progress. Retrieved November 7, 2012 from www.ihi.org/knowledge/pages/publications/partneringwithpatientsandfamilies.aspx.

Covey, S. R. (1990). *Principle-centered leadership*. New York, NY: Free Press.

Greenleaf, R. K. (1976). *The institution as servant*. Indianapolis, IN: Robert K. Greenleaf Center.

HCAHPS. (2005). Retrieved November 7, 2012 from www.hcahpsonline.org/home.aspx.

HHS. (2011). *Partnership for patients: Better care, lower costs*. Retrieved November 7, 2012 from www.healthcare.gov/compare/partnership-for-patients/.

Hoffart, N., & Woods, C. Q. (1996, November/December). Elements of a nursing professional practice model. *Journal of Professional Nursing, 12*(6), 354–384.

Institute of Medicine (IOM). (2001). *Crossing the quality chasm: A new health system for the 21st century*. Washington, DC: Author.

Institute for Patient- and Family-Centered Care (IPFCC). (2010). *Patient- and family-centered care: A hospital self-assessment inventory*. Retrieved November 7, 2012 from www.aha.org/content/00-10/assessment.pdf.

The Joint Commission (TJC). (2010). *Advancing effective communication, cultural competence and patient- and family-centered care: A roadmap for hospitals*. Retrieved November 7, 2012 from www.jointcommission.org/assets/1/6/ARoadmapforHospitalsfinalversion727.pdf.

May, E. L. (2011, March/April). The efficient healthcare organization: Creating a new standard in healthcare. *Healthcare Executive, 26*(2), 14–24.

McClellan, M., McKethan, A. N., Lewis, J. L., Roski, J., & Fisher, E. S. (2010, May). A national strategy to put accountable care into practice. *Health Affairs*, (6), 982.

Nelson, E. C., Batalden, P. B., & Godfrey, M. M. (2007). *Quality by design: A clinical microsystems approach*. San Francisco, CA: Jossey-Bass.

Resnick, A. S., Disbot, M., Wurster, A., Mullen, J. L., Kaiser, L. R., & Morris, J. B. (2008). Contributions of surgical residents to patient satisfaction: Impact of residents beyond clinical care. *Journal of Surgical Education*, (3), 243–252.

Robert Wood Johnson Foundation (RWJF). (2010, September 14). Patient-centered medical homes. *Health Affairs*, 1–6. doi:10.1377/hpb2010.17.

Silow-Carroll, S., Alteras, T., & Stepnick, L. (2006, January). *Patient-centered care for underserved populations: Definition and best practices* [White paper]. Washington, DC: Economic and Social Research Institute.

St. Francis Medical Center (SFMC). (2010). *Strategic plan*. Lynwood, CA: Author.

Chapter 12

Financial Considerations for Healthcare Leaders

Linda J. Gunn and John A. Orsini

LEARNING OBJECTIVES

By the end of this chapter, the student will be able to:

- Explain the importance of financial management in health care.
- Identify the components of effective financial management.
- Describe financial management models utilized in the healthcare industry.
- Discuss the financial implications of healthcare reform.

KEY TERMS

Benchmarking	Key drivers
Financial management	Management model
Healthcare reform	Performance reporting

INTRODUCTION

With the rapid growth of healthcare facilities, it is increasingly important to understand how to utilize financial information to make the best decisions possible to ensure sustainability and viability of the healthcare institution.

Financial Management Considerations

Financial management is vital to healthcare organizations' success. Financial performance management combines strategic and operational elements that allow healthcare leaders to develop, invest in, and implement effective and sustainable business models for their organizations. Intuition and professional experiences clearly inspire leadership vision. But by analyzing past and present financial performance and using those data and assessments to inform future projections and scenarios, leaders can reduce risks and maximize opportunities for successful achievement of the mission, goals, and objectives of their organizations.

MEASURE AND MONITOR KEY DRIVERS

Key drivers are factors that influence and direct the outcome of a process, mission, program, or strategic plan. Key drivers can be used to identify the steps to be taken toward the organization's goals and objectives and the data to be collected to assess effective performance and progress. Each industry has refined its key drivers, which are available from industry associations or rating agency reports and analyses. From these industry sources, healthcare leaders should select "the vital few" drivers that are most relevant to their operations and monitor those indicators on a regular basis. Following too many indicators, or measuring drivers unrelated to organizational performance, can result in management distraction and delay necessary action. For that reason, it is critical for healthcare leaders to identify and focus on the vital few.

Key drivers in health care include:

- Salary and benefits as a percentage of revenue or per unit of service performance
- Supplies as a percentage of revenue or per unit of service
- Contribution margin by product or service line
- Bad debt and charity as a percentage of revenue
- Market share percentage
- Cash collections as a percentage of net collectable revenue (net revenue less bad debt)
- Operating margin percentage
- Earnings before interest, taxes, depreciation, and amortization (EBITDA percentage)

Glossary of Key Drivers

Salary and benefits as a percentage of revenue or per unit of service performance: The percentage of the organization's budget allotted for labor, which includes employee salaries and also takes into consideration payroll and unemployment insurance taxes, benefits, reimbursements, overtime, workers' compensation, leave time, and holiday pay (Deeb, 2012).

Supplies as a percentage of revenue or per unit of service: Total supplies divided by net operating revenue.

Contribution margin by product or service line: A cost accounting concept that allows a company to determine the profitability of individual products or service lines. This figure can then be used to determine whether variable costs for that product can be reduced. The contribution margin is the revenue left over after paying variable costs (Investopia, n.d.a).

Bad debt and charity as a percentage of revenue: Bad debt expense plus charity writeoffs divided by net operating revenue.

Market share percentage: The percentage of an industry or market's total sales that is earned by a particular company over a specified time period. Market share is calculated by taking the company's sales over the period and dividing it by the total sales of the industry over the same period. This metric is used to give a general idea of the size of a company to its market and its competitors (Investopia, n.d.b).

Cash collections as a percentage of net collectable revenue (net revenue less bad debt): This is total patient cash collections divided by net collectible revenue. Over time, this should be 100%. If less than 100%, it informs you that your net revenue is overstated or accounts receivable are growing. If over 100%, accounts receivable should be declining or net revenue is understated.

Operating margin percentage: A measurement of what portion of a company's revenue is left over after paying all costs. A healthy operating margin is required for a company to pay for its fixed costs, such as interest on debt (Investopia, n.d.c).

Earnings before interest, taxes, depreciation, and amortization: These are intended to be an indicator of a company's financial position. EBITDA tells an investor how much money a company would have made if it didn't have to pay *interest expense* on its debt or *taxes*, or take *depreciation and amortization charges* (Kennon, 2012).

Functional Performance Reports

Financial performance in an organization can be assessed by monitoring its vital few key drivers. For example, it is a performance report that assesses productivity, a key indicator. Because labor costs are one of the top expense categories in healthcare organizations, such a report allows each business unit to identify its underperforming departments on a biweekly basis. This process depersonalizes performance issues and facilitates a culture of transparency and a commitment to rapid cycle improvement. Units and managers can use the data to understand "How we got here," and develop operational plans and specific actions to improve future performance—that is, "Where we want to go" (see **Table 12.1**).

Performance reporting can also be used as a learning tool that high-lights best practices within an organization. A best practice that has been successfully implemented by one unit or department can be shared with or adopted by other similar units to facilitate more rapid process improvement (Laurent, 2010).

Table 12.1 MOR Summary Report

Monthly Operating Review (MOR)

Summary Report

FY 2005—April 2005

Part I. Global Measures

Productivity Index*	CURRENT MONTH				YEAR-TO-DATE		
	ACT	BUD	P/YR	P/MO	ACT	BUD	P/YR
Adjusted Occupied Bed (AOB)	578	549	543	570	551	541	534
General ALOS	4.2	4.4	4.6	4.2	4.4	4.4	4.5
FTEs all man-hours	3947	3718	3716	3902	3842	3688	3573
FTEs per AOB	6.11	6.06	6.25	6.23	6.30	6.11	6.09
Salaries and benefits as % of net revenue	46.0%	45.3%	48.0%	43.9%	45.0%	45.1%	44.7%
Average hourly rate	$31.13	$27.82	$28.03	$29.28	$28.65	$27.41	$26.67

Part II. Challenges

Department	ACT FTEs	BUD FTES	FTE VAR
740000 Labor and Delivery	95.46	82.00	–13.46
856000 Admitting	68.39	55.54	–12.85
615010 Cardiac Telemetry	58.76	48.06	–10.70

Part III. Operational Plan

Please write your action plan below your cost center.

740000 Labor and Delivery
Continuing to flex labor care staff accordingly, based on census. Antenatal unit being used as a med/surg overflow.
Staffing for caregiver hours affecting department's productivity with no credit for midnight census.

*Legend: ACT = Actual; BUD = Budget; P/YR = Prior year; P/MO = Prior month; FTE = Full-time equivalent; VAR = Variance.

Benchmarking and Best Practices

For the vital few key drivers, performance can also be evaluated and compared among internal or external cohorts through the process of **benchmarking**. Comparing performance among units can highlight operational excellence, identify best practices for dissemination, uncover areas for potential growth, and facilitate an environment of continuous quality improvement. Benchmarking allows quantitative assessments that support the well-known adage, "You can successfully manage only what you measure." Examples of benchmarking reports are discussed as follows.

Balanced Scorecard

A balanced scorecard combines performance management and benchmarking. The tool reports the performance of a business unit's individual goals, but also allows the comparison of performance among all the units assessed. These comparisons can promote communication and information sharing, best practice implementation, performance consistency, and collaboration toward the achievement of common goals.

Trending

Benchmarking allows similar cohorts to compare performance on specific indicators as well as to monitor trends and variation in performance. Organizations often prepare a benchmarking report that groups together cohorts to facilitate performance comparisons and also allows individual units to track their own performance over time (Berger, 2003).

Department Specific Performance

Table 12.2 offers an example of a more detailed benchmarking tool that reports performance for specific similar departments in like cohorts. Such reports allow performance comparisons and opportunity identification on a microlevel.

LEVELS OF ACCOUNTABILITY

Accountability at every level of the organization is critical for effective performance and continuous quality improvement. Successful **management models** strive to create and advance accountability not only in the executive suite, but also on the "front lines," where employees are implementing the strategies to achieve the organization's mission and goals. "Lowest common denominator accountability" acknowledges that employees providing the organization's services are likely to have valuable insight about clients, procedures, issues, and such, and can suggest

Table 12.2 Benchmarking Summary for Transcription

Transcription FTEs	YTD Feb 09		FY 08		FY 07	
	Per Adjusted Patient Day	Per Adjusted Discharge	Per Adjusted Patient Day	Per Adjusted Discharge	Per Adjusted Patient Day	Per Adjusted Discharge
Our System						
Hosp. A	10.69	51.34	12.38	60.05	10.64	50.14
Hosp. B	10.54	35.70	12.36	43.30	11.73	40.28
Hosp. C	10.61	46.14	15.70	73.03	14.35	71.10
Competitor System						
Hosp. A			7.57	35.57	14.09	63.28
Hosp. B			4.55	19.30	6.51	27.95
Hosp. C			11.38	43.44	14.92	52.42

excellent ideas to improve performance. Granting frontline employees the authority to identify concerns and to formulate and implement solutions can promote accountability and enhance successful performance (Office of the Auditor General of Canada, 2008).

Some accountability questions are:

· What is the performance issue we have identified?
· What is the magnitude of the problem?
· What are some of the potential causes of the problem?
· What tools or resources do we need to solve the problem?
· What would be a successful solution to the problem?
· How can we measure success?
· How often will performance be assessed? Hourly? Daily? Weekly? Monthly?

Team Player and Facilitator

Healthcare leaders play a crucial role in problem solving by facilitating collaboration and teamwork to address issues. A traditional autocratic approach wherein the team leader directs the quest for solutions from the "top down" can result in lost opportunities. Effective leaders approach performance issues with the "beginner's mind"—that is, an openness to new ideas and learning; consider all alternatives suggested (especially from those who work most closely with the issue of concern); and encourage a climate of good will and trust.

Intellectual Curiosity and a Culture of Excellence

Performance management is not a destination, but a journey. Leaders who promote a culture of intellectual curiosity and excellence are most likely to enlist employees in collaborating to identify concerns and to develop and implement creative and effective solutions.

A commitment to excellence can inspire units and departments to aim for a higher level of performance. Benchmarking results demonstrate performance in a particular quartile; for example, median or top. Whereas median performance may be adequate in some settings, most units strive to provide services of superior quality. Setting performance expectations at the median is likely to result in median performance. With a commitment to excellence, operating units are frequently able to achieve upper-quartile performance levels despite limitations in funding, facilities, staffing, and technology. Reviewing benchmarking reports in detail to understand the current level of function, identifying areas for potential intervention, and developing strategies to improve performance can result in an excellent learning exercise and builds the foundation for a better business model.

This "reconciliation process" can lead to the development of strategies such as enhanced workforce training, investment in upgrading technology, and revisions of policies and procedures, which can benefit not only the business unit engaged in review but also other units in the organization.

Goals, Rules, Process, and Interpersonal (GRPI) (**Figure 12.1**) is an excellent tool to facilitate group performance reviews and questions and items for teams to discuss, and on which teams can vote and come to consensus.

Project Plan

Performance management also requires organizational skill and project management capabilities. Leaders must marshal and guide the most effective teams to assess and address issues and launch or revise projects to achieve performance outcomes and strategic objectives.

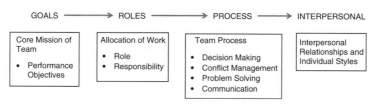

Figure 12.1 GRPI Model*

*This model provides a framework for diagnosing and improving team effectiveness. The model is hierarchical: start with goals, then allocated work/roles, then identify team processes, and finally deal with personalities, styles, and cultural differences to minimize process loss.

Some key considerations for project development include:

- What are the objectives of the project?
- What steps are necessary to implement the project plan?
- Who will be responsible for oversight and coordination of the plan and its steps?
- When will each step be implemented (timeline)?
- What resources are required for each step?
- What metric will measure success? How often will data be collected?
- If success is not achieved, how at what point will the project be reevaluated for a possible revision or course change?

Making Wise Decisions

As team and unit leaders, managers are tasked with making decisions about new strategies and directions to improve performance, often with limited information and data to help guide choices. Some choose to wait for additional input or instead opt to make incremental decisions with the input available and then monitor the results. Each approach has its pros and cons. Leaders do need to keep in mind that decisions made in an effort to improve performance can not only affect the livelihoods of unit employees and the future of the organization as a whole, but also the economy of the geographic region where the organization is located. Therefore, it is important for managers to consider all potential outcomes and consequences in their decision-making process. It is a good idea for leaders to establish ongoing performance metrics to be able to identify negative outcomes and to determine whether the decision was sound or needs review (ReadPeriodicals, 2010).

An effective approach includes these items:

- Understanding that the goal of performance management is to improve the organization
- Identify areas of concern and analyze the causes of identified problems and issues
- Focus efforts on strategies and solutions for these problems
- Use data collected to help drive decisions and recommendations
- Assess the effectiveness of strategies to address the problems on an ongoing basis and revise these strategies as needed

MANAGEMENT MODEL

Managers in healthcare organizations are entrusted to deliver high-quality services and programs to their clientele and are accountable for the efficient and effective utilization of resources. Executives must demonstrate that they have been "good stewards" of the organization's resources and have safeguarded the assets of the organization.

Managers must have support for their decision making; ensure the availability of timely, relevant, and reliable financial information; establish a supportive control environment; and make efficient and effective use of the resources of the organization. Management must also enable the organization to comply with various regulatory bodies and safeguard the assets of the organization.

The management model focuses on managing and directing the organization's resources economically and efficiently to achieve the organization's objectives. It includes strategic planning, analysis, and support for decisions.

Financial Management

Leaders must accurately represent an organization's financial status, including expenditures and revenue. Cash provides the corroboration for financial statements. If more revenue is recorded than cash collected, and the disparity cannot be explained via accounts receivable, there is risk of an overstatement.

Cash

Cash explains and justifies the expenses of the organization, which are generally routine, predictable, and ongoing. Cash is the lifeblood of any organization and must be properly safeguarded through a robust internal control system and monitored to ensure adequate levels are maintained to cover organization expenses.

Budgets

Budget management and review support effective monitoring of financial resources and successfully planning for an organization's future. The budget reflects the organization's financial and operational goals. By tracking and analyzing financial performance, management can develop strategic plans that align fiscal resources with the desired goals.

Before the start of the operating year, each organization must establish an accurate budget that integrates the organization's strategic plan into the financial plan. The financial plan documents cash/capital and debt levels, projects the amount and number of resources needed to maintain a sustainable future, and allows the implementation of the strategic plan.

During the operating year, managers should review the budget entries, compare actual expenses and revenue with previous estimates and projections, and analyze the variances between actual and projected data.

Variances can also be analyzed against the budget data for an earlier interval. For example, operating units can compare expenditures in the first quarter of this year to the first quarter of the previous year. Managers can be offered incentives to stay within their allocated budgets, be held accountable for unfavorable variances, and tasked to provide corrective action plans when actual results fall outside of the budgeted or planned range.

Variance Analysis

Executives aim to ensure the sustainability of their organizations and strive to increase productivity and performance without increasing expenses and costs. Variance analysis examines the difference, or variance, between projected/budgeted expenses and actual expenses and allows managers to identify areas of concern that need assessment or intervention. Variance data can also be benchmarked against equivalent data from like competitors such as hospitals and can aid managers in making decisions and developing more effective tactical initiatives that can control excessive spending and improve cost-efficiency and effectiveness. Variance analyses help management to set strategic goals and to explain the utilization of resources in support of those goals to stakeholders such as the Board of Directors, staff physicians, insurance companies, and stockholders.

Table 12.3 demonstrates an expense variance analysis that examines planned/budgeted expenses versus actual expenses for salary and hours worked.

Weekly Projections

Weekly projections are designed to accurately project current month revenue and expenses on a weekly basis to monitor the budget, capture fluctuations, serve as a guide to future financial decisions, and allow financial managers to address concerns in a timely manner.

Monthly Operating Reviews

Financial statements are also produced regularly at longer intervals (e.g., monthly, quarterly, and annually) and summarize the hospital's financial status during designated intervals. Management reviews the information on a monthly basis to ensure the hospital is running effectively and efficiently and to identify any variances between planned and budgeted goals and actual operating results.

The monthly operating review aids managers in pinpointing problems and implementing remediation if there are inconsistencies that deviate from the organization's operating plan. The statement of financial position or balance sheet displays the organization's assets, liabilities, and net worth

Table 12.3 Salary Variance Analysis

Actual Expense	$2000
Budgeted Expense	$3200
Actual Hours	400
Budgeted Hours	800

Financial Variance $3200 – $2000 = $1200 Favorable

There may be two possible causes of the variance between the actual values and the projections:

1. Differences in the hourly rate of pay (i.e., a lower salary)
2. Differences in the number of hours worked (i.e., fewer hours worked)

Actual Hourly Expense (salary paid per hour)	$2000/400 = $5.00
Budgeted Hourly Expense (salary projected per hour)	$3200/800 = $4.00
Hourly Variance	

Financial Variance $5.00 – $4.00 = –$1.00 per hour rate of pay Unfavorable

Price/Rate Analysis:

Budgeted Hourly Expense	$4.00
Actual Hourly Expense	**$5.00**
Hourly Rate Variance	*<$1.00> Unfavorable*
Actual Hours	**400**
Unfavorable Variance	*<$400>*

Usage/Efficiency Analysis:

Budgeted Hours Allowed	800
Actual Hours Used	**400**
Usage Variance	400
Budgeted Hourly Expense	$4.00
Favorable Variance	$1600

Variance Analysis Summary

Price Rate Analysis—Unfavorable <$400>

Usage/Efficiency—Favorable $1600

Total Variance—Favorable $1200

(net assets) during the specific period. The income statement or statement of activities reports the revenue and expenses of the organization during that term. The monthly operating review presents information that allows managers to easily define their progress. It is important for managers to set financial goals in advance of these ongoing assessments, otherwise the data collected is less meaningful.

Net Accounts Receivable Estimates

Funds due from patients or insurance payers that the organization expects to collect within 30 to 60 days of service are considered accounts receivable. These sums can be large and must be monitored carefully. It can be challenging for financial managers to estimate what percentage of accounts receivable are likely to be collected by the organization—that is, net collectible revenue.

Net Collectible Revenue

A good test of organization solvency is the monitoring of net collectible revenue. Revenue estimates should quantify projected cash collections. A total of 100% of net collectible revenue should be collected in a designated period and monitored via a rolling 6-month trend report. Variances below 100% net collectible should routinely be reconciled and explained. Reconciliation can provide insights into the accounting estimation process, which can then be used to refine future net revenue projections.

Capital Investment and Look-Back

In some cases, additional cash can be generated internally from prior years' capital investments. A Federal Depreciation Look-Back Analysis, which reviews the classification and categorization of assets, has the potential to improve cash flow by reducing current federal and state income tax. This process allows for an organization to accelerate federal tax depreciation into the current year from investments made in buildings and other fixed assets in the past (General Financial and Tax Consulting, LLC., 2009).

Certifications

The Sarbanes-Oxley Act of 2002 introduced major changes in the regulation of corporate governance and financial practice. Section 302 pertains to corporate responsibility and requires certification of financial documents and accountability for the financial reports that organizations produce. To ensure that there is no misrepresentation, a CEO or CFO must review all financial reports and guarantee their accuracy. Any material changes in internal accounting controls, and any deficiencies, accounting misrepresentations, or fraud must be reported immediately to the audit committee. Certification is done quarterly and/or annually and establishes an audit trail, which makes it easier to identify, correct, and track any organizational deficiencies (Sarbanes Oxley 101, 2012).

Senior management is responsible for compliance with these regulations. The signatures of the CEO or CFO signify the accuracy and integrity of the document—that is, that it correctly represents the financial condition of the organization at the time of submission and attests to the effectiveness of the accounting management controls of the organization (Sarbanes Oxley 101, 2012).

FINANCIAL IMPLICATIONS OF HEALTHCARE REFORM

On March 23, 2010, President Obama signed into law the Patient Protection and Affordable Care Act, and 7 days later, the Health Care and Education Reconciliation Act of 2010. The Patient Protection and Affordable Care Act and the Reconciliation measure (collectively, the "Act") expand healthcare coverage by providing the following:

- Expanded Medicaid eligibility to enroll an additional 16 million people
- Subsidies for insurance purchase through healthcare exchanges for approximately 16 million people
- Health insurance eligibility for individuals with preexisting conditions
- Extended dependent coverage in insurance programs through age 26
- A ban on lifetime limits and unreasonable annual caps on insurance coverage
- A requirement that states maintain current eligibility levels for a specified period for children in Medicaid and the Children's Health Insurance Plan

The Patient Protection and Affordable Care Act (H.R. 3590) is considered true **healthcare reform**. It is expected to enhance health services for an additional 30 million Americans and provide new revenue to the healthcare and health insurance industries. However, the Act is also likely to deliver significant financial challenges to healthcare organizations (Dunn, 2010). Some examples of these challenges are listed as follows.

Medicare Reimbursement

As of January 1, 2013, Medicare reimbursements for hospitalized patients may decrease if patients are readmitted. Hospitals with high readmission rates will have Medicare reimbursements for the original hospitalization reduced by 1% if the patient is readmitted for a preventable cause within the next 7 days. To demonstrate a lower readmission rate, some hospitals might consider extending a patient's initial stay.

Medicare Pilot Program

In 2013, Medicare will launch a national pilot program to provide and evaluate bundled payments for acute inpatient hospital services, physician services, outpatient hospital services, and post-acute care services for an episode of care from 3 days prior to hospitalization until 30 days following discharge.

Medicare and Medicaid Reimbursement Cuts

Beginning in fiscal year 2010, the Act reduced Medicare market basket updates for a number of services and inserted a productivity adjustment.[1] Reimbursements will be cut by $103 billion over 10 years. Medicare and Medicaid disproportionate-share hospital payments[2] for hospitals that offer services to large cohorts of underserved clients will be reduced by $44 billion over 10 years beginning in 2015 (Davis, 2010).

Independent Payment Advisory Board

In 2015, the Act will launch an Independent Payment Advisory Board similar to the existing Medicare Payment Advisory Commission (MedPAC), which will have Medicare rate-setting authority. Hospitals will be subject to the board's authority in 2019. This reform measure is expected to save $23.4 billion over 10 years (Davis, 2010).

Physician Integration

Physicians would like to achieve target incomes while assuming a manageable workload. At the same time, hospitals are experiencing physician shortages, especially in emergency care and specialty services, even as they are facing market challenges from local entrepreneurial physician competitors. Developing partnerships between physicians and hospitals could address the needs of both stakeholders and channel competition into collaboration toward common goals. Integrating physicians and hospitals could help both to share patient information and records, avoid

---

1. Market basket adjustments refer to adjustments that reduce reimbursement based on prospective improved productivity.
2. Medicaid disproportionate-share hospital (DSH) payments provide financial assistance to hospitals that serve a large number of low-income patients such as the uninsured and individuals covered by Medicaid. Medicaid DSH payments are the largest source of federal funding for uncompensated hospital care (Peters, 2009).

unnecessary tests and procedures, assess and demonstrate improved quality outcomes, and reduce healthcare costs.

There are several ways in which hospitals and physicians can work together, formally and informally. Hospitals can employ physicians or contract with them to provide services. Another type of partnership is a joint venture model, in which selected doctors in a hospital may co-own a hospital service, such as a pharmacy or laboratory. Additionally, physicians and hospitals can collaborate to integrate clinical services and procedures to avoid duplication and incorporate best practices to improve quality of care.

SUMMARY

The healthcare industry is growing in size and complexity. The role of financial information in the decision-making process is critical. Financial literacy is essential for healthcare leaders in the constantly changing economic environment. Understanding financial factors and influences will assist leaders in their ongoing assessment and evaluation of these industry changes and allow for preparatory and effective strategic planning.

Discussion Questions

1. What is the importance of analyzing past and present financial information?
2. What is a key driver in health care?
3. Identify the critical components in a project plan.
4. How does healthcare reform impact healthcare institutions from a financial perspective?

Case Study: Financial Management

You are the CFO of Amityville Hospital. It is a 250 bed, for-profit hospital, renowned for its cardiology unit. The hospital has 300 employees, including 125 physicians with staff privileges.

Amityville is located in a thriving community that represents its primary service region. There are many high-tech companies and industries in the area that attract families and retirees from around the United States. The area has a mild climate and offers an excellent educational environment that includes multiple community colleges and universities.

There are approximately 750,000 residents in the surrounding city, and its population is growing about 4% per year. Approximately 46% of the population is under 18 years of age, 42% is between the ages of 18 and 64 years, 12% is over 65 years of age; 49% of the residents are female and 51% are male.

Amityville has one competitor, Serenity Hospital, which is located 40 miles away. Serenity is a 350 bed not-for-profit hospital with an excellent reputation. It has strong orthopedic and cardiac services and also offers oncology services, which are poorly organized and not accredited. Serenity Hospital's financial performance is stable, and its market share is growing.

Serenity has no formal orthopedic or cardiology departments, though several popular orthopedic surgeons and cardiologists maintain privileges there. The community's premier orthopedic group practices are located near Serenity Hospital, making it inconvenient for surgeons to use Amityville Hospital for surgery except in rare cases. However, a few orthopedic practices are planning to open branch offices near the Amityville facility.

Cardiologists on Serenity's staff restrict their activity to performing consults for Amityville physicians whose patients have been admitted to the facility. Although Amityville Hospital has had moderate success in the burgeoning community, its leaders would like to ensure adequate preparation for the future, especially in the environment of health reform. You will assess key areas in Amityville's operations from a financial perspective and report your results to the Board of Directors in a PowerPoint presentation. Please address the following questions in your presentation.

Case Study Discussion Questions

1. What areas of Amityville's operations will be critical to review?
2. How will Amityville's financial data be used in the strategic planning and decision-making process?
3. How will healthcare reform impact Amityville and its strategic planning?
4. How do the community and Serenity Hospital impact Amityville's strategic planning?

OTHER SUGGESTED READINGS

Aptara. (2008). Chapter 8: Reporting and analyzing receivables. Retrieved November 7, 2012 from http://media.wiley.com/product_data/excerpt/19/EHEP0002 /EHEP000219-1.pdf.

Huron Consulting, Inc. (2010). Key healthcare reform initiatives: Medicare market basket productivity adjustments. *Healthcare Reform: A Huron Healthcare Series.* Retrieved November 7, 2012 from www.huronconsultinggroup.com/library /healthcare-reform-series-2.pdf.

Sarbanes-Oxley Act Presentation—Key Aspects. (n.d.). Retrieved November 7, 2012 from www.soxtoolkit.com/sox-pres.htm.

Sarbanes-Oxley Summary. (2003). A guide to the Sarbanes-Oxley Act: Sarbanes-Oxley Act summary and introduction. Retrieved November 7, 2012 from www .soxlaw.com/introduction.htm.

Stults, K. (2007). Understanding your revenue. *HSIHealth.com*. Retrieved November 7, 2012 from www.hsihealth.com/pdf/understandingrevenue.pdf.

The Library of Congress. (2010). Bill Summary & Status 111th Congress 2009–2010 H.R. 3590 CRS Summary. Retrieved November 7, 2012 from http://thomas .loc.gov/cgi-bin/bdquery/z?d111:HR03590:@@@D&summ2=m&|TOM:/bss /d111query.html.

References

Berger, S. (2003). Learning to ready financial statements. *The Grantsmanship Center.* Retrieved November 7, 2012 from www.tgci.com/magazine/Learning%20to %20Read%20Financial%20Statements.pdf.

Davis, C. (2010). Health reform's financial implications: HFMA details the issues. *Fierce Health Finance.* Retrieved November 7, 2012 from www.fiercehealthfinance .com/story/health-reforms-financial-implications-hfma-details-issues/2010 -03-24.

Deeb, C. (2012). Percent of a business budget for salary. *Houston Chronicle.* Retrieved November 7, 2012 from http://smallbusiness.chron.com/percent-business -budget-salary-14254.html.

General Financial and Tax Consulting, LLC. (2009). Federal depreciation look-back analysis. Retrieved November 7, 2012 from www.genfitax.com /Resources/GFTC%20-%20Federal%20Depreciation%20Look%20Back%20 Analysis.pdf.

Dunn, G. (2010). Healthy financial reporting and disclosure: A summary of the financial reporting and disclosure implications of the health care reform. *Deloitte.* Retrieved November 7, 2012 from www.deloitte.com/assets /Dcom-UnitedStates/Local%20Assets/Documents/AERS/ASC/us_assur _Heads_Up_040910.pdf.

Investopedia. (n.d.a). Contribution margin. Retrieved November 7, 2012 from www .investopedia.com/terms/c/contributionmargin.asp#axzz1iq2CL9tT.

Investopedia. (n.d.b). Market share. Retrieved November 7, 2012 from www .investopedia.com/terms/m/marketshare.asp#axzz1iq2CL9tT.

Investopedia. (n.d.c). Operating margin. Retrieved November 7, 2012 from www .investopedia.com/terms/o/operatingmargin.asp#axzz1iq2CL9tT.

Kennon, J. (2012). Earnings before interest, tax, depreciation, and amortization—EBITDA. *About.com.* Retrieved November 7, 2012 from http://beginnersinvest .about.com/od/incomestatementanalysis/a/EBITDA-on-income-statement .htm.

Laurent, W. (2010). Managing and improving quality with key performance drivers. *Dashboard Insight*. Retrieved November 7, 2012 from www.dashboardinsight .com/articles/business-performance-management/managing-and-improving -quality-with-key-performance-drivers.aspx.

Office of the Auditor General of Canada. (2008). Financial management capability model. Retrieved November 7, 2012 from www.oag-bvg.gc.ca/internet/English /meth_gde_e_19706.html#0.2.2Z141Z1.WKP23M.SXB89F.C.

Peters, C. P. (2009). The basics: Medicaid disproportionate share (DSH) payments. *National Health Policy Forum*. Retrieved November 7, 2012 from www.nhpf.org /library/the-basics/Basics_DSH_06-15-09.pdf.

ReadPeriodicals. (2010, January). Hospital strategies for effective performance management. *Healthcare Financial Management*. Retrieved November 7, 2012 from www.readperiodicals.com/201001/1975387781.html.

Sarbanes Oxley 101. (2012). Sarbanes Oxley Act summary of major sections. Retrieved November 7, 2012 from www.sarbanes-oxley-101.com/sarbanes-oxley -compliance.htm.

Chapter 13

The Physician Leader

Sharon B. Buchbinder and Dale Buchbinder

LEARNING OBJECTIVES

By the end of this chapter, the student will be able to:

- Describe physician education and training, licensure and certification, continuing education, and quality assessment.
- Identify common roles of physician leaders in healthcare organizations.
- Compare and contrast clinical versus nonclinical leadership roles in healthcare organizations.
- Describe the value of physician leaders to a healthcare organization.
- Suggest potential leadership roles for physicians in evolving healthcare organizations.

KEY TERMS

Bell Commission

Board certification

Chief Medical Officer

Chief of Medical Staff

Conflict of interest

Continuing medical education

National Practitioner Data Bank

Physician credentialing

Physician privileging

INTRODUCTION

Healthcare organizations employ a wide array of clinical, administrative, and support professionals to deliver services to their patients. The Bureau of Labor Statistics (BLS), which lists over 30 different categories of healthcare professionals on its website, notes that "as the largest industry in 2008, healthcare provided 14.3 million jobs for wage and salary workers," and that "most workers have jobs that require less than four years of college education, but health diagnosing and treating practitioners are highly educated" (Bureau of Labor Statistics, 2010a). In 2008, there were 661,400 physicians employed in the United States; that number is expected to grow by 22% in 2018 to 805,500 (Bureau of Labor Statistics, 2010b). While fewer in number than their nursing counterparts at 2.64 million, physicians have an enormous impact on healthcare organizations. Physicians not only provide critical direct healthcare services, but also serve in administrative and leadership roles that significantly contribute to the sustainability, quality, and success of a healthcare organization.

Healthcare administrators can expect to be actively collaborating with physicians who are not only clinicians, but also knowledgeable administrative colleagues. Physician leaders, drawing on their extensive training and expertise in medicine and management, can be outstanding liaisons between the executive administration and physician employee, contractor, and stakeholder groups. Healthcare organizations reap the benefits of utilizing these highly skilled professionals in their strategic workforce.

In this chapter, we will provide you with an overview of physician medical education, licensure and certification, continuing education, and performance management. We will provide an example of the roles and functions of physician leaders and discuss physicians' important current and future leadership roles in healthcare organizations.

PHYSICIAN MEDICAL EDUCATION, TRAINING, AND CONTINUING EDUCATION

Physicians begin their preparation for medical school as undergraduates in a variety of majors, but are often identified and labeled as "premedical students." Premedical students can obtain a degree in any field; however, according to the Association of American Medical Colleges (AAMC), the expectation is that they will graduate from university with a bachelor's degree, having successfully completed prerequisites in science subjects such as mathematics, biology, chemistry, and physics (AAMC, 2010).

Medical schools in the United States generally provide 4 years of academic and clinical instruction. Entry into U.S. medical schools is extremely competitive; successful applicants must earn high grade point averages and high scores on the Medical College Admission Test (MCAT). Some students opt to study medicine at medical schools outside the United States and return to the United States to obtain clinical experience and take the necessary examinations for U.S. licensure and entry into graduate medical training programs.

Though there are some shorter, combined Bachelor of Science/Medical Doctor (BS/MD) programs in the United States, the majority of American medical school graduates will have at least 8 years of post–high school education, including 2 or more years of clinical externships, before they go through the National Residency Matching Program (NRMP, 2010). The NRMP is a process whereby 4th-year senior medical students interview and rank their choices for graduate medical education (GME), also known as residencies. The residency training programs also interview and rank their choices for future residents, and program participants are then matched with the highest ranked choice available. Residency training programs, which provide intensive mentoring and clinical training in a physician's chosen specialty, are sponsored by teaching hospitals, academic medical centers, healthcare systems and other institutions (Accreditation Council for Graduate Medical Education, 2010a).

During their residency training program, physicians are primarily trained in either a general or specialized area of medicine. Depending on the specialty, the length of the residency training program can be as short as 3 years (for family medicine) or as long as 10 years (for cardio-thoracic surgery or neurosurgery). According to the Accreditation Council for Graduate Medical Education (ACGME), "When physicians graduate from a residency program, they are eligible to take their **board certification** examinations and begin practicing independently" (n.d., p. 2).

Residents spend many years in training before they can practice independently and, in addition, work extensive hours as part of their training programs. Not long ago, it was not uncommon for residents to be on-call every other night as often as several times a week, working continuously on duty for 36–48 hours per shift. Caps on hours of work for residents varied by residency training program, but were typically highest for the surgical specialties, often greater than 100 hours per week.

In 1984, Libby Zion, an 18-year-old college student, died while hospitalized at the New York Hospital in Manhattan. Among the factors alleged to have contributed to her tragic death were medical errors due to a lack of adequate supervision of the hospital residents responsible for her care, as well as the negative effects of overwork and fatigue on the residents' performance (American Medical Association, 2010). A criminal grand jury called to review the case did not bring forth an indictment, but did criticize the working conditions in the New York Hospital training program. The New York State Health Commissioner established the **Bell Commission**, which recommended the institution of limits on resident work hours in New York to a maximum of 80 hours per week and 24 hours per shift.

Physician educators and hospital administrators expressed concerns that limiting resident work hours would negatively impact resident learning. Residents would no longer be able to stay by a patient's bedside during the critical first 36 hours of a patient's admission and observe the natural course of many acute diseases. However, advocates of limiting resident work hours countered that this "no limits" agenda was also motivated by the active utilization of residents to cover hospital staffing at a pay rate well below the minimum wage.

In 1989, New York became the first state to institute limits on resident work hours and to require the physical presence of supervising attending physicians in the hospital 24 hours a day. Over the past 2 decades, various specialty societies, medical associations, and legislators across the United States have continued to struggle with the definition of "reasonable" work hours for physicians in training. Over the past 10 years, the Accreditation Council for Graduate Medical Education (ACGME) has adopted guidelines for U.S. accredited medical training institutions. Hospitals and residency training program directors are now required to limit resident work hours to no more than 80 hours per week, inclusive of in-house call activities and all moonlighting (i.e., side jobs or extra work in addition to the 80 hours per week). No first-year residents (PGY-1) are permitted to moonlight (ACGME, 2010). Furthermore:

> Duty periods of PGY-1 residents must not exceed 16 hours in duration. Duty periods of PGY-2 residents and above may be scheduled to a maximum of 24 hours of continuous duty in the hospital. Programs must encourage residents to use alertness management strategies in the context of patient care responsibilities. Strategic napping, especially after 16 hours of continuous duty and between the hours of 10:00 P.M. and 8:00 A.M., is strongly suggested (ACGME, 2010, p. 17).

The same document describes the need for continuity of patient care and appropriate patient "handoff" procedures; that is, when the resident goes home, the next doctor taking care of the patient must be briefed to ensure the transfer of all relevant information (ACGME, 2010). Although these new guidelines were supposed to become effective July 1, 2011, the ACGME has been under pressure to delay implementation (Iglehart, 2010). As of October 2012, these guidelines are still in dispute and have yet to be fully implemented.

Regardless of the final date of implementation, this controversy will not disappear. These work-hour rules and new patient handoff protocols, which emphasize the need for a culture of safety and patient-centric care, also underscore the fact that residents are on duty to obtain an education, not for the benefit of the hospital's bottom line. The Joint Commission has published a Sentinel Event Alert on healthcare worker fatigue (The Joint Commission, 2011). However, there are no published studies at this time that demonstrate the benefits of reducing work hours on resident performance.

Most physicians are eligible to obtain a license to practice medicine after only 1 year of postgraduate training. Just as for other members of the healthcare team, *licensure,* granted by the state, is required for physicians and certifies competency to perform within a designated scope of practice (National Council of State Boards of Nursing, 2010). Limited licensure is granted for PGY-1s in hospital practice under supervision. State Boards of Physician Quality Assurance (BPQA) establish the requirements for medical licenses. These requirements are lengthy and strenuous. For example, the state of Maryland requires the following (Annotated Code of Maryland, 2010):

- Good moral character
- Minimum age of 18 years
- A fee
- Documentation of education and training
- Passing scores on one of the following examinations:
  - All parts of the National Board of Medical Examiners' examinations, and/or a score of 75 or better on a FLEX exam, or a passing score on the National Board of Osteopathic Examiners, or a combination of scores and exams; or
  - State Board examination
  - All steps of the U.S. Medical Licensing Examination (USMLE)

Candidates must demonstrate oral and written English-language competency and supply the following:

- A chronological list of activities beginning with the date of completion of medical school, accounting for all periods of time
- Any disciplinary actions taken by licensing boards, denying application or renewal
- Any investigations, charges, arrests, pleas of guilty or *nolo contendere,* convictions, or receipts of probation before judgment
- Information pertaining to any physical, mental, or emotional condition that impairs the physician's ability to practice medicine
- Copies of any malpractice suits or settlements, or records of any arrests, disciplinary actions, judgments, final orders, or cases of driving while intoxicated or under the influence of a chemical substance or medication
- Results of all medical licensure, certification, and recertification examinations and the dates when taken

Thirty-six states now have the "authority to run criminal background checks (CBCs) as a condition for licensure" for physicians. "Fourteen (14) states, Puerto Rico and the Virgin Islands do not conduct criminal background checks as a condition of licensure" (Federation of State Medical Boards, 2012). The reasons for CBCs are numerous and include, but are not limited to, increasing societal concerns about alcohol and drug abusers, sexual predators, and child and elder abusers. If a CBC contains reports of criminal convictions, the licensure board will closely examine the physician's application and consider approval on a case-by-case basis. Criteria that will determine the board's decision include the extent and frequency of the criminal behavior and the presence of evidence, often submitted by the applicant him- or herself, and of intervention and treatment such as alcohol and drug abuse rehabilitation.

After successful completion of residency or a fellowship, which provides an additional 1–3 years of training in a medical subspecialty, licensed physicians are considered *board eligible* (that is, prepared to sit for the specialty examinations in their field). Physicians may voluntarily submit documentation of their education, training, and practice to an American Board of Medical Specialists (ABMS) member board for review (ABMS, 2010a). Upon approval of the medical specialty board, the physician is then allowed to take the examination for *board certification*. Successful completion of the examination(s) allows the physician to be granted certification, and he or she is then designated as *board certified* in that specialty or subspecialty (e.g., a board-certified pediatrician or a board-certified neonatologist). Board certification is a form of *credentialing* a physician's competency in a specific area. Most hospitals, HMOs, and other healthcare organizations require a physician to be board certified to be hired or obtain staff privileges, because board certification demonstrates the achievement of a designated standard of knowledge and practice. This assumption of quality is based on research that more education and training leads to a higher quality of service (Donabedian, 2005; Tamblyn et al., 1998).

Board certification is time-limited; physicians must demonstrate continued competency in their evolving fields. The purpose of the American Board of Medical Specialties Maintenance of Certification (ABMS MOC) initiative is to ensure that physicians remain up-to-date in their specialties (ABMS, 2010b). In most specialties, a closed-book examination is required every 6–10 years to maintain certification.

Additionally, most states require that physicians complete a certain number of **continuing medical education** (CME) credits to maintain state licensure and to demonstrate continued competency. Hospitals may also require a minimum number of annual CME credits for their staff and admitting physicians to remain credentialed to admit and care for patients at their institution (National Institutes of Health, 2010). Seven organizations—the American Board of Medical Specialists (ABMS), the American Hospital Association (AHA), the American Medical Association (AMA), the Association of American Medical Colleges (AAMC), the Association for Hospital Medical Education (AHME), the Council of Medical Specialty Societies (CMSS), and the Federation of State Medical Boards, Inc. (FSMB)—are members of the Accreditation Council for Continuing Medical Education (ACCME) (ACCME, 2010b). The ACCME establishes criteria for determining which educational providers are quality providers of CME, and gives its seal of approval only to those organizations meeting their standards (ACCME, 2010a). The ACCME also works to ensure "uniformity in accreditation" of educational offerings to maintain the quality of continuing physician education (ACCME, 2010b).

Because of this great investment in education, initial and ongoing training, and continuing medical education, physicians are viewed as national resources and are tracked in the American Medical Association Masterfile database from the day they enter medical school. Originally created a century ago to establish biographical records on physicians, the online database stores information on education, training, and certification for each physician throughout his or her professional career and lifetime. The Masterfile, which also maintains records on deceased physicians, is now "used by the medical community for credentials verification, research, manpower planning, and other public good efforts" (Eiler, 2006).

A comprehensive review of a physician's credentials involves making electronic queries to the **National Practitioner Data Bank** (NPDB). At one time, physicians who were disciplined or lost their license in one state could simply move to another state and obtain a license there. Other than person-to-person contacts, there were few ways to track "bad docs" who moved across state borders. The NPDB was created to have a system whereby state licensing boards, hospitals, professional societies, and other healthcare entities could identify, discipline, and report those who engage in unprofessional behavior.

> The intent of the NPDB is to restrict the ability of incompetent physicians, dentists, and other healthcare practitioners to move from state to state without disclosure or discovery of previous medical malpractice payment and adverse action history. Adverse actions can involve licensure, clinical privileges, professional society membership, and exclusions from Medicare and Medicaid (NPDB, n.d.).

One of the main criticisms of the NPDB is that a physician can be reported for having been sued, but the outcome of the lawsuit, even when dismissed, is not reported, and the lawsuit remains on the physician's record. In an era of increasingly litigious consumers of health care, this is not a minor complaint. Physicians may dispute the report, but it can take much time and effort, much like trying to get a correction on a credit report. Per the NPDB (n.d.), "The information contained in the NPDB should be considered together with other relevant data in evaluating a practitioner's credentials; it is intended to augment, not replace, traditional forms of credentials review."

The pressure on physicians to engage in active learning and to remain current and competent in their specialty and scope of practice is enormous. Physician livelihoods—and patient lives—are at stake. It behooves physician leaders and other senior administrators to be vigilant in promoting and facilitating physician continuing education and maintenance of certification for the benefit of both physicians and patients.

Despite the intensity and extent of physician training, most physicians have had little or no instruction or mentoring on organizational, team, and individual leadership and management. Physicians who step beyond the doctor–patient dyad into the role of leading an organization at a population-based, or macro-level, face challenges that may require additional training to enhance their skills and expertise.

PHYSICIAN LEADERS IN HEALTHCARE ORGANIZATIONS

Historically, physicians were among the first hospital administrators. It was not uncommon in the 1940s and 1950s for hospitals and clinics to be owned and operated by physicians. Their years of medical training, however, did not typically include the basic elements of business and finance, which play a critical role in the financial stability and sustainability of healthcare organizations. The recognition of the value of business skills and expertise led to the development of professional education programs for health administrators who could provide oversight and management of healthcare organizations. In organizations where health administration experts served as CEOs and CFOs, physicians often contributed to organization leadership as elected or appointed Chiefs of Medical Staff.

The **Chief of Medical Staff** often served both as ambassador and as negotiator between the executive administration and the physicians on staff. A successful Chief of Medical Staff could become a champion for the physician stakeholders in the organization and, by effectively representing his or her constituency, a valuable contributor and ally to the health administration executives. Unfortunately, at times, the Chief of the Medical Staff could also be viewed with skepticism by other physicians who believed that he or she no longer represented the perspective of the practicing doctor, but instead had been coopted by ("gone to the dark side" of) "administration."

Education and training of physician champions in the necessary business and management skills for successful leadership has helped to avoid these pitfalls and overcome such challenges. The financial and economic pressures that have triggered the breadth of changes in healthcare organizations over the past 30 years demand a skilled team of leaders at the helm, including trained physicians who are "bilingual," who can speak the language of business as well as the language of medicine.

Physician leaders are often drawn from a pool of highly competitive individuals who have been trained with a focus on individual patients and one-on-one case examination (i.e., the microlevel of care). Physician leaders must refocus their perspective from the micro to the meta—from the individual patient to the big picture of a complex healthcare organization. This change of perspective can be challenging for some potential leaders and intuitive for others, especially when additional training and mentoring are provided to encourage skills development.

Clearly, professional experience and training can play a major role in a potential physician leader's perspective. Physicians who graduated from medical school in the 1960s through the 1990s have faced seismic changes in the system of healthcare delivery. Many doctors find these changes frustrating and overwhelming, scrambling to cover costs and escape perceived burdens of practice. Some even opt to sell their practices to hospitals with an eye toward retirement rather than battle new paradigms of patient care.

A number of organizations that have purchased and/or consolidated practices to increase patient volumes have subsequently faced economic challenges because the buyers had not created a strategic plan for these new acquisitions or defined posttransition productivity expectations with the practicing physician, who may continue to operate from a microperspective (LeValley, 2010). In such a situation, the purchasing organization would be better served if a physician leader with both clinical expertise and business skills works with the practicing physician to plan and implement a smooth private practice transition into a consolidated healthcare organization.

Physician leaders may not only face challenges communicating with their practicing peers, but with executive administrators as well. A Chief Executive Officer (CEO) and Chief Operating Officer (COO) may not share the same strategic perspective on how an organization can provide cost-effective, high-quality health care. The use of evidence-based research and guidelines to promote quality improvement in health care and reduce unnecessary expenditures can bring administrative and clinical leaders together by suggesting effective common strategies to achieve a high quality of care.

Because of their education and training, many physicians tend to gravitate toward clinical leadership roles, wherein they can maximize the use of their medical expertise. Examples of such roles are medical directors of clinics and laboratories. Others physician leaders have moved into roles that demand business as well as medical expertise, such as **Chief Medical Officer** (CMO), Chief Executive Officer (CEO) and Chief Operating Officer (COO). Recent research on the 300 best hospitals in the United States found an association between the presence of physician CEOs and higher quality of patient care scores (Goodall, 2011). Additional research may be able to further identify the skillsets that successful physician leaders provide toward this goal.

Physician leaders can access certification, advanced education and training, mentoring and peer support, and employment opportunities through the American College of Physician Executives (ACPE) at www.acpe.org.

Among the leadership opportunities for physicians are service as chairpersons of clinical departments such as Surgery, Medicine, Obstetrics and Gynecology, Pediatrics, etc. Chairs are often responsible for **physician credentialing** and **physician privileging** in their department, developing and updating medical staff bylaws, promoting physician adherence to bylaws and regulations, ensuring standards of care are met by the unit's doctors through ongoing assessments such as peer review, disciplining physicians whose personal or professional behavior falls below accepted legal and practice standards, and coordinating quality assessment programs that use regular audits and evaluations to engage in continuous quality improvement. Credentialing and privileging must be repeated periodically, as frequently as every 1 to 2 years for most healthcare organizations, and require a review of the staff physicians' continuing medical education, certification, and performance. Some seek assistance for this demanding task from credential verification organizations, which can gather primary verification for credentialing criteria and can collate information from national databases about physicians' professional and performance history.

If a physician's performance or behavior falls below expected standards, chairs may be tasked with intervening to address this disparity. Medical staff bylaws, human resource services guidelines, and state medical board regulations must be adhered to during this process, as the impact of such intervention and possible discipline on a physician's professional career can lead to the loss of privileges to practice in the organization and even the loss of a license to practice medicine.

Spurred by the significant changes in the healthcare landscape, more physicians are pursuing education and training in leadership and management via business courses and executive MBA programs. There are now 50 MD/MBA programs in existence in the United States and an estimated 2000 physicians enrolled in business schools (Caffareni, 2008). Graduates of these business programs, many who become certified as Physician Executives, are well prepared to assume a variety of leadership roles in the healthcare industry. Some may choose clinical leadership positions in small or large healthcare organizations, but others may opt for other professional opportunities, for example, with insurance companies or government agencies, such as the Centers for Medicare and Medicaid Services, the Agency for Health Care Research and Quality, and the National Institutes of Health.

Insurance companies have long used physicians to perform utilization review, and this role continues to be critical. When physicians in practice request or advocate for insurance payment for specific services, the expertise of a physician employed by the insurance company can be invaluable in helping to assess or determine the medical necessity of those services (American Board of Quality Assurance and Utilization Review Physicians, 2011).

Some healthcare organizations have established the position of Chief Medical Officer (CMO), which is especially suited to candidates with multiple degrees and diverse professional training and expertise, such as an MD/JD (attorney). A CMO's duties may include negotiating the organization's contracts and, in light of our litigious society, supervising patient safety, quality assessment, and risk management programs.

Physician leaders can be an important asset for healthcare organizations. Those physicians who choose to expand their training and expertise into crucial areas such as finance, management, and law will continue to be sought after to help organizations survive and thrive in these challenging times.

PHYSICIAN LEADERSHIP AND CONFLICT MANAGEMENT SKILLS

Healthcare organizations share common characteristics with other diverse organizations, including similar patterns of communication, collaboration, and conflict. Many healthcare professionals chose their professions because they wanted to help people. Highly educated in their individual fields, each professional brings a different perspective to the healthcare team as to how to provide the best care for a patient or a population of patients. These diverse views can sometimes lead to conflicts. While conflict is often perceived as bad, healthcare managers and physician leaders should not fear or avoid it. With an understanding of individual and group differences that prompt the emergence of conflict, organizations can channel conflict into a positive mechanism that leads to productive change. In healthy, well-run organizations, conflict can be a means to bring fresh ideas to the table, to provide opportunities to air different points of view, and to help the organization evolve and grow.

The high stress environment in which healthcare professionals work can be a breeding ground for tension, miscommunication, and conflict, not only among staff, but among professionals and patients as well. Fires of conflict in healthcare settings can rage out of control and even lead to violence, unless managed properly. The consequences of unmanaged conflict could lead to negative patient outcomes and a drop in the quality of care.

This section will provide an example of a common conflict scenario in a hospital, discuss some of the underlying issues that created the challenges, and demonstrate steps that physician leaders can use to successfully manage conflict.

Scenario: Central Line Protocol

Current standards state that an infected central line should be a "never event," and therefore require a standardized protocol for central line insertion (The Joint Commission, 2010). Cutting Edge Hospital, through its medical executive committee, has approved a policy that mandates a protocol for insertion of central lines. Dr. Quik has been consulted to place a central line for intravenous (IV) access in a very ill patient who is headed to the intensive care unit (ICU). As he inserts the catheter, Dr. Quik omits a major step in the protocol. Agnes Bythebook, RN, attempts to inform Dr. Quik that he has not adequately followed the protocol. Dr. Quik becomes quite indignant and belittles Nurse Bythebook in front of the patient and staff.

Nurse Bythebook reports the incident to her supervisor, who reports it to the Quality Assurance Officer, who, in turn, sends the report to Dr. Quik's department chair and supervisor. Upon questioning, Dr. Quik states, "It was a life-threatening emergency and there was no time to follow the protocol."

Underlying Issues

Dr. Quik was trained as a capable independent practitioner, but is inexperienced in serving as part of a healthcare team. He is a dedicated, responsible physician who deeply cares about his patients, but is not used to answering questions or collaborating in the provision of treatment. Dr. Quik's greatest fear is losing a patient. He believes he did the right thing at the right time for a very sick patient and is the most qualified to make treatment decisions without being questioned or challenged.

Nurse Bythebook is a graduate of an MSN program, who completed an ICU nurse residency training program, and is preparing to take her advanced certification exams as an ICU nurse. Nurse Bythebook wants to avoid unintentionally hurting a patient either directly or indirectly. She believes that advocating for the protocol was the correct action at the right time for a very ill patient.

Healthcare delivery systems now demand that healthcare professionals work together with other health professionals to provide high-quality healthcare as members of healthcare teams. Clinical research has underscored the importance of excellence in teamwork in the operating room (OR). A multisite retrospective study of 74 Veterans Health Administration (VHA) facilities found that "participation in the VHA Medical Team Training program was associated with a lower surgical mortality rate" (Neily et al., 2010, p. 1693). The authors report an 18% *reduction* in annual mortality rates, representing lives saved through teamwork. The findings from this study are significant not only in a research sense, but also in a true clinical sense. Dissemination of these findings throughout surgical training programs in the United States will require enormous effort because surgeons often believe "they alone are responsible for patient outcomes" (Pronovost & Freischlag, 2010, p. 1721). It will take a major culture shift to move many physicians and surgeons from this "solo savior" mentality to the "There is no I in teamwork" approach.

Additionally, through collaborative discussion and review, collaborative teams provide a system of checks and balances that reduce the risk of unintentional medical errors that could result in an untoward or tragic patient outcome.

Conflicts between team members often come to the attention of the physician chair of a department, whose role includes serving as a mediator to improve and facilitate the effective communication and work of the team. Educating members of the healthcare team, especially those who have little experience with team function, about the benefits of collaboration for quality of care and patient outcomes, can promote buy-in and cooperation by previously reluctant participants.

Management of conflict today, just like the delivery of health care itself, requires a team—a team of skilled managers such as physician and nurse leaders. In the case given, the designated supervisors of the involved team members (e.g., physician department chair and the nursing supervisor) were recruited to assist with reviewing the team members' communications and function and, when indicated, coaching and mentoring the participants in improved team operations. If inappropriate or abusive behavior has been reported, and team members or patients perceive a hostile work environment, human resources professionals may assist physician and nursing leaders in defining and reviewing standards of behavior and, if necessary, implementing disciplinary action.

Physician Leaders' Steps for Conflict Resolution

1. Determine the facts of the case. Such investigations are best done by interviewing all involved parties and witnesses separately and privately.
2. Identify the areas of concern. These may include quality-of-care issues, communications issues, or violations of rules and regulations. Each area should be handled discretely—and discreetly.
3. Use medical expertise to come to a conclusion as to the appropriateness of the medical treatment and deviation from protocols and guidelines. Use management expertise to determine the appropriateness of the behaviors and the possible presence of a hostile work environment.

In the example given, the department chair reviewed the case and agreed with Dr. Quik's medical perspective that his actions were medically appropriate during such an urgent situation. However, the chair also validated the actions of Nurse Bythebook, recognizing that her questioning the deviation from protocol was a valuable contribution toward preventing medical error and ensuring a high standard of care.

Unfortunately, the private interviews conducted by the department chair confirmed that Dr. Quik had communicated inappropriately with his team colleague and that Nurse Bythebook now perceived that she was serving in a hostile work environment. After consulting with Human Resources, the department chair met with Dr. Quik for oral counseling and a written reprimand that clarified expectations for professional behavior and communications, and presented a training program for Dr. Quik to improve his communications, anger management, and team function skills. The chair also supported Nurse Bythebook's supervisor and Human Resources as they explored whether the hostile work environment persisted and additional steps needed to be taken to ensure a safe work environment for Nurse Bythebook. Finally, the chair advised Dr. Quik that repetition of unacceptable behavior may lead to further disciplinary action up to and including loss of hospital privileges and/or termination.

Many healthcare organizations are now proactive in educating and training their healthcare professionals in teamwork and collaborative practice to support a high-quality, patient-centric culture. Some organizations such as the American College for Physician Executives, the Center for Creative Leadership, and the Studer Group (2011) provide access to outside resources for coaching and mentoring of physicians. For example, the Center for Creative Leadership (CCL, 2011) conducts week-long on-site training for entire healthcare teams. Though such training may be expensive, the investment can save an organization millions of dollars by staving off grievances and other legal actions down the road.

FUTURE LEADERSHIP ROLES FOR PHYSICIANS IN EVOLVING HEALTHCARE ORGANIZATIONS

The ancient Greek philosopher Heraclitus wisely advised that "The only constant is change." Just as healthcare organizations constantly change with the times, so do the leadership roles for physicians. The following are some areas where we foresee increasing demands for physician leaders in evolving healthcare organizations.

- *Health Information Technology and Health Informatics*: With the adoption of Electronic Health Records in healthcare organizations, more physicians will be involved in the transition from paper charts to electronic records. Physician "superusers" can help select the best software and hardware for this process, as well as design templates that increase clinician efficiency while ensuring the documentation necessary for effective reimbursement and quality assurance.
- *Patient Safety*: The appointment of Donald Berwick, MD, a pediatrician and former CEO of Institute for Healthcare Improvement (IHI), to be the interim head of the Centers for Medicare and Medicaid, signaled an important shift in linking patient safety to payments from the country's largest healthcare insurance provider.
- *Performance Improvement/Quality Assessment*: Continuous quality improvement has been a staple of healthcare organizations in the past 30 years. Initiatives have included accreditation, audits, peer reviews, morbidity and mortality review boards, etc. Assessment findings are analyzed and used to "close the loop" in the QI process by informing intentional change in goals, objectives, and strategies. Since the publication of the IOM report, the focus has shifted toward prevention of errors and negative outcomes, and increased

use of evidence-based, performance-improvement methods, such as *poka-yokes*, which are "fail safe" backups that reduce medical errors and patient risks. Physicians trained in quality-improvement methodologies will be in high demand.

· *Consulting*: Physicians who have strong administrative and clinical skillsets can serve as independent contractors and private consultants to mentor and coach physician and nonphysician leaders and healthcare staff in organizations. Healthcare consulting firms are increasingly hiring or collaborating with broadly trained physician leaders with MBAs and JDs to expand their resource capabilities.

SUMMARY

Physician leaders play a critical role in successful health services delivery. This chapter has described physician education, training, and continuing education; compared and contrasted clinical versus nonclinical leadership roles in healthcare organizations; identified common roles of physician leaders in healthcare organizations; analyzed a scenario where conflict management skills are critical to effective physician leadership; and hypothesized future leadership roles for physicians in evolving healthcare organizations. The need for physician leadership will continue to grow. Wise healthcare managers will recruit, select, and work to retain good physician leaders.[1]

Discussion Questions

1. Delineate the steps in attaining state licensure for physicians.
2. What is the difference between licensure and credentialing?
3. Why is it important to have physician leaders who have both medical and managerial expertise?
4. Identify and describe two clinical and two nonclinical leadership roles for physicians.
5. What are the necessary steps that physician leaders can take to address healthcare team conflicts between physicians and other team members?
6. Identify and describe some of the future roles for physician leaders.

---

1. *Note*: Parts of the "Physician Education, Training, and Continuing Education" and "Physician Leadership and Conflict Management Skills" sections of this chapter were originally published in *Introduction to Health Care Management* (2nd ed.), 2012 by Sharon B. Buchbinder and Nancy H. Shanks and are reprinted here with permission of the publisher.

Case Study: Conflict of Interest or Quality of Patient Care?

Dr. Smith, head of orthopedics at Cutting Edge Hospital, insists on using only products manufactured by BoneMedCo, despite the existence of multiple comparable lines that are manufactured by other companies. If the hospital could shift to a different product line, it could mean a savings of over $1 million in the next fiscal year. Dr. Smith is adamant: he will not use any other products.

Dr. Richards, the Chair of Surgery, reviews the BoneMedCo website, and it is obvious to him that Dr. Smith has been involved in the development of several products and is receiving large royalties on sales. When Dr. Richards and Dr. Justus, the Chief Medical Officer, meet with Dr. Smith, they show him the website and state that they feel this is the reason Dr. Smith is reluctant to use or even evaluate other company products. Dr. Richards and Dr. Justus tell Dr. Smith that they feel this is a **conflict of interest** (COI), i.e., when an individual can be influenced by money or other considerations to act in a way that is contrary to the good of the organization for whom he or she works or the patient for whom he or she should be advocating in their best interests.

Dr. Justus points to the Cutting Edge Hospital policy manual and states, "All physicians and employees who make purchasing decisions must complete a COI form disclosing all potential conflicts. Furthermore, you filed a COI form, but did not note your relationship with BoneMedCo."

Dr. Smith replies, "Yes, I helped to develop some of the products, and I just began receiving royalties from BoneMedCo. I planned to update my COI form, but it slipped my mind. Furthermore, these products were developed to my exacting standards. I believe they provide a better quality of care for the patient. Are you saying you want me to give inferior patient care?"

Case Study Discussion Questions

1. Using the conflict management steps outlined in the scenario earlier in this chapter, what should happen next?

2. What potential consultation(s) should the physician leaders seek?

3. If this relationship between Dr. Smith and BoneMedCo was active at the time the COI form was filed, how should that discovery impact the administrator's decisions?

4. At a subsequent meeting, Dr. Smith provides three hot-off-the-presses peer-reviewed articles in prestigious medical journals that conclude the device he helped to create is superior to all others on the market. Do these data change things?

5. What should Drs. Richards and Justus do next? What should Dr. Smith do next?

6. Should conflict of interest be overlooked if doing so could potentially benefit a healthcare organization or its patients?

RELATED WEBSITES

ABIM Foundation: www.abimfoundation.org/default.aspx

American Association of Medical Colleges: www.aamc.org

American College of Physician Executives: www.acpe.org

Institute for Healthcare Improvement: www.ihi.org/ihi

Liaison Council on Medical Education: www.lcme.org

Medical College Admissions Test: www.aamc.org/students/applying/mcat/

National Board of Medical Examiners: www.nbme.org/

United States Medical Licensing Examination: www.usmle.org/

Online Resources for Leadership

ABIM Renewing Professionalism: A Challenge to the Health Care Community. Resetting the Social Contract (Part II)—In the Service of Patients: www.youtube .com/watch?v=A9WcAYrqKBI&feature=related

IHI Open School for Health Professionals: www.ihi.org/IHI/Programs /IHIOpenSchool/

IHI: Defining Quality: Aiming for a Better Health Care System: www.youtube.com /watch?v=5vOxunpnIsQ

IHI: Apologizing Effectively to Patients and Families: www.youtube.com/watch?v =kDfoJXq8BRA&feature=relmfu

Practicing Wise Stewardship of Resources (Part I): Embracing Stewardship in Daily Practice: www.youtube.com/watch?v=P3i2a91HxKA

Renewing Professionalism: A Challenge to the Health Care Community. Why Does Professionalism Matter? (Part I)—Perspectives on Professionalism: www.youtube .com/watch?v=2PIplMOIINg&feature=related

Renewing Professionalism: A Challenge to the Health Care Community. Improving Systems to Deliver High Quality Care (Part II)—Collaborating & Working in Teams: www.youtube.com/watch?v=Glhd7pxyPZg&feature=related

REFERENCES

Accreditation Council for Continuing Medical Education (ACCME). (2010a). *Board of directors.* Retrieved November 8, 2012 from www.acgme.org/acgmeweb /About/BoardofDirectors.aspx.

Accreditation Council for Continuing Medical Education (ACCME). (2010b). *Recognition requirements.* Retrieved November 8, 2012 from www.accme.org /accreditors/recognition-requirements.

Accreditation Council for Graduate Medical Education (ACGME). (n.d.). *ACGME fact sheet.* Retrieved November 8, 2012 from www.acgme.org/acgmeweb /Portals/0/PDFs/ACGMEfactsheet.pdf.

Accreditation Council for Graduate Medical Education (ACGME). (2010). *Common Program Requirements: Effective July 1, 2011.* Retrieved November 8, 2012 from http://acgme-2010standards.org/pdf/Common_Program _Requirements_07012011.pdf.

American Board of Medical Specialists (ABMS). (2010a). *What board certification means.* Retrieved November 8, 2012 from www.abms.org/About_Board _Certification/means.aspx.

American Board of Medical Specialists (ABMS). (2010b). *About ABMS maintenance of certification.* Retrieved November 8, 2012 from www.abms.org/Maintenance _of_Certification/.

American Board of Quality Assurance and Utilization Review Physicians (ABQAURP). (2011). *About ABQAURP.* Retrieved November 8, 2012 from www .abqaurp.org/about.asp.

American Medical Association (AMA). (2010). *Resident work hours: Background.* Retrieved November 8, 2012 from www.ama-assn.org/ama/pub/about-ama /our-people/member-groups-sections/medical-student-section/advocacy -policy/resident-work-conditions.page?

Annotated Code of Maryland (COMAR). (2010). *Licensure: Qualifications for initial licensure.* Retrieved November 8, 2012 from www.dsd.state.md.us/comar /comarhtml/10/10.32.01.03.htm.

Association of American Medical Colleges (AAMC). (2010). *Making the decision to study medicine.* Retrieved November 8, 2012 from www.aamc.org/students /aspiring/109796/considering_decision.html.

Bureau of Labor Statistics (BLS). (2010a). *Career guide to industries, 2010–2011 edition, healthcare.* Retrieved November 8, 2012 from www.bls.gov/oco/cg/cgs035 .htm.

Bureau of Labor Statistics (BLS). (2010b). *Bureau of Labor Statistics, Occupational Outlook handbook, 2010–11 edition, Physicians and Surgeons.* U.S. Department of Labor. Retrieved November 8, 2012 from www.bls.gov/oco/ocos074.htm.

Caffareni, K. (2008, August 4). *Do you need an MBA, or are there alternatives?* Retrieved November 8, 2012 from www.ama-assn.org/amednews/2008/08/04/bica0804 .htm.

Center for Creative Leadership (CCL). (2011). *About.* Retrieved November 8, 2012 from www.ccl.org/leadership/about/index.aspx.

Donabedian, A. (2005). Evaluating the quality of medical care. *The Milbank Quarterly, 83*(4), 691–729.

Eiler, M. A. (2006). Helping doctors help patients for 100 years: Happy birthday AMA physician masterfile. *AMA Physician Credentialing Solutions, 9*(2).

Federation of State Medical Boards (FSMB). (2012, April). *Criminal background checks: Overview by state*. Retrieved November 8, 2012 from www.fsmb.org/pdf /GRPOL_Criminal_Background_Checks.pdf.

Goodall, A. (2011, July 6). Physician–leaders and hospital performance: Is there an association? *Social Science and Medicine*. doi:10.1016/j.socscimed.2011.06.025.

Iglehart, J. K. (2010, October 21). The ACGME's final duty-hour standards—Special PGY-1 limits and strategic napping. *New England Journal of Medicine*. Retrieved November 8, 2012 from www.nejm.org/doi/pdf/10.1056/NEJMp1010613.

The Joint Commission. (2010, February 23). *Central line-associated bloodstream infections (CLABSI) - NPSG - Goal 7- 07.04.01*. Retrieved November 8, 2012 from www.jointcommission.org/standards_information/jcfaqdetails.aspx?Standar dsFaqId=199&ProgramId=1.

The Joint Commission. (2011, December 14). *Health care worker fatigue and patient safety*. Retrieved November 8, 2012 from www.jointcommission.org /assets/1/18/SEA_48.pdf.

LeValley, C. (2010, September 1). *3 Considerations for hospitals acquiring practices*. Retrieved November 8, 2012 from www.beckershospitalreview.com/hospital-physician -relationships/3-considerations-for-hospitals-acquiring-practices.html.

National Council of State Boards of Nursing (NCBSN). (2010). *About NCBSN*. Retrieved November 8, 2012 from www.ncsbn.org/about.htm.

National Institutes of Health (NIH). (2010). *Frequently asked questions*. Retrieved November 8, 2012 from www.nih.gov/news/calendar/calendarfaq.htm #cmecredit.

National Practitioner Data Bank (NPDB). (n.d). *About us*. Retrieved November 8, 2012 from www.npdb-hipdb.hrsa.gov/topNavigation/aboutUs.jsp.

National Residency Matching Program (NRMP). (2010). *How the NRMP process works*. Retrieved November 8, 2012 from www.nrmp.org/about_nrmp/how .html.

Neily, J., Mills, P. D., Young-Xu, Y., Careney, B. T., West, P., Berger, D. H., . . . Bagian, J. P. (2010). Association between implementation of a medical team training program and surgical mortality. *Journal of the American Medical Association, 304*(15), 1693–1700.

Pronovost, P. J., & Freischlag, J. A. (2010). Improving teamwork to reduce surgical mortality. *Journal of the American Medical Association, 304*(15), 1721–1722.

Studer Group. (2011). *About*. Retrieved November 8, 2012 from www.studergroup .com/.

Tamblyn, R., Abrahamowicz, M., Brailovsky, C., Grand'Maison, P., Lescop, J., Norcini, J., . . . Haggerty, J. (1998). Association between licensing examination scores and resource use and quality of care in primary care practice. *Journal of the American Medical Association, 280*(11), 989–996.

Chapter 14

Governance in a New Era

Salvador J. Esparza and Michael L. Wall

LEARNING OBJECTIVES

By the end of this chapter, the student will be able to:

- Understand traditional structures of governance and identify new structures in an environment of healthcare reform.
- Describe the skills and qualifications needed for ideal governance.
- Understand the issue of public scrutiny and its effect on governance.
- Discuss potential strategic alternatives with a quality emphasis.

KEY TERMS

Accountability	Governing body
Fiduciary duty	Trustee
Governance	

INTRODUCTION

Healthcare organizations today are moving from traditional structures to emerging corporate models. The **governance** of modern healthcare enterprises demands a new level of functioning; one that utilizes the knowledge, skills, and expertise of key individuals to provide the most cost-effective and highest quality of care to target patients and communities. These key individuals frequently make up the organization's governing board or **governing body**, whose responsibility is to govern on behalf of the organization's stakeholders or shareholders (Pointer & Orlikoff, 1999). Effective governance can only result if governing board members clearly understand the broad mission of the healthcare organization, as well as the organization's role as a stand-alone entity or as a part of a larger corporate health system. To address the enormous number of changes forecast in the years ahead due to healthcare reform initiatives, the governing board must possess highly-qualified members, a strong infrastructure, and decision-making capability and authority (Center for Healthcare Governance, 2010) that will help position the organization for success.

Governance can be defined as the state or act of governing and includes the implementation of formal authority and control over an organization. In the United States, most healthcare organizations are not-for-profit and thus are accountable to stakeholders such as the community, employees, management, medical staff, regulators, and other interested parties. Healthcare organizations that are for-profit, on the other hand, have shareholders, and thus governance **accountability** is to the owner or owners of the company (shareholders). Although there are other differences between not-for-profit and for-profit healthcare organizations, both types of organizations share a similar purpose, which is ensuring the deployment of organizational resources in a manner that protects and advances the interests of stakeholders and/or shareholders (Pointer & Orlikoff, 1999). This purpose is also known as **fiduciary duty**.

Board members of not-for-profit healthcare organizations are typically volunteers; they are given the title **Trustee** to acknowledge their role in safeguarding community assets held in trust for the benefit of the community at-large. For-profit healthcare organization board members are frequently compensated for their service and given the title *Director*. However, these titles are often used interchangeably, particularly in the not-for-profit sector. Governing body members in both sectors share common goals and objectives as they discharge their fiduciary duty.

Responsibilities

There are published guidelines that governing boards can adopt to maximize their performance and effectiveness. In more traditional settings, board or governing body responsibilities may include formulating the organization's vision—that is, the future pathway and goals of the organization, making an explicit commitment to high-quality patient care, ensuring the presence of a high-performance executive management team, safeguarding the organization's financial health, and evaluating the board's own effectiveness as a governing body (Pointer & Orlikoff, 1999).

Biggs (2011) described the overall responsibilities of a governing board, which include:

- Creation and/or guardianship of the healthcare organization's mission, vision, and values
- Evaluation of Chief Executive Officer performance
- Ensuring the provision of quality patient care
- Ensuring the organization's financial health
- Assuming some responsibility for the health of the community
- Assuming responsibility for itself

To allow a governing body to function effectively, its members must also assume individual responsibilities. Among these basic responsibilities are learning about and understanding the organization and its culture, learning about and understanding the target population/clientele, developing a working knowledge of the healthcare industry and the key drivers of the healthcare system, being prepared for and attending meetings regularly, making an active and positive contribution in meetings and toward initiatives, and maintaining confidentiality (Biggs, 2011). Tyler and Biggs (2001) identified five characteristics that individual board members must exhibit for personal effectiveness: (1) demonstrate commitment to their role, (2) set policy and yet not oversee or micromanage daily operations, (3) guard against self-dealing or its appearance, (4) take corrective action as dictated by circumstances, and (5) remain focused on the needs of the community.

Measuring the effectiveness of for-profit boards has been acknowledged as a standard process; governing-body effectiveness is normally reflected in metrics such as the organization's balance sheet, stock price, dividends, and overall return on investment. However, these metrics may not be applicable to not-for-profit organizations, making evaluation of their governing bodies' effectiveness more of a challenge (Bryant & Jacobson, 2006). For-profit board assessment is typically outcome-oriented, whereas not-for-profit board effectiveness is better measured in a process-oriented manner. Examples of process-oriented measurements include achievement of strategic planning initiatives and objectives, utilization and analysis of performance dashboards, development of governance competencies in senior executives and management, adherence to legal requirements; voluntary compliance with corporate conduct regulations, and avoidance of conflicts or dualities of interest (Bryant & Jacobson, 2006).

Legal Basics

The legal guidelines for and the obligations of governing bodies are well documented; there are three basic duties, described as follows. The first legal duty of a governing board member of a healthcare organization is called the *duty of care.* This duty requires the board member to act with due diligence when making decisions for the organization; that is, to do what a reasonable person would do in the same situation with the same information and to act in the best interests of the organization and its clients (Biggs, 2011).

The second legal duty of a board member of a healthcare organization is called *duty of loyalty.* Board members must act in the best interest of the organization and not on behalf of themselves, friends and family, or other organizations with which the board member might be affiliated. Board members must understand *conflict of interest* and *corporate opportunity* (Biggs, 2011). To avoid conflict of interest, board members must acknowledge and remove themselves from decisions that create an integration or conflict between their personal interests and the interests of the organization. Corporate opportunity requires that board members not personally accept business opportunities without making those opportunities available first to the healthcare organization (Biggs, 2011).

The third legal duty of a board member of a healthcare organization is called *duty of obedience.* Board members must comply with all federal, state, and local laws and must support the mission, vision, values, and bylaws of their organizations. Board members should not exceed their delegated authority and violate the trust of their organizations; such actions could endanger the tax-exempt status of nonprofits (Biggs, 2011).

STRUCTURES IN GOVERNANCE: WHAT SHOULD WE LOOK LIKE?

Many federal, state, and municipal laws and regulations impact healthcare organizations (HCOs), and can influence or determine their bylaws, configuration, and operations. Healthcare organizations are typically structured as business corporations, for-profit (taxable) or not-for-profit (nontaxable). Corporations are expensive to establish and operate under strict guidelines and reporting requirements. However, the advantages of incorporation include limited liability for stakeholders (community, not-for-profit) and shareholders (proprietary, for-profit); ease of transfer of ownership; and unlimited life.

Hospital Structures

As healthcare organizations have merged with or acquired other healthcare entities, several variations in HCO governance structures have evolved. Pointer and Orlikoff (1999) have described these varying structures as *decentralized*, *centralized*, or *modified centralized*. Decentralized structures

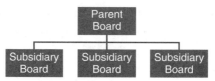

Figure 14.1 Decentralized Structure

(see **Figure 14.1**) typically have multiple boards or layers of governance, with a parent board retaining designated authority, oversight, control, and coordination over subsidiary boards that govern "operating units." Clear delineation of functions, authority, and scope, along with fruitful information-sharing and communication among all the boards, is critical for the parent board to be effective as a governing body (Pointer & Orlikoff, 1999).

In a centralized structure (see **Figure 14.2**), the parent board has the ultimate authority over its subsidiary entities, which are themselves considered the operating units. These subsidiary organizations are not formally governed by subsidiary boards, as in Figure 14.1, but they may establish their own advisory bodies, which, however, do not exercise any fiduciary or legal authority (Pointer & Orlikoff, 1999).

A modified centralized structure (see **Figure 14.3**) is a compound of the first two. In this model, the parent board will oversee some subsidiary entities that are managed as operating units and some subsidiary entities that are decentralized boards and serve as subsidiary fiduciary governing bodies.

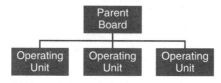

Figure 14.2 Centralized Structure

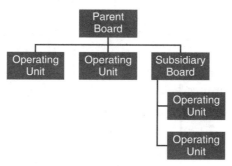

Figure 14.3 Modified Centralized Structure

The governance of HCOs in both modified centralized and centralized structures is complicated by the fact that, typically, an entire healthcare organization is:

- Licensed by the state
- Certified by the federal government to provide care to Medicare and Medicaid patients
- Accredited by national agencies such as The Joint Commission

Licensing, certification, and accreditation requirements hold the healthcare entity as a whole accountable for its operational components. Each unit must meet regulations and standards in areas such as quality of care and community service. The advisory bodies of these operating units may play a critical role in supporting organization-wide accountability initiatives by overseeing policy development and approval and provider credentialing and privileging. Pointer and Orlikoff (1999, p. 116) state that "the right structure is necessary to provide a liberating framework for the creativity, imagination, focus, big-picture thinking, and timely and meaningful action that is the hallmark of good governance."

Healthcare organizations that retain local boards need to practice shared governance—that is, to grant these local boards sufficient jurisdiction and authority to make decisions affecting their target communities and promote achievement of legal and accreditation standards (Center for Healthcare Governance, 2010). Elements of effective shared governance include informed and inclusive decision making, transparency and clarity of operations, open lines of communication, accountability, and mutual trust and respect.

Physician Structures

Physicians also have traditionally provided services through a variety of structures, such as:

- Sole proprietorship/solo practice
- Partnerships
- General partnership
- Professional corporation or professional association
- Professional limited liability partnership
- Professional limited liability company

Which of these medical practice structures is adopted by a healthcare provider or organization is usually determined by factors such as the size of the entity, its anticipated growth, its tax goals, and the liability concerns

Table 14.1 Medical Practice Structures

Type of Structure	Advantages	Disadvantages
Proprietorships and Partnerships	· Ease of formation · Subject to few regulations · Physician–owner has total control over money and decisions · No corporate taxes	· Limited life · Cash flow stops if physician–owner is absent · Difficult to transfer ownership · Unlimited liability · Difficult to raise capital
Professional Corporation (PC) or Professional Association (PA)	· Unlimited life · Easy transfer of ownership · Limited liability · Ease of raising capital · Tax deductible benefit expenses · Often used by individual clinicians	· Cost of formation and reporting · Requires a governance structure with a board and elected officers · Dual taxation for investor-owned corporations
Professional Limited Liability Partnerships (PLLP) and Professional Limited Liability Companies (PLLC)	· Treated as a partnership for tax purposes · Revenues and losses passed through to owners · Not subject to dual taxation · Partners liable for their own malpractice (PLLP) · Liability like that of stock-holders (PLLC)	· Difficult to establish strong governance · Physicians are not its employees and are not entitled to same benefits as with a PC · Requires special financial practices · Not all states allow creation for medical practices

Source: Adapted from Medical Group Management Association. (2009). *Body of knowledge—Governance*. Englewood, CO: Author.

of its owners or principals (Medical Group Management Association, 2009). **Table 14.1** outlines the advantages and disadvantages of the various types of medical practice structures.

Emerging Forms of Governance

Historically, there have been several regulatory barriers or limitations for hospitals and physicians who have endeavored to align themselves structurally, financially, or operationally. One of the federal statutes that has had the most significant impact in this area is known collectively as the Stark Law. This statute is actually three separate provisions that govern physician self-referral for Medicare and Medicaid patients (see www.starklaw.org) and is named after U.S. Congressman "Pete" Stark, who authored the initial bill. According to the Stark Law website, physician self-referral is defined as "the practice of referring a patient to a medical facility in which he or she has a financial interest, be it ownership, investment, or a structured compensation arrangement." Proponents of the Stark Law allege that physician self-referral is a conflict of interest and may encourage overutilization of services, which provide increased revenue or reimbursement that would increase the cost of care.

Another barrier to alignment is "corporate practice of medicine" statutes, such as those in California, which prohibit nearly all hospitals from directly employing physicians. Restrictions implemented by these federal and state laws spurred healthcare providers to develop work-around strategies and creative governance structures, such as tax-exempt foundations and independent practice associations (IPAs). In states where such prohibitions did not exist, hospitals began hiring physicians or purchasing physician practices. These approaches flourished during the early 1990s as an effort to protect revenue and market share in response to managed care penetration and anticipation of Clinton health reform initiatives (Menninger, 2010). Although some of these newer healthcare entities remained successful, the majority did not survive due to their utilization of market-driven-only strategies, ineffective governance structures, and poor communication and collaboration between hospital executives and physicians (Menninger, 2010).

The enactment of the Patient Protection and Affordable Health Care Act in 2010 has once again opened the door to physician–hospital integration via specific *clinical integration* strategies. Today, the emphasis throughout these partnerships is on the provision of quality of care through the practice of evidenced-based medicine, care coordination, and population and disease management. One of the vehicles for creating this clinical integration is through an *accountable care organization* (ACO). An ACO brings together various healthcare entities—primary care physicians, specialists, hospitals, ambulatory surgery centers, diagnostic centers, and home health agencies—to oversee and coordinate care for a defined patient population. ACOs promote access to care and value of care and are rewarded for meeting outcomes and benchmarks for quality of care and cost-effectiveness.

According to Michael Peregrine (2011), partner with the healthcare law firm of McDermott Will & Emery, a critical success factor of any ACO will be the creation of an effective governance structure. In addition to the traditional board responsibilities mentioned previously, Peregrine indicates that an ACO board must perform these 10 unique duties:

1. Development of performance criteria for the Chief Executive Officer
2. Evaluation of network provider performance against plans and budgets
3. Approval of the clinical integration program

4. Establishment of network provider criteria for participation
5. Oversight of performance incentive programs for participating providers
6. Monitoring network provider performance against benchmarks
7. Review and approval of payer contracts against standards
8. Oversight of quality reporting and auditing activity
9. Oversight of compliance plans and substandard care concerns
10. Oversight of implementation programs to meet external standards

Another critical success factor for ACOs will be their ability to adapt to changing circumstances and new regulations; these are currently evolving and will continue to do so in the near future. Peregrine (2011) warns that it is imperative for ACO governance to be ever-vigilant regarding the mission and operations of the organization and to develop and implement strong conflict disclosure and resolution processes.

Additionally, which type of legal entity is chosen for ACO formation will affect the governance structure and related fiduciary considerations (Peregrine, 2011). How the ACO's structure will form and develop may vary depending on its history of alliances, partnerships, mergers, and joint ventures.

Regardless of the governance structure established, healthcare leaders must learn from the failures of previous hospital–physician integration strategies and avoid repeating the errors of the past. **Table 14.2** provides an outline developed by Menninger (2010) for the California Healthcare Foundation to promote successful HCO–provider integration in today's era of reform.

Table 14.2 Key Elements of Successful HCO–Provider Integration

- A shared strategic vision that identifies the longer-term goals of the ACO within the contexts of community health, provider capabilities, and overall health policy.
- An organizational structure that supports ACO strategy through shared hospital-physician leadership, transparent decision making, and clarity about participants' roles.
- Respectful and trusting relations among ACO participants, with open channels of communication.
- Appropriate clinical and organizational infrastructure to implement coordination of medical care, information technology, and financial systems.
- Aligning provider financial incentives with achievement of ACO strategic goals and objectives, while simultaneously addressing issues of cost, quality, access, and choice.
- Sufficient capital and clinical/financial management capabilities to support the assumption of risk and plans to move from lower-risk payment models (i.e., shared savings) to higher-risk models (i.e., capitation).

Source: Adapted from Menninger, B. (2010). *Accountable care organizations: Avoiding the pitfalls of the past*. Oakland, CA: California HealthCare Foundation.

BOARD COMPOSITION: WHOM DO YOU WANT?

As Pointer and Orlikoff (1999) indicated over a decade ago, the individual members of a board can make the difference between mediocre governance and great governance. It is imperative for a governing body to retain a good balance of individuals with the requisite personal characteristics, experience, and skills that will contribute effectively to the organization. Tyler and Biggs (2001) add that respected community stature, volunteer experience, and excellent references from other board members are key criteria.

The American Hospital Association's Center for Healthcare Governance (CHG) has published a series of monographs on a wide range of governance topics. In its blue-ribbon report, "Building an Exceptional Board: Effective Practices for Healthcare Governance" (2007), the CHG outlines personal characteristics and experience considered important for board members (see **Table 14.3**).

Leaders should also make the case for diversity. Data from a 2011 survey by the American Hospital Association and the CHG showed that HCO governing boards are less diverse than the communities they serve. The CHG (2007) recommends that organizations strive to achieve board diversity in age, gender, and ethnicity in order to reflect the community and patients served and, even more importantly, to promote a diversity of thoughts and

Table 14.3 Effective Board Characteristics and Experience

Personal Characteristics	Reputable
	Big-picture thinker
	Intelligent
	Objective
	Open to new ideas
	Proactive
	Highly engaged
	Able to ask tough questions and challenge others in a nondisruptive way
	Embraces organization's values
Experience	Demonstrated leadership
	Board experience
	Community involvement
	Particular business experience
	Some members should have clinical experience (physicians and nurses)

Source: Adapted from Center for Healthcare Governance. (2007). *Building and exceptional board: Effective practices for health care governance*. Chicago, IL: Author.

ideas. Biggs (2011) expands on this notion of diversity by including individuals who have demonstrated achievement, the ability to be a team player, integrity, receptivity to training and evaluation, the resources to contribute, and a willingness to devote their time.

Selection

In most cases, board members can join the governing body via three basic methods: election, appointment, and self-perpetuation (Pointer & Orlikoff, 1999). Elected board members are selected by a vote of stakeholders. Stakeholders can include taxpayers in the county or district the HCO serves. Advantages of the election model include opportunities for constituents to exert control over the governing body and to demand accountability. The major disadvantage of this model is that the board position becomes politicized.

In the appointment model, board members are selected and appointed by another entity, such as a parent board or government body (e.g., board of supervisors). An advantage of this method is that board members who are appointed can advance the goals and objectives of the larger entity or governing body. One major disadvantage, however, is that appointees may be reluctant to make decisions that may be in the best interest of the local organization but conflict with aims of the larger entity (Pointer & Orlikoff, 1999).

A self-perpetuating board selects its own members and therefore, perpetuates itself. In this process, a current board member or nominating committee recommends a new member for selection as a member of the governing body. This model allows the board to ensure membership continuity, expertise, and qualifications that best meet the needs of the organization (Pointer & Orlikoff, 1999). Unfortunately, without outside influences, there is also a potential risk that a mediocre board will remain mediocre or that *groupthink* can become the dominant culture of the governing body.

Keeping the Board Engaged

Board engagement is a two-way street. The board chair and chief executive officer have a responsibility to create an atmosphere that encourages attendance and participation while remaining sensitive to members' time demands. Effective board leaders implement a well-defined governance process that is aligned with the organization's strategic focus, provide appropriate and ongoing education, inspire and motivate excellent performance, and create a culture of respect that survives professional disagreement and dissent.

Board members also have a responsibility to effectively promote the business and purpose of the organization by being prepared, understanding the organization in its larger context, respecting the other board members and the executive team, and appreciating the backgrounds and expertise of their colleagues and leaders.

GOVERNANCE SKILLS: WHAT DO YOU NEED?

The CHG (2007) has indicated that boards should recruit and appoint members who have the specific skills and abilities needed to help govern effectively. Among the necessary skills are expertise in developing and managing quality initiatives, business partnerships, and financial and legal issues. Emotional intelligence and proficiency in building and maintaining collaborative professional relationships are also critical.

Healthcare organizations that anticipate growth in strategic partnerships are wise to seek board members with backgrounds in mergers and acquisitions and in enterprise-wide risk management (CHG, 2010). Organizations whose clinical integrations result in the assumption of clinical and financial accountability for the health of defined populations should consider finding board members with expertise in public health, population health management, and health disparities (CHG, 2010). These new strategic partnerships will also demand that board members bring a systems-thinking mindset and objectivity to their governance activities.

Strategic Change Management

No skill is in greater demand during this turbulent era than the ability to strategically manage change for an organization. As the saying goes, "The only constant is change." The governing body has a responsibility to prepare and position the organization to adapt and respond to changes in the environment. Organizations with a high adaptive orientation, which includes taking advantage of new opportunities and innovation whenever possible, have a better chance of succeeding than those that take a wait-and-see approach (Brown, 2011).

This adaptation can only occur effectively through the use of a systems model, which acknowledges the organization as an open system influenced by the environment (Brown, 2011). A *system* is a set of interrelated and interdependent parts that are brought together by design to achieve a goal or purpose. Organizations are in continuous interaction with their environment (see **Figure 14.4**). The environment continuously influences the resource *inputs* (the items needed to create or launch a process), the

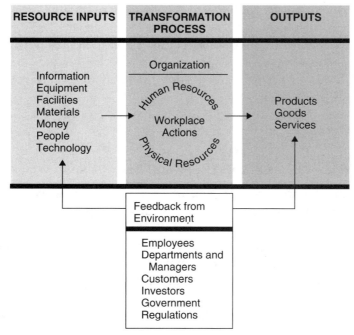

Figure 14.4 The Open System Organization

Source: Courtesy of BROWN, DONALD R, EXPERIENTIAL APPROACH TO ORGANIZATION DEVELOPMENT, 8th Edition, © 2011. Printed and Electronically reproduced by permission of Pearson Education, Inc., Upper Saddle River, New Jersey.

transformational *processes* (the activities or functions performed to produce products or services), and *outputs* (the products and services produced) (Brown, 2011).

Change can be radical or incremental. *Radical change* is an acute and major *revolutionary* change, whereas *incremental change* is slower, more limited, and *evolutionary* in nature. Regardless of the type of change introduced, however, resistance to change is a typical response. The greatest resistance will come from changes that have a high impact on the culture of the organization and demand a major degree of change (Brown, 2011). The organizational changes that are anticipated under healthcare reform fall into this category, and governing boards should be fully prepared for this challenge. The governing body of a healthcare entity can support the executive management team and increase the chances of a successful change process (Brown, 2011) by ensuring that their organization has:

1. Created a climate that is conducive to change
2. Clearly articulated a vision for the change
3. Provided the appropriate leadership for the change

4. Understood the politics of the change and negotiated with appropriate stakeholders
5. Effectively and continuously communicated the change to all stakeholders
6. Allowed for participation of appropriate organizational members in the change process
7. Developed reward systems to promote and reinforce the change process

The Chief Executive Officer: The Pivotal Point Person

One cannot discuss the roles and responsibilities of a governing body without acknowledging the key individual who represents the board to the organization and represents the organization to the board—the Chief Executive Officer (CEO). The relationship between the board and the CEO cannot be underestimated and can "make or break" the performance of the governing body and the institution (Biggs, 2011; Pointer & Orlikoff, 1999; Tyler & Biggs, 2001). For effective governance, this relationship must be based on mutual trust and respect. Open lines of communication should be maintained; the chair of the governing board and the CEO should meet regularly to keep the relationship reliable and productive.

The CEO's role is to run the organization in a manner consistent with its mission, vision, values, policies, and procedures, as approved by the governing body. Because of their skills, knowledge, and expertise, CEOs can be a crucial source of information for their boards about industry trends; with the information provided, the governing body can make better-informed decisions regarding the strategic direction of the organization. Boards may often request the presence of other experts from the executive team as well, such as the Chief Financial Officer, Chief Nursing Officer, and Chief Medical Officer, to provide additional information and insight. Ultimately, however, it is the CEO alone who is accountable to the governing body for the effective and efficient operation of the organization and for the appropriate execution of the board's short- and long-term strategies.

TRANSPARENCY: EVERYONE IS WATCHING!

Triggered by the less-than-stellar governance of some institutions, primarily in financial and for-profit healthcare sectors, increased government and public scrutiny has resulted in regulatory changes that "shine a spotlight on board practices and accountability" (Orlikoff, 2009, p. 72). The not-for-profit healthcare sector has not been immune to this scrutiny. For example, recent legislation now requires not-for-profit healthcare organizations to complete the newly revised Internal Revenue Service (IRS) Form 990. Form 990 not only asks for reports of income, but also for disclosures of governance information, including an organization's number of voting board members and specific organizational or governing body policies addressing issues such as conflict of interest and whistleblower protection.

In health care, transparency allows stakeholders and shareholders to remain aware of hospital quality, safety, pricing, and financial performance (Totten, 2011). Organizations promote transparency by publishing quarterly financials for investor agencies, by providing internal monthly financial reports to department heads and medical staff, by publicly reporting clinical quality/patient safety outcomes and patient satisfaction data, and by quantifying the level of community benefit provided each year (CHG, 2007).

However, transparency encompasses much more than data reporting. A transparent organization is honest, open, and accountable with regard to how its business is conducted. Transparency is reflected by an organization's willingness to allow greater internal and external visibility and to communicate effectively with the people it serves (Totten, 2011). The tone for transparent behavior must be clearly set by the governing body.

Transparency carries risks and benefits. According to Totten (2011), the benefits of transparency include the opportunity for:

- Patients to make informed decisions about the organization
- Payers to make accurate determinations regarding cost-effectiveness
- Staff and physicians to monitor their organizations' performance
- Organizations to develop best practices to improve care

There are also risks that exist with increased transparency (Totten, 2011). These risks include:

- Leaders and organizations being held to higher expectations
- "Once the door is open, there is no turning back"
- Demands for information continue to grow
- Leaders can no longer shun accountability

Measuring and Monitoring What Matters

Healthcare organizations, particularly hospitals, are tasked with a multitude of mandatory reporting requirements. These requirements are driven primarily by the federal government via the Centers for Medicare and Medicaid Services (CMS) and, to a lesser extent, by state legislatures and public health departments. For example, hospitals must report hospital-acquired conditions and present-on-admission information for all diagnoses of Medicare patients admitted to the hospital. Additionally, hospitals are required to annually report quality-of-care data so that reimbursement rates can be updated and readjusted. Board members should understand their organization's reporting requirements and how these reports reflect on the organization's performance and reputation.

Clearly, boards should be kept apprised of their organizations' performance and quality of care through rigorous assessments and reports, which provide a breadth of information and data. Without adequate information, the governing body may not be able to provide the necessary leadership to ensure the organization is achieving its mission. Sometimes, however, boards may be inundated with information that is peripheral or irrelevant to their tasks (Biggs, 2011). Boards should receive information critical to governance rather than management information more relevant to day-to-day operations, such as daily staffing reports, monthly operating reports, risk-management reports, and unit accounting summaries. Governance reports should focus on strategic information, which, according to the CHG (2010, p. 18), may include:

> ... trends, forecasts, emerging technologies, regulatory and legislative requirements, and other environmental issues, threats, and opportunities ... [and] organization-specific information in the context of local and broader environmental issues ... in a manner that allows decisions to be made regarding the organization's audit and financial statements, executive compensation, and clinical quality and patient safety.

One way to organize governance information is through the use of standardized reporting formats such as balanced scorecards and dashboards, which can display the organization's performance as compared to established targets or metrics. Balanced scorecards should ideally focus on four primary dimensions: organizational, executive, quality of care, and financial (CHG, 2010). **Table 14.4** shows the various elements that may be included in these dimensions. By spotlighting and monitoring these four dimensions of performance, the governing body can focus on issues that are most critical for the organization's success (CHG, 2010).

QUALITY: IS THERE SKIN IN THE GAME?

Renowned investor Warren Buffett coined the term "skin in the game" to describe a situation in which high-ranking executives use their own money

Table 14.4 Elements of a Balanced Governance Scorecard

Dimension	Intent	Elements
Organizational Performance	To ensure the organization is achieving its mission, goals, and objectives	· Formulating a mission and vision to maximize stakeholder and client benefit · Developing key goals the organization must achieve · Assuring that management strategies align with these goals
Executive Performance (fiduciary boards only)	To ensure that C-level executives such as the CEO are empowered and able to contribute to organizational success	· Recruiting and selecting the CEO · Assessing CEO performance · Determining CEO compensation · Overseeing CEO succession planning · If necessary, terminating the CEO
Quality of Care Performance	To ensure that the organization provides excellent service and a high quality of care in a safe environment to its patients/clients	· Developing clinical quality, safety, and service objectives · Credentialing and privileging members of the medical staff · Ensuring effective quality management and improvement systems are implemented and regularly assessed · Monitoring all aspects of quality and ensuring corrective action is implemented if needed
Financial Performance	To ensure the organization is financially sound and remains so in the future	· Specify financial objectives · Review management's financial plans and budgets, ensuring alignment with strategic goals · Ensure effective capital allocation · Ensure the accuracy of financial statements · Ensure the creditworthiness of the organization · Monitor financial performance and implement corrective action as needed

Source: Adapted from Center for Healthcare Governance. (2011). *AHA health care governance survey report*. Chicago, IL: Author.

to buy stock in their company. This personal investment (and assumed risk) will increase the chances that these executives will remain committed to promoting the success of their business. Inviting the board of a healthcare organization to make a personal investment in the quality initiatives of their organization can have a similar positive effect.

Unfortunately, of the four dimensions of organizational performance, *quality* can be the most vexing for board members, particularly those who lack a clinical background or knowledge base. Although most board members see themselves as unqualified to pass judgment on matters of patient care or quality, changing regulations and accreditation standards have made it clear that hospital board members are now being held accountable for the quality of care delivered in their organization (CHG, 2010). Governing boards must embrace this change, assume the responsibility of overseeing quality, and ensure that their organizations' services are delivered in a safe, effective, and reliable manner (Biggs, 2011).

Even though many board members will not become experts in clinical care, they can still contribute to quality improvement within their organizations via a number of strategies. In some organizations, governing boards acknowledge and accept responsibility for the care and safety of their organizations' clients (Biggs, 2011). These boards facilitate close relationships among board members, the medical staff, and executive management, which allows for open, honest, respectful, and productive discussion about quality initiatives and patient care outcomes—even when outcomes are negative.

Another effective strategy for board members striving to interpret and analyze quality data is to educate themselves about the main drivers of quality, to understand data provided as they relate to those drivers, and to ask executives and medical professionals to clarify queries that may arise.

A third strategy is to determine specific outcomes, as guided by appropriate benchmarks, for medical, nursing, and other clinical staff. These targets should be aggressive in order to dramatically improve the quality of care and reduce potential harm to patients (Biggs, 2011).

A fourth strategy is to demand clear and unambiguous accountability for quality outcomes. Many organizations are holding CEOs accountable for quality outcomes and tying a large portion of executive compensation to their achievement. Governing boards must make quality a priority and address quality issues as comprehensively as they do financial and operational issues (Biggs, 2011).

Healthcare reform trends include the promotion of greater accountability for quality of care through *pay for performance* or P4P (CHG, 2010). Healthcare organizations are being rewarded, by both public and private payers, for achieving quality outcomes. Conversely, organizations are also being penalized financially for reporting hospital-acquired conditions, errors, or poor outcomes. These "never events" are monitored by the CMS and, if recurrent, can cause a hospital to lose its Medicare certification—and even its operating license.

One of the greatest challenges to quality improvement is variability and misalignment in the reimbursement process, which limits collaboration toward a common goal. For example, hospitals are paid a lump sum by Medicare per case or diagnosis, whereas physicians are paid on a fee-for-service or piecemeal basis. If a patient's condition worsens and discharge is delayed, the hospital is placed at economic risk; the patient stays in the hospital extra days and consumes additional resources without additional reimbursement. The physician, on the other hand, can continue to bill Medicare for his or her daily visits to the patient. As long as hospitals and physicians are not partnered financially in the quest to provide excellent care and service to patients, there will be little progress in dramatically improving quality.

Nevertheless, at no time in the history of health care has there been a stronger business case for improving healthcare quality. Not only are hospitals pursuing improved quality because it's "the right thing to do," but also because their enhanced reputations are becoming a competitive advantage in the healthcare marketplace. Better quality, fewer errors, and less harm means greater cost savings; improving quality may be the "most powerful value strategy on the board governance scorecard" (Biggs, 2011). In this era of reform, governing bodies are implementing clinical integration to align hospitals and physicians and improve outcomes by fully sharing risks and rewards through more effective reimbursement methods such as bundled payments, shared savings, and other benefit-sharing arrangements.

SUMMARY

All elaborate organizations require some form of governance, and, in light of their size and complexity, healthcare organizations are no exception. Traditional forms of governance have been effective in the past, but now, as a result of changes in the industry, government regulation, and market forces, we are seeing new, nontraditional forms emerge.

Governing bodies play a critical role in ensuring the success and quality of healthcare organizations. The responsibilities of governing boards in this regard have been well articulated by researchers, consultants, and legal experts. Measuring and evaluating organizational performance is a key collective function for boards of both not-for-profit and for-profit entities. As individuals, board members have specific obligations and accountabilities as well, including fiduciary duty, duty of loyalty, duty of obedience, and avoidance of conflict of interest.

The composition of the board or governing body will be critical for navigating the turbulent waters of a new era in health care. Recruiting board members with the requisite characteristics and experience via the most effective selection method is essential for governance effectiveness.

Different healthcare organizations have different governance structures. Hospitals traditionally follow a corporate model and can be stand-alone entities or part of a larger, multihospital/health system. Medical groups tend to structure themselves as traditional and hybrid business entities. As a result of health reform legislation, healthcare organizations must learn to adapt to changing circumstances and develop structures that provide opportunities for provider/clinical integration to promote more efficient and effective healthcare delivery. Accountable care organizations (ACOs) are an example of this evolving governance structure.

The governing board will be required to lead the organization in making the strategic changes necessary for adaptation and response to this new environment. Boards must take a systems approach to facilitating the changes needed, whether they be incremental or radical. Resistance to change is common; successful change management requires a positive and trusting relationship between the governing body, the executive leadership, and the medical staff to effectively develop successful change strategies for the organization.

Finally, transparency is the name of the new game. Information about quality of care, patient safety, and pricing is now publicly available via the Internet and other sources. The demands for efficiency and effectiveness by stakeholders, regulatory agencies, and clients fall on the shoulders of the governing body; healthcare organization boards must know how and what performance measures to monitor and assess to promote and ensure success.

Governance is facing an exciting and challenging future in this era of reform. Understanding the roles, responsibilities, and value of governance is critical for competence in the field of modern health administration.

Discussion Questions

1. How are nontraditional forms of governance affecting the efficiency and effectiveness of organizational performance?
2. Have the demands for quality and accountability changed in governance? Why and how?
3. How can members of the governing body assist the organization to prepare for change in the new environment?
4. There are many types of agencies that oversee healthcare organizations. Do you think there will be more agencies created or do you anticipate a consolidation of these agencies? Why or why not?

Case Study: Conflicts in Governance

[This case study was contributed by Hildy Aquinaldo, JD, MPH.]

Approximately 10 years ago, South Bridge Health System (SBHS) allocated Noble Regional Medical Center (NRMC) a capital budget that was commensurate with its poor financial performance. The medical staff at NRMC believed that if the hospital became more profitable, SBHS would likewise make more funding available. Accordingly, the medical staff worked in concert with NRMC's leadership to improve the hospital's financial situation and, in the meantime, got by with what they had.

Today, NRMC is one of the strongest cogs in the SBHS wheel. Yet, SBHS has not lived up to its end of the promise. In fact, total capital expenditures at NRMC rose only 2% between 2002 and 2012. On the ground, this meant that many of the medical staff's requests for the purchase of new or replacement medical equipment had been deferred to "next year." The medical staff commented that it felt unappreciated and disincentivized from future improvement.

With this sentiment, the medical staff drafted a letter to SBHS, but wisely sought the advice of NRMC's president and CEO, Raymond Collins, before firing it off to the powers that be. Mr. Collins suggested that because the medical staff reported to the hospital's Community Board, that they should seek the latter's support, and indeed they did. As a result of their efforts, the Chair of the Community Board, Bridget Andrade, drafted a letter to Ethan Christiansen, SBHS's Chief Operating Officer. Her letter detailed the medical staff's concern over capital budget allocations and invited Mr. Christiansen to meet with the Board that following month.

Prior to that meeting with the Board, however, Mr. Christiansen took an unusual step by meeting with the medical staff. Following their frank discussions, Mr. Christiansen volunteered to dip into his own reserves to grant the hospital $200,000, with consideration for additional funds. He also agreed to revisit the issue of SBHS's distribution formula so that the system's high performers would be encouraged to continue their progress. By the time the board meeting came around, the fire had been extinguished.

Case Study Discussion Questions

1. When hospitals are part of a larger system that must allocate its capital equitably among its other entities, what would be considered a "fair" formula for allocation? What criteria might be included?

2. Why might the medical staff of a hospital organization feel that they have some say in the distribution of capital?

3. What is the responsibility of the Board in this case? Whose interests must they be concerned about and why?

RELATED WEBSITES

Center for Healthcare Governance: www.americangovernance.com/
Great Boards: www.greatboards.org
Stark Law: www.starklaw.org
Trustee Magazine: www.trusteemag.com

REFERENCES

Biggs, E. L. (2011). *Healthcare governance: A guide for effective boards* (2nd ed.). Chicago, IL: Health Administration Press.

Brown, D. R. (2011). *An experiential approach to organization development* (8th ed.). Upper Saddle River, NJ: Pearson Prentice Hall.

Bryant, E. L., & Jacobson, P. D. (2006, December). Ten best practices for measuring the effectiveness of nonprofit healthcare boards. *Bulletin of the National Center for Healthcare Leadership.* Supplement to *Modern Healthcare, 36*(48).

Center for Healthcare Governance. (2007). *Building and exceptional board: Effective practices for health care governance.* Chicago, IL: Author.

Center for Healthcare Governance. (2010, November). Governance implications of healthcare reform. *Great Boards Newsletter.* Retrieved November 8, 2012 from www.greatboards.org/newsletter/2010/Governance_Implications_of _Healthcare_Reform.pdf.

Center for Healthcare Governance. (2011). *AHA health care governance survey report.* Chicago, IL: Author.

Medical Group Management Association. (2009). *Body of knowledge—Governance.* Englewood, CO: Author.

Menninger, B. (2010). *Accountable care organizations: Avoiding the pitfalls of the past.* Oakland, CA: California HealthCare Foundation.

Orlikoff, J. E. (2009, May/June). Are you ready for greater transparency and accountability? *Healthcare Executive, 24*(3), 72–73.

Peregrine, M. (2011, February 15). ACO formation & operation: Principal governance issues [Podcast]. *McDermott Will & Emery, LLP.*

Pointer, D. O., & Orlikoff, J. E. (1999). *Board work: Governing health care organizations.* San Francisco, CA: Jossey-Bass.

Totten, M. K. (2011, September/October). Transparency: Considerations for CEOs and boards. *Healthcare Executive, 26*(5), 76–77.

Tyler, J. L., & Biggs, E. L. (2001). *Practical governance.* Chicago, IL: Health Administration Press.

Chapter **15**

Leadership and Community Outreach

David Cockley and Timothy Putnam

LEARNING OBJECTIVES

By the end of this chapter, the student will be able to:

- Delineate the role of leadership in outreach to small/rural communities.
- Identify outreach roles of community-based health organizations.
- Transition from stand-alone community facilities to networked partners.
- Provide models and methods of outreach leadership.

KEY TERMS

Collaboration

Community benefit

Community needs assessment

Community outreach

Critical access hospitals

Federally qualified health center

Partnerships

INTRODUCTION

Leaders in healthcare organizations (HCOs) are expected to be involved in strategic activities within the organization. For several important reasons, executives and managers should also be aware of and involved in community-oriented outreach activities *beyond* the HCO. Such outreach activities enhance the HCO's networking, augment the organization's role and reputation in the community, and serve to promote marketing for the HCO, its service line, and its mission.

The reputation and image of an entity can be influenced by a variety of issues, including customer satisfaction, workforce development, and recruitment of patients and insurance plans. **Community outreach** increases opportunities for **partnerships** with other organizations and extends the HCO's footprint and mission. The local media as well as business and educational communities also recognize HCOs by their community-wide reputation. Organizations often expend substantial resources to enhance the public image of their facility in to the wider community.

Where does the responsibility of a healthcare leader end? Is it at the threshold of the facility? Is it to the organization's primary service area, to the local or extended community?

A profit-motivated leader might utilize every opportunity to drive profitable business to the healthcare organization. An altruistic leader might simply answer that the HCO would continue to promote, provide, and improve healthcare services in any way it could, regardless of the financial impact on the organization. Outreach activities can allow leaders to carve a middle ground between these two positions by leveraging the resources of an organization to serve the health needs of a community without compromising the financial viability of the HCO.

Organizations and Communities

All HCOs exist within the milieu of one or more specific communities. Some smaller facilities, such as community hospitals or small physician groups, may have been established and developed through the efforts of a specific locality or city. Their business and services are typically branded with the culture, values, and local politics of those localities, and their staff and patients are generally residents of those communities. Even in larger, more urban areas, healthcare facilities are still molded by local or regional characteristics. Additional neighborhood influences that have an impact on HCO's include the existence of adjacent health-related training academies (such as medical schools, nursing programs, and specialized ancillary training programs), the proximity to one or more military bases with active duty or retired personnel, or the presence of special populations (such as university students, immigrants, or "snowbird" populations). A general adage in government is that *"all politics are local."* Understanding the demographics, expectations, and challenges of a local population is also necessary to develop outreach opportunities and to fully serve the community's health needs.

The mission of healthcare organizations is one prominent place wherein this local flavor can be displayed. While most HCOs have mission statements that acknowledge the patient populations that will be served by the organization, many statements also speak to the role of the community and its unique patient subpopulations. This is especially true of many freestanding community hospitals or community clinics that were initiated as county, city, or district facilities and may answer to local governmental bodies. The mission statements of such HCOs set the strategic parameters that guide the operations of the organizations, which include outreach efforts with community-based partners.

The laudable goal of addressing the health-related needs of a local community can be promoted through involvement in specific community-oriented programs and by allowing representatives or administrators from these community stakeholders to have a voice in addressing healthcare concerns. Various types of **collaborations** can be established, from one-time partnerships with community groups to address a particular community need, to ongoing formal linkages of organizations, including program affiliations or joint ownership of a community resource.

A community-oriented vision can also provide a way for an HCO to test and market its services. Successful outreach endeavors can blossom into new services or full-blown service lines for the HCO. Innovative programs or modes of service delivery catch the attention of the public, area media publicity, and monitoring groups such as state governments or the Joint Commission. Community outreach projects can also build or improve organizational reputation and demonstrate **community benefit** required for the not-for-profit status of many HCOs.

An outreach orientation also helps the HCO become a significant leader in broader networks of medical, healthcare, and social service providers in an area. Organizations such as county health departments, senior centers, and long-term-care facilities may become network partners and expand an HCO's service delivery options. With the recent federal focus on transitions of care for patients who receive health and social services from multiple organizations, such multidisciplinary collaborations are paramount.

As health organizations are increasingly advised to link with other providers in their region, the leaders of these organizations benefit from adopting such a collaborative perspective. The positive results for the organization and its leadership include favorable community publicity, opportunities for interorganizational leadership in the local health environment, and achievement of the organization's mission of serving the healthcare needs of the community.

Providing healthcare services in nontraditional sites (i.e., schools, industrial workplaces, mobile health units, or long-term-care facilities) can address both the identified health-related concerns of the locality and increase the community esteem for the HCO and its partners. In a community with, for example, elevated adolescent obesity rates or an excessively high incidence of Type 2 diabetes, a local hospital may take a leadership role in sponsoring a community-wide weight monitoring program. A smaller physician group practice may provide influenza vaccines at multiple community sites, such as schools, places of worship, community centers, or workplaces. In each case, the HCO moves beyond its physical location into the community to address a particular community need.

OUTREACH ROLES OF HEALTH ORGANIZATIONS

Outreach includes the many ways that organizations go beyond their organizational walls to address population needs or expand services. Many of the healthcare conditions that bring patients to HCOs have their antecedents or causes in environmental or community factors. Addressing those causal factors may require the HCO to move outside its borders.

One widely noted outreach activity involves organizations that offer treatments for cancer. The HCO and sponsors support annual or periodic community-based initiatives or "walks" to highlight their concern for patients and families impacted by this health condition. Many other outreach programs are initiated by an organizational marketing campaign and provide critical services in a new venue. The services provided may not be unique, but the places where they are provided may be new for the HCO. School-based health centers are no longer novel, but have become a widely accepted way to address the physical, chronic, and behavioral concerns of children and adolescents at a location convenient to children. Many workplaces have been transformed in a similar way by offering workplace healthcare and wellness programs, exercise facilities, and breastfeeding support for employees.

Outreach programs can also allow HCOs to reach new populations of patients. Although the healthcare industry has widely assumed that patients who need healthcare services will arrive at a facility's door, a more proactive approach is to extend needed healthcare services to the patients in accessible locations, such as schools, workplaces, community centers, and shopping malls. Studies have shown the value of such healthcare initiatives, often led and directed by executives of local healthcare organizations, in the positive development of communities (Alexander, Comfort, Weiner, & Bogue, 2001). Because the provision of healthcare services is central to the robust economic and service infrastructure of a community, organizational leaders will continue to be drafted for input or oversight of such community initiatives.

Examples of successful outreach partnerships include:

- A large statewide hospital system has an agreement with the state's Department of Health to manage many of the state's local public health clinics.
- A small physician practice operates the only pharmacy in a large rural county.
- A **federally qualified health center** (FQHC) partners with the local school system to offer in-school health centers to provide primary care and behavioral health services to county adolescents.
- A regional public health district promotes annual flu shots at a large number of workplaces to increase the rate of immunization and reduce the incidence of influenza and employee absences.
- Urgent care or primary care clinics are temporarily or permanently located in shopping malls to provide easy access for clients/patients with health concerns.

Even if a local health organization is not leading an outreach initiative, it may play a role in supporting the initiative's financing. If funding is needed, the HCO, as a major stakeholder and employer, will often be asked to provide approval or endorsement for the project and to contribute available resources. HCOs may also have fundraising or marketing expertise that can assist the outreach endeavor and its partners.

This collaboration can provide benefits *within* organizations as well. Smaller HCOs or health-related businesses that join these efforts can access the training, skills, and experience of leaders in larger HCOs. Through this mutual effort, the smaller entity can potentially gain valuable expertise, and the larger HCO can enhance recognition or enlist allies in outreach and marketing.

THE ROLE OF LEADERSHIP IN OUTREACH INITIATIVES

Healthcare industry leaders recognize that outreach is essential to the success of not only health services organizations, but also large corporate networks. *Money matters* has become a truism throughout the American business world. In the altruistic milieu of healthcare, the common adage is *no margin, no mission*. Even smaller HCOs need to generate adequate revenues for survival and sustainability. Without the proven value of outreach initiatives, HCOs may face drops in revenue that result in *no mission, no margin*. Effective HCO leaders should be aware of this risk and should strive to enhance their organizations' economic and mission "fitness" by remaining engaged in their communities and addressing their neighbors' needs and concerns.

HCOs such as hospitals, physician practices, or skilled nursing facilities typically play a significant leadership role in their neighborhoods, especially in small or rural communities where HCOs may not only be the area's primary healthcare providers, but also the primary employers. For that reason, city planners often strive to include HCOs in local community planning initiatives (Alexander et al., 2001).

Involvement of HCO leaders is often a critical factor in the success and sustainability of outreach programs. HCO leaders bring the positive reputation of their organizations to the table, adding value to the initiative and its objectives, and inspiring and motivating the program participants. Healthcare providers, administrators, or ancillary staff may be the implementers of a successful HCO outreach program, but the organization's top managers or executives can guide its development and strategic planning and can facilitate the coordination of key program elements. Leaders' involvement can also draw greater media attention, build the reputation of the participant stakeholders, and enhance internal and external collaboration and networking to promote program success.

HCO leaders can bring their partners and competitors to the table to address a mutually agreed-upon health concern and can encourage and support initiative participants in the discussion and resolution of common problems. Even highly competitive organizations understand the value of putting aside their differences and working together to serve the community's greater needs. Larger HCOs are often viewed as the dominant player in such multiparticipant groups, but the directors or leaders of smaller healthcare organizations can also contribute critical data or skills to positively influence the partnership and play pivotal roles in building consensus and developing mutually agreed-upon solutions.

In many communities, HCO leaders have formalized partnerships to address community needs with local or regional associates and continue to inform and support them on an ongoing basis.

Greater Cincinnati Health Council

One example is the Greater Cincinnati Health Council (GCHC; www .gchc.org), a network of HCOs within 50 miles of Cincinnati. GCHC members range from academic medical centers such as Cincinnati Children's Hospital and the University of Cincinnati to community hospitals such as Dearborn County Hospital in Lawrenceburg, Indiana. Though individual Council member institutions typically compete with each other on a variety of fronts, including staff recruiting and client marketing, the Council has developed outreach initiatives that address common goals and objectives, and benefit the participants in the group and the patients that they serve. An example of a successful GCHC initiative was the development of HealthBridge, a Health Information Exchange that allowed all member healthcare providers to electronically share patients' personal health information. As a result, the GCHC network of member institutions has implemented an integrated model for patient records management ahead of the timeline proposed in the 2010 Patient Protection and Affordable Care Act.

Remote Area Medical Clinic

Another example of a successful outreach partnership is the large annual Wise County Remote Area Medical Clinic. The Clinic, located in Southwest Virginia, is sponsored by multiple providers of health and health-related services. These partners include local health, dental, and vision providers; the state medical schools and their students; and social service agencies for uninsured and low-income families in the region. Each year, the Clinic, which runs Friday through Sunday, reaches thousands of underserved low-income patients in this economically challenged region (Huttlinger, Schaller-Ayers, & Lawson, 2004; Merwin, Snyder, & Katz, 2006).

OUTREACH AND COLLABORATION

Outreach efforts to address community-based health concerns may require more resources than a single organization such as a community hospital can provide. In these circumstances, organizations may need to collaborate temporarily (or on an ongoing basis) to address a mutually identified concern. For example, overweight and obesity intervention in a local population is not typically within a single organization's scope. Goal-focused partnerships can draw discrete organizations together around a particular issue, such as obesity rates in the community, and engage them in both short-term and long-term collaboration to benefit their clientele.

When multiple independent or linked organizations collaborate to address an identified outreach project, leadership skills that facilitate effective team operation and function are required (Alexander et al., 2001). Leaders can help participants overcome barriers to collaboration, such as divergent missions or populations, or issues regarding competition, and help collaborators build formal and informal networks for implementing and providing services.

Some examples include:

- To address behavioral health needs in the community, a mid-sized community hospital facilitated the launch of a collaborative network of area safety-net providers.
- After a natural disaster ravaged a community, local public health services became unavailable. Under the leadership of the state Department of Health, healthcare providers in adjacent communities stepped forward temporarily to fill in the service gaps.
- To monitor high-risk pregnancies in a small community, its Community Health Center instituted a telehealth link with a medical center over an hour's drive away, saving time and reducing necessary travel for pregnant women for prenatal care.

Skillsets for Outreach Leadership

The leadership skillsets required to accomplish successful outreach goals include looking strategically beyond the organization, categorizing the wider community as the customer, and understanding the central role of needs assessment in that community. Additionally, team-building skills that enhance collaboration across disciplines and organizations are of great value.

Population Orientation

When an organization turns its attention to groups beyond its normal patient population, its leader must adopt a different perspective, a population orientation distinct from the patient or consumer orientation central to most healthcare facilities (Huttlinger et al., 2004). The leader needs to learn about, understand, and empathize with the specific needs and challenges of the larger group the HCO is aiming to serve. Public health agencies function with this broader population perspective, and their operational models can be adopted by private HCOs for outreach initiatives. The following list presents examples of the ways in which HCOs can partner with public health agencies.

- A nursing home wishes to identify and address the home healthcare needs of its region. To make a judicious decision about expanding into home health services, the nursing home examines the population data for its county or region to assess the demand for regional home health care.
- A community health center wishes to provide additional services to the homeless population in a midsized city. It assesses the specific

healthcare needs of this population, identifies those needs not being currently or adequately addressed, and partners with other service providers such as public health and social service agencies to help fill in the gaps.

HCOs have traditionally relied on individual patients, either by choice or by referral, to come to the HCO doors and access the services provided. A population orientation sends the HCO or a collaboration of organizations to the community first to assess unmet needs and then to strategize how services can be figuratively or literally delivered to the patient. Data analysis of population assessments, available from local and state public health departments, and national agencies such as the Centers for Disease Control and Prevention, can allow the identification of specific characteristics or needs within a subset of the larger population and can drive the development of interventions that more appropriately address the needs of that discrete group.

The health needs of populations or communities will be formulated differently than those of an individual. For example, to address the rapidly escalating problem of Type 2 diabetes, an individual healthcare provider treating an individual patient might focus on diet, exercise, and prescription medication. An HCO with a population orientation, on the other hand, might build community exercise facilities, monitor school lunch programs, provide nutrition education sessions, and advocate for improved food labeling at the supermarket. Both the individual and population efforts address Type 2 diabetes, but the outreach initiative has the potential to improve the health of many individuals in a community and facilitate a population-wide response.

Collaboration and Negotiation

Outreach activities of HCOs often involve partnerships with other organizations, including those outside the healthcare industry, coming together to implement an initiative or achieve a short- or long-term goal. Outreach partners may be direct competitors (e.g., two hospitals within a small city), healthcare providers of different types (e.g., home health agencies, physician group practices, long-term-care facilities), or they may be social service agencies or private businesses that do not provide direct healthcare services.

Interagency collaboration in the healthcare arena can develop referral networks and linkages for patient care. Most HCOs already have established linkages with other health providers (e.g., specialists, therapy practitioners, the regional tertiary-care facility) to facilitate additional care for patients with specific health needs in areas beyond the scope of the specific HCO.

These linkages with ancillary providers may be formal or informal and involve multiple organizations. For example, a community hospital facility may offer state-of-the-art cardiac imaging and establish a secure communications pathway with the private cardiology practices in the region to transfer patient test results quickly and confidentially.

Not every HCO manager has the skills necessary for successfully building a team of such diverse partners. HCO leaders may opt to recruit capable members of their management team or other HCO professionals with these skillsets to implement collaborative outreach programs or may purchase these services through external contractors qualified and experienced in operationalizing strategic plans. Training in team building and facilitation skills can allow leaders to successfully navigate the challenges of guiding a multifaceted group. This investment by an HCO that promotes successful outreach partnerships can provide valuable returns in enhancing both the organization's reputation and its bottom line.

Multidisciplinary clinical teams, led by a capable manager trained and skilled in negotiation and medication, are being promoted as a method for bridging the array of disciplines providing healthcare. But multidisciplinary administrative groups are also recommended to manage complex administrative problems in and across organizations and disciplines (Anderson & McDaniel, 2000; McDaniel & Driebe, 2001). Though these internal teams share many aspects in common with outreach partnerships, they are distinct from teams built from multiple organizations, especially those representing diverse industries. Setting up a management team within a community hospital, for example, is different from engineering a multi-entity task force spanning a hospital, several independent physician practices, and an elder retirement community.

Jeffrey Alexander and colleagues (2001) identified specific leadership skillsets necessary to successfully develop partnership arrangements across organizations. They identified five categories of factors necessary for effective community partnership. These included a system perspective, the ability to promote vision-based leadership, collateral leadership, power sharing, and process-based leadership.

Trauma Project for the University of Mississippi Medical Center

Advanced trauma centers across the country offer life-saving multispecialty resources for critical patient treatment. Unfortunately, not all traumatic injuries occur in locations close to an academic medical center and its trauma unit. In Mississippi, for example, rural hospitals receiving trauma cases would often transport their injured patients over long distances at high risk to the trauma center at the University of Mississippi Medical Center in Jackson (UMMC). UMMC leaders realized that many of the patients transferred could be best stabilized and treated at their local hospital if trauma evaluations could be performed locally with a high level of confidence. UMMC developed a plan to partner with seven rural hospitals throughout the state via a telemedicine service, which allows the local emergency department team to consult with the trauma team at UMMC to evaluate patients remotely and determine the most appropriate care.

The study of the telemedicine trauma project at UMMC (Duchesne et al., 2008) demonstrated some dramatic results. In the 30 months prior to the implementation of the telemedicine service, 351 patients were transferred from these seven hospitals for trauma care. In the next 30 months, the UMMC team evaluated 463 trauma patients through the Internet-based telemedicine system; only 51 patients required transfer to the trauma center at UMMC. Additionally, the study found that there was a dramatic decrease in the total cost of care for patients treated in the telemedicine era.

It is important to recognize that such an outreach program is not successful solely due to the use of modern technology. The vital ingredient in the program's success is the relationship developed among the medical professionals and healthcare leaders in the participating organizations. Constant refinement of processes and procedures are critical to maintain and improve the success of such a program. If the team at UMMC were to lose confidence in the capabilities of a rural hospital's staff, they would have little choice but to recommend more patients be transferred for trauma care. Ongoing active communication and education can promote and enhance the quality of care provided via this outreach partnership.

Clearly, UMMC realized that its responsibility to care for patients did not end at its emergency room door or even at the city limits of Jackson. As the leader in trauma care for Mississippi, UMMC recognized the need to reach out to rural areas and develop a partnership that better met the needs of patients throughout the state. However, few other programs have attempted to duplicate this telemedicine trauma program. For this type of outreach to expand around the country, healthcare leaders will need to accept that their responsibility to patients extends far beyond the front door of their facility.

Excellent communication skills become a heightened priority when leaders work with multiple organizations in collaborative networks. The HCO leader can mentor staff in how to best communicate and collaborate with other organizations. Clear communication among organizations prevents misunderstandings and promotes program success, especially in the delicate but critical area of resource allocation. Partners must clearly understand and agree on the contributions of personnel, time, and funding toward the project, before and during its implementation.

Needs Assessment

Many community-based HCOs incorporate periodic **community needs assessments** to identify areas of unmet need, new opportunities for organizational collaboration, and new directions for strategic planning and service delivery. Additionally, many healthcare organizations, independently or in collaboration with other local/regional organizations, carry out such assessments to evaluate how the HCO is meeting the healthcare needs of the locality.

The value of needs assessment for leaders and HCOs is underscored by new requirements within the Patient Protection and Affordable Care Act (PPACA). The PPACA stipulates that hospitals conduct a community health needs assessment at least once every 3 years beginning in 2012 (PPACA, 2010). The purpose of this requirement is to identify the healthcare needs in the community served by the HCO and to stimulate the development of strategies through which the HCO can address these community health needs. HCOs are being tasked with the responsibility to serve their communities, and their action plans and strategic outcomes will be assessed in the future to document implementation and effectiveness.

Needs assessment can be performed as an internal exercise for individual organizations to identify potential markets for new or expanded services, evaluate client satisfaction, or guide future organizational mission and goals. Needs assessment may also be undertaken by external groups, including collaborations of multiple community organizations, seeking to assess healthcare or social service needs and identify healthcare gaps.

Such assessments are an excellent means for multiple health-related organizations within one locality or region to pool resources to obtain a mutually beneficial product. A needs assessment coordinated by a specific community group, such as a community mental health center, would typically assess the community from one perspective (mental health) and not identify unmet health needs for, say, acute care providers or other interests in the community. A broadly targeted needs assessment, sponsored by a partnership of health-related groups, or separate community-based resources, such as the Chamber of Commerce or a community action agency, can develop an assessment that spans multiple areas of interest and identifies new areas wherein HCOs may direct their attention and efforts.

The process of bringing multiple organizations together to formulate the assessment instrument and collect and analyze the results is in itself a significant outreach endeavor. Distinct and unaffiliated organizations can learn the various skillsets and strengths of community partners, resources that lay the groundwork for future joint activities. Coordinating needs assessment projects with other healthcare providers can also help eliminate duplication of effort and help develop a common vision and "message." Some examples are:

- A small group practice partners with a continuing care retirement community (CCRC) to open a satellite clinic at the CCRC that expands direct service delivery to a larger population of retired individuals.
- A community hospital sponsors radio talk shows by local physicians on local health issues to educate the general public.
- A university's student health center contracts with a primary care practice in the college town to provide extended services to the university's student and employee populations.
- **Critical access hospitals** and affiliated healthcare practices develop telemedicine connections with a large tertiary medical center to increase community-based specialty services.

MODELS AND METHODS OF OUTREACH LEADERSHIP

HCOs are involved in a wide variety of outreach activities. Models for outreach programs include individual HCOs intent on building alliances within a local community or expanding services by partnering with other agencies, and multiple organizations seeking to achieve common missions and objectives. Two specific examples of successful ongoing outreach activities are presented below.

Critical Access Hospitals

Throughout much of the rural United States, small hospitals serve as the main source of healthcare, including emergency services (see **Figure 15.1**). Leaders of these institutions face specific challenges such as a lack of human and financial resources, overwhelming patient demand, time-intensive and difficult-to-implement government regulations, and falling reimbursements. Historically, small hospitals have struggled to survive; from 1980 to 1990, some 330 rural hospitals closed in the United States. Hospitals with fewer than 100 beds demonstrated less profitability than larger hospitals, and outreach efforts were often seen as an unaffordable luxury. The failure rate for rural hospitals was 29% higher than for urban facilities, often creating an additional healthcare void that was left unfilled (Drain, Godkin, & Valentine, 2001).

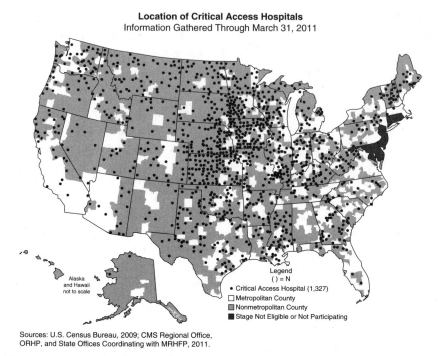

Figure 15.1 2011 Distribution of Critical Access Hospitals

Source: Courtesy of the Rural Assistance Center.

In an effort to help stem the rising tide of rural hospital closures, the federal government implemented the Critical Access Hospital (CAH) program in 1997 (Roop, 2008). The CAH program allowed small rural hospitals to be cost-based reimbursed—that is, paid 101% of their allowable costs, for Medicare patients. The program was offered to healthcare facilities that were typically the only hospital in their region and had fewer than 25 inpatient beds. Today, over 1300 CAHs are in existence. These facilities are often the sole hospital in their community, and the CAH program has stabilized their financial performance and reduced the closure rate of the previous decades (Holmes, Pink, & Slifkin, 2006).

The CAH program also provided common guidelines for the operations of the member institutions. Though services varied from hospital to hospital, the program encouraged consistency in areas such as bed capacity and length of patient stay. Hospitals that had functioned like solitary islands now felt they were part of an archipelago in which there is a level of interdependence and information sharing. Participants not only communicated informally, also but formalized cross-hospital groups into networks to develop programs and services of use to all.

One such organization is the Illinois Critical Access Hospital Network (ICAHN; www.ICAHN.org). This network of over 50 CAHs has worked together to accomplish several projects that would have been very difficult for any of its hospitals to accomplish individually. The network does not function like a traditional healthcare system with its standard corporate hierarchy and structure. ICAHN is governed and directed by a small group of hospital leaders elected by the entire group; this governance council oversees the operation of the network and the work of the employed ICAHN staff. Each hospital retains its own level of local control that is not encumbered or usurped by the governing council.

ICAHN is empowered to develop services of value to the group as a whole. A few examples include:

1. *Information Technology Expertise*: The Illinois CAHs identified that the technological revolution in healthcare augmented the demand for electronic health records, telehealth linkages, and other health information technology (HIT) advances. Unfortunately, managing these technologies demanded a broad HIT skillset with part-time availability that was difficult for most participants to obtain in their small towns. ICAHN was charged with developing an IT team that could be used to support the needs of the individual hospitals in the network, which is assigned to assist individual hospitals as needed.

2. *Sharing Best Practices*: Small hospitals with limited resources fazed by operational challenges used to hire expensive outside experts to consult and help develop solutions. Today, these hospitals can query the other members of the network, (many of whom have faced similar challenges and have developed successful solutions), for advice and recommendations. Methods for sharing include:
   a. Computerized listservs that allow hospital leaders to communicate with their counterparts at other ICAHN hospitals.
   b. User groups that communicate online and meet in person to share ideas and exchange information.
   c. Annual conferences that focus on educational and operational needs as well as updating members on relevant industry trends and projections.

3. *Physician Peer Review*: For reaccreditation and licensure, as well as if a concern arises regarding the care provided by a physician to a patient, healthcare organizations set up formal peer-review programs within their institutions. Peer providers review selected cases and render an opinion about the care and treatment provided and, if necessary, offer recommendations for future care.

Unfortunately, in small hospitals, there may not be a physician peer available to review cases in certain specialties. For example, even if there are several family medicine/primary care providers in local practice, a community may have only one cardiologist or neurologist, whose cases would need review by another specialist in those fields. Additionally, in the interdependent environment of a small hospital, physicians are often hesitant to scrutinize or criticize their close colleagues, so smaller hospitals often utilize national firms to perform peer reviews. Unfortunately, there are drawbacks with this process; first, external review is expensive and may limit the number of cases submitted for review. Second, the external reviewers, who are often located in large urban areas, are not always aware of the challenges and limitations their peers face in CAHs; they may provide recommendations that are difficult to implement in a small hospital.

For ICAHN hospitals, a better option was to utilize physicians across the ICAHN network to peer review cases from sister CAHs. This option was not only more affordable for the member hospitals but, because the reviewers hailed from similar smaller institutions, it also resulted in more relevant and helpful recommendations.

The ICAHN network is an excellent example of the value of collaboration in enhancing healthcare delivery and addressing challenges that could overwhelm an individual institution. HCO leaders in the ICAHN network have been able to organize and develop their network and promote cooperation among its members by demonstrating the benefits of this partnership for all the involved institutions. The key to its success is the development of trust among the members. A hospital would hesitate to share information or engage in collaborative initiatives if it sees its partners as competitors. Building trust among members and demonstrating the benefits of working together is the primary task of the effective HCO leader.

Pendleton Community Care

Pendleton Community Care (PCC) is a comprehensive primary care clinic located in rural West Virginia. PCC began as a small private nonprofit practice in the early 1980s, evolved into a Rural Health Clinic (1986), and, in 1998, became a federally qualified health center. Because the providers who launched the practice wanted to address the health concerns of the broader community, they began assessing the healthcare needs of their community early in the clinic's history.

PCC initiated several community-based outreach projects to address these identified community needs. Funding for these projects came from sources such as grant funding, direct reimbursement, or the clinic's operational budget. Another PCC goal was to ensure the initiatives' financial sustainability. Initiated from an assessment of their community populations, specific new healthcare services were provided external to the health center's normal operations.

- PCC's clientele included many noninstitutionalized community elders as well as their adult children caregivers. Clinicians observed that the elders' health status was directly related to the health condition of the caregiver. Overburdened and exhausted caregivers were unable to provide the best care for either their parents or themselves. To address this issue, PCC launched a community-based program to train and support homemaker aides for elders who needed home services, which also allowed routine monitoring of the elders' conditions. In addition to easing the caregivers' burdens and providing additional elder care, these aides could keep clinicians apprised of their patients' home situations and functional status between office encounters. After its launch, the state Medicaid program offered financing for the initiative in the hopes of reducing early nursing home admissions for Medicaid-eligible adults.
- Working with the county school system and parental contacts, PCC proposed and developed a series of school-based health centers (SBHCs). PCC now operates four school sites staffed by physician or nurse practitioners for regular hours each week. This outreach endeavor has proven successful at bringing primary care services to the students' location. The current SBHCs are addressing comprehensive primary care and behavioral health needs in this vulnerable population.
- PCC partnered with county employers to begin a series of worksite wellness initiatives, which provided health assessment exams for workers and offered a series of worksite health initiatives, including exercise competitions, diet and weight-loss classes, and health education modules on food and exercise. Initially funded from the PCC budget, this project evolved into a statewide health initiative for public employees.

OUTREACH CHALLENGES

Despite the acknowledged value of outreach initiatives for HCOs, challenges to participation remain. These include organizational factors such as limitations of resources or shortages of specialized personnel, regulatory obstacles in the industry, or issues in the community. HCO leaders must face and overcome challenges to build a successful outreach program.

Healthcare managers and organizations often cite a lack of sufficient resources to undertake outreach initiatives. HCO leaders owe a fiduciary loyalty to their organization and understandably focus on attaining the mission and goals set forth by the organization's governing body and/or owners. Outreach proposals that could eventually enhance the organization's reputation or financial stability may be met by confusion and resistance from organization executives and governing boards. The leader trying to focus attention on community needs or collaborative efforts with other organizations may hear "This is not our core purpose," from the Board. Demonstrating the value of outreach initiatives in achieving organization goals, along with the advantages for the organization of reaching out beyond its property line and expanding its footprint, is critical to assuaging such concerns and gaining acceptance and support.

The value of outreach activities and network development should be viewed in a longer-term strategic environment—positive results and revenue returns may not be immediate, but should be visible over the medium to long term. Among the demonstrable benefits that can improve acceptance of outreach initiatives are evidence that separate community groups, including actual or potential competitors, build ongoing relationships or partnerships that provide partner organizations with new service lines or revenue streams; barriers to service availability and utilization are weakened; new referral patterns for existing services are built; and the community or subpopulations within the community see improved health.

Another challenge for HCO leaders aiming to tackle community-wide or nontraditional initiatives is the need for specialized management expertise that may be lacking in all but the largest organizations. A community hospital, for example, may not have the experienced personnel to forge meaningful linkages with a nearby skilled nursing facility or home health agency.

The field of healthcare management has evolved to the stage wherein multiple layers of management expertise may be necessary within a single HCO to maximize its revenue or service lines. Many health services administrators begin their careers as management generalists, but the increasing pressure to specialize has influenced healthcare executives just as it has physicians and nurses. In fact, one of the key drivers for stand-alone HCOs to join larger networks or chains is the opportunity to tap into specialized management expertise.

In addition to shortages of management specialists, local healthcare organizations, especially those in smaller communities and rural areas, may also face shortages of clinical staff such as nurses, ancillary personnel, and specialty physicians. A nursing shortage, for example, will negatively impact the delivery of specific hospital services in the area, as well as put the hospital in direct competition with skilled nursing facilities, home health agencies, and local physician practices. Though sharing of resources may help alleviate a shortage, competition to recruit new hires may hamper attempts at organizational collaboration among these separate healthcare groups.

HCO leaders should be prepared for such challenges as they develop and implement outreach initiatives. Collaboration among HCO leaders to exchange best practices and skillsets that can help overcome challenges can promote greater success in facilitating outreach collaborations.

SUMMARY

Leaders of health care organizations (HCOs) become involved in outreach activities through their strategic planning initiatives in the HCO. An organization's specific goal may be to enhance its image or to market services to new populations of users. Strategically designed outreach activities, involving organizational leadership, employees, and the community, can provide marketing and partnership prospects for the HCO.

HCO leaders are influential in creating partnerships and in encouraging colleagues in their community to construct partnerships to address identified healthcare needs. However, the specific management skillsets required to build and sustain such partnerships and collaborations may be distinct from the skills taught traditionally in management. A population orientation, skills for building collaborations across multiple disciplines or provider groups, and methodologies to assess the healthcare needs of populations and communities are critical.

Multiple examples of outreach activities by distinct types of HCOs help exemplify the range of opportunities available to HCOs and their leaders. Among them are the Critical Access Hospital program, outreach endeavors of specific federally qualified health centers, and initiatives of specific academic medical centers. These examples highlight both the range of programs and the best-practice opportunities available to HCOs.

Engaging in nontraditional and innovative initiatives is not without challenges for leaders of HCOs. Obtaining the differing management skills, understanding effective resource allocation, and recruiting the necessary stakeholders and partners will allow leaders to successfully sustain outreach activities beyond an initial pilot phase for the benefit of the HCO and its community.

Many HCOs become providers of outreach activities, either as part of their declared mission to meet the healthcare needs of a community or through short- and long-term partnerships to address specific goals and objectives with other healthcare organizations. Understanding the value of outreach initiatives and the benefits of successful collaboration are critical for successful HCO leaders. Effective healthcare leaders will understand how to make use of all the organizational, financial, and collegial resources at their disposal to provide outreach to serve their communities via synergistic collaborations.

A shift in focus beyond a facility or organization may be necessary for healthcare leaders as they move to include outreach in their strategic planning efforts. Participation in a variety of collaborative linkages and partnerships will expand the vision of the organization outside the focus on its internal operations. The managerial skillsets necessary to lead an organization's involvement in outreach initiatives may differ from the skillsets required to manage an organization internally. Successful outreach orientation will require knowledge about how to assess and analyze the healthcare needs of a community, a willingness to look beyond the organizational boundaries for partners and delivery sites, team building and facilitation skills, negotiation skills effective across multiple organizations and industries, and the ability to facilitate creative solutions to fiscal and other challenges.

Many industries pursue outreach initiatives to enhance market share and revenue streams. Yet, in healthcare, outreach and collaboration can have a profound positive impact, not only on organizations but on the lives of individuals and communities. This reality motivates HCOs to consider and develop outreach programs that improve health and quality of life for individuals and populations, even at a cost to the bottom line. As they engage in strategic planning decisions, HCO leaders must consider and include the benefits of outreach programs on human lives.

Discussion Questions

1. Why should healthcare organizations consider outreach programs to address identified healthcare needs in their communities? What are the strategic and marketing benefits of outreach efforts?

2. Hospitals in urban markets routinely compete, sometimes aggressively, for market share and workforce. What are some specific outcomes that would benefit the community's health from the HCOs' collaboration?

3. In what ways do the outreach challenges differ for hospitals in highly competitive urban markets versus sole hospitals in smaller communities?

4. What skills are necessary for leaders in competing organizations to be able to work together and share resources to benefit the health of the community?

5. Why is a partnership with other community organizations necessary for many successful outreach initiatives? What are some of the potential pitfalls of initiating an outreach project without the support of other community organizations?

6. Answer the following questions as an HCO leader who understands the value and benefits of outreach:

   a. If your HCO develops a new procedure that significantly reduces nosocomial (hospital) infections, should you as its leader share that information with other HCOs, or parlay your improved outcomes for competitive advantage to increase market share?

   b. Your HCO's primary service area has a new and growing population of non-English speaking individuals with little ability to pay for healthcare services. What responsibility do you have as a leader to serve the health needs of this population?

Case Study: Mobile Dental Services

St. Mary's Medical Center is a tertiary-care hospital located in Evansville, Indiana. For several years, the hospital has coordinated a novel outreach program—Mobile Dental Care for Kids—which provides full-service dental care for children who would otherwise have little or no access to dentists (see **Figure 15.2**). This program reports over 3000 patient contacts in 2010, primarily from elementary age children at the rotating school sites.

St. Mary's is an acute care medical center that does not provide any other dental services. Why have they chosen to coordinate an outreach program in a field in which they have little expertise? The steps below provide a pathway toward the implementation of this successful initiative.

Identification of the problem:

· An existing partnership with area schools and school nurses identified a problem that could not be readily solved given limited school-district resources. Low-income elementary school children would come to school with acute tooth pain, unable to be cured by the school nurse. The lack of dental care often allowed these acute problems to become chronic, and students in constant pain were unable to study and learn effectively.

Courtesy of St. Mary's Medical Center.

Figure 15.2 St. Mary's Mobile Dental Care for Kids

- Many of the affected children were eligible for Indiana Medicaid dental services. Research showed that few dentists in the area accepted Medicaid patients because
  - Medicaid reimbursement rates were significantly lower than private insurance reimbursement rates.
  - Transportation and accessibility challenges for Medicaid patients resulted in a high incidence of patient late arrivals and no-shows, costing dental practices vital revenue.

Resources available in the community:

- St. Mary's, the local acute care medical center, offered to help and worked with leaders in the schools to coordinate resources.
- School nurses and support staff worked with parents to:
  - Ensure eligible students were registered for Medicaid dental services.
  - Obtain the necessary consents for treatment.
  - Schedule students for exams during the school day to make the best use of the dental unit and staff.
- Area civic organizations and churches offered to help families with care logistics when school was not in session.
- A mobile dental service van was outfitted and launched to improve accessibility of dental care.
- Area dentists agreed to work shifts to provide care when the mobile unit's full-time dentist was unavailable.

The success of this program is due to the effective partnership among St. Mary's and the other partner organizations. Together, the collaborators identified a problem (health concern), researched the causative factors, and developed creative strategies to address these factors. Each partner contributed different resources to the initiative, allowing the development of a successful solution to address this challenge.

Case Study Discussion Questions

1. What information and personnel resources are available to St. Mary's Medical Center to aid in planning and development of this outreach program?
2. Ongoing partnerships were developed with key stakeholders in the community. How can the leadership at the Medical Center sustain these partnerships with the school personnel, area dentists, and the multiple civic organizations?
3. What other benefits does St. Mary's Medical Center gain from this outreach endeavor? Are there financial, marketing, or promotional benefits that can accrue to the Medical Center?

RELATED WEBSITES

AHA annual survey, American Hospital Association: www.ahadata.com/ahadata/html/AHASurvey.html

Caring for Communities (AHA program of community outreach): www.caringforcommunities.org/

Center for Disease Control and Prevention: www.cdc.gov/datastatistics/

Center for Medicare and Medicaid Services (CMS) Critical Access Hospitals Certification and Compliance Guidelines: www.cms.gov/Medicare/Provider-Enrollment-and-Certification/CertificationandComplianc/CAHs.html

Guidelines for Community Benefit: www.irs.gov/Charities-&-Non-Profits/Charitable-Organizations/Hospitals-and-Community-Benefit—Interim-Report

HealthBridge Health Information Exchange: www.healthbridge.org/

Health Resources and Service Administration (HRSA) Federally Qualified Health Center Guidelines: http://bphc.hrsa.gov/about/requirements/index.html

Illinois Critical Access Hospital Network: www.icahn.org/

Pendleton Community Care and the North Fork Clinic: www.pccnfc.org /PCChistory.html

PPACA Needs Assessment Guidelines: www.ruralcenter.org/tasc/resources /ppaca-tax-exempt-hospital-status-requirements-9007

Rural Health Clinic Guidelines: www.cms.gov/Center/provider-Type/Rural-Health -Clinics-Center.html

Rural Health Clinic Program: www.hrsa.gov/ruralhealth/

REFERENCES

Alexander, J. A., Comfort, M. E., Weiner, B. J., & Bogue, R. (2001). Leadership in collaborative community health partnerships. *Nonprofit Management & Leadership, 12*(2), 159–175.

Anderson, R. A., & McDaniel, R. R. (2000). Managing healthcare organizations: Where professionalism meets complexity science. *Healthcare Management Review, 25*(1), 83–92.

Drain, M., Godkin, L., & Valentine, S. (2001, Fall). Examining closure rates of rural hospitals: An assessment of a strategic taxonomy. *Health Care Management Review, 26*(4), 27–51.

Duchesne, J. C., Kyle, A., Simmons, J., Islam, S., Schmieg, R. E., Jr., & McSwain, N. E., Jr. (2008). Impact of telemedicine upon rural trauma care. *Journal of Trauma, 64*(1), 92–97.

Holmes, M., Pink, G. H., & Slifkin, R. T. (2006, November). *Impact of conversion to critical access hospital status on hospital financial performance and condition.* Retrieved November 9, 2012 from www.flexmonitoring.org/documents /PolicyBrief1.pdf.

Huttlinger, K., Schaller-Ayers, J., & Lawson, T. (2004). Healthcare in Appalachia: A population-based approach. *Public Health Nursing, 21*(2), 103–110.

McDaniel, R. R., & Driebe, D. J. (2001). Complexity science and healthcare management. *Advances in Healthcare Management, 2*, 11–36.

Merwin, E., Snyder, A., & Katz, E. (2006). Differential access to quality healthcare: Professional and policy challenges. *Family and Community Health, 29*(3), 186–194.

Patient Protection and Affordable Care Act (PPACA). (2010). Pub. L. No. 111-148, 124 Stat. 119. Retrieved November 9, 2012 from www.healthcare.gov /law/full/.

Roop, E. S. (2008, January). A litmus test for critical access. *Hospital Health Network, 82*(1), 42–44.

Chapter 16

Emerging Trends in Health Care: Implications for Leadership

Andrew N. Garman and Christy Harris Lemak

LEARNING OBJECTIVES

By the end of the chapter, the student will be able to:

- Identify macrotrends affecting the U.S. health sector that have significant implications for leadership.
- Understand the implications of the Institute of Medicine's recommendations concerning continuing education, electronic health record adoption, and the concept of the learning healthcare system.
- Describe key trends in healthcare leadership development practice.

KEY TERMS

Knowledge management

Leadership development

Population health

Trends

INTRODUCTION

As we write this chapter, the health services sector in the United States is in a period of turbulent change, preparing for an unclear future. The Affordable Care Act legislation, often referred to as "Healthcare Reform" or "Obamacare," is being enacted; however, there are efforts among some legislators and lobbyists to put the brakes on many of the

Act's mandates. Meanwhile, high unemployment rates and rising health insurance premiums are leaving many healthcare consumers uninsured or underinsured, even as healthcare organizations are being negatively impacted by federal, state, and local deficits, which are limiting financial resources available for support of health services delivery.

We can get a clearer sense of future directions—and their implications for healthcare leaders and administrators—by taking a longer-term view of the industry's fundamental **trends**. Part of the work of the nonprofit National Center for Healthcare Leadership (NCHL) focuses on understanding these trends and assessing their impact to better inform current and future leaders. In this chapter, we will discuss these trends and their potential impact on the healthcare industry and its leadership. In addition, we will provide a glimpse of how organizational approaches to leadership training and development are evolving as a result of scientific advances in industrial psychology and education.

FUNDAMENTAL TRENDS IN HEALTH CARE

Change in the healthcare sector is highly complex and hyperdimensional. Our goal in this section is not to comprehensively document the changes that are likely to take place over the coming years—such a task would easily fill volumes. Instead, we identify six trends we believe will have the greatest impact on the learning needs of future healthcare leaders.

Trend 1: Growing Emphasis on Cost Constraints, Transparency, and Value-Based Reimbursement

Despite many uncertainties about how health reform will unfold, it is widely accepted that reimbursements for care will flatten, if not decline. There will be considerable pressure to move health services to settings where they can be provided most cost-efficiently. Additional savings in the system will be pursued through the implementation of financial incentives for improving the quality of care. Value-based purchasing approaches are placing increased attention on clinical and other systems that can influence quality outcomes. For hospitals, these outcomes include 30-day readmission rates, healthcare-associated infections, and other markers of safe and high-quality care. Healthcare systems will continue to publicly report their performance on a variety of metrics, including clinical quality, patient experience, and access to care. Leaders will spend more time understanding the perspectives of patients and their families and designing systems that simultaneously improve quality, lower costs, and enhance patient satisfaction.

Trend 2: Moving Toward Population-Based Health

There is growing recognition that high healthcare costs in the United States have not been associated with better health outcomes. Although inefficiencies in the system are partly to blame, there is also an underinvestment in the prevention of illness and the management of chronic diseases. There is some truth to the old saying that "an ounce of prevention is worth a pound of cure." In the future, we are likely to see greater attention to systematic investment in preventing and more effectively managing chronic conditions such as diabetes. The work of improving **population health** will require leaders of health systems, clinics, social service agencies, public health leaders, and policymakers to work together in new ways.

Trend 3: Increasing Importance of Knowledge Management

The availability and depth of electronic health information is likely to expand at a dramatic pace, creating unprecedented opportunities for evidence-based practice as well as challenges in effectively managing information storage, retrieval, and use. The Institute of Medicine has called for health systems to transform themselves into "learning healthcare systems," capable of routinely working with data from electronic health information systems to continuously improve care (Olsen, Aisner, & McGinnis, 2007).

Beyond the simple mechanics of information management comes the challenge of **knowledge management**—processes for turning information and experience into accessible "inputs" to support more effective decision-making. Knowledge management requires mastery of dissemination techniques such as *positive deviance*—identifying and facilitating the spread of locally created solutions to common challenges (Pascale, Sternin, & Sternin, 2010) and building a culture that values and supports professionals in actively sharing lessons learned. Knowledge management is also an essential component of the Malcolm Baldrige National Quality Award, a widely respected national award designed to recognize excellence in total quality management (Banaszak-Holl et al., 2011).

Trend 4: Changing Demographics and Needs of Patients

The U.S. population is expected to grow by a total of 63 million people (20%) between 2010 and 2030 (U.S. Census Bureau, 2008). Almost half of this growth will be among people between the ages of 65 and 84, which will increase the number of people in this age range by 84%. The number of the "oldest old" (age 85 and older), a group associated with multiple complex health and social support needs, is projected to more than double.

In addition to the aging population, growth in the numbers and severity of chronic conditions is also expected, due in part to lifestyle choices. Conditions such as diabetes, heart disease, stroke, high blood pressure, and some cancers will increase, driven by unhealthy diet and poor nutrition, sedentary lifestyles, and smoking. Between 2003 and 2023, the proportion of Americans with diabetes is projected to increase by 53%, heart disease by 41%, hypertension by 39%, and stroke by 29% (Bodenheimer, Chen, & Bennett, 2009). These trends will put new strains on healthcare leaders to improve the ability to manage patients with complex needs and provide care coordination and care management services to support patient needs across the continuum.

In addition to these growing needs, both the approaches to treatment as well as patients' level of participation in decision-making processes are also evolving. Advances in genetics are leading rapidly to new approaches to treating cancer and other diseases, giving some patients new hope but also increasing cost pressures on the system (Kolata, 2012). As the emphasis on population health continues to grow, clinicians and systems leaders are also increasingly recognizing the need to more actively engage patients in taking greater responsibility for their own health, as well as the redesign of the care systems they utilize (HFMA, 2011).

Trend 5: Changing Demands of the Healthcare Workforce

The increased demand described previously is also predicted to exacerbate shortages in the clinical workforce, particularly in rural and underserved areas. These domestic shortfalls could be further exacerbated by the modernization of health systems in other countries. International medical graduates, physicians who received their training outside the United States and Canada, account for 25% of the U.S. physician workforce (American Medical Association, 2010). Although U.S. nurses and general practitioners earn the highest incomes in the world (Fujisawa & Lafortune, 2007; Peterson & Burton, 2007), other countries are catching up, particularly in the home countries of many of these immigrants (Garman, Johnson, & Royer, 2011), suggesting that, in the future, immigration trends may slow or even reverse. Fortunately, the U.S. market-driven system has shown itself to be remarkably adaptable to shortages (Auerbach, Buerhaus, & Staiger, 2011). With growing pressures on both the supply and demand sides, however, the limits of this adaptability may be tested in the years to come. Healthcare leaders will need to pay close attention to population-based estimates for various clinical services and the resulting requirements for clinical resources.

Trend 6: Increasing Globalization and Global Innovation

A recent analysis of global trends in health service delivery concluded that most of the macrotrends affecting health services in the United States are also affecting other countries. To fully benefit from the innovative solutions other countries find in addressing these challenges, healthcare leaders will need to monitor what is going on outside of the United States (Garman, Johnson, & Royer, 2011). Historically, differences in regulations across borders significantly slowed the diffusion of innovations globally, but recent years have brought increased efforts to align regulatory requirements. For example, the International Conference on Harmonisation of Technical Requirements for Registration of Pharmaceuticals for Human Use is a collaboration between the United States, Japan, and Europe to reduce duplicative testing that is currently required for research and development and to bring new products to market in multiple countries (Cortez, 2009). These trends will require leaders to have an awareness of global perspectives and the skills to operate and collaborate across borders.

LEADERSHIP COMPETENCY IMPLICATIONS

The trends outlined in the previous section are likely to have profound implications for the competencies expected of future healthcare leaders. Future leadership roles will require specific competencies in order to help manage and even capitalize on these trends.

The trend toward transparency and value-based purchasing suggests that leaders will need to be particularly strong in *accountability* (setting clear expectations and holding people to them). At the senior level, leaders will need to establish management systems that help ensure a culture of accountability throughout the organization. Pressures for higher value (quality outcomes per resources expended) suggest that health systems are going to need leaders who are particularly skilled in process and performance improvement and in the application of *Industrial and Systems Engineering*—the continuous improvement of system reliability and efficiency (Grossman, Goolsby, Olsen, & McGinnis, 2011; Valdez, Ramly, & Brennan, 2010). These system-redesign efforts are also likely to see an increased focus on engaging patients in the redesign process, which will require leaders to learn effective approaches to collecting patient input through design-development approaches as well as advisory councils. Future leaders will also have greater opportunities as well as responsibility to leverage *information technology management* to pursue efficient, evidence-informed approaches to process improvement. The complementary competency *change leadership* (helping others see change as imperative and building the will within them to take the steps needed to redesign their work) will also be important in this hyperdimensional, complex healthcare industry. Important components of this competency include the ability to proactively identify high-priority areas for change and to communicate a clear and compelling vision for the desired future-state that the initiative will allow the organization to reach. It also involves ensuring that communications about the change process reach intended employees and that they are provided the opportunity to support the process as participants.

The trends toward population-based health care suggest that health system leaders will need to develop new competencies in *community orientation*—proactively engaging their communities' public health needs. Leaders will need to be able to effectively develop and facilitate diverse stakeholder coalitions, which may include community centers, social services providers, religious organizations, businesses, and government organizations such as park districts and school systems. There will also be a greater need for competency in managing *collaborative competition*—developing and managing relationships with organizations to create efficiencies, while still competing with them for market share. Trends toward increased globalization and more diffuse innovation suggest future leaders will need to have particularly well-honed skills in *information seeking*. High-performing leaders will be those who become adept at systematically scanning for promising emerging innovations that may benefit their organizations. Equally important will be the capacity to rapidly and critically assess these innovations, to maximize the attention spent on those with the greatest real potential, and minimize the time spent on those that may ultimately not pan out.

Taken together, these trends also suggest that healthcare providers in the future will need leaders who have a strong *strategic orientation*, who are able to identify the 5- to 10-year trends that are likely to affect health services delivery and assess their implications through approaches such as futures task forces and scenario planning (Garman, Johnson, & Royer, 2011; Marcus, 2009). To turn these efforts into meaningful action, leaders will also need competency in both *self-development* and *talent management*— a capacity and orientation toward continuous improvement of the skills of oneself and others. Given the magnitude of evolution we are forecasting for the future of health care, we will need to learn new ways to approach their work, and methodical but efficient retraining will be essential to success. With this in mind, we now turn to a consideration of how future leaders are likely to be developed.

EMERGING TRENDS IN LEADERSHIP DEVELOPMENT

As the scientific underpinnings of effective **leadership development** continue to evolve (Garman & Lemak, 2011), organizations' approaches to developing leaders are likely to change in some of the following ways.

Leadership development is increasingly tied to corporate strategy. Key organizational outcomes, such as care quality and patient experience, are significantly associated with the extent to which health systems successfully tie their staff development agendas to their corporate goals (Garman & Lemak, 2011; Garman, McAlearney, Harrison, Song, & McHugh, 2011), and leadership development is no exception. Successful alignment requires that training and human resource operational leaders be involved at a strategic level within the organization; however, this is still frequently not the case in health care. In many healthcare organizations, the training function is viewed primarily, if not entirely, as a compliance function. In such structures, leadership development may focus mainly on basic supervisory training, with a goal of ensuring that leaders are aware of employment laws and regulations. Organizations with a more strategically aligned training operation, in contrast, will have a systematic approach to turning corporate strategy into learning and performance management practices, such as those depicted in **Figure 16.1**.

Greater emphasis on team and systems-based development rather than individual leader development. Throughout most of modern health care's existence, formal leadership development activities have focused on the individual leader. A leader might join a professional association, go offsite to attend conferences, and bring lessons learned back to his or her team. In recent years, there has been growing recognition that an individual-focused

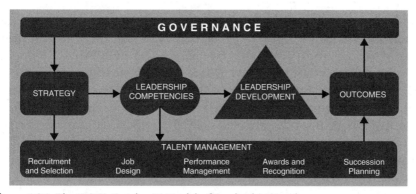

Figure 16.1 The NCHL Catalyst™ Model of Leadership Development

Source: Reprinted with permission from the National Center for Health Leadership (www.nchl.org), Chicago, IL.

approach has limited impact, particularly when leadership goals involve the need for intense collaborative leadership efforts. Sending teams through shared developmental experiences, which is becoming more prevalent among clinical staff, is still less common among healthcare leaders. This approach has started to draw more attention in recent years, a trend that is likely to continue, given the substantial team efforts required by the trends described previously in this chapter.

Increasing emphasis on enhancing on-the-job learning. Healthcare organizations are starting to shift away from an emphasis on classroom training and toward more "learning by doing." Many organizations with formal leadership training programs now require participants to complete an applied project, which can account for half or more of the total hours spent in the program. Identification of "stretch assignments" is also becoming a more routine part of talent-management programs. Such assignments are matched to leaders based on specific competencies they need to develop. Coaching, mentoring, and peer-learning approaches are also being used to ensure participants gain the maximum learning benefit from their experiences.

Developments in simulation-enhanced education. For many types of health services, particularly those for which errors pose significant risk of life or health, a student clinician's first experiences are with simulated rather than actual patients. Simulated patients allow a clinician to practice in an environment free from the potential for patient harm until the procedure can be performed with a high degree of reliability. There are many leadership-development activities as well, in which direct experience may be less desirable, either because it is too expensive, too risky, or too scarce. With advances in technology, simulations are becoming increasingly viable alternatives to direct experience. The widespread availability of Internet and mobile technologies have helped drive down the cost of computer-based simulations. Evidence supporting their effectiveness has been accumulating rapidly, to the point at which they now compare favorably to other types of training, particularly when added to a traditional course (Sitzmann, 2011).

In addition to helping student leaders gain experience in risky or rare contexts, simulations may also help leaders prepare for environments that do not yet exist. In other industries, simulations have been used to test possible future strategic directions as well as the implications of impending changes in a given market. They can also be used to examine alternatives to currently entrenched operating models, such as those toward which the Affordable Care Act seeks to help the health system transition.

SUMMARY

Regardless of the specifics of what the future holds for health care in the United States, it is safe to assume that all healthcare leaders will be called upon to help the system work more reliably and efficiently to deliver higher-value care and better health for our diverse population. It is also safe to assume that leadership expectations will be different 5 to 10 years from now. Change is imperative, and as a future healthcare leader, you will need to actively continue to develop your skills, through participation in continuing education as well as developing the discipline of continuous skill development. Doing so will help ensure that you stay current and relevant, and that you are helping to build a modern health system that provides the very best care possible for the people we all serve.

Discussion Questions

1. Now that U.S. healthcare reform has been rolled out, what other changes are needed in the system that are not addressed already?
2. What other trends besides those addressed in this chapter have surfaced that will affect health care?
3. Are there global implications from changes occurring in the U.S. healthcare system?
4. Speculate how healthcare leadership expectations might be different 5 to 10 years from now.

RELATED WEBSITES

Global Infobase, World Health Organization: https://apps.who.int/infobase/
Institute for Healthcare Improvement: www.ihi.org
Institute of Medicine: www.iom.edu
Kaiser Health Reform Source: http://healthreform.kff.org/
Malcolm Baldrige Performance Excellence Program: www.nist.gov/baldrige/
National Center for Healthcare Leadership: www.nchl.org
TED MED: www.tedmed.com/home
U.S. Census, population projections: www.census.gov/population/projections/

REFERENCES

American Medical Association. (2010). *International graduates in American medicine: Contemporary challenges and opportunities.* Retrieved November 9, 2012 from www .ama-assn.org/ama1/pub/upload/mm/18/img-workforce-paper.pdf.

Auerbach, D. I., Buerhaus, P. I., & Staiger, D. O. (2011). Registered nurse supply grows faster than projected amid surge in new entrants ages 23–26. *Health Affairs, 30*(12), 2286–2292.

Banaszak-Holl, J., Lemak, C. H., Griffith, J. R., Fear, K., Lammers, E., & Zheng, K. (2011). *Use of knowledge to support evidence-based management in high-performing health care organizations.* Presentation at the 2011 Academy of Management annual meeting, San Antonio, TX.

Bodenheimer, T., Chen, E., & Bennett, H. D. (2009). Confronting the growing burden of chronic disease: Can the U.S. health care workforce do the job? *Health Affairs, 28*(1), 64–74.

Cortez, N. (2009). International health care convergence: The benefits and burdens of market-driven standardization. *Wisconsin International Law Journal, 26*(3), 646–704.

Fujisawa, R., & Lafortune, G. (2007). *The remuneration of general practitioners and specialists in 14 OECD countries: What are the factors influencing variations across countries?* Organisation for Economic Co-operation and Development, Working paper No. 41. Retrieved November 9, 2012 from www.oecd.org/dataoecd /51/48/41925333.pdf.

Garman, A. N., Johnson, T. J., & Royer, T. C. (2011). *The future of healthcare: Global trends worth watching.* Chicago, IL: Health Administration Press.

Garman, A. N., & Lemak, C. H. (2011). *Developing healthcare leaders: What we have learned, and what is next.* National Center for Healthcare Leadership White Paper. Retrieved November 9, 2012 from www.nchl.org/Documents/NavLink/NCHL _Developing_Healthcare_Leaders__Nov_2011_uid11212011137292.pdf.

Garman, A. N., McAlearney, A. S., Harrison, M. I., Song, P. H., & McHugh, M. (2011). High-performance work systems in healthcare, part 1: Development of an evidence-informed model. *Health Care Management Review, 36*(3), 201–213.

Grossman, C., Goolsby, W. A., Olsen, L., & McGinnis, J. M. (2011). *Engineering a learning healthcare system: A look at the future.* Washington, DC: National Academies Press.

Healthcare Financial Management Association (HFMA). (2011). *Building value-driving capabilities: People and culture.* Westchester, IL: Author.

Kolata, G. (2012, July 8). In treatment for leukemia, glimpses of the future. *New York Times,* p. A1.

Marcus, A. (2009). *Strategic foresight: A new look at scenarios.* New York, NY: Palgrave-Macmillan.

Olsen, L., Aisner, D., & McGinnis, J. M. (Eds.). (2007). *The learning healthcare system: Workshop summary.* Washington, DC: National Academies Press.

Pascale, R., Sternin, J., & Sternin, M. (2010). *The power of positive deviance: How unlikely innovators solve the world's toughest problems.* Cambridge, MA: Harvard Business Review Press.

Peterson, C. L., & Burton, R. (2007, September 17). *U.S. health care spending: Comparison with other OECD countries.* Washington, DC: U.S. Congressional Research Service. Retrieved November 9, 2012 from http://assets.opencrs.com /rpts/RL34175_20070917.pdf.

Sitzmann, T. (2011). A meta-analytic examination of the instructional effectiveness of computer-based simulation games. *Personnel Psychology, 64,* 489–528.

U.S. Census Bureau. (2008). *Projections of the population by selected age groups and sex for the United States: 2010 to 2050* (NP2008-T2). Retrieved November 9, 2012 from www.census.gov/population/projections/data/national/2008/summarytables .html.

Valdez, R. S., Ramly E., & Brennan, P. F. (2010, May). *Industrial and systems engineering and health care: Critical areas of research—Final report.* AHRQ Publication No. 10-0079. Rockville, MD: Agency for Healthcare Research and Quality.

Glossary

360 evaluation: An assessment of skills and competencies that is taken by an employee and all or a subset of stakeholders he or she interacts with, such as direct reports, peers, supervisors, clients, vendors, patients, and the like, in order to obtain multiple perspectives on abilities and demonstrated behaviors. Paired with coaching for debrief and the formation of employee development plans and follow-through.

Accountability: Assumption and acknowledgement of responsibility for decisions and actions through setting clear expectations and holding people to them.

Accountable Care Organization (ACO): An organization that can provide primary care, specialty care, and inpatient care for a population of patients. An ACO and its physicians are collectively willing and able to take responsibility for the overall costs and quality of care for a population.

Agenda: A list of things to be done, especially the program or plan for a meeting.

Aims for Improvement: In their landmark publication, *Crossing the Quality Chasm*, the Institute of Medicine called for a shared vision of six aims for improvement: safe, effective, patient-centered, timely, efficient, and equitable.

Balanced scorecard: A strategic performance management tool, first described by Kaplan and Norton, which presents a mixture of financial and nonfinancial performance measures reflecting an organization's strategic priorities.

Baldrige National Quality Award: National recognition awarded to U.S. organizations for performance excellence through the Baldrige

Program, which was established by Congress in 1987 to recognize U.S. companies for their achievements in quality and business performance.

Bell Commission: New York State appointed panel of experts led by Bertrand Bell, MD, convened to examine the circumstances surrounding the death of Libby Zion. The recommendations of the Bell Commission led to the Accreditation Council on Graduate Medical Education (ACGME) reforms of medical resident work hours. All postgraduate residency training programs are required to adhere to the new requirements or risk major consequences, up to and including loss of accreditation status.

Bench strength: A term used to refer to the growth of new leaders who can provide backup and eventually replace the current leaders in charge.

Benchmarking: The process of comparing one's performance metrics or business processes to industry bests or related industry's best practices.

Board certification: Documentation of proficiency in a specific specialty or specialties within the practice of medicine. Prior to sitting for a board certification examination, physicians must complete a residency training program in a specialty or subspecialty. In surgery, physicians must provide documentation of successful completion of an adequate number of cases for a specific board certification. The American Board of Medical Specialties' (ABMS) Maintenance of Certification (ABMS MOC) requires physicians to demonstrate continuing education, ongoing continuous quality improvement, monitoring of patient outcomes, and retaking of board certification examinations at given intervals, usually every 10 years.

C-suite: The designation of an area where the higher executives have their offices. For a hospital this could include examples such as CEO (Chief Executive Officer), COO (Chief Operation Officer), CNO (Chief Nursing Officer), CIO (Chief Information Officer), CMO (Chief Medical Officer), and CFO (Chief Financial Officer).

Care delivery model: Method by which an organization delivers care to patients and families.

Character: A combination of qualities or features that distinguishes one person, group, or thing from another emphasizing one's values and ethics.

Chief Medical Officer (CMO): A physician who serves at the executive level in a healthcare organization, and whose duties may include negotiating contracts and supervising patient safety, quality assessment, and risk management programs. CMOs often have additional degrees in law (JD) or business administration (MBA).

Chief of Medical Staff: An elected position within the physicians who serve on the staff of a hospital. The Chief of Medical Staff acts as the advocate for physicians and liaison to administration for physician concerns.

Codes of conduct: Sets of rules describing proper practices or responsibilities of individuals or organizations.

Collaboration: A process in which two or more people or organizations work together to achieve a common goal.

Collaborative alliances: Creating interdependence among organizations for complex problem solving.

Collaborative leadership: Leadership skills and attributes needed to successfully develop and manage interorganizational strategic alliances and other forms of partnership.

Community benefit: The provision of charity care that distinguishes not-for-profit hospitals and health systems from for-profit healthcare organizations.

Community collaborators: Leaders who can influence diverse groups of stakeholders to work together.

Community needs assessment: A method of gathering information about a community's opinions, needs, and challenges that is used to determine which projects or services can be used to meet the needs of the community.

Community outreach: The process of providing time or resources to benefit a community in an effort to improve the quality of life for community residents.

Competency: The ability of a person to do a job properly.

Conflict of interest (COI): When an individual can be influenced by money or other considerations to act in a way that is contrary to the good of the organization for whom he or she works or for the patient whose best interests he or she should be advocating.

Consensus: Collective opinion or agreement.

Continuing medical education (CME): Lifelong learning undertaken by physicians in a variety of delivery modes to stay current with their specialties, sustain clinical proficiency, adhere to professional organization requirements, and maintain their state licensure.

Core values: Internal principles that make up the underlying foundation of a person or agency and guide relationships with others.

Creative thinking: Creating something new or original.

Critical access hospitals: Small, generally geographically remote facilities that provide outpatient and inpatient hospital services to people in rural areas.

Cultural competence: The ability and willingness to respond respectfully and effectively to people of all ethnic, cultural, and religious backgrounds.

Cultural diversity: The quality of diverse or different cultures as opposed to a single culture.

Cultural synergy: Describes an attempt to bring two or more cultures together to form an organization or environment that is based on combined strengths, concepts, and skills.

Culture: Shared beliefs, values, customs, practices, and social behavior of a particular group or population.

Diversity management: A strategy for fostering or embracing a positive workplace environment.

Emotional intelligence: Ability to identify, assess, and manage the emotions of oneself, of others, and of groups.

Empowerment: Sharing information, rewards, and power with others so that they take initiative.

Ethics: The study of standards of conduct (behavior) and moral judgments.

Executive coaching: A confidential set of consultations between a qualified coach and an executive, which focuses on improving the executive's leadership skills.

External environment: Entities that exist outside an organization's boundary but have significant influence on its survival and growth.

Federally qualified health center (FQHC): An entity that has entered into an agreement with CMS and is receiving a grant under §330 of the Public Health Service (PHS) Act, or is an outpatient health program or facility operated by a tribe or tribal organization under the Indian Self-Determination Act or by an Urban Indian organization receiving funds under Title V of the Indian Health Care Improvement Act.

Fiduciary duty: Ensuring the deployment of organizational resources in a manner that protects and advances the interests of stakeholders and/or shareholders.

Financial management: The planning, organizing, directing, and controlling of the financial activities of a business enterprise.

Governance: The state or act of governing; includes the implementation of formal authority and control over an organization.

Governing body: A group of individuals who make up a body for the purposes of administering or governing.

Group think: The phenomenon when people in a group tend to agree with each other.

Health disparities: Health differences in individuals' or the public's (population) health that can be ascribed to social, economic, or environmental factors.

Healthcare Executive Competencies Assessment Tool: A self-assessment instrument developed by the American College of Healthcare Executives to assist managers in identifying areas of strength as well as areas in which they may wish to improve their performance.

Healthcare Leadership Alliance (HLA): A consortium of six major professional membership organizations, which promotes identified competencies that support excellence in healthcare management across diverse professional roles.

Healthcare reform: A reference to major health policy creation or change— that is, recent government policy that affects changes in the organization, reimbursement, scope, and delivery of health care.

Healthcare teams: Small groups brought together for a discernible purpose.

Healthcare value: Cost effective, high-quality health services.

High potentials: Employees identified as strong candidates to groom for promotion to upper management levels. Often they are offered development opportunities and are identified in succession plans.

Human resources metrics: A set of measurements used to determine effectiveness and value of human resource strategies.

Key drivers: Factors that influence and direct the outcome of a process, mission, program, or strategic plan.

Knowledge management: Processes for turning information and experience into accessible inputs to support more effective decision making.

Leadership: The process whereby an individual influences a group of people to accomplish a common goal.

Leadership competencies: The skills and abilities necessary to influence people to achieve a mutually satisfying goal. Some examples are problem solving, communicating effectively, and developing a vision.

Leadership development: The required growth of a leader to adapt to and anticipate changing needs of the industry.

Leadership leverage points: Changes, which can be made by a healthcare leader, that have a big impact considering the time and effort invested.

Leadership models: Various approaches to determining how leaders act or behave.

Leadership pipeline: How leaders are selected and groomed for upper management positions.

Lean: A methodology to increase value and efficiency through a reduction of waste; based on the Toyota Production System.

Learning organization: An organization that is skilled at acquiring, creating, and transferring knowledge and modifying its behavior to reflect new insight.

Limited English proficiency: An individual who comes from an environment where a language other than English is dominant.

Management model: A model that focuses on managing and directing the organization's resources economically and efficiently to achieve the organization's objectives.

Mental models: Images, stories, and assumptions about aspects of the world, which determine what we see, how we see it, and how we act.

Minorities: A smaller party or group as opposed to a majority.

Mission, vision, and values: Statements of organizational purpose, future, and philosphy that provide direction to the organization.

Multidisciplinary team: In healthcare, generally refers to groups consisting of various professional disciplines.

National Practitioner Data Bank (NPDB): A central repository of information on physicians, dentists and other healthcare providers whereby state licensing boards, hospitals, professional societies, and other healthcare entities can identify, discipline, and report those who engage in unprofessional behavior.

Nursing Magnet Recognition Program: A program established by the American Nurses Credentialing Center to recognize healthcare organizations for quality patient care, nursing excellence, and innovations in professional nursing practice.

Obligation: A course of action that one is required to take, whether legal or moral.

Organizational culture: Shared values and norms that guide how people in an organization interrelate within and beyond.

Partnerships: An arrangement whereby two parties agree to cooperate with one another to advance their mutual interests.

Patient and family partnerships: True and equal collaboration between patients, families, providers, and administrators in the planning, implementation, and delivery of care at the individual and organizational levels.

Patient Protection and Affordable Care Act (ACA): Enacted in 2010, it is a series of reforms to the U.S healthcare delivery system that roll out over a period of time. The Act goes fully into effect in 2014 with the main goal of increasing the availabilty of health insurance for citizens and providing better coordinated care.

Patient- and family-centered care (PFCC): An approach to the planning, delivery, and assessment of healthcare grounded in mutually beneficial partnerships among healthcare providers, patients, and families. Four concepts comprise PFCC: (1) dignity and respect, (2) information sharing, (3) participation, and (4) collaboration.

Patient- and family-centered leadership: Individuals in formal or informal positions who are able to implement positive change and who are patient- and family-centered. They listen to and value the individual and collective voice of patients and families, empower patients and their families to take charge of their own health and welfare, and recognize that patient and family partnerships inform and shape the healthcare organization's operational policies, staff interactions, facilities, services, and programs.

Performance evaluation: The process of a formal, systematic assessment of how well employees are performing in their jobs in relation to established standards.

Performance Reporting: Documentation that communicates results obtained. Often used to compare prior results, goal obtainment, and/or to identify trends.

Physician credentialing: The process of verifying information that a physician supplies on an application for staff privileges at a hospital, HMO, or other healthcare organization. Most healthcare organizations have protocols that they have established. It is ususally required to obtain primary (i.e., first hand and original) verification and documentation, such as transcripts with raised seals, by contacting each place of education, training, and employment individually by phone.

Physician privileging: When physicians apply for privileges at a hospital, HMO, or other healthcare organization, they must specify the scope of their practice, not only by specialty, but also by procedure. Using extensive documentation, the physician must demonstrate competency for those privileges.

PIE^2: Personal (internal and external) and professional (internal and external) professionalism.

Population health: The health status of a group of individuals, inclusive of health outcomes and disease burden. Its scope exceeds traditional, individual-level medicine by focusing on factors that affect whole populations such as the environment, social structure, and economic wellbeing.

Process improvement: A systematic approach to improving a process or system performance through streamlining and cycle time reduction, and the identification and elimination of the causes of substandard quality, process variation, and nonvalue-adding activities.

Professional practice model: A practice system comprising specific structures, processes, and values that supported registered nurse control over the delivery of nursing care and the environment in which the nursing care was delivered.

Professionalism: Professional quality, character, or conduct; a professional system or method. The conduct or qualities that characterize or mark a profession.

Psychological contract: A person's beliefs, formed by the organization, regarding the terms and conditions of a reciprocal agreement between that person and his or her organization.

Recruitment: The process of attracting, interviewing, and hiring new employees.

Retention: A set of activities designed to reduce turnover and retain the talent necessary for effective organization performance.

Rounding: Talking face to face with employees for the purpose of gathering information in a structured, consistent format.

Selection: The process of selecting an individual or group of individuals who are a good fit for the organization.

Servant leadership: A leadership model in which the leader supports and facilitates the work, mission, and goals of the employees and the organization.

Shadowing: A formal technique that invites a high-potential employee to follow (or shadow) a leader for a designated period of time, observing and learning about the leader's daily duties.

Situation analysis: Analyzing the current situation by evaluating the strengths and weaknesses internal to the organization and the opportunities and threats in the external environment.

Six Sigma: A data-driven, statistical methodology that focuses on improving quality by identifying and eliminating defects in a process.

Strategic management: The process of assigning responsibility to implement and monitor the activities that must be accomplished to reach the organization's goals.

Strategic planning: A method used to define the tasks and operationalize activities that must be accomplished to reach an identified or agreed-upon goal.

Strategic thinking: A mental process of synthesizing and analyzing information to envision the strategies and tactics needed to achieve an ultimate goal.

Strategy formulation: The process of determining appropriate courses of action for achieving organizational goals and objectives.

Strategy implementation: The effective execution of strategic goals and objectives.

Stretch assignment: A form of on-the-job learning that requires employees to extend beyond their comfort zone and develop new skills or strengthen existing competencies.

Succession planning: The process taken to ensure that qualified employees are in place and ready to fill key roles in an organization as needed for smooth transitions in leadership.

Talent management: An internal structure and process for developing and nurturing leaders within an organization.

Team charter: A document that outlines the purpose and function of a team.

Virtual team: A group of individuals who work across time, space, and organizational boundaries with links strengthened by webs of communication technology.

Theory X: Theory on motivation introduced by Douglas McGregor in the 1960s to describe the idea that people are generally lazy, do not really enjoy work, and only work for the paycheck.

Theory Y: Theory on motivation introduced by Douglas McGregor in the 1960s to describe the idea that employees are ambitious, self-motivated, and self-controlled, and work because they want to.

Top box achievement: Achieving the highest performance level.

Total rewards model: A set of strategies to attract, motivate, and retain employees.

Training and development: A set of activities designed to assist employees in maintaining and enhancing their knowledge, skills, and abilities.

Transactional leader: A person whose leadership style promotes his or her own interests and assumes that all employees are motivated by the same things (i.e., pay raises).

Transformational leaders: Individuals who possess and communicate a compelling vision that inspires followers to change expectations, perceptions, and motivations to work toward common goals.

Transparency: The act of being open, honest, and providing full disclosure.

Trends: The movement of the industry over time toward an idea, practice, or goal.

Trustee: A legal term describing a person who holds property, authority, or position of trust or responsibility for the benefit of another.

Turning Point Leadership Development National Excellence Collaborative: A partnership of local, state, and national public health organizations working to increase collaborative leadership capacity at all levels of public health practice.

Value-based purchasing: A payment methodology that bases inpatient hospital reimbursement on the provider's performance results in clinical quality, patient experience, and the cost of care provided.

Will-Ideas-Execution: The core elements of a framework to achieve better performance as suggested by the Institute for Healthcare Improvement. Successful leaders must develop the organizational will to achieve results, generate or identify effective ideas or strategies for improvement, and then execute those ideas.

Workforce planning: A process used to align the needs of the organization with the availability of human resources.

Index

Note: Italicized page locators indicate figures/photos; tables are noted with t.

Agendas
  meeting, 151
  team, 142
Aging population, growth in, 337–338
AHA. *See* American Hospital Association
AHCA. *See* American Health Care Association
AHIMA. *See* American Health Information
  Management Association
AHME. *See* Association for Hospital Medical
  Education
AHRQ. *See* Agency for Healthcare Research
  and Quality
Aims for Improvement (IOM), 166
Alderfer's ERG theory, 16
Alexander, Jeffrey, 320
American Association of Medical Colleges,
  website for, 286
American Board of Medical Colleges, 275
American Board of Medical Specialists, 235,
  274
American Board of Medical Specialties
  Maintenance of Certification initiative,
    purpose of, 274
American College for Physician Executives, 283
American College of Health Care
  Administrators, website for, 20
American College of Healthcare Executives, 7,
  37–38, 199
  code of ethics and conduct, 86
  demographic profile of Members and
    Fellows, 32–33
  ethical behavior codes and statements of, 17
  website for, 20, 206, 225
*American College of Healthcare Executives' Code of
  Ethics*, 19
American College of Health Executives, training programs provided by, 42*t*
American College of Physician Executives, 7,
  278
  training programs provided by, 42*t*
  website for, 20, 286
American College of Physicians, 235
American Health Care Association
  code of ethics, 86–87
  website for, 93
American Health Information Management
  Association
  code of ethics, 86
  training programs provided by, 42*t*
  website for, 93
American Hospital Association, 233, 275
  annual survey, website for, 333
  assessment tools, 236
  Center for Healthcare Governance, 298

American Medical Association
  founding of, 218*t*
  Masterfile database, 275
American Nurses Association, 172, 235
American Nurses Credentialing Center, 183, 189
American Organization of Nurse Executives,
  7, 20
American Osteopathic Association, 171
  Healthcare Facilities Accreditation
    Program website, 173*t*
American Recovery and Reinvestment Act of
  2009, 225
American Society for Healthcare Human
  Resources Administration, 42*t*, 106
Americans with Disabilities Act of 1990, 98*t*
America's Health Insurance Plans, training
  programs provided by, 42*t*
ANA. *See* American Nurses Association
Appointed board members, 299
Appraisals, 103
Arango, Polly, 235
ASHHRA. *See* American Society for Healthcare
  Human Resources Administration
Assessment, of organizational cultural compe-
  tence, 69–70
Assessment Plus, website for, 53
Association for Hospital Medical Education,
  275
Association for the Care of Children's Health,
  232
Association of American Medical Colleges,
  270, 275
Association of University Programs in Health
  Administration, 40, 53
Assumptions, questioning, 123
Audit committee, 262
AUPHA. *See* Association of University
  Programs in Health Administration
Australian Commission on Safety and Quality
  in Healthcare, 235
Authentic leadership, 5, 5*t*
Authoritarian leaders, 9, 9, 10
Autonomy, 18

B

Baby Boomer generation
  aging of, healthcare industry and, 137
  healthcare services and, 107
  retirement of, 24
Baccalaureate level programs, 39–40
Bachelor of Science/Medical Doctor (BS/MD)
  programs, 271
Bachelor's degree, 39–40